RAISING GIANTS

MY EXTRAORDINARY JOURNEY WITH **TWO** NFL SONS

LEE SCHWARTZ

Copyright © 2025 by Lee Schwartz

All rights reserved. Published in the United States of America. No part of this book may be reproduced or transmitted in any form or by any means, graphic, electronic or mechanical, including photocopying, recording, taping or by any information storage or retrieval system, without permission in writing from the publisher.

This edition published by Highpoint Executive Publishing. For information, write to info@highpointpubs.com.

First Edition
ISBN: 979-8-9908488-7-0

Library of Congress Cataloging-in-Publication Data

Schwartz, Lee
Raising Giants: My Extraordinary Journey With TWO NFL Sons
Includes index.

Summary: "The story of two sons, Geoffrey and Mitchell, whose paths to NFL success could not have been more different, but whose journeys are united by grit, resilience, and, above all, a father's unwavering love and commitment. What ties Geoffrey and Mitchell's stories together is the relentless support of their father, Lee Schwartz." – Provided by publisher.

ISBN: 979-8-9908488-7-0 (paperback)
1.Sports 2. Memoir

Library of Congress Control Number: 2025900979

Cover design by Heather Schwartz.
Interior design by Sarah Clarehart.

Manufactured in the United States of America

CONTENTS

PREGAME

Foreword 3

Preface: Who Would Have Thunk It? 5

FIRST QUARTER

1 A Career In The Balance 11

2 When Did You Know? 15

3 Sights On College—Our Recruiting Odyssey 31

4 UCLA—A Dream Dashed 49

SECOND QUARTER

5 Geoffrey's Journey To The Draft 59

6 Society Of Doubters (No Respect) 81

7 Mitchell's Journey To The Draft 87

8 Through The Turnstiles 101

9 The Most Memorable Games 123

10 Stadium Highlights 133

11 The More, The Merrier 161

HALFTIME
My Journey Through Photos 177

THIRD QUARTER

12 Football And Food—A Special Combination 191

13 Football Intelligence 203

14 "Do You Celebrate Thanksgiving?"—Sports And Being Jewish 221

15 Shoe Dog—My Interactions With Phil Knight 241

16 Super Bowl LIV—A Dream Come True 251

FOURTH QUARTER

17 Inevitable: Football And Injuries 271

18 Don't Be Fooled—It *Is* A Business 301

19 Eat My Schwartz 313

20 What's Next? 319

21 The Changing Landscape Of Collegiate Football 331

OVERTIME

22 From Boys To Men—The Building Of Character 343

23 Stories Without A Home 355

24 The Final Whistle: Acknowledgments 363

GLOSSARY 369

INDEX 375

PREGAME

FOREWORD

Do you have a dream that your son will one day play in the NFL? What about two? This book is the story of *Raising Giants*—two sons, Geoffrey and Mitchell, whose paths to NFL success could not have been more different, but whose journeys are united by grit, resilience and, above all, a father's unwavering love and commitment.

Two different paths, one incredible family. What ties Geoffrey and Mitch's stories together is the relentless support of their father, Lee Schwartz. Whether it was traveling with his wife Olivia to watch their sons' games, missing career milestones to be there for them, or simply being a steadfast presence in their lives, Lee's dedication to his boys was nothing short of extraordinary. It's the kind of love and guidance that turns challenges into opportunities and setbacks into stepping stones.

As someone who had the privilege of representing both Geoffrey and Mitch during their NFL careers, I've had a front-row seat for their journey. What I can tell you is this: their success is a testament to the values their parents instilled in them—hard work, determination and the idea that commitment to excellence starts at home.

This book isn't just about football. It's about family, resilience and the ability to overcome whatever life throws your way. If you've ever doubted yourself, you'll find inspiration here. If you've ever thought about quitting, you'll find reasons to keep going. And if you've ever wanted to scream out of frustration, you'll learn why sometimes you should—and how to move forward after the scream fades.

Lee's story, and the stories of his sons, are a reminder that life is a team sport, and the bonds we build with our loved ones are the most important victories of all.

Enjoy the journey.

Deryk Gilmore
Day 1 Sports & Entertainment
Advocate for Excellence

PREFACE
WHO WOULD HAVE THUNK IT?

If you're about to read this book, be prepared. You will find plenty of examples of my taking liberties (thunk) with the English language. Do I know better? Of course. But this book, this story, is all about the fun I've experienced enjoying a front row seat watching my two amazing sons blossom from Little League tots to NFL pros, including a Super Bowl champ.

As the original Schwartz athlete, I grew up a jock. Following my father's love of the game, playing stickball as a youth in the streets of the Bronx and resting his arms on the railing in the short right-field porch of Yankee Stadium, I early on took a hankering to baseball. I began playing Little League at seven or eight. I also developed, at about the same age, a love of basketball while snuggling with my father and watching the famed Boston Celtics perform their court magic. My first organized basketball experience was as a towering twelve-year-old. I was a six-foot-tall center playing for my sixth-grade elementary school team.

I developed into a decent athlete, typically chosen for all-star teams, who early in life benefited from a genetic advantage: I stood taller than all of my classmates. Coupling my height and apparent athleticism, I had visions of playing collegiate sports. Being a professional? Seemed unlikely, but why not dream?

I completed my ninth-grade year still standing taller than my classmates. Then something curious happened. When I walked into my first day of high school after summer vacation, I shockingly discovered that two of my basketball teammates from our ninth-grade team had experienced a summer growth spurt that stretched them to six feet, four inches and above. Not possible! Others were almost looking me in the eye. I waited for my next growth spurt. Disappointingly, it never arrived. I don't think I grew another millimeter thereafter.

As a six-foot, one-and-a-half-inch hoops player with skills limited to the center position, I had zero chance for a "career" beyond high school. Baseball wouldn't be an option either as I didn't throw hard enough or hit for any average. I was destined for intramurals in college and adult recreational leagues post-college. I continued playing basketball into my fifties.

The birth of my first-born rekindled thoughts of my past. Geoffrey (I believe I'm the only person in the world who doesn't refer to him as Geoff, a parent's privilege) arrived in this world on July 11, 1986, weighing nine pounds, seven ounces, and measuring over twenty inches in length—95 percentile for both. Our second son, Mitchell, popped out on June 8, 1989, (they were both born at 1:03 p.m., a statistical improbability) at "only" eight pounds, twelve ounces. He might have been ten pounds according to the pediatrician if Mom (Livie) hadn't been induced early. Both had a jump start on me at birth.

From the earliest years, both Geoffrey and Mitchell showed evidence of athletic ability, whether it was smacking a baseball off a tee or dribbling a basketball around the house. As I was a decently talented baseball and basketball player, I would like to think that my genetics were the blueprint for these physical gifts. But then Livie believes she deserves some of the credit. This from someone who, during her formative years, wouldn't have known the difference between a baseball field and a basketball court. (She is a decent ping-pong player and can actually shoot a basketball...from close range.)

As I shared, the boys arrived genetically mutated, as I like to joke. They were always inches taller than their contemporaries. Unlike me, they continued to grow well into their teenage years. With the combination of size and talent, plus a sprinkling of tremendous desire and determination that, I'd like to think, they learned from Mom and Dad, they have both achieved what I only dreamed about. They played major Division 1 football and then went on to lengthy and fulfilling careers in the National Football League (NFL), including that Super Bowl appearance.

Who Would Have Thunk It?

This book is a labor of love, written to detail my twenty-year experience as the father of two extraordinary sons and athletes, sharing personal stories, commentary and perspectives along the way. It has been an unexpected journey, but one that has enormously enriched our lives.

I watched football from afar for two-thirds of my life. Now, having lived vicariously through the boys, I understand more intimately how the game is played plus the naked truth about how much of a business it truly is. I also understand what it takes to support a child through a process for which very few are prepared.

For lifelong jocks like me who once had fantasies of being a collegiate or professional athlete, for families who have offspring who might follow a similar path as my boys, for the moms who wish to be inside the huddle, I welcome all of you to join me as I describe life as the very proud father of two former professional football players and dole out some very important lessons learned along the way.

Although this memoir is a far cry from the daunting 1,440 pages of *War and Peace*, it is not a short novella. Whether you read cover to cover, specific chapters or portions thereof, as the clock winds down to 0:00 and you've turned that last page, I sincerely hope you have smiled a bunch, laughed out loud often enough, stumbled upon a few "aha" moments, gained a greater understanding of football, maybe learned some related parenting skills, and found the time spent reading this book to be worthwhile.

Time to tee it up for kickoff.

P.S. You will see throughout the book a football icon 🏈 after certain phrases or words. For those who wish to learn more about these topics, please refer to the glossary section that trails The Final Whistle chapter.

FIRST QUARTER

A CAREER IN THE BALANCE

It was NFL Draft Day 2012, and the professional career of my youngest son, Mitchell, hung in the balance. His older brother, Geoffrey, had already been playing in the National Football League for four years.

The NFL altered the schedule of the draft two years prior to Mitchell's draft. The first round in 2012 was scheduled for Thursday night, April 26, rather than a Friday night. Rounds two and three would take place Friday, with the remaining four rounds conducted on Saturday. Given that the preponderance of input pegged Mitchell as a second- or third-round selection, we watched the broadcast Thursday night with more of a passing interest rather than being riveted to the screen. And that turned out to be the appropriate approach. The first round ended without Mitchell being selected.

We truly believed that Friday night would be *the* night. At the prescribed time, the family gathered in our family room. Mitchell was sprawled out on the couch facing the television. Geoffrey, my brother and Livie occupied the other spaces on the sofa. I dragged a chair from the kitchen table and strategically positioned myself to watch the screen but also to have a clear view of Mitchell.

The show began with the St. Louis Rams making a selection with the thirty-third overall pick of the draft. The first night I remember there being fifteen minutes between picks. On the second night that was reduced to ten minutes. In either case, it seemed like an eternity. The Indianapolis Colts followed the Rams. Next up would be the Baltimore Ravens. As we watched the crawlers at the bottom of the screen, we noticed that Cleveland would be on the clock two picks later. Hmmm.

Given that they attended Mitchell's Pro Day, and then invited him to their facilities after the Combine (in both events the best college players run through drills in front of NFL scouts and coaches), maybe they had more than a passing interest. They had already selected running back Trent Richardson the night before with the third pick of the first round, and then with pick number twenty-two they chose quarterback Brandon Weeden. The Browns had eleven overall picks in that year's draft. Would they take an offensive lineman that high in the draft?

For a thirty-seventh pick, a team must want the player. Might it change? Sure. Let's say the two teams preceding Cleveland did not select a player that the Browns thought would be off the board by their pick, so the Browns scramble and instead draft someone else. Or possibly another team calls Cleveland and makes a trade offer that the Browns believe they couldn't pass up. So it wasn't an absolute; however, the likelihood had been very high that Mitchell would be taken.

We waited for the Broncos to make their selection. Chris "Boomer" Berman was the lead commentator on ESPN's telecast that night. Once the Browns were on the clock, we waited. As time closed in on that ten-minute window, Berman began speculating on what positions Cleveland needed, specifically mentioning a tackle. Then, in what seemed to me to be an abrupt move, Berman announced they were going to commercial but would be back in time for the Browns' pick.

We were now waiting for the commercial to end. I really hate commercials. I record almost all TV shows for the express purpose of fast forwarding through commercials. Combining my distaste of these pointless promotions with the anticipation of what we believed was forthcoming, returning to the draft show couldn't come soon enough. And then the doorbell rang.

We have some very dear friends who have known the boys their entire lives. We celebrate all of the major Jewish holidays with Joel Weinstein (Joel was a partner with Livie at her law firm) and his wife Deborah Eisen. Joel was born and raised in Ohio. We had been sharing with him Cleveland's interest in Mitchell leading up to the draft, so we invited them over to watch the broadcast, believing that maybe Mitchell would be selected by the Browns at some point that night. We encouraged them to arrive at our house by 5 p.m. when the show was scheduled to begin. But that didn't happen.

But as fate would have it, the doorbell rang during the commercial immediately before Cleveland's pick. Hearing the bell and knowing it had to be Joel and Deborah, I rushed to the door. I dispensed with the normal pleasantries and urged, "Hurry, follow me." Of course, they had no idea why I was virtually dragging them to the family room. I tried to explain but was interrupted by the sound of Berman's voice.

"It's time to go to the podium for the Browns' pick," Boomer declared. The camera shifted to the stage with Commissioner Roger Goodell at the podium. That particular year the NFL invited former players to join Goodell to announce selections. I don't recall who announced the Browns' first two choices but, for the thirty-seventh pick, Gary Collins, a former receiver who was chosen as the fourth pick in the 1962 draft, was invited to join Goodell. All those years of dedication to helping our sons attain success as professional athletes were about to come to fruition. But what form would that take?

2
WHEN DID YOU KNOW?

This question was asked routinely during our journey. "When did you know that the boys would become college athletes and possibly professional football players?" Nothing was ever certain until a tangible event occurred, like signing the National Letter of Intent after committing to a college, being selected in the NFL draft or receiving input from a credible source. It was kinda like my not knowing I was college bound until the day a letter appeared in the mailbox from UCLA containing my acceptance.

Let me begin by putting this journey into perspective. The odds of becoming a professional football player are abysmal. Is that a surprise to anyone? Over a decade ago, I caught Pat Haden, Athletic Director (A.D.) of the University of Southern California (USC), on a sports radio talk show answering a question on this exact topic.

In response to "What are the chances of playing in the NFL," Haden revealed that there were approximately 1.1 million high school football players in the United States at that exact moment in time. He then progressed to how many of those would play any level of college football, followed by how many of them would even play a down in the NFL.

So let's jump to the final statistic. How many of the 1.1 million would enjoy ten years in the NFL? Why ten years? Because it's a badge of honor to have lasted for that length of time. The average career of all NFL players is about 3.4 years. Offensive linemen are a tick higher at 3.5 years. It's not long. Since first contracts are four to five years, most players don't reach a lucrative second deal that would likely create long-term financial security for them and their families.

Before I provide the final number, care to take a guess? Of all the people I've teased with this question, only one or two have guessed correctly on their first attempt. The answer...11. That's a percentage of .0001. How many activities would you attempt if you knew the odds of success would be so infinitesimal? For the overwhelming majority of high school players, the road to the NFL is a dead end.

We had indications along the way that Mitchell and Geoffrey had the physical skills to become special athletes. I remember the boys' elementary school coach, Hal Kurtzman, a former minor league baseball player and major league scout, being impressed with their early athletic skills. But there's so much more to reaching the mountaintop than physical talent alone. Athleticism provides a great foundation; however, early, precocious development can be fleeting, and not indicative of future success. An individual must package mental, emotional and psychological strengths with extraordinary physical talent to grasp the golden ring.

It didn't hurt that Geoffrey and Mitchell popped out of Mom's womb so large. The average newborn boy measures 19.7 inches. My two were right around 22 inches. At the 95th percentile for height and weight at birth, they were physically ahead of the curve from the beginning, and never looked back.

As toddlers, they gravitated toward sports, maybe with a tad bit (haha) of encouragement from their dad. As they grew, their love for sports grew. By the time each was five they were playing Little League baseball, two or three years earlier than my introduction. At about seven, we enrolled Geoffrey in a recreational park basketball league. Mitchell never showed interest in competitive basketball.

At all levels of youth sports, they certainly were the biggest for their age and often played well enough to be named to the league's all-star team. Was this any sort of indicator of their future sports achievements? No. It was way too early to be predictive.

Soccer, Baseball, Football and Basketball

The boys weren't great at all sports. Our next-door neighbor was a soccer fan. One season he registered his son to play soccer and asked if Geoffrey would like to sign up. Geoffrey had never expressed an interest in the game, but at seven or eight years old, he was up for trying anything, and Mom and Dad weren't going to stand in the way.

The next question was a real head-scratcher. He inquired if I would be his assistant coach. Me? He knew I had never played soccer. Not to insult any readers, but I'd rather watch grass grow. I was never shy about my feelings for the game, but that didn't prevent him from asking. (He must have been awfully desperate.)

I said yes. How difficult could it be? I had coached youth baseball and basketball and was considered better than average at it by the kids and their parents. I accepted. What a mistake! If any of you have attempted to coach a sport or mentor in a subject with no previous experience, you'll know what I mean.

We quickly learned soccer was not Geoffrey's sport. Trying to run up and down a full soccer field, especially given his, shall we say, solid body type, similar to his dad at the same age, was not what Geoffrey considered fun. For me, trying to coach a sport that I knew nothing about was boring, joyless and, most importantly, not productive for the kids. It was the only season that Geoffrey and I were involved with soccer. Mitchell, having possibly watched his brother labor, never made it onto the pitch.

There was an important lesson to be learned in all this. Every sport requires unique physical characteristics for the participant to be successful. Look at some of the more productive soccer players. They are agile. They are typically lanky and more diminutive, like Lionel Messi. Quite the contrary when contrasted against the characteristics associated with successful football players, especially offensive linemen like my boys. It's vitally important for parents to understand the genetic makeup of their kids when helping them choose a sport.

As the boys grew and matured, their respective baseball and basketball skills continued to improve, but I don't remember that ever translating to dreams of professional opportunities. Maybe thoughts of a college baseball scholarship, but that was the extent of our daydreaming. And, therefore, Livie and I stressed balanced lives rather than burdening them with extracurricular activities to chase what we believed at the time would be some fantasy.

The boys were busy enough. Regular school and homework. Hebrew school and Bar Mitzvah lessons. Friends and social activities. School athletics, which bled into holidays and vacations. Their plates, as well as ours as actively involved parents with full-time professional jobs, were plenty full. We were somewhat outliers compared to many other parents who dreamt of future stardom for their young athletes. Not until late high school was time set aside for supplemental coaching. And whereas many contemporaries were actively involved in travel ball (as it suggests, teams of top-tier athletes are assembled and travel to locations far and wide to compete), that was limited for my two.

It was imperative that Livie and I establish realistic expectations for the boys, having seen what harm unrealistic expectations could produce. Following are two compelling examples of how early, improbable dreams can be so easily derailed.

An eleven-year-old was the talk of Little League. His abilities far exceeded his years. He wasn't exceptionally sized for his age, yet he hit baseballs a distance not usually seen in that age group. The coaches in the league fawned all over him. His hitting proficiency and tape-measure home runs were signs to this group that stardom was knocking on his door, almost a fait accompli.

Ultimately, the only notoriety awaiting this young man was being known for not achieving what so many had predicted. Genetics cannot be overlooked, playing a significant role in what ultimately is achieved on the field, court or rink. This boy's father may have stood five feet nine inches and his mother was no taller than five feet four inches, unlike Geoffrey and Mitchell, who had a six-foot-one-and-a-half-inch father and a five-foot-nine-and-a-half-inch mother, both offspring of six-foot-one-inch fathers and five-foot-seven-inch mothers (very tall for their generation).

He graduated high school no longer possessing the physical advantages he once enjoyed. He received a baseball scholarship to a four-year college program, but within three years was no longer playing the game he once dominated.

A second example of unrealized expectations involved another Little Leaguer who also played in the same league as Geoffrey. He was, unquestionably, the best pitcher in the league. Unhittable. But not only was he on the hill twice during a Little League week, he was also toeing the rubber for a travel team typically once a week. His body was still maturing. Just think of the overuse his arm experienced by all those pitches at such a delicate age. Plus, proper pregame and postgame arm care was the exception at the time. He pitched into high school, where his elbow blew up, requiring surgery. He never threw competitively again.

But let's get real here. It's one thing to deal with the physical toll on these young bodies. Often the injured body part will fully recover. But what about the emotional and psychological damage done? In both cases, I am sure these youngsters wrapped their futures around an expectation of high-level success in their chosen sport. They lived and breathed baseball almost every day of their lives. They were constantly reminded of their on-field achievements and, therefore, who they may become.

Then, one day, poof, it was all gone. At such a young and critical age, how is one to replace their identity and purpose in life? These two would have been far better served by parents, coaches, and other influential people in their lives setting more realistic and attainable goals.

Livie and I were committed to not overhype expectations. Enjoy the moment in time. We allowed the boys to play multiple sports. Geoffrey baseball, basketball and football; Mitchell football and baseball. I remember parents and coaches telling us that the boys "needed" to focus on one sport, and one sport only. Bah humbug to that. Geoffrey has adopted the same approach. My grandkids, Alex and Emmy, at the ripe ages respectively of ten and eight, have already experienced baseball/softball, flag football, tennis, basketball, gymnastics and swimming.

The future is unknown. If your son or daughter wants to participate in multiple sports, then, by golly, encourage them to do so. What might be a strength at, let's say, eight years old, might no longer be a gift as they begin their teenage years. I remember competitively running track, shot putting and throwing the discus in junior high school. I was sure glad that I had baseball and basketball to fall back on, as track was but a blip on my radar screen.

I also firmly believe that such diversity will make youngsters better all-around athletes. I'm convinced that Geoffrey's football footwork was enhanced by his hoops play. The hand-eye coordination required to hit or field a baseball led to improved dexterity in other sports. Geoffrey can already see the added strength in Alex's upper body when throwing a baseball as a result of all of his swimming.

Life balance was also supremely important to us. We encouraged sports participation but made sure it didn't interfere with their academic pursuits. Fortunately, Mitchell and Geoffrey are both intelligent and were excellent students. Mitchell's 4.3 GPA in high school and 3.4 at Berkeley were proof positive. If a future in sports beyond high school wasn't in the cards, they had the smarts to follow other routes, like walking in their mother's footsteps as an accomplished lawyer.

Our principles were validated some years later. The National Collegiate Athletic Association (NCAA) sponsored a series of TV commercials to bring attention to the limited professional sports opportunities facing collegiate athletes. One commercial stated there were 360,000 NCAA student-athletes. Another offered 400,000. Regardless, both closed with a student-athlete proclaiming the same hard fact: "Just about all of us are going pro in something other than sports." Academics must trump athletics. It's just the reality of life.

I've talked about balancing everyday life and sports. For Livie and me it was essential, but not an absolute. Our concession? Travel ball. It wasn't a "thing" when I grew up. As I look back, travel-ball participation was a particularly good indicator of the boys' athletic abilities, as these teams were comprised of the best of the best, an all-star team for lack of any other description. But, as opposed to other families, we made sure it wasn't all consuming. It was seasonal/occasional rather than year-round and participation didn't get in the way of essential activities in their lives. The costs were minimal. And not only did my boys enjoy their experiences, but I'm convinced it made them better players, enriched their lives and taught them invaluable lessons.

Mitchell was invited to join a West Los Angeles–based travel baseball team during his middle school years. He was the Johnny-come-lately entrant, as the majority of the team had already been formed. I know that he had fun on the field, but something much more significant resulted from his participation. He found a bestie. Mitchell and teammate Andy Megee both ended up attending the same high school, where their relationship flourished. Today, after this chance meeting almost twenty years ago, they are like brothers from different mothers.

Geoffrey was also a member of a travel baseball team during his later Little League tenure. It was the first time he had traveled out of state to play a sport, to a tournament held in Phoenix, Arizona, during mid-summer. The days were a sweltering 100-plus degrees, even after the sun went down. As the tournament progressed, it was obvious that the players were wilting. And so, apparently, was the head coach.

Sparing you the nasty details, this coach got a bug in his bonnet with the umpires late one game. Ironically, besides coaching he was also an experienced umpire. After some charged words between this coach and

When Did You Know?

an ump, an exchange that he, as an umpire, would have never tolerated, the coach pulled his team off the field and forfeited the game. For what purpose? To this day I have no clue. But what a message to his team, huh? Instead of working through whatever was bothering him and being a mentor to his pupils, he forgot it wasn't all about him and let his anger dictate his actions.

At the time I also was coaching Little League. What a lesson for me. I swore that I would be a shining example for my sons and players and never let my emotions dictate my actions on the field. I'm proud to say I succeeded throughout my almost twelve years of coaching.

Traveling Club Teams

Geoffrey was on the roster of another baseball travel team about three or four years later, this one sponsored by the Police Activities League (PAL). Whereas I was a parent chaperone on his first travel team, this time I was invited to be an assistant coach. The tournament was also held in Phoenix at one of the sprawling Major League spring-training facilities in the area. It was quite a jolt to Geoffrey's confidence, competing successfully for the first time against top-tier talent on a field designed for professionals. He pitched well and was an anchor at first base. And for me, it was a dream week watching Geoffrey's raw delight in his accomplishments.

One of the team's coaches was a staffer at PAL. Kermit Cannon was, and still is, an amazing athlete. Played baseball. Ran track. Today he trains athletes from high school to professional leagues. That trip was the beginning of a long-term bond between Kermit, Geoffrey and me. Because of this relationship, Geoffrey turned to Kermit to put him through his training paces before heading off to Eugene for his freshman football season at Oregon. To this day, Kermit can lay claim to being the only drill sergeant to have worked Geoffrey so hard that he threw up. And my relationship with Kermit blossomed as well. We now have an annual routine. He comes to the house for the NCAA championship basketball and football games, where we fine dine on El Pollo Loco chicken, enjoy several refreshing frozen Greek yogurt dessert bars and view the games on side-by-side sixty-inch TVs.

Geoffrey's basketball travel team experience was also very rewarding. His high school basketball coach, James Palino, never fully appreciated his talents on the court, hardly ever positioning him for success. The travel-team coach, DeWitt Cotton, approached his players very differently. Big guys can be much more than just post players. Some can step out and accurately shoot from three-point land. Regrettably, Geoffrey was discouraged from doing so by his high school coach. Coach Cotton encouraged him to be a more well-rounded player and pop from the outside. (I sure wish the three-point line was in existence when I played high school ball. I was known to have a decent stroke from the far corners of the court.) Wow, did that change Geoffrey's mental attitude on the court. Having the freedom to use his multiple talents, he thrived during travel ball.

There does come a time, though, when having a better idea of what the future may hold is more essential. Geoffrey was a three-sport high school athlete, jumping from football, to basketball, and then to baseball during a school year. Summertime involved all three in some fashion or another.

By the age of fifteen or sixteen Geoffrey was already six feet five inches tall and closing in on 300 pounds. Would he grow more? If so, and with his body type, for which sport would he be best suited? At the time, there were few offensive linemen standing six feet six inches or above. Few professional pitchers back then stood at that height. Six feet four inches is considered more of an ideal size for right-handed throwers. Geoffrey was already on the plus size. With his thick body, basketball was not his future, unless he spurted another four to six inches, and thinned out while growing. Maybe Geoffrey was at a crossroad and would need to focus on one sport because of his ultimate size.

Geoffrey Focuses on Football

I had heard it was possible for a pediatric orthopedic surgeon to x-ray the left wrist of an adolescent to assess their growth plates—closed, almost closed, or open (suggesting more growth to come). I had gotten to know such a surgeon during Little League days, so I called him when Geoffrey was a junior. He confirmed that this approach was not pie in the sky. We scheduled an appointment to take the needed x-ray.

His plates were almost closed. Maybe one inch more to grow, two inches optimistically. (He was right on. Geoffrey topped out at six feet six inches.) If there was any lingering thought that a growth spurt was in the offing, that door was shut. No basketball. And given that Geoffrey's "heater" from the mound was yet to top ninety miles an hour, a key threshold for upper-tier right-handed pitchers, the future was now evident. Focus on football. If he was to continue playing baseball or basketball it would be purely for enjoyment. But at that time high school basketball wasn't fun, thanks to the constraints placed on him by Coach Palino, so he "retired" after his junior year.

During Geoffrey's tenure, his high school football team at Palisades Charter High, located in one of Los Angeles's tony enclaves, Pacific Palisades, was a cellar dweller. It was standard practice for prized athletes in Southern California to consider greener athletic pastures when their teams were not competitive, which typically meant a transfer to a private school. Playing in a historically successful, higher profile program was, and still is, believed by some parents to enhance their kid's future prospects.

As a result of Geoffrey's travel-team participation, I got to know the dad of one of his teammates. His son attended a well-respected private West Los Angeles high school. One day during Geoffrey's junior year, the dad engaged me in conversation. He floated the idea of Geoffrey transferring from Pali High to this private school for his senior season. He believed Geoffrey could quickly become big man on campus. He also asserted that, from an academic perspective, a private school would open more doors to upper-tier colleges. Geoffrey's athletic abilities coupled with his GPA gave this dad reason to believe the transfer would be rubber-stamped by the private school administration.

I truly believe this dad had Geoffrey's best interests at heart. However, there may have been an underlying, maybe even selfish, motive. The private school was looking to improve their football roster. Players of Geoffrey's caliber, even at that stage in his career, were few and far between at this school. He would have been a real prize.

Livie and I were products of public schools and thus were their advocates. We appreciated the cultural diversity that public schools provided. We also felt that the boys could receive an excellent education at the right public school. Fortunately for us, we found the right schools. Following all guidelines, we enrolled Geoffrey and Mitchell in three nearby public schools outside of our neighborhood trio. All three—elementary, middle and high schools—ranked academically within the top three to four for their respective levels in the Los Angeles city school district. And although not as close to our house as the neighborhood trio, they were still within reasonable distances.

Though flattered by the thought, the answer to the transfer invite was very simply, "Thanks, but no thanks." It was the same response to anyone else suggesting a transfer from Pali to a private school strictly because that school was thought to have stronger sports programs. The light will shine brighter on their talents and therefore throw open more future doors of opportunity, they claimed. Great, but what about the educational component, or the broader cultural experiences?

As I alluded to earlier, Livie and I were firm believers that academics stood at the top of the totem pole, then athletics. The value of an education was impressed upon us by our parents. All four were very bright. I'm convinced that my mother could have been a lawyer had the door been open to women of her generation. And my father-in-law was recently described to us by a ninety-eight-year-old former high school classmate and friend, who founded and still runs an extraordinarily successful recycling company, as possibly being the brightest person he ever knew. But none had a college education. They wanted for us what wasn't available to them. Livie and I were the first generation in our respective families to earn a college diploma. Our kids would be the second.

Maybe we both were naïve at the time; however, we knew that Pali was a top-flight academic school. If the boys would be good enough to athletically stand out and have careers beyond high school, that would be icing on the cake. We firmly believed in the adage, "The cream rises to the top." A more broadly defined adage is, "A good person or idea cannot go unnoticed for long, just as cream poured in coffee or tea eventually rises to the top." Even though Pali's football program was less than prime time during their tenure, if the boys had the requisite abilities, we believed they would be appropriately noticed. We were ultimately proven correct. The cream did rise. They were noticed. They received fine educations. And today they enjoy very fortunate lives.

Since Geoffrey and Mitchell were primarily baseball players growing up, the prospects of them finding life-altering success in football never crossed our minds. When Geoffrey decided to give football a try as a high school freshman, he was a clod. Not very mobile. His first couple of years playing the sport provided us with zero indication of what was to come. It wasn't until his third high school season that we began hearing "he might have the talent" to climb to the next level.

That first demonstrable input was voiced by one of his assistant coaches. I frankly cannot remember the triggering event, but one day Coach Don Blatt (may he rest in peace) simply proclaimed, "Geoffrey has the ability to play at the next level." Wow! At that stage in my evolution of football knowledge, I had no clue what it might take to jump from the high school gridiron to college stadiums. But truth be told, as the jock I was, and still am, I walked away from that interaction very excited, thinking, "My son could be playing college football one day."

There was a second indicator, also during Geoffrey's junior campaign. Another Pali assistant coach, Dorrick Roy, began riding him very hard during practices. He would get in Geoffrey's face, exhorting him to try harder, to push himself. Geoffrey did not receive all this "encouragement" well. He would complain to me about the treatment being doled out. I urged him to forge ahead. I was reminded of my days on the basketball court, when I was pushed beyond my comfort level. I could have walked away, but that wasn't a choice per my father. I was a better player and person for having stuck it out. Roy had the pedigree to exhort Geoffrey, as he was a member of three National Championship teams with the University of Nebraska in the 1990s. He saw potential in Geoffrey that no one to that point had identified and wanted him to be the best he could be.

And then there was Pali High head coach Jason Blatt, who also knew a thing or two about big-time football. He played four years for the Colorado Buffalos and was a member of their 1990 NCAA National Championship team. Geoffrey credits Coach Blatt with providing him with the best advice he's ever received from a coach: "Don't lie to yourself." Coach Blatt wanted his players to be completely accountable for their actions on the field and for understanding who they were as football players. If you talk with Geoffrey about his football career, you'll find him refreshingly honest about his level of skill and athleticism. So when Coach also began talking about Geoffrey earning a college scholarship, the messaging began to feel more real than hype.

And thus began the more tangible and reliable signs that maybe, just maybe, Geoffrey was destined for a football career beyond high school. But, still, what did I know? Nothing really. I relied on the input of those who knew much more than I to calibrate my expectations. With this newfound "knowledge" I began sharing the same with friends and family who were following the journey. I did my level best to ascribe these opinions to their true sources. Lord knows I had no firm ground to stand on to make such prognostications.

Unfortunately, all the qualifiers in the world did nothing to assuage Livie's discomfort with any pronouncement that implied the boys would have success beyond what was a *known* fact. Maybe that was the lawyer in her. You may have heard about the advice a seasoned lawyer will give to newbies when in a trial: "Do not ask a question for which you don't know the answer." Since we had no tangible clue of what was to be, she was a whole lot more comfortable living in the present.

Mitchell's Career Kickoff

Our sense of Mitchell's probable ascent to the next level was clearer than Geoffrey's, and earlier. (Gee whiz, not a surprise. This will be the first of many instances throughout this book affirming the theme that while their journeys were similar, their paths were often different.) Amazingly though, Mitchell's football career almost never kicked off.

Heading into his freshman high school year, Mitchell wasn't very keen about playing football. And if he were to play, he didn't want to follow in his brother's lineman's footsteps, preferring the role of quarterback. There wasn't much reality in that happening, given his size, approximately six feet four inches, and body type. He, like his brother and father, was on the thicker side, but if that had to be the initial path, so be it.

Geoffrey and I knew the junior varsity coach, Ted Baker, well. We hatched a plan. We asked Ted for a meeting. We shared Mitchell's resistance to playing the line. We asked Coach Baker if he'd give Mitchell some reps at QB if he indeed came out to summer workouts. In my gut I believed that if we got him to the workouts, he would ultimately see his best path.

Mitchell was present on the first day of camp. Without divulging this previous backdoor meeting, Ted had a conversation with Mitchell and promised him QB reps. Ted kept his word. Mitchell was on the QB depth chart, albeit I believe he didn't see as many reps during practice as the other roster quarterbacks.

Fast forward to the first game of the season. Mitchell started at both offensive and defensive tackle. Late in the game, I noticed that he wasn't in the lineup. Peering over to the sidelines, I saw the tape on his hands had been removed. (All linemen wear tape to protect digits from injury.) I knew what this meant. When the offense next appeared, Mitchell trotted onto the field. The team huddled. A play was called. And there was Mitchell standing in shotgun, several feet behind center, as the quarterback.

He barked out the signals. The ball was hiked. Mitchell snatched the pigskin and looked downfield. It was to be a pass play. Typically QBs set their feet in such a way to make a successful throw. Mitchell hardly moved his feet. Instead, he flicked the ball downfield. It traveled some thirty to thirty-five yards, landing comfortably in the receiver's hands for a completion. And that was it. Mitchell jogged off the field. The final whistle soon blew.

Mitchell had the weekend to ruminate about this experience. Monday rolled around with the team's first practice since the Friday contest. By that time, Mitchell had seen the "error of his ways." He told Coach Baker that he was all in as a lineman. The itch to be a quarterback had been scratched. Imagine, we may never have seen his incredible career. Might not have witnessed his iron man consecutive snap streak. Might not have attended a Super Bowl. I guess a little timely deceit ain't half bad.

After this experiment, Mitchell quickly became a two-way starter his freshman year. This was the first clue that Mitchell was on a faster track than Geoffrey. Remember, Geoffrey didn't join the starting lineup until his junior year.

In the spring of that junior year, Geoffrey must have performed well enough during the fall football season, as he received invites to two or three regional camps for "rising" stars, where they can strut their stuff to college coaches. With those doors opened, he shined during his drills and one-on-one activities, where he demonstrated his natural strength and mobility for his size. His participation was most definitely a positive sign of what might happen in the coming year and change.

Knowing the lay of the land through my experience with Geoffrey, I relied on a relationship that I had cultivated with Marty Martindale to get Mitchell invited to these camps. Marty was co-founder of eDuck, the first website to cover University of Oregon sports. He took the initiative to contact someone with juice at one of these camps for an exemption to allow Mitchell to participate as a sophomore. Mitchell became a rare sophomore participant. He was talented enough to be worthy of an invite, but I suspect genetics played a part. Having an older brother as a collegiate starter just might suggest that the younger lad has some skills as well.

Not only did Mitchell seem to have a leg up on reaching the next level simply by his participation in these camps as a sophomore, his standout performances in front of all the college coaches made the case stronger. I'm sure it didn't hurt when Mitchell was paired with one of the top defensive recruits in the nation in a one-on-one, mano-a-mano blocking drill, someone who went on to play for USC and enjoyed a twelve-year NFL career.

It was my assessment that day that Mitchell got the best of this opponent on two out of the three reps they faced each other. But what did I really know back then? It was so early in the boys' football careers that I was rather clueless. But I had Marty, who was also at the camp that day, to turn to. He, too, was watching the tussles between Mitchell and this stud recruit. He had a similar assessment. And he shared that afterward, when talk among the coaches got around to discussing the day's top performers. A number wondered, "Who was so and so?" Marty was happy to fill them in. So maybe I knew more than I gave myself credit for.

Opportunity Ahead

As I look back, there were signposts along the way that read, "Opportunity ahead." Some were more subtle than others, while some were as unmistakable as a slap in the face. I did my level best to rely on the experts—coaches, players with collegiate experience and others connected to professional football—to set expectations. My biggest challenge was to not count the chickens before they hatched. Admittedly, there were times when I failed in this regard.

I remember so clearly opening an envelope sent to Geoffrey during his recruitment period. It was from the Notre Dame Fighting Irish, one of the more historically preeminent football programs in the country. Wow. The message inside the card was not some generic preprint but rather handwritten. And it included the signature of the head coach, Tyronne Willingham. I excitedly thought, "There must be legit interest if the head coach is reaching out himself." Yeah, right. Most around me tried their best to shake my gullibility, but I was undeterred.

Months later, once I learned a few valuable lessons about the realities of recruiting practices, I, with egg splattered all about my face, accepted the reality that the head coach had nothing at all to do with sending this card. It was prepared by a staffer with permission to autograph on behalf of the head coach. The funny part of this story, at least to me, is that I'm not sure why I got so excited. A Jew from West Los Angeles attending Notre Dame?

Livie and I did what we thought was appropriate to navigate through this recruiting process. Where it made sense—that is, it wasn't a financial burden, it didn't interfere with studies, it might enhance their performance—we engaged coaches outside their school teams for special instruction. Pitching and hitting instructors for baseball. Offensive line specialists. A basketball mentor.

When Did You Know?

So here's the conundrum for parents of aspiring athletes. Given the mounds of evidence that earning a college scholarship or signing an NFL contract is a remote possibility, how does a parent proceed? How are expectations set? What importance is placed on athletics versus academics? What's the investment in time and money in the pursuit of limited opportunities?

It's not my intention here to tell anyone what to do. I understand that each situation is unique. I know that my West Los Angeles, white, upper-middle-class life has far different needs and wants than Inner City USA objectives.

Nevertheless, here is my seven-part playbook, formed from firsthand experience, which I firmly believe could universally and fundamentally help parents and their aspiring athletes better navigate their way through the challenges that everyone is sure to face.

- Education is first, second...and last. The chances that your offspring will succeed in life with a college degree are much greater than what sports can deliver.
- Allow your children to play any and all sports that tickle their fancy. Only if they develop a kinship with a particular sport or demonstrate extraordinary skills in one sport might their exposure to other sports be limited.
- Be realistic. Don't follow your heart but rather be led by the gray matter between your ears. Remember Coach Blatt's advice: "Don't lie to yourself."
- Seek outside counsel. Let those with expertise provide *objective* input as to future potential.
- Create balance in your children's lives. School. Athletics. Social activities. Church/synagogue. Down time. Ultimately a well-rounded individual has a greater chance for success in life.
- Make sure your kids are having fun! It's a requirement.
- It's not about you, the parent. Divorce yourself from your emotional baggage. Make decisions about them for them.

There you have it. We didn't know what we were doing back in the day, but we kinda did. Along the way we had our suspicions but didn't want to pull the trigger too quickly. In the end, it all worked out for the best...for all concerned.

3

SIGHTS ON COLLEGE—OUR RECRUITING ODYSSEY

As Mitchell and Geoffrey worked their way through their high school careers, it became apparent that playing college ball was a real possibility. But what path would ultimately deliver them to a collegiate gridiron? At the time, we were clueless. Having followed college football since I was a kid, I knew about recruiting in a general sense but wasn't versed in the details. I was about to learn "by the seat of my pants."

Looking back, I think it's fair to say that the key to being recruited is exposure. At the time Geoffrey and Mitchell fancied themselves as collegiate football players, colleges were becoming more sophisticated with their recruiting practices. Player data was more universally available. Recruiting services had sprung up to provide visibility. Camps for the athletes, sponsored by some of the biggest names in sporting apparel, were much more commonplace, providing venues where coaches and staff could put eyes on prospects. And the internet was just beginning to be a valuable tool. There was a chance that a high school player with collegiate level talent not necessarily considered prime stock could be discovered. But that's a very passive approach. Sit back and see what happens? Not my style.

My first direct exposure to the world of recruiting happened before there was any talk of Geoffrey being a potential prospect. During his freshman junior varsity season at Pali High in 2000, I would remain at the stadium after the game to watch the varsity team compete. During those contests I noticed one of the dads constantly on his feet, racing from one end of the field to the other with a camcorder pressed against his eyeball as he videotaped his son's every movement on the field. At some point during the season, we fortuitously bumped into each other. We've been friends ever since.

Norm Beegun's son Eric was a senior that year, the starting varsity tight end, and was being recruited to play at the next level. Much more out of idle curiosity initially, I began asking Norm questions about the recruiting process. He was very generous with his responses. His answers became the foundation for my understanding of recruiting.

Eric earned a scholarship. In one of the many "small-world" stories that I've experienced throughout my life, and especially on this journey, Mitchell and Eric became teammates during Mitchell's first year at Cal. Although it was purely coincidental, "Uncle Normie" has always taken credit for the pairing.

Watching Pali football on Friday nights with Norm continued after Eric's graduation. Whenever Cal's schedule allowed, Norm would attend the Friday night Pali game, asking me to save him a seat. We'd sit side by side, talking all things football. During Geoffrey's junior season, our conversations began to focus on recruiting. Norm apparently saw something in Geoffrey's play to suggest the next level was possible.

The insights provided by Norm were absolutely invaluable. One piece of advice stood out then and has ever since. Don't be suckered in. College recruiters are trained to make recruits feel like they are prospect number one for their position. However, as Lee Corso, former college head coach and currently (as of 2024) part of ESPN's Saturday *College GameDay* staff, is prone to say, "Not so fast."

The warm and fuzzy feeling recruiting coaches try to generate with a prospect is, for most recruits, subterfuge. Each position group, that is, quarterbacks, offensive linemen, etc., is evaluated by the full coaching staff, after which they rank prospects. Indeed, there is always a number one. However, there might be nine others being pursued who are not. A coach's objective is to make a recruit feel like they are number one, regardless of where they may actually reside in the position rankings. If numbers one through five decline their scholarship offers, they want number six to feel like they were number one the entire time. It was quite an eye-opening revelation.

Sights On College—Our Recruiting Odyssey

Geoffrey's junior season was his turning point. Before then, although gargantuan for his age, playing football beyond high school was just a pipe dream. But then his coaches started to whisper, "He may have a chance."

Seemingly out of the blue, Geoffrey started receiving attention from college coaches visiting campus. In fact, our mailbox became a daily repository for recruiting materials from colleges across the country. Some came from blue-blood institutions. Others arrived from schools I'd never heard of or couldn't fathom Geoffrey, or later Mitchell, ever attending, for a whole host of reasons, such as academic standards, location and distance from home, the football team's competitiveness or the talent of its coaches. But these schools had nothing to lose. Cast a wide-enough net and maybe they catch some unexpected fish.

Collecting the daily mail was never more fun than during Mitchell's and Geoffrey's recruiting periods. The guys agreed that I could open the envelopes. One by one I'd tear them open to read the contents. Some were just generic advertising, promoting the institution and football program. Others were personalized, specifically addressed to one of the boys. "Come play for us Geoff/Mitchell." Some were typewritten, others handwritten with a faux signature, like the one from Notre Dame.

On the Radar

Exposure is the key to opportunities at the college level. Back then, in the early 2000s, the options for the athlete and/or their family to create visibility beyond their play on the field were limited. You could submit videotapes, but that was dicey. There was no assurance that they would be viewed. And more than likely the tapes were highlight reels. Coaches want to see the unvarnished truth, that is, the good, the bad and the ugly. Attending a camp was a possibility, but that was by invitation only. There was word of mouth, which, hopefully, encouraged coaches to visit campus or attend a game. Or maybe the high school coaches were burning the midnight oil promoting their stars.

Apparently, one or more of the above spurred some action because college coaches began showing up at Pali to talk with coaches about Geoffrey or to talk with him directly when recruiting rules would allow.

Should an athlete, during their junior season, appear on the radar screen and be deemed a higher-level prospect, they are considered for an invite to Junior Day. All big-time colleges schedule these one-day affairs.

Coaching staffs identify their top prospects and invite them, with their parents, to a day on campus toward the end of the athlete's junior year. The day is spent meeting with coaches and touring campus facilities, both academic and athletic. Staffs enthusiastically promote their school, attempting to demonstrate why their football program is ideal for the athlete and to tout the care your son will receive if part of their program. It's an all-out promotional blitz.

Geoffrey was invited to two Junior Days, both quite memorable and remarkable in their own ways. His first visit was to Palo Alto, California, and the beautiful Stanford University campus. When the invitation arrived there wasn't a moment of hesitation. Although at the time Stanford was not a football powerhouse, we were talking about one of the finest academic institutions in the world. The prospect of our son one day attending Stanford fit so well into our academic goals for the boys. Mom and Dad were super excited.

In the middle of May 2003, all other plans were put on the back burner for that weekend trek up to Palo Alto. The activities began Saturday morning. We made our way to Stanford's humongous campus, the second largest in the world behind the University of Georgia in the former Soviet Socialist Republic. Being there gave me goosebumps. The campus was beautiful. I was in awe as we toured the property.

We met the coaches and staff. They gave us a comprehensive tour of the campus, visiting the stadium, the weight and locker rooms, the student store and their trophy room, which included their numerous Sears Directors' Cups, awarded to the nation's top athletic program. Stanford basically owned the cup for over two decades, winning twenty-five consecutive trophies from 1994-95 through 2018-19.

It was while we were touring the weight room that a staffer approached and asked us to follow him. We bounded up a flight of stairs, took a hard left turn at the top, and were escorted into Head Coach Buddy Teevens' office. We had no idea why our family, or Geoffrey specifically, had been singled out. We were soon to learn.

We walked into the office with our feet solidly planted on terra firma. We departed and felt like we were walking on air. Geoffrey had been offered a scholarship to attend and play for the Stanford Cardinal. Oh my!

Even if Geoffrey wanted to accept the offer to play for the Cardinal at that moment, he couldn't. Stanford, as we were told at the meeting, was the only Division 1 institution, at least at the time, that required athletes to complete the admission package and gain acceptance before the offer is considered official. No rubber stamping. The only concession made was to have the application, submitted in a pink or red envelope to highlight its contents, fast-tracked once received. (The athlete admission practices at Stanford have since been modified to streamline the process.) We were told that a decision would be forthcoming in a couple of weeks. And so we waited.

The more you read the book the more you will learn that this journey was replete with small-world experiences, commonplace for Livie and me. That Junior Day at Stanford was a perfect example.

Livie and I were roaming the student store when I noticed another family also attending Junior Day. The father looked familiar, but I couldn't place him. I mentioned this to Livie. She, too, thought he looked familiar but also didn't know from where. As we wandered about the store, Livie, who can talk to any stranger, approached this family and engaged them in conversation.

Livie will tell you that I have an uncanny ability to remember faces. I once again demonstrated my talent. A year into our marriage, 1978 to be exact, we moved into a townhouse. Neil Kay was our next-door neighbor in that complex. It had been almost twenty years since we last saw Neil. His son, Jordan, a place kicker, was also a Stanford recruit.

Amazingly, that was not the end of this small-world story with the Kay family. Neither of our sons attended Stanford. But a few years later Mitchell, as an incoming freshman, and Jordan, a junior at the time, became teammates...at Cal, Stanford's archrival. How bizarre? Two neighbors, one not even married at the time, find their sons playing football for the same team two decades later. What were the chances?

Leaving Stanford that day and knowing that Geoffrey's admittance was not guaranteed, we continued to explore other possible opportunities. That led Geoffrey to accept an invitation from UCLA to attend its Junior Day a few weeks later.

It was a rather surreal experience. Every attempt was made by the coaching staff of the very school Livie and I both graduated from to make us feel special. And being there that day was a possible foreshadowing that Geoffrey would, one day, wear Bruin blue and gold. It was a day to treasure. (Unfortunately, that turned out to be the high-water mark in our experience with UCLA, which I describe in the following chapter.)

Raising Giants

I can't fully explain why, but Mitchell was not invited to one Junior Day. Very befuddling considering Mitchell was a starter during his sophomore year, accorded himself well at his sophomore spring camps and was recognized as a talent in his junior campaign. But yet no invitations. I can explain why two schools, seemingly obvious candidates, did not extend an invite.

Based on a heartbreaking UCLA experience with Geoffrey that I will detail in the next chapter, I put out word through channels that the Bruins should move on. So long as the same coaching staff was in place, DO NOT recruit Mitchell. That door was shut. I guess they heeded my directive.

The other school that curiously didn't invite Mitchell was Oregon. This didn't quite make sense. At the time an invite would have been fitting, Geoffrey was a two-year starter for the Ducks. Logic would suggest that the younger brother of a two-year starter might be worth strong consideration. Just look at the NFL and the numbers of brothers holding roster positions. Mitchell was a two-way starter as a sophomore. He attended those camps a year earlier than the norm and accorded himself well. Plus, the coaches had seen Mitchell in the flesh when he traveled with us to Eugene for Geoffrey's official visit. He was an imposing figure back then. And yet, no invite.

It was sometime later that we learned the reason for the absence of an invite. The Oregon offensive line coach, Steve Greatwood, thought Mitchell wasn't talented enough to be considered. Are you kidding me?! I can't help but think that there was an underlying reason that was never publicly stated.

By the way, the Oregon coaching staff did finally come around during Mitchell's senior season, joining the hunt for his commitment. It was a full-scale onslaught. Head Coach Mike Bellotti even visited the house one day to make his case. In retrospect, I don't think Oregon ever got out of the starting gate with Mitchell. First, I believe that their original handling of him struck a nerve. Mitchell felt disrespected and unappreciated. Secondly, and maybe more of a contributor, I think that Mitchell wanted to chart his own course without being in the shadow of his big bro.

Junior season is sort of the appetizer in advance of the main meal during senior season, when recruiting activity significantly ramps up. Visits to Pali High by college coaches. Calls to the house (text messaging wasn't a thing back then). Mailbox jam-packed with letters and marketing pieces. Official, as well as unofficial, visits to campuses. Decisions, decisions, decisions!

Sights On College—Our Recruiting Odyssey

Contact by collegiate coaches with high school prospects was, and still is, highly regulated by the NCAA. The NCAA compliance book outlines, in great detail, when a college coach is permitted to visit a high school campus, and when and how often the prospects can be contacted otherwise. "Dark periods" are calendared, when there can be no communication between coaches and prospects. Schools have been punished by the NCAA over the years for violations. But it's not always so cut and dried.

There's such a thing as an "accidental" contact. I believe it happened at least once to one of the guys. A college coach was allowed to visit the high school campus at a time when direct contact with the prospect was not allowed. But miraculously, the coach and prospect crossed paths as they respectively journeyed about campus. While not technically allowed to converse, a few words were exchanged, along the lines of "We're watching you." Coincidence? I think not.

The phones were busy during the early months of the boys' senior football seasons. Some coaches called rather randomly. Others were quite regimented.

Geoffrey, for a time, was being courted by USC. Yes, that's right. In some ways it was a tough pill to swallow, this UCLA Bruin family thinking about their son wearing the cardinal and gold of our hated cross-town archrivals. (To this day I still root against the Trojans, regardless of the sport.) But how could we stand in the way? At the time, USC was one of the premier programs in the country. If Geoffrey was good enough to earn a spot on the Trojan roster, it likely would be an avenue to the NFL. Numerous USC players were being drafted. But it ultimately wasn't to be.

Every Monday night around 7:30 the phone would ring. Often, I would be the one picking up the receiver. It was USC coach Ed Orgeron. Although his voice was clearly distinguishable the moment he spoke, he politely introduced himself and asked to speak with Geoffrey. I'd turn the phone over to Geoffrey, who would nonchalantly, yet purposefully, slip away into another room. He wanted his privacy. That was understandable. The call lasted maybe a handful of minutes, ending with "talk with you next week."

Then one week the tenor of the conversation changed. Coach Orgeron informed Geoffrey that USC had but a couple of offensive line openings and they had their sights set on two or three other recruits, all of whom were of higher profile than Geoffrey. USC had to end their pursuit of Geoffrey. Frankly, it wasn't such a disappointment given our UCLA affiliation. But I will forever appreciate the coach's approach to dealing with Geoffrey. To directly explain the situation rather than leaving a message or ghosting him entirely spoke volumes about Coach's character. There are indeed some upstanding guys out there, regardless of what you may hear. The last conversation ended with a very warm, "I wish you luck."

Mitchell had one particularly memorable conversation during recruiting. Toward the end of his recruiting journey Mitchell was very fortunate to be pursued by three of the top academic institutions in the country—Stanford, Cal Berkeley and Virginia. Perfect for Mitchell, given he's such a bright guy. There was a fourth team in the picture, the Tennessee Volunteers, making quite the push to convince Mitchell to attend their school. But when compared academically with the other three, the Vols weren't in the same zip code.

Consistent with how we appreciated the candor from Coach Orgeron, we told Mitchell it was important for us/him to be candid with Tennessee. Livie and I typically didn't give the boys much direction during recruiting as to which school to choose, but in this case we did. Tennessee was not an option. "You need to call the head coach and let him know so they'll stop recruiting you," we directed Mitchell.

That was to be a very tough conversation for Mitchell, given his introverted personality, but it was a conversation he had to have. So Mitchell called to explain. When Coach Fulmer asked why, Mitchell repeated a fact we had earlier shared with him after we read college rankings in *U.S. News and World Report*, which is that Tennessee did not possess the academic chops of the other three schools. I suspect I shouldn't have been surprised by what came next. The coach disagreed and told Mitchell that his school was on par academically with the other three. I believed that this was a desperate attempt to keep Mitchell in the fold. For Livie and me, we felt the right decision had been made, as was borne out by Mitchell's success academically and athletically at Cal.

Official Visits

NCAA rules allowed football prospects to visit up to five campuses during their senior season for what was termed an "official visit." All expenses for the prospect were paid by the school. Parents traveling with the athlete had their lodging and meals covered, but the cost of travel had to be assumed by the parent(s).

Sights On College—Our Recruiting Odyssey

Festivities began Friday night, and concluded after a send-off breakfast/brunch Sunday morning. This schedule was problematic. High school football games typically take place on Friday nights. (Remember the movie and TV series *Friday Night Lights?*) How can the athlete be in two places at one time? Our solution? High school football seasons are completed by Thanksgiving, so we made our official trips in December. These excursions were special weekends, as the schools tripped over themselves putting on their Sunday best to show the athlete and his family the love that would persuade them to choose the host school over all the others.

We attended three official recruiting visits with Geoffrey (Oregon, Arizona and UCLA) and four total visits with Mitchell (Virginia—one official, one unofficial—Cal Berkeley, and an unofficial to Michigan). The two unofficial visits were made during the summer between Mitchell's junior and senior years, thus not missing a high school game. Beyond the five official visits allowed by the NCAA, prospects and their families could arrange unofficial visits to any college on their own dime in coordination with the team's coaching staff.

So why spend the time and money?

Sometimes respective interests don't initially align. In these instances, where the prospect's desire to attend a particular school is greater than the school's desire to have them on the team, visiting might help to align interests, thus opening the door for a possible scholarship offer. In some ways it was a crapshoot but, in certain instances, sometimes it was worth the effort and the expense.

During official visits, we and the other prospects/families in attendance were all housed at top-tier hotels. We feasted at the finest restaurants in the local area. We were transported in luxury buses. We were treated as if we were heads of state. And where they could, the team orchestrated activities that were designed to tug at the heartstrings, such as our experience with UCLA.

Saturday morning included a brunch at Gladstones, a historic, renowned restaurant overlooking the Pacific Ocean where Sunset Boulevard dead-ends into the Pacific Coast Highway and, literally, rests three miles from Pali High. It was ironic that Gladstones was chosen. The Pali football teams, both varsity and junior varsity, devoured their pregame meal before all home games at Gladstones. Once satisfied, we boarded our buses for a trek to Pasadena, California, home of UCLA's home turf, the

Rose Bowl. The buses drove up to the southern entrance of the stadium, the side of the Bowl where the iconic Rose Bowl sign draws all eyes. It was fully lit, although daytime, and nary a soul was on site otherwise.

As we neared the stadium, we noticed below the sign, on ground level, something that, frankly, brought tears to my eyes. There, resting on easels, was a series of baby blue UCLA jerseys, the very same worn by the Bruins for home games. The backs of the jerseys faced outward toward us. And there it was. I don't remember the jersey number because all I could focus on was the name "Schwartz." I will never forget the emotion of that moment. My son, a Bruin! My alma mater. Well, possibly.

Upon exiting the bus, the staff walked us by the uniforms. We took pictures. Livie and I and the other parents were then escorted through a tunnel and down dozens of steps leading to the lush green field of the Bowl, fully prepared as if a game was about to kick off. Once we reached the gridiron, we were told to look back up toward the tunnel from which we came. There, one by one, each recruit appeared, wearing "their" jersey that just moments ago lay on an easel.

UCLA had arranged for the official stadium announcer to be present. As each player exited the tunnel and began walking down the stairs to the field, we heard the blare of, "and now, playing for the UCLA Bruins, [insert name]." As Geoffrey's name was announced and he carefully ambled down the stairs, his size-eighteen shoes bigger than the step itself, tears once again streaked down my cheeks. I couldn't contain my emotions, as much as I tried. Dads don't cry. (Haha.) Oh my goodness. At that point, all I could envision was spending Saturdays at the Rose Bowl, proudly eyeballing Geoffrey from the stands, adorned in baby blue and gold, playing his college football for my beloved UCLA Bruins.

The unofficial visits were nothing like the official versions. No wining and dining. Much more business-like, but what we believed was necessary at the time. One was quite enjoyable. The other not so much.

At some point during Mitchell's junior season, Ron English, a coach from the University of Michigan Wolverines, visited Pali High. Mitchell was summoned from whatever he was doing at the time. By conversation's end, Mitchell had received a verbal offer to attend Michigan. Wow! That was the highest profile program to make an offer. But as we learned by this experience, verbal offers can be as valuable as a $3 bill.

Coach English indicated that a formal offer would be forthcoming from Michigan's Head Coach Lloyd Carr. As the weeks passed, nothing arrived.

Sights On College—Our Recruiting Odyssey

I kept hounding English, asking him about the formal offer. Each time he assured me it was on its way. Being people of our word and expecting the same from others, we believed the letter would surely arrive. That being so, Livie, Mitchell and I decided to journey to Ann Arbor, Michigan, for an unofficial visit. I scheduled a weekend with Coach English.

It was August 2006. All three of us were so amped to be visiting Ann Arbor and the Michigan campus. This was one of those programs that I had followed from afar since I was a youngster. Their fight song, "Hail to the Victors," is immediately recognizable to me. Frankly, it gets my blood pumping when I hear it. And The Big House is historic, at the time seating the most fans of any football stadium in the country at over 100,000.

We arrived on campus and headed to the administration building as arranged with the coach. Things went downhill from there. We were quickly informed that the players were not on campus that day. What? That's an important part of any visit. Watch practice. Interact with players. How could they schedule our visit on a day without players on site? It wasn't like they didn't know in advance we were coming. That set the tone for the rest of the day.

We were shepherded into Coach Carr's office. A huge room. Not very warm and inviting. We sat several feet apart (as was the norm years later during early COVID). The conversation was not very engaging. There was some mention of receiving a formal offer but, as we now know, that was a bunch of malarkey. Concluding the meeting with Carr, we were introduced to Offensive Line Coach Andy Moeller, whose duty that day was giving us a tour of the expansive campus, from his vehicle. As he drove, Coach Moeller attempted to engage us in conversation. I think by then, though, we all realized we were simply going through the motions, our enthusiasm destroyed in Coach Carr's office. The final straw? We weren't even taken to the stadium. I was so upset. Their actions that day were simply disgraceful.

At the end of the day, the trip was a complete waste of time. The formal offer letter never arrived. Coach English ultimately claimed that he never made the offer, which seemed disingenuous to me. And Coach Moeller complained that Mitchell was not very enthusiastic. Gee whiz. I wonder why not. Why couldn't they be honest? If they didn't intend to recruit Mitchell, then tell us so!

Fast forward several years. Mitchell was in the NFL playing for the Cleveland Browns. During Mitchell's four years with Cleveland, there was a revolving door of coaches, coordinators and front-office staff. Two presidents. Three head coaches. Four offensive coordinators. And two offensive line coaches. (Any wonder why Cleveland was such a bad team during this period?) Care to take a guess who ended up being Mitchell's o-line coach his last two seasons as a Brown? The former Michigan o-line coach, Andy Moeller—the very one who questioned Mitchell's enthusiasm. I frankly never asked Mitchell if the two of them ever had a conversation about that wasteful day. I suspect not. To what benefit?

Recruiting visits were, to some degree, a poor reflection on the NCAA. Livie and I both attended those very special weekends. Once, and only once, did we split duties. Livie accompanied Mitchell to the visit at Cal while I attended one of Geoffrey's Oregon games. However, that wasn't the case for all prospects. Some arrived by themselves, without being accompanied by an adult. Some were joined by just one parent. How unfortunate. Here you have a teenager involved in a potentially life-altering decision-making process that could transform their life and they are doing so without adult counsel. Why?

The NCAA does not cover travel costs for the parents. Imagine having to trek, for instance, from somewhere in the south to Eugene, Oregon, to visit the University of Oregon. That's at least a two-legged trip across country, if not three. Many parents simply can't afford that expense. Others can't afford to miss work. So the prospect travels alone or with just one of their two parents.

Back in 2015, two college coaches from prominent programs were quoted on the topic, mirroring my thoughts about parental travel for official visits. Arkansas's then-coach Bret Bielema offered, "We really should pay for at least one parent."

> *I think kids, when they are on official visits to these schools, they can so easily be fooled by coaches or people they are in touch with that really isn't reality. They get promised these things that don't ever happen or don't come true.*
>
> *If there's a parent around that can monitor everything, first the kid can make better decisions. And in the process, you'd have better relations down the road. I think that's very apparent.*

LSU's then-coach Les Miles was also right in line with my thinking when he stated the following to New Orleans' *Times-Picayune:*

Sights On College—Our Recruiting Odyssey

> *I think having a prospect's parent with them on a visitation is a tremendously important piece, and I think that should be made available for at least one parent—no matter what the length or distance is.*

> *If you're going to bring in a guy from California, you might as well bring in his mom or dad with him. If you need both parents, then maybe the family buys the ticket. But if it's the decision-maker, they need to come because [the family] needs to be comfortable, especially if there's long distance involved.*

If you can encourage parental interaction in any way in recruiting, then I'm for it.

The NCAA is a huge enterprise. In 2022-2023, the organization earned almost $1.3 billion in revenue. That's right. Why not carve out funds to cover travel costs for at least one parent to accompany a prospect to an official recruiting weekend visit? I haven't spent any time crunching the numbers, however, I believe that offering this benefit would not materially impact the NCAA's bottom line, whereas extending this financial assistance would be of great value to the prospect and his family.

As the weeks of their senior years passed, the wheat was separated from the chaff. Those schools truly interested continued to connect with the boys as much as was legally permitted. The intensity grew because each school wanted a commitment. But neither Mitchell nor Geoffrey would cave in to any pressure, and we as parents supported that approach. They would make their commitment decision when *they* were ready to do so. No sooner.

Another ploy coaches used to further bond with a prospect and their family was to request a home visit. As I recall, we had two head coaches to the house for a living room sit-down. Coach Mike Bellotti from Oregon came calling for both Geoffrey and Mitchell while Coach Al Groh from the University of Virginia rang the doorbell for Mitchell. Plus, we welcomed recruiting coaches Don Pellum from Oregon and Ron Gould from Cal for dinner. Livie's an excellent cook. She shined both nights. The meals were scrumptious. Remarkably, Oregon and Cal were schools the boys ultimately selected. We heard for years thereafter how much of a hit Livie's cooking was, especially the teriyaki-marinated flank steak she served to Coach Pellum.

Having head coaches sitting in our living room was surreal. Both seemed very familiar, as I had seen them on TV numerous times. Now they were in my house in the flesh. Of course, they pulled out all the stops trying to convince us, most particularly Mitchell or Geoffrey, that theirs should be the school of choice.

Days before Coach Bellotti's scheduled visit to see Mitchell, I had read *U.S. News and World Report*'s annual ranking of the top colleges and universities in the country. When Coach Bellotti walked through the door, I was very familiar with the rankings. As would be expected, at one point the conversation shifted to academics. When hearing about Mitchell's trio of preferences, Coach Bellotti, just like Coach Fullmer of Tennessee, suggested that his school was academically on par with Cal, Stanford and Virginia. That just wasn't the case. Oregon was ranked outside the top fifty while the other three were all listed in the top twenty-five. Oregon's marketing program was nationally recognized, having won numerous awards for research excellence. If Coach had focused on that one area of instruction, then his boast would have had more legitimacy. The exaggeration didn't help his cause.

Decision Time—Choosing a School

Ultimately, a decision had to be made. For Geoffrey, it came down to Arizona and Oregon. Livie and I felt comfortable with both. It was strictly up to Geoffrey. As we know, Oregon was victorious. Now it was time for Geoffrey to inform both coaches of his choice. How that was to be done was critical. Livie and I talked with Geoffrey about the process. Arizona's Coach Stoops was the first to be called, a difficult conversation for any seventeen-year-old. In a tweet, Geoffrey once shared, "I did not want to call the coaches to tell them so. My dad (rightfully so) made sure I did."

Geoffrey called Stoops, I'm sure with nerves off the charts. Coach was very professional. He expressed his disappointment, yet understood, and wished him well...after informing Geoffrey that he was with his entire family for Christmas and was hoping for a call with a different outcome.

Then it was time for the victors to hear the news. Geoffrey called Coach Bellotti. As I recall, the team had just landed ahead of their bowl game that season and the coach was walking down the stairs departing the airplane when Geoffrey's call lit up his phone.

When told of his decision, Coach Bellotti was ecstatic. So was Geoffrey. And so were Mom and Dad. Geoffrey's recruiting journey was a success. On one hand it was exhilarating. On the other, nerve-racking. In retrospect, Oregon was the right choice for Geoffrey. To this day, he's a

Sights On College—Our Recruiting Odyssey

Duck to his core and recalls his time as a student and athlete fondly. He grew into a man during those four years.

Mitchell had three options at the end: two West Coast schools and another that was 3,000 miles away. We once again left the decision to Mitchell, privately praying that his choice was not the one school across the country. Our prayers were answered. But the final decision took a rather circuitous route.

As the eleventh hour approached, Mitchell was leaning toward Stanford, with Cal being a close second. And then the news broke. It was late December. Stanford's Head Coach Walt Harris was given his pink slip. That usually means the entire staff would be released as well. All the relationships Mitchell had developed would vanish. Counselors will advise potential scholarship athletes to not make their college decisions based on coaches. Their argument? Coaches change, but not colleges. Location remains constant. Academic orientation remains consistent. Culture is unchanging. But then there's reality.

A seventeen- or eighteen-year-old teenager isn't thinking about these more universal considerations. They're basically focused on one thing. Football. They will be spending more time with their coaches than any other adult figure during their college tenure. So, it's not surprising that much of their decision-making comes down to the relationships they've developed and believe they will maintain with their prospective coaches.

When Mitchell learned of the Stanford staff's firing, his level of commitment took a big hit. He had no idea when a new head coach would be hired and who that person might be, much less who the offensive line coach would be. He could wait and try to get to know the new staff. But if that didn't work out his other opportunities might vanish.

Option number two was Cal. Mitchell had developed a solid relationship with Head Coach Jeff Tedford and an even better one with Offensive Line Coach Jim Michalczik. I, too, had developed a relationship with Jim, enough so to ask him for a consideration. At the time Cal had filled four of their five available offensive line slots. Only one was left. So, I asked, "Can we have right of first refusal?"

Ever heard of this concept? Basically, if another recruited high school lineman called Jim wanting to accept their offer, Jim was to check with us first before awarding the final scholarship. At that point it was either a yea or nay from Mitchell. No more "let me see." It was a tremendous ask, but what's the worst case? "No." Fortunately Jim kindly responded with "yes."

We would be called. Could I be absolutely sure the call would be made? No. But in my gut I felt Jim was ethical and would keep his word.

With all the unknowns at Stanford and the recruiting cycle coming to an end, Mitchell made his decision. He was to be a Cal Bear. And my instincts about Coach Michalczik turned out to be correct. He was always honest with Mitchell, and he demonstrated his integrity in other ways as well.

Like Geoffrey, Mitchell now had to contact the other schools. As I recall, the reaction from Coach Groh was not as gracious as Geoffrey's experience with Arizona Coach Stoops. And there was no Stanford head coach yet to call, so Mitchell contacted the recruiting coordinator, who pleaded with Mitchell to hold out. (Ironically, the coach hired was Jim Harbaugh, who transformed the Cardinal program into an eleven-game winner a handful of seasons later.) Nevertheless, I am convinced that Cal's staff, led by Coaches Tedford, Gould and Michalczik, was much better suited for Mitchell's personality. It was the best choice and allowed Mitchell to thrive, athletically as well as academically.

A peek into how the Cal staff might act presented itself soon after Mitchell's verbal commitment. Livie, Mitchell and I were in Las Vegas attending the season-ending Las Vegas Bowl in which Geoffrey was playing. As you might know, Oregon has become well known for pioneering creative uniform designs. That chilly night in Vegas they introduced a new set. The color scheme missed the mark. The helmet was a putrid mustard color. While sitting in the stands pregame, Mitchell's phone buzzed. It was Jim Michalczik. Knowing that Mitchell was in attendance, Jim inquired, "Are those helmets as ugly in person as they are on TV?" Mitchell's answer was a definitive "Yes!!" We all burst out laughing.

About a month later we received the very unfortunate news that my brother Paul, forty-six years old with two young kids, had passed away. We loaded up the car and headed for the suburbs of Phoenix, Arizona, where he had lived. Joining us was my father. I can't begin to imagine what it was like for Dad having to attend the funeral of his youngest son. The day after arriving in Arizona we spent the afternoon with my sister-in-law Tammy and two nieces, Rebecca and Rachel, at their home. While passing the time, Mitchell's phone rang. It was Coach Gould from Cal.

Ron had promised Livie and me several times during our interactions with him that he would always be there to support Mitchell if the need arose. He passed the first test. Somehow the staff caught wind of Mitchell

Sights On College—Our Recruiting Odyssey

losing his uncle. The call was to extend condolences and offer his and the staff's support.

At this point in time, Mitchell had not even signed the paperwork making his commitment to Cal official. That was another month away. All I could think was, if they would show such interest before he officially became a Bear, imagine how they would conduct themselves when it was official. It was a very comforting feeling for both Livie and me.

Once verbally committed and all interested parties informed of the decisions, there wasn't anything else to do until official signing day. That is, unless the prospect wanted to change his mind, or the school(s) left at the altar didn't accept a "no." Nothing was official until the prospect submitted his signed, and binding, National Letter of Intent (NLI) on National Signing Day (NSD). Until 2017, NSD was the first Wednesday in February. (It has since been expanded to two separate days.) So, for both Mitchell and Geoffrey, the final step was that first Wednesday in February.

To be expected, given his personality as viewed through a distant lens as head coach of Stanford, my beloved San Francisco 49ers and his alma mater Michigan Wolverines, Jim Harbaugh wasn't one to give up easily. He called Mitchell soon after being named Stanford's head coach. Couldn't blame him. Mitchell was a prized recruit. It would be a real coup to flip his commitment, especially from Stanford's archrival. His try was unsuccessful. At that point Mitchell knew nothing about Harbaugh and understood that taking the time to get to know him would likely eliminate Cal as an option. A bird in the hand is worth two in the bush, as they say. Mitchell held firm.

Harbaugh wasn't the only coach who didn't give up easily. Coach Stoops of Arizona called Geoffrey about a week before signing day. When Geoffrey answered, Coach asked if a decision had been made, as if he had no recollection of being told otherwise. We'll never know whether that was a ploy to take one more shot, or he simply forgot the prior conversation.

The window to submit a signed National Letter of Intent began at 7 a.m. on that first Wednesday morning in February. We worked with the boys to have all the documentation prepared the night before. As the clock struck the prescribed hour, the papers were inserted into the fax machine (no such thing as scan and email back then), the telephone number entered and the send key pressed. In mere seconds it would be official. I wasn't aware of the Cal receipt process, but there was a definite hierarchy at Oregon. Alum, benefactor, supporter number one and co-founder of Nike, Phil Knight would stand at the fax machine awaiting the NLIs to spit out. (Given what he has meant to the University of Oregon, it only seemed right that he was the sentry.)

Those two Wednesday mornings were the culmination of years of emotional ups and downs for the boys—as well as for their mother and father–physical and mental growth and tough decisions. It was also an awesome journey working our way through the twists and turns of recruiting. I'd say that entering this odyssey, not knowing a thing about the process, it all turned out wonderfully. The boys had extraordinary experiences at their respective schools. Both graduated with degrees. Both played football at the highest possible levels in college. Both made lifelong friends. Both made their way into the NFL.

And little did we know until years later that their decisions had set in motion our retirement plans. There's an argument expressed rather consistently that athletic scholarships financially benefit the student-athlete. How so? I found an article summarizing a study asking about parents' contributions toward college costs. According to that survey, 85 percent of college students had some form of financial help from their parents. Proves my point. Scholarship benefits largely accrue to the parents. In our case, unscientifically crunching the numbers, I would offer that the two scholarships saved us more than $250,000 of after-tax dollars. Those dollars saved helped support the financial foundation that Livie and I built to retire in our sixties and paid for our many trips to watch our sons play football in person.

I understand that, for many, this journey isn't always so positive. Fortunately, all four of us are supremely blessed.

4
UCLA—A DREAM DASHED

My fascination with UCLA began long before I officially became a Bruin.

As a twelve-year-old, I played organized basketball for the first time. Being six feet tall, I was the starting center for my sixth-grade elementary school team. I remember so clearly that I could hardly fit into the uniforms available back then. The bottoms were old school, hardly extending beyond my derriere.

My love for basketball led me to follow the best team in the country back then, the UCLA Bruins. I couldn't wait for Saturday afternoons to watch the Bruins in action. That was the season (January of 1968) when, for those who might recall, Elvin Hayes and his Houston Cougars broke UCLA's forty-seven-game winning streak in the Astrodome in what some describe as The Game of the Century. Lew Alcindor, who four years later assumed the name of Kareem Abdul-Jabbar, played with a scratched eye and was not his usual exceptional self. Later in the year, fully recovered, he avenged that loss during the semi-finals of the NCAA tournament.

I was hooked on UCLA from that time forward. When it came time to apply to college, it was UCLA. I also applied to San Jose State, but truth be told, I do not know to this day whether I would have attended SJS if denied by UCLA. Maybe instead the local junior college. Fortunately, UCLA opened their doors to me.

Raising Giants

If memory serves me correctly, I likely attended at least 95 percent of the football and basketball home games during my four years on campus. Back then UCLA shared the Los Angeles Memorial Coliseum for football home games with the USC Trojans. Basketball games were held on campus at Pauley Pavilion. Long before there were lotteries and the like to attend games, students lined up outside Pauley on a first come, first served basis, waiting for the doors to fly open. The earlier you arrived, the better chance you had to secure prime seats. I was typically one of the early arrivals. When I started dating Livie in my sophomore year, she joined me in line, and together we made the mad dash to our "selected" seats once those doors flew open.

In 1978, one year after graduating and Livie and I tying the knot, we bought four season tickets to UCLA football games. We held on to those tickets until 2021. Those fall Saturdays were sacrosanct, whether the Bruins played in the Coliseum or ultimately in the Rose Bowl after moving there in 1982. Nothing else got in the way.

When Geoffrey was five years old, we began taking him to games. When Mitchell turned five, he joined us. The boys truly loved the outings. They became huge UCLA fans. What a surprise, huh? Learned the eight-clap cheer made famous by UCLA. Had all sorts of UCLA-themed shirts and sweatshirts in their closets or dresser drawers. They treasured the one jersey and many hats we collected over time, adorned with UCLA player autographs. When the Bruins played an away game that was televised, we all jumped on the family room couch to watch.

As Geoffrey progressed in high school and playing college football was becoming more and more of a possibility, you likely wouldn't be surprised to learn that UCLA ranked number one out of the schools he wished to play for. And, of course, that would be the absolute dream come true for Dad. So when Geoffrey received that Junior Day invitation from UCLA, oh my. He was possibly one step closer to realizing a football dream.

As with Stanford, UCLA pulled out all the stops. All day long during that Saturday in early June, Dad couldn't stop thinking about his son, one day soon, jogging onto the football field wearing blue and gold. My first impressions of Head Coach Karl Dorrell were positive. Nice enough guy. Somewhat subdued. Very business-like, which seemed to be a departure from most coaches; however, being the businessperson I was, I appreciated that approach. At some point during the festivities, Geoffrey was

UCLA—A Dream Dashed

approached and invited to attend an upcoming multi-day camp on the UCLA campus. He must have impressed the staff with what they saw during his junior season. His schedule would only allow for one day of participation. We committed to that day, a Sunday. I dropped Geoffrey off at campus that morning, awaiting a call to pick him up.

The call came much sooner than expected, maybe ninety minutes into camp. There was an uncommon excitement in Geoffrey's voice on the other end. He shared that the coaches seemed to like him, and he thought it would be wise for me to return to campus ASAP. Being the dutiful dad, plus thinking that maybe a scholarship offer was in the offing, I dashed out the door, sped up the 405 freeway (I'm sure exceeding all speed limits) and was on campus in about twenty minutes.

Geoffrey was right. Linebacker coach Don Johnson, responsible for recruiting Pali High and the surrounding area, did verbally offer Geoffrey a scholarship that day. Geoffrey was elated. And, of course, Dad was over the moon. We left the campus ecstatic.

Later that evening Geoffrey received a call from Coach Johnson. Geoffrey had spent little time with Coach Dorrell while at the camp. They wanted to schedule an in-person visit with Coach Dorrell for a more intimate conversation later in the week.

Wednesday was the day. It couldn't arrive soon enough. Livie, Geoffrey and I were clock-watching until the appropriate time to leave. We followed instructions as to where to park on campus and where to meet the coaches. We spent about ninety minutes with Coach Dorrell, joined by the offensive line coach Mark Weber and then were escorted around the facilities, weight room and such. The three of us left campus believing that the meetings went well. Were we so, so wrong.

The Offer That Wasn't and Other Setbacks

A couple of days later, Friday morning to be exact, an email appeared in my inbox from Coach Dorrell. I truly wish I had retained that message but, unfortunately, I did not. The email retracted the offer, claiming that it was not the right time to proceed and suggested the parties reconnect at some future time. My heart sank. We were devastated.

I first shared the news with Livie. We huddled together to map a course of action. Geoffrey was at school when the email arrived, so we had some time to react before he returned home. I first called Coach Dorrell. No answer, so I left a message. I then tried several of the other coaches who we had met at Junior Day. No luck. Not one of them had the good graces to take or return my call. They hid, like cowards. No different than sending an email to share such shocking information rather than demonstrating professionalism, and a spine, to call us with what they had to know would be devastating news. (A similar scenario to what you'll read about in Chapter 18, "Don't Be Fooled—It *Is* a Business.")

I finally got through to one of the coaches. We arranged to talk with Coach Dorrell that afternoon. I believe it was 3:00 p.m. Dorrell was joined by Coach Weber. They attempted to explain themselves.

Geoffrey, they claimed, did not show much enthusiasm during the Wednesday meeting. How ironic, given that Coach Dorrell was referred to in print articles as "dullard." Additionally, they were upset that Geoffrey attended a day camp at USC the day after UCLA offered the scholarship. "We know about these things," they boasted. And the problem with that? Before being invited to UCLA's camp, we had committed to have Geoffrey attend this one-day USC camp. A commitment is a commitment in my book. Plus, in the world of recruiting, as we learned throughout this odyssey, in some cases the hard way, one needs to cover every base. Never know what's going to happen. But the "best" was yet to come. We had informed both coaches during our in-person meeting about Stanford's scholarship offer and that Geoffrey would not make any decision until we heard from Stanford about Geoffrey's admission application. News would likely arrive within two weeks.

Apparently, that did not sit well with the coaches. When the topic of Stanford arose during the call, Coach Weber offered the most outlandish comment we ever heard during the entire recruiting process. To quote, he said, "I guess you value academics over athletics because you're waiting to hear from Stanford."

Wait a minute. Did I really hear what I thought I heard? How dare we value academics over athletics because we all know that every collegiate football player will ascend to the NFL and make life-sustaining money. Oh my goodness.

The conversation changed nothing. They still wanted to table any further discussion about another scholarship offer.

We ultimately learned that the coaching staff had an expectation of an immediate acceptance given our ties to the institution. Basically, we would kiss the ring without any further evaluation. I guess they did not know who they were dealing with.

Of course, we were all devastated by the events of that five- or six-day period. We had no choice but to put this episode behind us and continue with the recruiting process. But, I'll tell you, I was so angry my blood was boiling.

We ultimately heard from Stanford. It took a few more weeks than expected, but word finally reached us. As fate would have it, Geoffrey's application was denied. Although the Stanford coaches could not, would not, guarantee admission, they were very confident he would be admitted. That confidence was misplaced.

Livie called the admissions office to ask why. She was told that, regardless of Geoffrey's overall GPA, regardless of his notable extracurricular activities, regardless of the overall strength of his application, they could not accept him because he received a "C" grade in a freshman Spanish class. Wow. That was a double whammy for all of us. No UCLA. And now no Stanford.

As with many of the experiences on our odyssey, this was not the end of the story. A few months later, late in Geoffrey's senior high school season, Coach Johnson unexpectedly returned to Pali one day to talk with him about resuming the conversation. He apologized for the previous withdrawal of the scholarship but did not have a new offer in hand. If we were open to the idea, they wanted to invite us to a recruiting weekend in December. We accepted.

Friday night we checked into the five-star Century Plaza Hotel in Century City, a mere four miles from our house and across the street from Livie's office. Once settled in, we gathered downstairs for an introductory meal with UCLA coaches, other recruits and their parents.

Saturday morning began with that breakfast at Gladstones, followed by the Rose Bowl visit. After leaving the Rose Bowl, we spent the afternoon at the hotel, before joining the coaches and staff for dinner at a fashionable Beverly Hills restaurant. Nothing remarkable about that evening. It was the events of Sunday morning that, shall we say, "took the cake." And that is saying a mouthful given what we had experienced over the previous six months.

Sunday morning, the three of us gathered for breakfast in the hotel restaurant with the coaches and fellow recruits. As the festivities were seemingly winding down, one of the coaches beckoned us to meet with Coach Dorrell in a private room. I was anticipating a mea culpa after the bungling of the initial scholarship offer and then expected a new offer to follow. I believe regrets were extended.

But the scholly? They did not have a traditional scholarship to offer. Instead, he proposed a grayshirt. Without getting into the nitty-gritty, a "grayshirt offer" is really not an offer. It is more of a placeholder. They wanted us to wait until later that school year to see if a legitimate scholarship would open up. Are you kidding me?!?

With two legitimate scholarship offers in hand at that point from Oregon and Arizona, and after UCLA retracted one offer and then made a phantom second, UCLA selfishly wanted us to give up the known for the unknown. NOT A CHANCE! This was strike three. We were done. We declined and walked out, once again with dreams dashed.

A few years later, I attended a UCLA networking event in the backyard of a UCLA booster. By happenstance I ran into a fellow Bruin, Andy Hill, a member of Coach Wooden's three straight NCAA championship teams from 1970 to 1972, who I did not know at that time, but because of a common acquaintance we knew of each other. (We have since become very dear friends.) Andy was familiar with the circumstances of Geoffrey's recruiting journey.

After we completed our pleasantries, he noticed UCLA's Athletic Director Dan Guerrero amid the guests. He knew Dan well enough to approach him. Andy pointed in Dan's direction and said, "Follow me." I did.

Once corralled, Andy began detailing all that happened with Geoffrey's recruitment. He also threw in the fact that we were life-long Bruin supporters, season tickets holders for decades and had financially contributed to the school for the thirty years since our graduation. After completing his accounting, he urged me to give Guerrero one of my business cards, which I did. He then encouraged Dan to reach out for a more detailed conversation. I have never seen anyone scurry away so quickly, like a squirrel chasing its next meal. He wanted nothing to do with the Schwartz family and never reached out after that day. Gee, any wonder why the coaches were so resistant to talk to me the day the retraction email arrived? This was a first-hand example of the adage, "A fish rots from the head down."

I entitled this chapter "A Dream Dashed," but you know what? It all worked out for the best. Both Geoffrey and Mitchell thoroughly enjoyed their collegiate years at Oregon and Cal, respectively. They received their degrees and played football for staffs who wanted them as part of their teams. And maybe they benefited by being far enough away from their sometimes overzealous but well-meaning father.

SECOND QUARTER

5

GEOFFREY'S JOURNEY TO THE DRAFT

I discovered that the path from the college gridiron to the stadiums of the NFL is a multi-tiered process:
- Finish college strong.
- Select an agent.
- Participate in an all-star game.
- Prepare for and compete at the Combine.
- Head to the Finish Line.

As I previously noted, the odds of becoming a professional football player are miniscule, as offered by USC's Athletic Director Pat Haden.

From a 40,000-foot perspective, Mitchell's and Geoffrey's paths from high school football to the NFL gridiron were very similar. They both were drafted, became starters and enjoyed a successful eight or nine years in the league. However, their respective journeys, up to and including draft day, were often quite dissimilar. One as smooth as glass. The other turbulent, challenging, anxiety-ridden, akin to white-water rafting. I'll start with Geoffrey, simply because he was the first drafted.

Finish Strong

After Geoffrey's first three seasons at Oregon, he was not NFL worthy. I didn't need an assessment from an expert to understand that. His first season in 2004 was a waste, Oregon "burning" his redshirt-eligible

Raising Giants

season by trotting him out on the field for only eighty snaps over the course of an eleven-game season. It was a damn shame. His freshman-season offensive line coach, Neal Zoumboukos, came clean after the season, admitting that Oregon made a huge mistake playing Geoffrey instead of redshirting him. We'll never know the full impact of Oregon's ill-advised decision, given the fact that he sustained a back injury during his 2006 junior year, requiring surgery. With the extra season, the injury and surgery would have taken place in his redshirt sophomore season, giving him two full healthy years before the draft. I'm convinced losing the year made a difference in where he was drafted.

Sophomore year found Geoffrey a starter at right tackle. Unfortunately, the team sort of reneged on a promise made to us during recruiting. They committed to being watchdogs when it came to his weight. Geoffrey arrived in Oregon already a big human, tipping the scales at around 335 pounds. He played his sophomore season carrying 370, reducing his agility and mobility. Realizing that the added poundage was unhealthy and counterproductive to being the best player he could be, Geoffrey, on his own accord, shed almost forty pounds during the offseason, curbing his caloric intake while daily hopping on an exercise bike in his dorm complex to sweat away the unnecessary weight.

For the greater percentage of college football players, like Mitchell and Geoffrey, they generally first appear on the NFL radar during their junior year. This highly critical season is typically when the NFL begins watching film, talking to coaches, possibly attending games and gathering the megabytes of information necessary to conduct player evaluations.

Geoffrey began his junior year at Oregon without distinguishing himself during his freshman and sophomore seasons. I assure you he was a complete unknown to the NFL at that point in time. His junior season had to be a statement year. Unfortunately, it was not.

Geoffrey suffered throughout the year from a genetically bad back. It runs in the family. His grandmother. His pops. I used to watch him after games shuffling his feet, like some eighty-year-old worn down by the decades and in pain as he walked off the field. It would have taken a superhuman effort for him to perform at a level needed to attract any kind of NFL attention.

Geoffrey's injury contributed to him being benched twice during this critical year at the start of games by offensive line coach Steve Greatwood, who I felt was less than understanding. I give Geoffrey a whole lot of credit for trying to push through the pain, but in reality it did him more harm than good. However, that was the culture. Tough it out. Play with pain. The problem is that the NFL wants nothing to do with nonstarters, or players who find themselves benched during the season. Anyone from the NFL watching Oregon film to evaluate other Duck players simply would not have paid much attention to Geoffrey.

At the conclusion of his junior year, Geoffrey's back was surgically repaired, the first of many surgeries he would encounter during his playing days. I took a few days off from work to fly up to Eugene to be with him pre-surgery and then spend a few days post-op to help with his initial recovery. Livie held down the fort back home. I remember so clearly his first moments after being wheeled back to his hospital room. I was sitting in a nearby chair. He seemed comfortable. While talking with him, he coughed. No big deal, right? He immediately shouted words not appropriate for these pages. I gasped, thinking it was a spike of pain in the repaired area. Not the case. With a big grin on his face, he excitedly explained that this was the first time in what seemed like forever that when he coughed, or sneezed, and his back did not hurt. Thank goodness for modern medicine.

Fortunately, under the guidance of a well-qualified Oregon medical and training staff, led by Kevin "Chief" Steil, and the best facilities in the land, Geoffrey fully recovered in time for July summer camp heading into his senior season. He took his rightful place at starting right tackle as camp kicked off. If the NFL was to beckon, a monster year was a must.

Geoffrey had a mammoth season. By this time in my evolution, I knew a thing or two about good play. He was playing at a high level. At the end of the season, my assessment was confirmed. Geoffrey was recognized by the Pac-10 as a second-string all-conference honoree. That translated to being the third or fourth best tackle in the conference out of twenty starting right and left tackles.

Not to sound like "one of those fathers," because second team is a wonderful accomplishment, but it could have been better. According to someone I knew with credibility and first-hand knowledge of the selection process, I was told that Geoffrey was initially voted to the first team. That didn't sit well with one Pac-10 coach. Exerting his influence, and with some hornswoggling, the final vote found Geoffrey demoted to second team so this coach's tackle could receive first-team recognition. Oh, the reality of life.

Selecting an Agent

With an NFL career much more likely based on his senior-year performance, Geoffrey needed to hire an agent. Why? Because it's a must to be represented. These agents know the lay of the land, the ins and outs of the entire draft process. They personally know, sometimes very intimately, NFL coaches, staff and management. They know how to market and promote the athletes to help them possibly ascend the draft ladder. And, most importantly, they negotiate "the deal."

As Geoffrey's senior-season campaign progressed, and he played like he was draftable, two big questions arose in our minds. What agent would be interested in a player like Geoffrey, who, legitimately, had one productive college season? And, secondly, how would interest be generated?

As the season progressed, calls from agents or their minions began to trickle in. But just like with college recruiting, we were novices, knowing virtually nothing about this vital process of selecting an agent. It was very unnerving. Fortunately, we had some unexpected assistance.

During Geoffrey's first high school year, Livie and I had decided to engage an independent college counselor to help the boys with college selection, irrespective of football. While Palisades High was a first-rate academic institution in the Los Angeles Unified School District, their ratio of internal counselors to students was not acceptable to us.

Our decision to engage outside counselors proved to be invaluable. From an academic perspective, the two women we worked with were excellent, worth every penny spent. They really knew their stuff. As we worked more closely with them, we learned, purely coincidentally, that one of them was married to a giant in the field of football agents. His stable of players was the who's who of the NFL. As if that wasn't enough, their son was employed by an NFL team. So not only did we benefit from the counselors' extensive knowledge of colleges and the admission processes, we also received guidance years later when it came to selecting an agent and the draft. We are forever grateful for their generosity.

Of all the advice we received, one piece was especially key. We were strongly advised to shield the boys from direct contact with agents, as they tended to push boundaries when it came to pursuing a potential client. They would attempt to make contact at any time, day or night. During classes. While at practice. Late evening. While studying. During family time. Parents, we were told, needed to be the barrier, at least initially, between their sons and agents on the prowl. Nothing more to say. As I had been doing since birth, I was their protector.

Any agent who made initial contact with Geoffrey was quickly given my contact information and told to work through me. I believe most abided by this direction. If they fell off the wagon, they were reminded of the protocol by Geoffrey or ultimately by me, in no uncertain terms.

Early on during Oregon's recruiting of Geoffrey, we were introduced to their recruiting coordinator and Director of Player Development, Deryk Gilmore. Deryk's role was multifaceted. Among his responsibilities, he was an interface between the team and prospective scholarship candidates. He was responsible for developing all marketing materials that found their way into our mailbox. Deryk was extraordinarily good at what he did. Extremely creative. His marketing skills were so advanced at the time that he occasionally ran into headwinds with the NCAA.

So, looking back, unknown to us at the time, the hunt for an agent was not really an open casting call. We had developed a strong relationship with Deryk during his time at Oregon that continued when he left to become an agent. In retrospect, I truly believe he had the inside track from the beginning. Nonetheless, it was only prudent to consider all comers before a final decision was made.

From the moment we all met him, we formed an immediate bond with Deryk. And it only grew stronger over time, during Deryk's remaining tenure with Oregon. Geoffrey arrived on campus in 2004. Deryk left for what was to him greener pastures after the 2005 season. No, not to another collegiate athletic program. He became an agent, joining a well-respected agency headquartered in Chicago, Priority Sports and Entertainment.

Having "inside" information on us as a family, but more importantly about Geoffrey, Deryk let his intentions be known early on. He wanted to represent Geoffrey. Before anyone else had given him a lick of a chance to graduate to the NFL, Deryk believed in Geoffrey the person and his abilities on the field. Obviously, you will not find Deryk's name on the list of doubters Geoffrey carries with him. For more on this, see the next chapter, "Society of Doubters."

Conducting himself ethically, morally, professionally and legally, Deryk actively pursued Geoffrey. He knew that although a relationship existed between them, signing Geoffrey would not be a slam dunk. It had to be earned. And Livie and I knew that we would do Geoffrey a horrible disservice if we/he did not consider a broader field of agent candidates.

Others did ultimately join the pursuit. As I recall, I whittled down the list of possibilities to four or five agencies, including Priority Sports and Deryk. I would receive regular calls from all these groups. When the time was appropriate, we scheduled in-person visits for each to present their "dog and pony show" to the family.

As agents conducted their due diligence on Geoffrey, we also completed our homework on each respective agency. Slowly we trimmed the list. The first one out was an agency from Northern California. The fact that this agency was a single-shingle operation with just one agent, did not automatically disqualify them. What ultimately led to their elimination from consideration was embellishment of their accomplishments.

During our numerous conversations, this agent boasted of negotiating contracts greater than $120 million. On the surface, this aggregate over the course of an agent's career actually sounded impressive. Remember, this was back in the late 2000s when salaries of $20, $30, $40 million per year were unheard of, unlike in today's NFL, where a single NFL player contract could easily exceed $200 million.

Digging deeper, I discovered that this agent's stable was largely comprised of Women's National Basketball Association (WNBA) players and that he represented one NBA player who had signed an $85 million contract, about two-thirds of the aggregate total of his negotiated deals.

Knowing all this, I subsequently inquired, "Who have you represented in the NFL?" He offered some names. One or two were remotely familiar. The others complete unknowns. That was the point at which we said, "thanks, but no thanks," believing this agency was not right for Geoffrey.

Early on in this process, I received a cautionary word from someone who had walked in these shoes previously. They warned, "Be careful with the exaggerations." Agents, in their normal course, were not inclined to blatantly lie; however, they were not immune to stretching or manipulating the truth to serve their purposes, trying to appear more influential and successful than they really were. Our experience with this one agent corroborated the warning.

We continued to dialogue with Priority and two other well-qualified agencies. To be fair though, it wasn't exclusively the relationship with Deryk that tipped the scales in Priority's favor. Mike McCartney was a senior member of the agency. Does his last name sound familiar? Mike's father, Bill, was the head coach of the NCAA 1990 National Championship Colorado Buffaloes for whom Coach Blatt played.

Mike grew up with football in his genes. Before representing NFL players, he had two college coaching stints, one of those with his father at Colorado. Mike then moved on to the NFL, where he was a scout for one team and director of pro personnel for another. He spent the better part of a decade intimately involved in personnel evaluations and draft selections. That was key for me. Having first-hand knowledge of the goings-on in a team's war room◉ gave me comfort that there was legitimacy to Geoffrey's draft prospects and that, if signed with Priority, he would be properly represented.

Also, unlike the single-shingle agency, Mike and Priority had a huge stable of elite NFL players for whom they negotiated noteworthy contracts. Combining Mike's extensive NFL experience and Deryk's engaging enthusiasm and depth of belief in Geoffrey's abilities, this felt like a perfect team to engage and represent Geoffrey. As time passed, we learned just how right Geoffrey's choice was.

All-Star Game

With this all-important decision now in the rearview mirror, the next critical step in Geoffrey's draft journey? An invite to a postseason college all-star game. These showcases gather the best NFL prospects for first-hand evaluation by NFL staff. There are typically two ways to be invited. A direct invite as a reward for stellar performance, or an agent's advocacy helping to open the door.

While there are several of these games played after bowl season, two are considered the best and most influential. The Senior Bowl, played every year in Mobile, Alabama, was and still is considered the jewel of collegiate all-star games. An invitation to this game almost assures an athlete an invite to the upcoming NFL Scouting Combine◉, where the best college players perform physical and mental tests in front of NFL scouts and coaches. Unfortunately, Geoffrey's level of performance at Oregon didn't qualify him to participate.

The second respected contest was, and remains, the East-West Shrine Bowl game, that year held in Houston, Texas. Unlike the Senior Bowl, the Shrine game doesn't have an anchor location. I'll never know whether Geoffrey's invite was based solely on his on-field performance or whether Deryk's active advocacy to the organizers helped seal the deal. Regardless, it was a great honor to be included, although Geoffrey was soon to face some strong headwinds.

Oregon's offensive approach during Geoffrey's career was not well suited for the NFL. The scheme was progressively revolutionary, beginning with the aggressive spread offense introduced by Offensive Coordinator Gary Crowton. The innovation culminated during Geoffrey's senior season with the groundbreaking system introduced by then Oregon Offensive Coordinator and future Duck, NFL and UCLA head coach Chip Kelly.

Chip's scheme was initially nicknamed "The Blur" by the coaching staff, then shifted to the acronym "F.U.J.I." When asked what the acronym stood for, Head Coach Mike Bellotti had no answer. Basically, he explained, "spot the ball and get out of the way." It was extremely fast-paced. No huddle. Up tempo from the first whistle. The intent? Wear down the defense with the offensive pace and complexity of the playbook. Physically and mentally fatigued, the opponent's "D" would give up big plays, leading to an avalanche of touchdowns.

When Geoffrey was draft eligible, NFL offenses were much more deliberately paced, except for the two-minute drills preceding halftime and the end of the game, when the offensive pace dramatically picks up. Even in today's no-huddle NFL world, watch closely and you'll see the offense quickly line up but then spend the great majority of the play clock evaluating the defense and possibly audibling—changing the play call to adapt to the defensive positioning.

Without getting too nerdy here, the distinctive factor in Oregon's offensive approach that gave Geoffrey trouble during his Shrine game week, as well as early on in his NFL career, was his pre-snap stance. For four seasons at Oregon, he was positioned in a two-point stance with knees bent, both hands resting on his thigh pads. Didn't matter whether the play was a run or a pass, this was the starting posture.

When Geoffrey was draft eligible, three-point stances, with a forearm leaning on a thigh, the other hand resting on the turf, were the norm in the NFL. (Over time the NFL has morphed into a combination of the two as the newfangled college spread offenses crept into the NFL game.) Given these college all-star showcases are intended to provide scouts, coaches and management with a chance to evaluate collegiate talent in an NFL environment, Geoffrey was forced into using the three-point version the entire week of Shrine practice and, of course, during the game. What a departure from his four years of exclusive two-point stances while at Oregon!

Geoffrey's Journey to the Draft

As I recall, the week of practice and the game itself were not especially noteworthy. But that may be more a father's attempt to forget reality rather than face what happened on the field. While once again listening to Geoffrey on the radio recently (I do that a bunch), the topic of the draft arose. He was asked by his cohost to describe his East-West Shrine Game experience. "Rough week," he revealed. "My first time in a three-point stance against an edge rush in three years."

You might be familiar with journalist and author Malcolm Gladwell and his rule of 10,000 hours. Gladwell asserts that to achieve true expertise in any activity, it takes 10,000 cumulative hours of correct repetition to achieve the "muscle memory" needed for that goal. While there are those who have debunked this rule, you get the idea. For Geoffrey, while it didn't amount to 10,000 hours, he did spend every single practice and game for three years in a two-point stance. Now he was forced into using a three-point stance at a most critical time in his football career. Imagine spending your entire life cutting meat with a knife in your right hand and then being asked to cut with your left, without any practice.

Geoffrey came away from the Shrine game taking Coach Blatt's advice to heart. Being brutally honest with himself...and others...he was quick to share that he had underperformed. He knew what he was talking about. Geoffrey got his hands on his Shrine game evaluation. It wasn't pretty. The evaluators declared his "struggles throughout the week of practice... and during the game will push him down the board." The "board" is a reference to the draft board that all teams use to arrange their picks before the draft. How prescient that was to be when it came to the draft.

On the positive side though, the week in Houston did provide NFL personnel with affirmation that Geoffrey's back was completely healed from his surgery. Extracted from the evaluation, "he struggled with a back injury throughout his junior season and his play improved when healthy as a senior."

The Shrine week also served to corroborate the genetic mutation that is Geoffrey. Geoffrey was described as a "massive man whose size and upper body strength make him an imposing drive blocker." The experience overall was a blend of good and not so good, but it did confirm that he possessed the physical tools to play in the NFL.

At this point, was the glass half full or half empty? Geoffrey had a less-than-stellar junior campaign but exorcized those demons during his senior year. He had hired a well-respected agency that would serve him well during his career. He attended the Shrine all-star game, albeit to mixed reviews. However, as I learned while researching for this book, a touch over 50 percent of the players who participated in the Shrine week were ultimately drafted. His performance was not necessarily a deathblow. The ducks (pardon the pun) were beginning to line up for him. Next?

The Combine

The NFL Scouting Combine, also known as the National Invitational Camp, is a week-long invitation-only showcase held annually in late February, early March. For Geoffrey, it was the period from February 20 to 26, 2008. It gathers the best of the best college football players in Indianapolis, Indiana, to strut their stuff in front of NFL coaches, scouts and, in most cases, senior management, up to and including owners. Each athlete is present for four days, depending on their position group.

This Combine originally kicked off in 1982, its prime purpose then to provide a central location where clubs could poke and prod the athletes, not unlike cattle, to evaluate first-hand their medical condition. Previously, medical ailments could be hidden or disguised from teams, only to be discovered once drafted and after a substantial investment has been made in the player.

For instance, Geoffrey sprained his knee at the end of his first training camp. He played every game and apparently was never on the weekly injury report, so the public was unaware of the injury. At the Combine, a doctor, testing the stability of his knees, asked Geoffrey if he had previously sprained his medial collateral ligament (MCL)🏈. Almost four years later, the doctor could feel some joint instability. Had he not personally checked, no one would have ever known. Fortunately, no harm, no foul.

The Combine format, in the four decades since its inception, has morphed into a spectacle. Several days are now televised on the NFL Network. Behind the scenes, players all take a psych evaluation. Some are invited to fifteen-minute interviews with team personnel. When Geoffrey participated, 330 players attended, about the same number as Mitchell's year.

Geoffrey received one interview invite, but it was a very telling experience. First, one invite suggested he was not generating a whole lot of interest from teams. Then there was *the* question. These coaches and evaluators take their jobs seriously. They thoroughly watch film. "Did you play hard in that game?" One game during Geoffrey's senior season caught their eye. They thought Geoffrey hadn't given his full effort.

They were right. He wasn't going full speed. Geoffrey answered honestly. He explained that the game was against a weaker team and the opposing defensive linemen were some of the weakest in the league, so he performed accordingly. That was the end of any contact with this NFL team.

You would think that this experience would have taught Geoffrey a lesson. NEVER, ever adjust your level of play to conform to the ability of the player across the line of scrimmage. NEVER. But it hadn't.

In either his first or second year with Carolina, the Panthers were playing one of the weaker teams in the league. Not only was the team weak, so was the defender who would likely line up against Geoffrey. Or so he thought. He did not properly prepare for that game. And he got schooled. Beaten on numerous pass rushes. He also gave up several pressures on his quarterback.

One of his teammates, all-pro offensive lineman Jordan Gross, yanked Geoffrey aside after the game. In terms not appropriate for these pages, Jordan made it crystal clear to Geoffrey that he can never underestimate his opponents. They are all professionals. Their livelihood, just like Geoffrey's, depends on their performance, so they are going to play hard every snap. That was the last warning Geoffrey needed. He realized that this wasn't college any longer, where he "could get away operating at 85 percent"—his words—because the talent level was frequently weak.

Combine athletes participate in several on-field drills intended to provide club staff with measurables that can result in an elevated assessment, confirm pre-Combine assessments or, in the worst of cases, cause a player to drop on draft boards, to the point of even being dropped from draft consideration altogether.

Interestingly, these drills are not position specific. All players in attendance are required to bench press. Makes sense for a QB, huh? In this discipline, much more stock is placed on offensive linemen, like Geoffrey and Mitchell. O-linemen are expected to be studs, to have the capacity to pump a whole lot of iron. Not meeting expectations could have draft consequences. But how fair is all this?

A lineman with shorter arms will always have an advantage over those with longer arms. Lifting 225 pounds an additional six inches multiple times will take a toll on an upper body and likely result in less reps overall.

Does that mean that the longer-armed linemen are any weaker than their short-armed counterparts? I certainly think not. Plus, when does an offensive lineman ever bench press a body during a game? If they are doing so, it means they are sprawled on their backs. Not the ideal blocking position.

Or how about the forty-yard dash? When is an offensive lineman required to run, much less "dash," forty yards on a football field? Virtually never. Unless you are Geoffrey Schwartz. When his New York Giants teammate Odell Beckham Jr. made one of the most spectacular catches in NFL history, back turned to the end zone, falling backward, snatching the pass one-handed behind his head with only three fingers, Geoffrey bolted downfield in excitement. He was the first to reach Beckham, elevating his teammate skyward in celebration.

Even though many of these drills will not illuminate position-specific abilities, all players in attendance are expected to participate. (In recent years, players have opted out of some or all of these drills, while healthy, without any consequence.) The cumulative effect of the four days takes an enormous toll on the players, which is the diabolical intent of the Combine organizers. To perform at their best, participants must overcome the physical, emotional and psychological rigors of the week.

About 250 Combine invitations are sent to prospects before bowl games are completed. Geoffrey received one of those invitations. Underclassmen, those who have notified the league that they are concluding their collegiate career after three years, will subsequently receive invitations if qualified. Additional invitations to graduating seniors come later.

Geoffrey receiving his invitation was an additional indicator that he was on a path toward being drafted, along with 329 others who joined him during Combine week. How important was an invitation to a player's draft prospects? A total of 252 players were drafted that year. Of those, 214 had participated in the Combine. Do the math. Only thirty-eight collegians were drafted who were *not* at Lucas Stadium in Indianapolis. Yes, I'd say being at the Combine is a critical step toward being drafted.

Given this reality, it is imperative that attendees arrive in tip-top shape, having thoroughly prepared before they step foot in Indianapolis. Players can either establish their own workout plan or they can attend a formal training program. If they have signed with an agent, it's common practice for the agency to send players to proven workout programs and foot the bill for this training. It's no small investment. My understanding is that in 2022 the cost of a six-week program was $15,000.

Geoffrey's Journey to the Draft

Let's take a moment to put that investment into perspective. Agencies receive a 3 percent fee from their signed players. Geoffrey's first contract with the Carolina Panthers covered four years and was worth $1,746,600, with only a paltry $41,000 guaranteed. If indeed he played the four years (it was possible to be cut at any point and not be owed another dime) the agency would receive from Geoffrey $52,398 in fees.

So, in the best of all cases, the agency spends almost 30 percent of its projected income to fund its player's training. And, of course, the training program was not the only associated cost for the agency. During the dating period prior to signing, the agency is spending money on travel, lodging and other related expenses, attempting to convince the athlete to sign on the dotted line. It's said that agencies do not make money until a player signs a second contract. These numbers prove that reality. And thus, my purposeful use of the word "investment" above.

Priority Sports had a relationship with an outfit out of Franklin, Tennessee, a suburb of Nashville, where they sent their athletes. D1 Sports Training offered a pre-Combine training program providing "VIP treatment, including elite facilities, a full meal plan, physical therapy and daily workouts," all designed to "provide draft prospects the best chance to make it as a professional football player." And so Geoffrey hopped on a plane to spend six weeks in Tennessee.

Geoffrey was born and raised in West Los Angeles, where we still live. The weather is so ideal. Occasional rain. Snow in the local mountains. The thermometer hardly ever dips below fifty degrees and rarely climbs above eighty. Hurricanes, never. Earthquakes, of course. Because the weather is moderate throughout the year, residents joke that Southern California does not experience the traditional seasons of fall, winter, spring and summer, but rather earthquake, fire, flood and drought. Tornados are unheard of.

But in Tennessee, it's a different story. There are an average of thirty tornados a year in the state. These wild windstorms typically occur during October, November and December. So imagine Geoffrey's reaction when, in February, he hears the whine of the tornado warning sirens. He is in his hotel. What is he to do? Like any millennial, he began searching the web. He also called friends who had lived in tornado alleys for input.

He's told to hunker down in the tub of his hotel room should he hear what sounds like a train heading his way. I am sure his heart was pounding just thinking about the prospects. Fortunately, the area around his hotel was spared.

We heard from Geoffrey occasionally during his training. Attendees worked out six days a week. Goals are established for all the activities measured at the Combine—the ten- and forty-yard dash, shuttle, bench press, broad jump, vertical jump and so forth. During Combine training the players perform these drills, and their results are measured against the goals set.

The program was quite vigorous. From behind the scenes, I was in communication with Deryk, who was closely monitoring Geoffrey's progress. I'm hands on, and good thing I was.

Near the end of the six-week period, Deryk and Mike visited D1 for one more peek at Geoffrey's development. After watching Geoffrey carefully, Deryk frantically gave me a call. There was concern in his voice. What I heard over the phone almost floored me. "Maybe we should pull Geoffrey from the Combine." What the f***!!

Deryk proceeded to share that he thought Geoffrey looked slow in his forty-yard dash and other speed drills. Surprising? It shouldn't have been a shock to Deryk. Geoffrey was not a speed merchant. His "forty" times while at Oregon never raised eyebrows for fleetness. As a matter of fact, while this was never medically tested, and I'm no expert in the field, I have always believed that Geoffrey was born with a greater ratio of slow-twitch to fast-twitch muscles. A "twitch" refers to the contraction of muscles, how quickly and how often the muscle moves. Those with a greater concentration of fast-twitch muscles tend to be more suited for short, intense activities, such as...sprinting.

Deryk's other big concern was the bench press. Geoffrey did not bench press in high school. He claims that I was responsible for this—something to do with my belief that bench pressing would interfere with his pitching efforts. For the sake of peacekeeping, I won't endeavor to dispute his recollection. So Oregon was his introduction to this weight-lifting staple.

Even from his early days, Geoffrey struggled with this discipline. I could never understand why, given his size and girth, but that's the way it was. Throughout the six weeks at D1, Geoffrey's bench press numbers were underwhelming, and not improving. Deryk and I would talk about adjusting his technique. We wondered aloud whether, at this point in his football career, much of anything could be done to increase his repetitions enough to satisfy those observing him at the Combine.

For some reason, that day really stoked Deryk's concern. Geoffrey was struggling to complete more than a handful of reps. Average for linemen is upper twenties to low thirties. Deryk was contemplating pulling Geoffrey completely out of the Combine. I was not sure I was hearing him correctly. "No, no way!" I snapped back to Deryk. "Do not do it!"

Before continuing, allow me to share the back story. I was not aware of this situation until working with Geoffrey on his and Mitchell's book, *Eat My Schwartz: Our Story of NFL Football, Food, Family and Faith.*

Early in Geoffrey's senior season at Oregon, he was bench pressing. The traditional technique has the bar holding the weights resting in both palms, the pinky through index fingers wrapped over the bar, the thumb wrapped from below. A suicide grip is an open technique where the thumb is positioned next to the index finger. Once lifted, the barbell rests fully on the lifter's palms.

"Suicide" is such an appropriate name for this alternative grip. While not uncommon, it does come with definite risks. On the plus side, this grip version keeps the wrist neutral and aligns the shoulders in a safe position. However, to me, the negatives far outweigh any positives. Without the thumb wrapped around the bar, there's less command of the weights, creating a high risk that the barbell can fall from the lifter's hands.

Geoffrey didn't use a spotter. If he had, maybe this wouldn't have happened. During one of the reps, the barbell slipped from Geoffrey's palms, causing 225 pounds to crash onto his chest, causing him to scream in pain.

That was the end of Geoffrey bench pressing for the entire season; the injury prevented him from lifting the bar. He was also forced to wear a custom-made metal breast plate under his pads throughout the season to lessen the pain and discomfort from charging defensive linemen striking him in the chest. Any wonder why a handful of reps during Combine prep was all he could complete?

I was convinced that extracting Geoffrey from the Combine would completely devastate him. I was equally confident that doing so would absolutely destroy his draft chances. Deryk and I talked further to strategize. What options existed?

Anyone who knows me would characterize me as an extremely honest person. Livie will tell you that one of the reasons she married me was my honesty. That day, for this very special circumstance, to allow my son to retain his draft chances, I compromised my morals. Maybe not my proudest moment.

Deryk and I decided to move ahead with Geoffrey attending the Combine. He would participate in all activities, with one exception. No bench press. In what I thought was a lie at the time, Deryk would inform everyone who needed to know that Geoffrey had a pectoral injury prevented him from benching. And so he did, to numerous looks of doubt and skepticism from team staff.

I had no idea on the day we hatched our plan that we really weren't lying. Maybe Deryk simply forgot about Geoffrey's bench press accident, or maybe he did not want to let the cat out of the bag, so to speak. He had to have known. Geoffrey had not told Livie or me about the injury when it happened. My suspicion is that he swore Deryk to secrecy, and so when Deryk and I talked that day, Deryk was caught between the proverbial rock and a hard spot.

I take credit for how we resolved Deryk's concerns. I could have easily acquiesced to his wishes and allowed Geoffrey to be pulled from the Combine. As fellow parents know, we fight with every ounce of our being for our children. This was my ultimate fight. In my mind, Geoffrey deserved the opportunity to achieve his wish of being a professional. As I noted earlier, I truly believed that his opportunity would have shriveled up and washed away without participation in the Combine. That day, that decision, without a doubt in my mind, changed the trajectory of Geoffrey's life.

The six-week program at D1 came to an end. A few weeks later Geoffrey packed his gear and headed to Indianapolis with mixed emotions. Excitement. Anxiety. Maybe a touch of fear. Imagine being poked and prodded after stripping to your skivvies. Imagine being deprived of sleep and yet expected to shine mentally and physically. Imagine having to optimally perform every waking moment over four days. That's what he faced.

Geoffrey's combine results were not newsworthy, but not so terrible either. His forty-yard dash time of 5.36 seconds was quicker than only six other offensive tackles out of a total of twenty-seven, but it was only .06 seconds slower than what was expected of offensive linemen (5.30). Pleasingly, at least for me, Geoffrey was faster than the offensive tackle who ultimately received the first team All-Pac-10 honors instead of Geoffrey.

Do forty-yard dash times impact draft potential? I suspect yes, and no. If Geoffrey was projected as an NFL tackle, then maybe more so. Tackles are seen as more mobile. If seen as a guard, maybe not so much. Many of the better guards are referred to as "telephone booth" 🏈 players, implying they operate within smaller confines.

Ten-yard splits are the better indicator of o-line athleticism. As the player performs their forty-yard dash, their ten-yard time is recorded. Geoffrey's split was 1.8 seconds. The expectation was 1.8 seconds. This was clearly additional evidence that he possessed the athleticism of an NFL lineman.

One last Combine story. Another test performed is to evaluate metabolism rates. After Geoffrey received his results, he called his mother. "Thanks, Mom! I just tested with the slowest metabolism of everyone here." Why thank Livie? Because it's known within our family that Livie's metabolism is paced like a snail, whereas Mitchell is like me, a metabolism that burns like a furnace. No wonder why post-career Geoffrey remains a large human being.

Approaching the Draft

At this point in his journey, Geoffrey had one more audition to complete before the draft. It's known as Pro Day. These Combine-like days are held on college campuses for athletes of that college to repeat many of the Combine drills, but without lack of sleep, all-day medical testing and formal interviews. They are attended by masses of pro scouts and coaches and serve multiple purposes.

Those who may not have performed optimally at the Combine get a second bite of the apple. Players not invited to a postseason all-star game or the Combine are afforded an opportunity to showcase their skills. And the day serves as a chance for players who, by all accounts, had a productive Combine to shave another tenth of a second off their forty times or press the 250 pounds a few more reps, hoping to improve their draft status. Geoffrey participated in Oregon's Pro Day, but it changed nothing.

Everything under Geoffrey's control was done. Now it was up to Deryk to advance the needle. Ever since Geoffrey signed with Priority Sports, Deryk was advocating for him with NFL personnel in the hopes of elevating Geoffrey's position on their respective draft boards, otherwise known as *value boards*.

Months before the draft, every team begins their evaluation process. They assess their player requirements. Some teams are in greater need of receivers while other organizations need offensive linemen. They evaluate prospects for their value to the team—what contribution they can make toward a successful season. The value boards complete assessments of each player's "fit" into respective offensive or defensive schemes. Teams gather all the input and then set their draft priorities.

As we headed into draft week, Deryk called to share his assessment of where he thought Geoffrey would be drafted. Third to fifth round was his projection. He obviously could not make any promises. However, based on his numerous conversations with teams and his personal assessment, this seemed to be the consensus. I wish he had been a better soothsayer.

The format of the draft has changed over time. There once were thirty rounds. It was progressively whittled down to seven rounds as of 1994. To parlay this event into a TV spectacle in order to broaden its following and create greater revenue, the NFL expanded the draft to three days in 2010 with the first round held on a Thursday night, rounds two and three on Friday and the remaining four rounds completed on Saturday.

Geoffrey's draft year, 2008, was a two-day event held on a Saturday and Sunday. The first three rounds were completed on Saturday, April 26. The remaining four were held on Sunday the 27th. Based on all the input we had received, we believed that round three was the earliest Geoffrey would be drafted, so he elected to spend that Saturday morning watching his buddy Dylan Cohen play baseball rather than sit in front of the tube. Seemed like a very wise move. I joined him. It was a lovely morning. Clear blue skies. Very comfortable temps. But Geoffrey's attention was not on the baseball game. He was following the draft results.

The first round was thirty-one picks. Of those, seven were tackles, an unusually high number for round one. So, maybe, just maybe, Geoffrey might be selected higher than anticipated. But only one tackle was taken in the second round and only two more were chosen in round three. That first day found 10 tackles drafted, leading us to believe that Deryk's third-to fifth-round projection would become a reality the next day.

We woke up Sunday morning and turned on the telecast. The fourth round ended without Geoffrey being selected. So did the fifth. Same with the sixth, although Geoffrey received calls during this round from several organizations telling him that he would be their team's next selection, and to expect a call. We would sit riveted to the TV waiting for the selection, which, I ultimately found out, is preceded by a call from the head coach. Geoffrey had his phone resting right next to him. And time after time, cruelly, the phone did not ring. I understand from Geoffrey that these teaser calls are done to establish a relationship in advance of free

Geoffrey's Journey to the Draft

agency, the team having some level of interest in signing the athlete after the conclusion of the draft. Seems kind of cruel to me.

That Sunday had to be one of the most grueling days in my life. My anxiety was over the moon. I felt so bad for Geoffrey. He so wanted to be drafted. Were his dreams to be realized? Or dashed? We had no choice but to wait. My brother was with us. He coaxed Geoffrey outside to shoot some hoops. At some point during round six, I couldn't sit and watch any longer. I found myself aimlessly wandering the neighborhood. I simply could not settle down. I sat on the curb at the top of our cul-de-sac agonizing over what might be.

Six rounds in the books. The final forty-four selections remained. As the seventh round progressed, the phone rang with more empty promises from several teams. I called Deryk. What now? At this point in the draft, any player selected was likely a toss-away pick, that is, no expectation that they would survive the first camp, but a pick had to be made.

As the seventh round marched forward without Geoffrey being selected, another of my off-the-wall ideas came to mind. I called Deryk to ask if it was possible for him to contact teams with a selection remaining who would not be a good fit for Geoffrey and ask them to pass on him. Setting aside the shock to Geoffrey's ego, I felt it was better for him to go undrafted and then sign a free agent contract with a team that was more suited for his talents. Deryk said it was possible, so he began dialing.

I found out later in the day that Deryk's efforts did pay off. Two or three ill-suited teams who showed interest in selecting Geoffrey with a lower seventh-round pick agreed to not pull the trigger. But one brushed off Deryk's request. They claimed they had sincere interest in selecting Geoffrey and, if still available, would make him their last pick of the day.

The more I've thought about this, the more I'm convinced that the Carolina Panthers were indeed familiar with Geoffrey and his abilities. They had selected Oregon running back Jonathan Stewart as the thirteenth pick in the first round. To do so they had to spend a significant amount of time watching film of Jonathan. And who was in most, if not all, of those clips? Yup, Geoff Schwartz. He was the right tackle.

They were not blind. They had to see Geoffrey's production on the field. So why did they not select him earlier? In my thinking, a couple of circumstances contributed to Geoffrey's free fall. To begin, injuries or ailments are red flags to NFL brass, often leading to a precipitous drop in draft position for the formerly impaired player. In the eyes of the NFL, although he had fully recovered from his back surgery, Geoffrey was "damaged goods." Their thinking was why "waste" an earlier pick on someone who may not be physically capable of handling the rigors of the NFL? I believe that all thirty-two teams shared the same mindset. Wait, wait and wait until the last minute.

I believe my interpretation was validated during the draft of 2021. The Kansas City Chiefs selected Trey Smith in the sixth round of that year's draft. Number 226. This was a player who, while playing for Tennessee, was an all-SEC (Southeast Conference) honoree. So why was he drafted so low?

Seven games into Smith's sophomore season he was diagnosed with blood clots in his lungs. He was put on the shelf for the remainder of the year. Trey was cleared to return for his junior campaign and then, instead of bolting to the NFL after that season like many speculated, he elected to return to Tennessee for his senior year.

See parallels with Geoffrey? Smith's injury occurred during his sophomore year. Geoffrey's back flared in his junior season. Geoffrey would be a seventh-round pick by Carolina, although forecasted no lower than the fifth round. While Smith was graded by independent evaluators as having first-round pick qualities, he nosedived to a sixth-round selection.

In Smith's case, was a sixth-round selection warranted? Not based on his rookie season performance. Smith was named by the Pro Football Writers Association to their all-rookie team for 2021. He was a first-game starter for K.C. and was on the field for every single offensive snap during the season. And an outside grading service rated him as the sixteenth-best guard in the league. Doesn't seem like a sixth-round pick to me. Was Geoffrey, who ultimately enjoyed an eight-year career, deserving of being drafted where he was? You know my opinion.

These decisions have financial implications. Smith being drafted in round six, even though he was first-round capable, saved the Chiefs enormous amounts of money. Smith's first contract was a four-year deal for approximately $3.6 million. The payout to the last pick of the first round in 2021 was $11.17 million. That's a savings of $7.5 million. If drafted mid-first round, add another five to six million dollars saved. Carolina, certainly not to the same degree, saved money as well on Geoffrey.

The second factor likely contributing to Geoffrey's low seventh-round selection was his East-West Shrine game evaluation. Although it was recognized that he was "healthy as a senior," it was also asserted that his "struggles throughout the week" will "push him down the board." His back and his evaluation. A double whammy. And so it came to pass.

As the draft wound down with few picks remaining, Geoffrey's phone rang. He was not in a good mental state at that time. Hugely disappointed. Frustrated to no end. Feeling disrespected. He answered, probably thinking it was another team with an empty draft promise. But this call was different. On the other end was someone from Carolina who, after a brief introduction, turned the phone over to John Fox, head coach of the Panthers.

Of course, coaches present themselves as excited to be drafting the player, regardless of draft position. After the initial introduction and pleasantries, an excited-sounding Fox told Geoffrey that the Panthers were about to select him. "Are you excited?" Fox asked. Prepared for free agency, as Deryk had had conversations with several teams interested in signing Geoffrey post-draft, Geoffrey, being true to form, responded, "I don't really care." At that point he really didn't, dealing with the disappointment of the weekend. Fox didn't allow Geoffrey's less-than-enthusiastic response to deter him or the Panthers. Geoffrey was selected as "promised," number 241 out of 252 total picks that year.

At least Geoffrey was not Mr. Irrelevant. Beginning in 1976, the final draft selection was anointed with this nickname. Although possibly humiliating to some, the last person selected is still an NFL draftee, forever able to boast of such. Plus, they are celebrated in ways most others are not. They and their family enjoy a trip to Disneyland. Mr. Irrelevant is invited to attend a golf tournament, a regatta and a roast. And if that wasn't enough, they receive an award. The Lowsman Trophy mimics the Heisman Trophy® whereby the figure is of a player fumbling a football rather than the traditional trophy pose with the high knee and extended arm. All in good fun.

It is said that hard work pays off. Geoffrey is a shining example. He busted his tail for years to achieve his dream of playing professional football. He overcame all obstacles and doubters. Now, regardless of whether he was the number-one pick or number 241, he was in the NFL.

What was left? Time to celebrate! Livie and I, in the days leading up to the draft, planned a celebratory gathering for Sunday night, believing that Geoffrey would have been drafted long before he was. Email invitations were sent to family and close friends who had joined us for this journey.

Raising Giants

> *Hello Everyone!*
>
> *Draft weekend is upon us. All indicators suggest that Geoffrey will be drafted on Sunday...we just don't know what round. So we're being positive and planning a celebratory party. And you...and your spouses...are all invited.*
>
> *Geoffrey's football career has been an extraordinary journey. Livie, Geoffrey and I are so happy that you've been on the journey with us. We look forward to celebrating the beginning of this next chapter with everyone. Hope you can make it.*

Now, as the day progressed and disappointment firmly set in, Geoffrey was having second thoughts about a party. We considered cancelling, even if he was selected later in the day. We held off sending any further communication. Then Geoffrey received the call from Coach Fox. Reality set in. He was drafted. He was going to the NFL. True to his basic positive and resilient nature, it was party on!

> *Hi All!*
>
> *Later than we thought but Geoffrey was drafted in the 7th round by the Carolina Panthers. He wants to celebrate. So we're partying!! 6 at El Torito Restaurant on Ocean Park Blvd. in Santa Monica.*

Although the notice was very late in the day, I can still see the faces of all who joined us at El Torito. We took over the entire bar area. Those attending, immune to the anxieties of the day, were so, *so* happy with the ultimate result. We had one friend visit three different local sporting goods stores on his way to the party, where he secured three Panther baseball-style caps. One went to Geoffrey, of course. I took the second, of course. The third hat was presented to my dear father. Geoffrey's "Papa" (Norman Schwartz) was the proudest person in the room. We hold dear a picture from that night of Geoffrey with my wheelchair-bound father, who was beaming with a permanently pasted ear-to-ear grin that lasted the entire night.

We had no idea that day how long a professional career Geoffrey would have. What we did know was that his dream had come true. All his hard work and determination had paid off. Forever and a day he could claim to be among the few who could call themselves a professional football player.

6
SOCIETY OF DOUBTERS (NO RESPECT)

Throughout Geoffrey's athletic career, he came across nonbelievers, who I dubbed the Society of Doubters. Naysayers who, whether with their words or by their actions, attempted to throw cold water on Geoffrey's dreams, dismissing his abilities and potential to climb the ladder of football success. Maybe up to twenty-five in number.

Geoffrey's varsity high school football coach was the first doubter, telling my son during his sophomore season that he would never amount to anything on the gridiron. As it turned out, what did he know? His team that year won a single game. A pink slip arrived at the conclusion of the season, sending that coach on his way. Yet Geoffrey played years in the NFL.

Spurred by this completely erroneous slight, and others to come over the years, Geoffrey carried in his wallet a list of all the cynics. Anyone who belittled him, however trivial it might have seemed at the time, was added to the collection. Ultimately, being a Millennial and living his life through technology, he lightened his wallet load and transferred the names to his cell phone. To this day, if Geoffrey needs a bit of added motivation, that list sees the light of day.

One of the Society members was his Oregon line coach Steve Greatwood, a multiple-time offender. I suspect, if on the list, his name appears only once, but maybe it's in bold and highlighted to accentuate his clear disregard for Geoffrey.

The first instance was maybe more subtle than the others. Remember Geoffrey's resilience as he played in agony throughout his junior season? After a rough outing that season against USC, Geoffrey's reward for "toughening it out" was riding the bench at the beginning of the next game. Admittedly, he played poorly versus USC, giving up two sacks. But another offensive lineman gave up one sack and did not have his best game, yet he was not benched. A bit of a double standard?

Geoffrey, by any measure, is a large human being. I've talked about him being a genetic mutant, born of decent-sized parents, but our heights were not suggestive of his, or Mitchell's, ultimate proportions. Maybe their grandparents deserve the credit. Both grandfathers stood six feet one inch while both grandmothers were five feet seven inches. For their generation, they were outliers for height.

Or maybe it was the food they ate that caused the mutations. When the boys were young, Livie and I decided to source our meats, poultry, seafood and other foods from a home-delivery service boasting restaurant quality, healthful fares. For all we know, maybe the "nutrients" fed to the animals got into the boys' bloodstreams.

Incidentally, this membership required us to buy six months of provisions at one time, to be stocked in an industrial-sized freezer located in our garage. Customers would customarily pay six monthly installments, then reorder. Not the Schwartz family. Three months after the first order arrived, the freezer was almost bare. We called to reorder. They checked their records. "It's only three months. Nobody reorders so quickly!" Promising to make a lump-sum payment for what we owed, our reorder was accepted. The boys had to fuel their growing bodies somehow.

It was no surprise that as the boys left the house for college, the food lasted longer. With Geoffrey gone, the same volume that previously was consumed in three months took about four and a half months. Then Mitchell headed for college and we became empty nesters. At some point after Mitchell's departure, we received a call from the service. Now we weren't buying *enough*. They threatened to cut us off. Maybe it's Livie's charm, but we continue to buy from them to this day.

With size comes some potential complications. Geoffrey was always the tallest and biggest kid among his fellow classmates and friends. And not by a small margin. Being both physically imposing and athletically gifted, Geoffrey almost always found himself winning whatever sport he played. The game or event made no difference.

While being the victor so frequently is seen in some circles as the ultimate outcome, it can negatively impact bonds with friends and fellow competitors. We discovered that some of Geoffrey's childhood friends shied away from playing with him because they knew he would always win. Livie and I sat him down to explain the importance of balancing his physical gifts with the challenging realities of life. Playing for fun and not consistently outdueling his buddies would actually lead to stronger friendships. This was not an easy concept for a youngster to understand. We did our best to counsel Geoffrey about the benefits of letting others feel the exhilaration of winning.

And so here is the rub. One of the complaints offered early on by some of Geoffrey's football coaches was that he lacked a mean streak, did not exhibit the uber-aggressiveness expected on the field. Probably a fair observation. Maybe, in retrospect, our advice about dialing back his intensity did Geoffrey a disservice when it came to football. For life in general though, I firmly believe our parenting helped him become the mensch◎ he is.

The Punch

Fast forward to Oregon's opening 2005 contest against Houston. It was Geoffrey's first start. Trying to employ a new resolve to be more aggressive, Geoffrey accomplished what many o-lineman fantasize about. He pancaked◎ his opposing defensive lineman. They found themselves sprawled on the turf with other players piled on. The d-lineman, taking exception to being manhandled and pancaked, somehow took a swing at Geoffrey.

In the week following any game, players in their position groups gather to review film to evaluate their performance. Watching from the stands, I don't believe anyone saw the pugilism that took place under the pile of humanity, but the eye in the sky tends to capture everything.

On the day the offensive linemen gathered to watch game tape Coach Greatwood was not paying much attention to the film. While watching, one of Geoffrey's linemates hollered, "Did you see that?" Everyone in the room, including Greatwood, snapped to attention. The film was rewound. With all eyes riveted on the screen, there, for all to see, was Geoffrey landing a punch to the chest of the provocateur in retaliation.

Raising Giants

To this day no one knows what prompted Geoffrey's teammate to call out the punch. Was he proud of Geoffrey? Was it his way of tattling on him? Let's be clear. Punching is a no-no. The irony in this situation, however, was that Geoffrey was consistently urged to be more aggressive on the field. And so, after being slugged in his groin (which was not visible on the tape), he was. Shielded by a pile of humanity, I suspect Geoffrey thought no one would see the exchange of blows. But, if indeed discovered, I believe he figured he'd hear an "atta boy." He pancaked his defender. He defended his manhood. Instead, Greatwood banished Geoffrey to roll from one end of the practice field to the other...and then back. Two hundred yards. Think about that for a moment, if your stomach can handle the thought.

While initially writing this section of the book, I was listening to Geoffrey on a radio show. Coincidentally he was recalling this episode when his producer pleaded, "Please stop!" His stomach was feeling queasy just listening to the accounting. Imagine how Geoffrey's body reacted to the rolling. I will leave it to your imagination, but it wasn't pretty. This was his "reward" for busting out of his basic temperate behavioral tendencies.

Apparently two demonstrations of Greatwood's lack of support were not enough. A third was waiting to surface. It took place at the conclusion of Geoffrey's senior campaign. Oregon had been invited to play in a post-season bowl game in El Paso, Texas, known as the Sun Bowl. The routine before a bowl game has the team traveling to the game site days before the contest to prepare, finding a local field to hold practices.

During one of the practices, Geoffrey was warming up with his o-line mates. Greatwood was walking toward the group. In a demonstration of pride for his friend and teammate, one of his buddies stopped the coach, excitedly sharing the news of Geoffrey's Shrine game invite.

"Really?" Greatwood uttered, with complete surprise in his voice. Back at ya coach. Really? The fact he had no awareness of Geoffrey's invite spoke volumes. Ideally, coaches are advocates for their players. The lack of awareness of Geoffrey's invitation strongly suggested that Greatwood did not believe Geoffrey was worthy of such an honor, and therefore did not lift a finger to promote Geoffrey. What a slight.

If a trifecta of insulting behavior was not sufficient to spotlight Greatwood's lack of belief in Geoffrey and his abilities, might as well make it a four-peat. This was the most egregious. It happened heading into Geoffrey's senior season when he approached Greatwood and asked if

Society of Doubters (No Respect)

he could provide some film from his junior season. Geoffrey wanted to piece together a highlight film to submit to NFL scouting departments. The response to Geoffrey's request was, and still is, incomprehensible to me. It was emphatically denied. The explanation was very matter of fact: "You're not NFL material."

I am so proud of Geoffrey's fortitude. Instead of allowing these doubters to lay waste to his football career goals, he figuratively, and maybe literally, at least in private, lifted his middle finger to all of them and persevered. I remember having similar doubters in my life while playing high school basketball. I never created a list, but I can tell you that I worked harder and found myself more motivated to prove the coach wrong, all the while mentally offering a one-finger salute. Without a doubt Geoffrey's ultimate success was fueled by these experiences.

7
MITCHELL'S JOURNEY TO THE DRAFT

I began this book's Second Quarter by asserting that one of my sons had a smooth draft journey while the other's passage was rather bumpy. By now it should be obvious who had which experience.

Mitchell arrived at University of California, Berkeley (Cal) a more polished player compared with Geoffrey when he entered Oregon. Even so, Cal did the right thing and redshirted Mitchell, giving him the benefit of a full year to grow—physically, mentally and emotionally—before being thrust into active duty.

By the time Mitchell entered his junior season, he had started all twenty-six games in his first two years. As a matter of fact, he was on the field for every single offensive snap during those first two seasons and was highly recognized for his play in both campaigns.

In 2008 Mitchell was named as a second-team Freshman All-American by College Football News, received the Bob Tessier Award as Cal's "Most Improved Offensive Lineman" and was named honorable mention Pac-10 All-Academic. Building on the year-end honors, Mitchell began 2009's sophomore season named to Lindy's® second-team preseason All-Pac-10, Athlon's® third-team preseason All-Pac-10 and Phil Steele's® preseason third-team All-Pac-10. Steele continued to recognize Mitchell throughout the season, listing him on his midseason and postseason third-team All-Pac-10 teams. By the end of the season, Mitchell received

All-Pac-10 honorable mention, Pac-10 All-Academic honorable mention and was Cal's Brick Muller Award honoree as its Most Valuable Offensive Lineman. I'd say he was off to a very notable start heading into the critical third year.

By the time Mitchell completed his sophomore year, Geoffrey was already in the NFL. I had under my belt six collective seasons of football observations, so I felt I was no longer a novice when evaluating the guys. Nonetheless, I still relied on coaches and other football-savvy people to give me added perspective.

During Mitchell's time at Cal I got to know one of the team's more ardent fans, Bob Hink. We became friends and remain so to this day. One of his best friends is Ed White, a former NFL offensive lineman who played in the league for seventeen years, was a consensus collegiate All-American in his senior year at Cal and was fortunate to have participated in multiple Super Bowls. He has been inducted into several Halls of Fame. With all these awards and accomplishments, I would say that Ed knew a thing or two about offensive line play.

Bob shared a conversation he and Ed held from the stands during one of Mitchell's first games at Cal. I believe it was actually before Bob and I met. As I've come to understand, most offensive linemen, playing or retired, when watching a game are honed in on the offensive line. I know that's Geoffrey's and Mitchell's orientation. No different this day for Ed. He was focused on Cal's offensive line. Apparently Mitchell's play caught his eye.

According to Bob, it wasn't typical of Ed to comment on other players, but this time something was different. Ed turned to Bob and, with an air of absolute confidence and effusive positivity, said (paraphrasing), "Number 72 is going to play in the league." What made him so sure? Mitchell's footwork for one. Ed shared that he had seen few linemen at this stage in Mitchell's career who had the technical footwork that Mitchell possessed. And Ed knew that Mitchell would only get better.

So, whereas Geoffrey needed a monster junior season to create a buzz, it sure seemed that Mitchell had placed himself on the NFL radar screen heading into his third campaign. That was confirmed with the preseason recognition he received from various pundits. Athlon, Lindy's and Phil Steele all included Mitchell on their respective second-team preseason All-Pac-10 teams heading into his third season.

Mitchell's Journey to the Draft

How reliable are these prognostications? Questionable. Heading into the season, Phil Steele listed Mitchell as the nation's number sixty-three draft-eligible tackle. Yes, sixty-three. He was ultimately off by "only" sixty positions.

By season end, Mitchell had once again started every game. In addition, he earned Cal's Andy Smith Award for the player with the most "Big C" time, that is, the most snaps during the year. This was Mitchell's third consecutive season being on the field for every offensive play. He was named to the All-Pac-10 second-team squad. Cal honored him for the second consecutive year as the team's Most Valuable Offensive Lineman. Lastly, he was also an honorable mention Pac-10 All-Academic selection, for the third consecutive year.

Mitchell completed an outstanding fourth season and four-year career at Cal, being recognized as Cal's Most Valuable Offensive Lineman for the third consecutive year. He was a season-long offensive captain. He was on the watch lists for two prestigious offensive linemen–oriented awards, the Outland Trophy® and the Lombardi Award®. He was finally voted by the conference to the Pac-12's (by this time the league had expanded from ten to twelve teams) first-team squad. Adding to this list of accomplishments, Mitchell was also named first-team All-Pac-12 by ESPN Pac-12 Blog and Phil Steele.

For the fourth year in a row, Mitchell started every game. Unfortunately, his consecutive snap string was ended by a wardrobe malfunction that pulled him off the field for one lousy play, preventing him from receiving the Andy Smith Award for a second consecutive year.

It was the opening series of the UCLA game. His shoelace came undone. If you have ever paid attention to a lineman's hands during a game, you will have noticed that the only flesh visible is their fingertips. The rest of their hands are mummified in layers upon layers of white adhesive tape. It would have been impossible for Mitchell to retie that lace before the next snap, so he trotted off the field for help. A damn shoelace coming unfastened prevented Mitchell from playing four full years without missing a snap. We learned during his pro career that "streaking" was a part of Mitchell's DNA.

In 2014 we built a "bonus room" in our house, in part as a shrine to the boys. Beyond the two side-by-side sixty-inch TVs, the room contains many of Mitchell's Cal awards, trophies and other memorabilia. Shelves also contain numerous trophies for both Mitchell and Geoffrey dating back to youth sports and several helmets worn during their careers. Several jerseys hang on the wall. And for good measure, you'd find some of my youth trophies on the shelves.

Selecting Mitchell's Agent

By the end of his third season, without question, Mitchell had established an amazing collection of credentials that would springboard him to being a much-sought-after NFL prospect. I knew that agents would soon be descending upon him. It wasn't a matter of if, but when. Certainly a far more comfortable position than for Geoffrey, who at this same point in his career still needed to prove himself.

The agent selection process for Mitchell was quite different as well. There was already an incumbent. Deryk and Priority Sports were representing Geoffrey and doing a fine job. So was there really a need for the courtships that would arise as agents began pursuing Mitchell? I didn't think so. Neither did Livie. But the most important person in this process wanted to leave the door open for all interested. And so, we did.

As Mitchell's senior season progressed, those inquiries began to stream in. As I recall, the two who made the final cut with Geoffrey outside of Priority came calling. So did several others who had not shown interest in Geoffrey. I once again played protector, having all inquiries and conversations channeled through me. This time, though, I was more experienced and knew better how to evaluate and deal with the interested agents. In the end, it came down to the same three as it had with Geoffrey.

Frankly, it was a rather tortuous process for me. I truly felt the decision was quite easy. First, I believed deep down that Deryk, Mike and Priority had represented Geoffrey well. Since contracts are so formulaic, that is, standardized by the Collective Bargaining Agreement©, there's not much flexibility in what agents can negotiate. It actually might be more challenging to negotiate for a lower-level draftee than one more toward the top of the totem pole.

I also had a bias because I thought it would be awfully awkward to have the two guys represented by different agencies. It just seemed to me that, both being offensive linemen, there could be potential conflicts with two different agencies possibly having separate agendas.

Per NCAA regulations, a player cannot formally announce their agent selection while still having college eligibility. They may come to a decision at any time during their final season, but it needs to be held under wraps and shared only with trusted sources, like immediate family, who won't prematurely spill the beans. As long as neither party acts upon the information, the player can inform the agent/agency of their decision before the formal announcement is made.

Mitchell's final season included a postseason bowl game. The thirty-fourth edition of the Holiday Bowl, played at Qualcomm Stadium in San Diego, California, pitted the Cal Bears versus the Texas Longhorns. Cal's anemic performance that night resulted in a 21-10 defeat. Not an ideal way to conclude a season, much less a college career, but the night did not end on this sour note.

At some point during Holiday Bowl preparation, Mitchell finally reached his decision. What a relief for me. He made the "right" choice, selecting Deryk, Mike and Priority Sports. Deryk had informed us that he wanted to attend the Holiday Bowl but needed an "incentive." Of course, that was code for celebration. When Mitchell solidified his decision, he called Deryk. Of course, Deryk was thrilled...and relieved. During the course of the season, Deryk and I would talk. He, too, thought Mitchell's decision would be made more quickly than it was. But in the end, all parties were extremely happy. To celebrate, dinner was scheduled for after the game.

During the season, teams had to return to their home city no later than midnight of game day. One of the thousands of NCAA rules. Teams were only allowed formal activity six days of a seven-day week. If wheels up took place after midnight, it technically crossed over into that seventh day, so teams did their level best to comply with the rule. But in this case the season ended when the game clock struck 0:00.

Soon after Mitchell's announcement to Deryk, plans were hatched for a celebratory dinner at a local restaurant after the Holiday Bowl game. We ate like kings that night (thanks Priority). That evening was a great way to close that segment of Mitchell's career. But the night wasn't over.

As part of post-bowl-game plans, Cal rented a nightclub in downtown San Diego for the team along with their parents and friends to celebrate together. After wishing Deryk a good evening with a big hug, Livie, Mitchell and I headed to the after-game festivities. Performing that night was the Tightwad Hill Band, a cover group featuring Cal football team's operations manager Mike (Huge) McHugh. (Quick background: The band name was appropriated from a hill just beyond the east walls of Cal's football stadium. Students, and I suspect nonstudents as well, who chose not to pay to enter the stadium would scale the hill and watch the game for free. All those doing so became known as tightwads.) The band was quite good, playing a combination of oldies but goodies plus the popular music of the day. Great way to put a bow on Mitchell's Cal career.

All-Star Game

In the previous chapter about Geoffrey's journey, I spoke to the year-end all-star games. Being invited to the East-West Shrine Bowl game was a fantastic honor for Geoffrey. Being invited to the Senior Bowl was the ultimate. It brought together, in Mobile, Alabama, the best of the best. It is the crowning achievement for the most talented players in the land. It is a chance for each athlete to test their skills against NFL-caliber talent before they get into the league. Mitchell deservedly received a Senior Bowl invite, becoming the thirty-first or thirty-second Cal player to participate in this prestigious game.

Being curious to see if the talent level of the Senior Bowl participants was indeed better than the Shrine game, I've crunched some numbers—to a reasonable degree of scientific certainty—comparing Mitchell's Senior Bowl roster to Geoffrey's East-West Shrine roster. I didn't take too deep a dive. I simply looked to see if a player was drafted and, if so, how many years they played in the NFL.

What's that old saying about figures don't lie? Well, the numbers I crunched made it clear. Those who participated in the Senior Bowl were far more likely to spend time in the NFL and, once there, had a longer career than Shrine Game participants, at least in this limited sampling. I won't bore you with all the details, but here are a few specifics to validate my contention.

- First, interestingly enough, total rosters for both games in which the boys played amounted to 103.
- Thirty-five out of 103, or 34 percent, of the Shrine Game players did not get drafted. Of those on the Senior Bowl roster, only 16.5 percent did not.
- Exactly 53.4 percent of Shrine Game participants either didn't play a single season in the NFL or no more than two years.
- To the contrary, a full 71.8 percent of the Senior Bowl rosters played three years or more.
- Lastly, ten more Senior Bowl players than their Shrine Game counterparts reached the magical ten-year career threshold.

Mitchell's Journey to the Draft

The fact that Mitchell was a Senior Bowl participant was further validation that an NFL career was in his future.

Just like there was no way I would miss Geoffrey's East-West Shrine game, there was absolutely no way I wouldn't be in the stands for Mitchell's Senior Bowl game. I booked lodging and my flights to and from Mobile. I had never been to Alabama.

I was able to attend the Senior Bowl practice, albeit my vantage point was from the rather uncomfortable metal benches of 33,471-capacity Ladd-Peebles Stadium. For the Shrine Game, I was on the field in their indoor practice facility accompanied by a colleague from the area who had followed Geoffrey's journey. In Mobile, I ran solo as I knew not a single local soul who could join me. Mitchell and I hung out briefly, however, there was no formal dinner. Practice and the game itself were eye-opening given the level of talent that was on the field.

Here's an interesting tidbit about practice versus game attendance at these all-star contests. I had always thought that the stands on game day would be full of NFL scouts, coaches and staff, stopwatches in hand, binoculars fixed on players, information being gathered. But that's not the reality. Practice sessions prior to the actual game garner more attention than what happens on game day. As a matter of fact, it's standard practice that by Saturday game time, most NFL personnel have flown the coop. They have seen what they needed to see during the week of practice. Interesting.

My eyeballs told me that Mitchell had accorded himself well during Senior Bowl competition. Postgame reports related to Mitchell's performance during the week of practice and the game once again confirmed my ever-improving evaluation skills. Here's a sampling.

- "...at the Senior Bowl, he made a name for himself by taking on the draft's top pass rushers and handling them well....he looks like the prototypical NFL tackle."—www.turfshowtimes.com
- "...Mitchell Schwartz put the clamps on Quinton Coples and Courtney Upshaw. Schwartz enjoyed a good week prior to the contest, so he did a good job in solidifying his Day 2 potential." —www.walterfootball.com (These named defenders played four and five years, respectively, in the NFL.)
- "Schwartz climbing at Senior Bowl—Overshadowed in the Pac-12 due to the presence of two elite prospects...Schwartz has stood out this week due to his size (6-5, 317), long arms (33 1/8"), strength and

surprising agility. He's held up well at right tackle in pass blocking drills and has done a nice job of sealing off defensive linemen in the running game and has been able to get to the second level, as well. Schwartz has been especially impressive in pass blocking drills, where he's repeatedly stoned Penn State's **Jack Crawford** and Virginia's **Cam Johnson**, among others."—**www.espn.com** (These named defenders played ten and five years, respectively, in the NFL.)

I left Mobile confident that Mitchell had set the foundation to be a top-tier selection. Numerous reports suggested that, particularly based on his Senior Bowl performance, he could be a second- or third-round pick. Mitchell's job moving forward was to do nothing that would cast doubt among his NFL admirers.

The Combine

Next up after the Senior Bowl for Mitchell was Combine prep. It was so uneventful that I literally have no memory of what took place. I had to contact Mitchell and ask. "Was the Combine as uneventful as I remember?" "Did you train at D1?" "Yes" and "Yes" were his responses. Frankly, that gave me some relief. The fact I couldn't remember anything made me wonder if old age was creeping in.

Priority Sports had maintained their relationship with D1 Sports, so Mitchell also trained at D1 in Tennessee. He didn't have any of the drama encircling Geoffrey. His goals for his six weeks at D1 were rather simple. Improve his conditioning. Get stronger. Learn how to navigate the many drills he would be forced to complete while at the Combine. Be ready to compete.

An honest look at my two sons would draw me to the conclusion that they are not the most athletically gifted humans walking the face of the earth. They're obviously gifted enough to play professional football, which is more than most can say. To overcome any physical shortcomings, they relied on what rests above the neckline.

The Wonderlic Test was developed in 1936. It was created to measure intelligence, asking the test taker to try to answer fifty questions in a span of twelve minutes. (Most don't get close to completing all fifty.) Legendary NFL coach of the Dallas Cowboys, Tom Landry, is credited with introducing the Wonderlic test to the NFL in the 1970s. It was thought to be a predictor of player performance. It remained a Combine staple until 2022 when it ceased being administered. I've seen no official statement from the league as to why. I imagine its removal suggests that the test did not adequately or accurately predict future success of players in the league.

To provide some background, an average score is 20, roughly equivalent to an IQ of 100. Guess which NFL position achieves the highest average score? Maybe surprisingly to some, it's the big hogs of the front line. Based on a random sampling of 622 different players by Wonderlic, the offensive line averaged 26.8 correct answers, followed by the tight ends at 26.7 and quarterbacks at 25.9. In comparison, investment analysts average 27.

It was no surprise to his mom or me, given what we personally know about Mitchell's smarts and the multiple comments offered by teammates and coaches over the years, that Mitchell scored a 35.

Otherwise, his Combine results were pedestrian at best. Remember, I previously referenced expected forty-yard dash and ten-yard split times for offensive linemen: 5.30 and 1.8 respectively. Mitchell was timed at 5.38 and 1.88 respectively, leaving bragging rights to his brother. I suspect the eight hundredths of a second difference for each distance had no impact on the NFL's already established view of Mitchell.

Of course, one significant difference for Mitchell is that he did bench press at the Combine. Affirming my assertion about Geoffrey's and Mitchell's basic athleticism, Mitchell only pressed the 225-pound bar twenty-three times. Average for linemen is upper twenties to low thirties. The most ever is fifty-one in 1999. To demonstrate that brute strength is impressive but not always a predictor of NFL success, that defensive tackle went undrafted and was only in the league for one year. On the flip side, another defensive tackle logged a mind-numbing forty-nine reps, was drafted in round two and enjoyed a seven-year career.

Mitchell achieved what he set out to accomplish during this "audition week." He did nothing to damage his status. On the contrary, I think he solidified his standing in the eyes of the NFL teams. Yet some seemed to want more. Several teams, including the Browns (a foreshadowing of what was to come), Atlanta and Philadelphia attended Mitchell's Pro Day on Cal's campus.

Goal Line in Sight

With the draft but a few weeks away, it was time for Deryk to have conversations with teams to understand their thinking relative to drafting

Mitchell. What Deryk was hearing and what we were reading in reports was quite promising. But hold on a moment.

Remember that the general consensus for Geoffrey was that he'd be selected somewhere in the third to fifth rounds. And look where he ultimately was drafted—at the very end. One of the lessons we learned through that draft process is that one simply cannot rely on what's being publicly disseminated by NFL organizations. First of all, much is fluid during the pre-draft period. And, quite frequently, teams want to create smokescreens to mask their real draft intentions. If they can get another team to think that they have little interest in a player, then possibly that team, or other interested parties, might adjust their plans and wait until later in the draft to select the prospect. This slight pause would then allow the player to be available when desired to the team providing the deception.

All this being said, there was another clue that Mitchell might be drafted in the early rounds. By this time, NFL staffs had been given three opportunities to evaluate Mitchell in person. There was the Senior Bowl. There was the Combine. And then there was Pro Day on the Cal campus. One might conclude that three bites of the apple would satisfy their cravings. Apparently not.

Step back and think for a moment how consequential these selections are for a team, particularly in the first couple of rounds. There's a whole lot of money at stake. If they botch the choice, then they've blown that money and missed out on a real contributor, and possibly impacted their roster for years to come. Maybe that's why teams don't simply settle for a trio of personal interactions. They want one more.

So for those players who are being considered as a first- or second-round selection, teams will bring that prospect to their facilities for more in-depth conversations, spending more time with the head coach and general manager, and possibly a workout or drills to confirm what's been initially addressed at the Combine, Pro Day or in other ways. Mitchell visited four teams—the Cleveland Browns, Pittsburgh Steelers, Atlanta Falcons and Kansas City Chiefs. In retrospect, it's maybe no surprise that Mitchell played for two of these four teams.

Draft Day

As I described at the beginning of the book, that night of the NFL draft in April 2012 was intense. Family and friends had gathered to watch the proceedings on the television.

We all jumped as Mitchell's phone rang while Denver, whose turn immediately preceded Cleveland's, was making it's pick in the second round.

"Hello?" Early in the conversation Mitchell's face lit up. Geoffrey and I knew at that moment Mitchell was told that Cleveland intended to draft him with their pick, number thirty-seven overall in the 2012 draft. What was said thereafter is frankly a blur. Mitchell hung up the phone beaming. He confirmed what Geoffrey and I had assumed.

I've talked about draft promise reliability, or rather lack thereof. Why might this experience with the Browns be different? I can only speculate; however, I believe that selections in the first couple of rounds are made with much greater purpose and forethought. Homework has been completed. Vetting has been thorough. I will believe to my dying day that what seemed to me to be a hastily placed commercial was prompted by the broadcast production team learning that Mitchell would be Cleveland's pick. It's apparent, watching as many draft telecasts as I have, that the production team prepares data and video highlights of the players in anticipation of their selections. When a name is called, they then queue up what they've prepared for the benefit of the broadcast team and the viewing audience. This happens for all first rounders, typically all those drafted in the second round, and sometimes for third-round selections.

As I described earlier, the broadcast had quickly broken to a commercial just before the Browns' selection slot. I've always suspected that Mitchell was not expected to be chosen so high and therefore his highlight reel wasn't readily accessible. They needed the commercial time to place it front and center. Mitchell, and Geoffrey for that matter, vehemently disagree with me but I've watched enough TV to have a sense when something seems to lack fluidity.

The commercial ended and the Browns were up!

"With the thirty-seventh pick in the 2012 NFL draft, the Cleveland Browns select Mitchell Schwartz, tackle, California." (ESPN draft analyst guru Mel Kiper said of Mitchell's selection that it was "the key pick" of the Browns' draft.) The house erupted. I was as close to tears as possible without them flowing down my cheeks.

We all approached Mitchell for congratulatory hugs and kisses. Even now, more than twelve years later, the skin on my arms is full of goosebumps as I recap that night's experience. That was the end of our draft viewing for the evening. What an extraordinary, almost mind-numbing experience, particularly when compared to what Geoffrey went through.

All that was left was to celebrate. We all put our heads together to come up with a plan. Mitchell didn't want the fanfare that accompanied Geoffrey's celebration, so whatever we did would be with a small, intimate group.

Ultimately, we made reservations for the following evening at one of those Brazilian steakhouses. That night our family and the Weinsteins celebrated at a Mexican restaurant up the street.

For a handsome charge, it was all one could eat at the steakhouse. Several varieties of steak, in addition to pork, lamb and chicken, plus a salad bar that made us drool. The group included Mitchell, Livie, and me, my brother Fred, his wife Brenda and my two nieces Amanda and Heather, Geoffrey and his wife Meridith, and one of Geoffrey's BFFs Duke Manyweather. That's a total of ten—about three-quarters of whom had ravenous appetites. I suspect most fasted all day in order to gorge themselves that night. While the salad bar was tempting, most of us concentrated on the roving waiters who served the meats from skewers directly onto the seated diners' plates. A coaster is given to each patron. Place the card green side up and the servers continue to offer. Turn it red and the servers pass you by, a chance to let some of the food digest.

We all had an absolutely wonderful time that evening. We consumed multiple plates each, and were close to food comas by the time we left. Too bad there weren't wheelbarrows to cart us out. It wasn't surprising that the guys around the table held their own. The women did their best to keep up. The surprise of the night was one of my nieces. In those days, Amanda was a meat eater. She's subsequently become vegan. But that night, we joked how she gave Mitchell a run for his money with how much she devoured.

We had gobbled down all we could. Our stomachs were distended. Another bite of food or sip of a beverage might require a hasty trip to the bathroom.

That evening reminded me of an experience we had with Mitchell while visiting Geoffrey during his time at Oregon. At some point during that particular weekend, Mitchell, Geoffrey, my brother, Livie and I visited a local Olive Garden restaurant. I don't believe I've ever seen Mitchell consume so much food in one sitting. Started with endless salad. Main course a four-cheese pasta dish. At least a handful of breadsticks to accompany both. That's all I can specifically remember.

Toward the end of our meal Mitchell needed to excuse himself. When he returned to the table, he topped off the previous courses with some provided chocolate mints. He then excused himself one more time. He obviously was having some intestinal issues. When he returned a second time, he settled back into his seat, knowing that we knew what was happening. Instead of associating his discomfort with the mounds and mounds of food he had consumed, he proclaimed, "It was the mint." All of us at the table, with the obvious exception of Mitchell, almost fell off our chairs laughing so hard.

The bill for dinner arrived. Fortunately, we're not a family that drinks much, so basically we were paying for ten base rates—still not an insignificant amount. I had the check directed to me. It was our treat. As I'm pulling out my credit card, I see Geoffrey patting his pants pockets, then his jacket. Not finding what he was looking for, he looked at me and declared, "Dad, I was going to pay for half, but I left my wallet at home." How convenient. Seriously though, it was a nice gesture nonetheless.

While Mitchell's and Geoffrey's journeys would end similarly, they each took different paths to reach their ultimate destinies. It was also a journey during which I learned much about this passage from high school football to the college gridiron to the professional ranks.

It is very easy to want to rely, maybe too blindly, on those who have been engaged to guide one through the journey. They are the experts. However, one truth has become very apparent. Even the experts don't know. All indications were that Geoffrey would be drafted no later than round five. And forecasts for Mitchell had him being selected in the lower second round, into the third. As you now know, neither was accurate.

It's not my intention to assign any blame here. It is the reality of prognostication in this arena. My brother and I have spoken frequently about the lack of reliability with predictions and polls. I never saw the value of looking deeper into our shared hypothesis until writing this chapter. Coincidentally, it occurred while the NFL 2022 draft was underway and at the same time as I received my May 2022 print version—yes, still old school—of *Sports Illustrated*'s 2022 NFL Draft Preview. With the draft completed, I could easily compare the magazine's first-round draft predictions against actual.

The effort was quite enlightening. Using an arbitrary condition where accuracy is pegged to having the actual selection position within a plus/minus of two spots of the prediction, *Sports Illustrated* was accurate only 28.13 percent. Given that this was an extremely limited sampling, I researched further, capturing the predictions of two other nationally known sources. One was slightly more accurate, the other slightly less so. The aggregate rate of accuracy of the three was a tick under 30 percent.

Using this still-limited sampling, but enough for me for this conversation, the boys' experiences were not unexpected. The truth is that these kinds of predictions are not steeped in science. They are art and conjecture, and subject to a very diverse universe of input. Not dissimilar to the NCAA polls that try to predict the top twenty-five football teams in the country.

Before the 2021 NCAA season kicked off, the Associated Press (AP) published their preseason Top 25 list. Comparing that list with the final AP Top 25 listing published after Georgia won the national title, the outcome was even more inaccurate than the draft results. Of the twenty-five teams chosen in the preseason, only ten were on the list at season's end. And of those, only two met the same criteria I established above for success. Two out of twenty-five! Yet, there are untold numbers of people who live and die, figuratively, based on these numbers. They are used for betting purposes. They are debated at the water cooler throughout the season. They ultimately determine which teams are bowl bound, and which will play for the national championship trophy. And yet they are mostly wrong.

In the end, the only thing that mattered to me was...were my sons drafted? From there, the numbers that meant anything were years in the NFL and money earned. While Geoffrey and Mitchell were not drafted when predicted, they both were drafted. They spent many years in the NFL. Their accomplishments while in the league and money earned proved they were worthy of being selected.

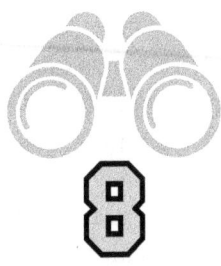

THROUGH THE TURNSTILES

My youth. Black and white television. Only two competing stations for football viewing. ESPN? It would be 1984 before they televised their first football game, a college contest between BYU and Pittsburgh. Crawlers across the bottom of a TV screen with real-time score updates? Decades away. This is how I began watching football.

My father worked every Saturday, so I watched college games with my brother(s), or alone. Dad worked an occasional Sunday but was home for most. When I was young, we would nestle side-by-side on his recliner watching NFL games. As I got older, and the chair shrunk, I was banished to sit alone in a nearby rocker recliner. Of course, there were no remotes, so changing stations required a junior member of the family to get up, walk to the TV and turn the knob on the front panel. Since this took some "effort," what's become known as channel surfing was a very infrequent practice.

As I've shared, I didn't play football growing up. Like the boys, I was oversized for Pop Warner youth football, and then there was my Jewish mother and Bar Mitzvah lessons. She was so concerned about my health and wellbeing that she slammed the door shut on poor delicate me playing football. Based on my size at the time, had I played I would have been the one causing the damage. One day I did put on pads, a jersey, and a helmet and pretended to play football on a local muddy school field with a buddy of mine. It didn't light a fire for me. Otherwise, the closest I got to a gridiron was watching my high school team practice through a classroom window, or a very occasional foray to campus for a Friday contest.

Later, while at UCLA, I was a member of my fraternity's intramural football team. I played quarterback and offensive line. Sound familiar? I had no clue what I was doing. My pass protection technique was completely contrary to what I would ultimately learn was correct. The result? I remember being gut-punched twice, knocking the wind out of me.

Ironically, I was closer to the game than I knew. For years, the Oakland Raiders commandeered an entire hotel in my hometown of Santa Rosa, California, for their preseason camp. I have no clue if practices were open to the public. We just never made the drive to find out. Instead, my father would come home after work to regale us with stories about Raiders visiting the market he worked at. One day, one of the better-known players wandered into the market after practice. He made a beeline to the soda pop section. Nutrition in those days wasn't a thing.

This Raider bought a sixty-four-ounce bottle of full-octane soda, along with several packets of processed deli meat slices. He tore open a pack, pulled out the entire contents, and shoved this clump of meat into his mouth. Once down the hatch, it was time to cleanse his palate with the soda. He twisted off the cap, lifted the bottle to his lips and drained the contents, continuing until there was not a drop left. I can only imagine the belch that followed.

My first year of college at UCLA began in the fall of 1973, just in time for football season. I pledged a fraternity (Zeta Beta Tau) upon arrival. On football Saturdays the fraternity would arrange for buses to schlep us from the fraternity house on campus to the game. In those years, UCLA's home field was the Los Angeles Coliseum, home then and still today to the University of Southern California (USC) Trojans. We'd make the fourteen-mile trek from Westwood to the stadium located a few miles south of downtown Los Angeles.

Unbeknownst to me at the time, this was the beginning of the hundreds of football games I would attend over the course of the next four-plus decades. UCLA played an eleven-game regular season schedule between home and away contests. By the time I graduated in 1977, I likely made that trip to the Coliseum twenty-two times.

The year after graduating from UCLA, Livie started law school at USC, our hated rivals. We talked at length about how to handle school allegiances, as school loyalties are formed during undergraduate years. We are both Bruins through and through, so we agreed, somewhat like a prenuptial agreement, that although Livie was attending USC law, she would never, *ever* root for the Trojans.

During her time at USC, the Trojans had scheduled a home football game against their other hated rival, Notre Dame. As a USC student, Livie was able to buy two tickets for us to attend that game. USC jumped ahead quickly, dampening our spirits initially as we sat silently watching the Trojans fans hooting and hollering. Behind 24-6 heading into the fourth quarter, Notre Dame quarterback Joe Montana led a furious comeback, ultimately throwing a deciding touchdown with forty-five seconds remaining to win 25-24. It turned out to be a glorious day after all. As we returned to our car, I felt giddy as I gleefully watched the sullen USC fans grousing about the shocking outcome. Fortuitously, Montana was drafted by "my" San Francisco 49ers, leading the team to four Super Bowl victories between 1982 and 1990.

The Laid-Back Pro Bowl

Between my college graduation and when the boys began playing high school football, I attended several professional games. I don't remember which came first. The 1993 NFL Pro Bowl game in Hawaii, or the Los Angeles Rams traveling to Chicago to take on the Bears.

The Pro Bowl is a postseason NFL all-star game matching the best players in the American Conference against their brethren in the National Conference. Between 1980 and 2016, the games were played at Aloha Stadium on the island of Oahu in Hawaii.

In 1993 I was the president of a wholesale distribution company. We became one of the top customers in the United States for a vendor with international tentacles. As a reward, the vendor invited Livie and me to travel with their regional sales manager for an all-expense-paid trip to Honolulu. Gee whiz. Twist my arm.

We arrived, picked up our rental car and drove from the airport to the hotel, a Hilton on Waikiki Beach. When we pulled up to the property it was instantly apparent that this hotel was the weekend home to the Pro Bowl players. Talk about being excited. Walking the hallways, I was rubbing elbows with these football icons.

Raising Giants

Saturday, the day before the game, we had nothing better to do than bask in the sun on Waikiki Beach. I couldn't relax. My head was on a swivel. Who would I see? The game roster read like a who's who of the NFL at that time, as it should have, given the purpose of the game. That afternoon many of these NFLers were also on the sand, a good number within spitting distance of us. Oh, there's Steve Young and Troy Aikman and Jerry Rice and ... Oh my. I was in heaven.

The game itself on Sunday was simply not memorable. Participating players see this game as an exhibition, so they really aren't going full steam. The goal for the day is to have fun, enjoy time with their peers and, most importantly, walk away at the final whistle uninjured.

Then there's the financial reward for participating. Some players have handsome incentives built into their contracts as a bonus for being chosen. All Pro Bowlers, regardless of contract terms, do walk away with some extra cash for their day's efforts. Back in 1993, the winning team earned $30,000 per player, the losing team $15,000 each. Not chump change, but then again let's keep things in perspective.

Back in 1993, the average NFL salary was $666,400. It grew to $860,000 in 2021. So, for some, this money is more meaningful than for others. In a 1993 Associated Press article, one Pro Bowl player was quoted, "I don't care if you're a housewife or a CEO of a large company, $15,000 is $15,000." However, at least according to the article, a greater percentage of those quoted seemed to discount the importance of the money. "But for me it's just going out here, having fun and playing with some of the guys on other teams and building a bond." Another lamented, "I don't think about the money. All these guys here make a lot..." And lastly, "The money is nice, but not the main motivator for me." Bottom line, the usual competition and aggression of a pro game was not evident during those few hours.

The most notable memory from that afternoon was the weather. It was a very unseasonably cool Hawaii day. As the sun went down and the shadows crept in, it actually was on the chilly side. Of course, being Hawaii, packing a jacket was almost sacrilegious, so I hadn't done that. I remember spending a good part of the second half, especially when the sun hid behind the stadium, rubbing my arms, sitting on my hands, doing whatever I could, short of jumping jacks, to stay warm. However, all in all, it was a great time. I still have hanging in my closet, and worn very occasionally, a Pro Bowl T-shirt that I bought that weekend over thirty years ago.

Fun at the Games

Soldier Field, Chicago, Illinois. An iconic stadium. The oldest in the league and one that was designated as a National Historic Landmark in 1987. It was architecturally distinguished by colonnades along the east and west sides with thirty-two columns supporting the structure. But it was delisted nineteen years later when a controversial renovation destroyed the original character that made the stadium so special.

Over the years I had watched on TV many Chicago Bears' games played on that field. I remember seeing Hall of Fame linebacker Dick Butkus demolish opposing running backs and wide receivers who dared to cross his path. I remember watching a game that was suspended in the third period as a monsoon descended upon the stadium, making the field unplayable. I remember watching in absolute amazement as 330-plus-pound defensive lineman William "Refrigerator" Perry lined up as a fullback in the offensive back field during goal line situations. He set the record at that time as the heaviest player to score a touchdown, and he remains the heaviest player to ever score a Super Bowl touchdown.

A Weighty Topic

The game of NFL football has changed in so many ways over the past several decades, with the size of these professional players demonstrably different. When the Green Bay Packers won what was referred to as Super Bowl I in 1967, their largest roster player weighed 260 pounds. In 1970, only one NFL player weighed as much as 300. Then in 1985, William "Refrigerator" Perry was drafted by the Chicago Bears, pushing the scales at 335 pounds.

Jumping to the 2019-2020 season, almost 25 percent, or 427, of those in the NFL weighed at least 300 pounds. I think we'd be hard pressed today to find an offensive lineman below that 300-pound threshold. And to think that once was considered so outlandish. As a matter of perspective, Geoffrey joined the NFL weighing a touch above 330 pounds and Mitchell played most of his career between 320 and 325 pounds. Neither was considered fat, other than by each other. The boys to this day are constantly making jokes and tweeting about the girth of themselves and the other.

Fortunately, in today's world the body composition of the players has dramatically changed...for the better. Due to a combination of advanced training techniques, emphasis on nutrition and a general shift in genetics, a player weighing in at over 300 pounds is in much better shape than years ago. Their percentage of muscle mass to fat has greatly increased. One of the tests administered to the boys throughout their careers was body-fat composition. There are three methods that I'm aware of for computing body fat. I'm not sure which of the three methods the NFL teams employ; however, the resulting number is carefully watched by training staffs. Too high and a player would find himself on a program to drop some pounds, such as happened to Geoffrey once or twice during his career.

As an example, in 2016, in a final attempt to salvage his career, Geoffrey was trying to play his way onto the Detroit Lions roster. For spring camp he reported at a weight unacceptable to the team. His body-fat content was also unacceptable. They told him to lose fourteen pounds before reporting to summer camp but said that if he lowered his body fat, they'd be "OK" with it. When he reported to camp, he had lost thirteen of the fourteen required pounds and trimmed his body fat from 24 percent to 21 percent. He was told that wasn't good enough. Until he dropped the one extra pound, he was fined daily. I believe it was $500 per pound. And to "encourage" the loss, he was required to ride the exercise bike before and after practice. All this to an eight-year veteran. For ONE lousy pound.

More Fun in Chicago

The very same vendor who hosted Livie and me on the trip to Hawaii once again showed their appreciation for my business by inviting me to join the principals of their Southern California sales agency to attend a game of their hometown Chicago Bears versus the Los Angeles Rams. I suspect, being from Southern California, they presumed that I followed the Rams.

Through the Turnstiles

I accepted the invite, knowing—wink, wink—that I'd be rooting for the Bears to prevail because of my attachment to the San Francisco 49ers.

That was quite a memorable weekend. We flew back to Chicago and found ourselves staying at a Westin Hotel downtown. Upon arrival we soon discovered that the Rams were hotel mates. Sunday morning, the two other guys and I went downstairs to wait for our car from the valet. At the same time, two or three buses were idling on the curb in front of the hotel belching disgusting exhaust. One by one, the Rams' players exited the hotel through the front revolving doors, making their way to the buses. It was the first time I had ever been that close to human beings of such large proportions. (Amazing to think that years later my two guys would grow to behemoth proportions like these players.)

I do not want to be rude, but I watched in amazement. Many of the guys, probably linemen, looked grossly overweight to me. Seemed like they would have been hard-pressed to look down and see their toes because of their ample midriffs. Yet these were professional players. I could only marvel how men of that size could be so agile and move with such fluidity on the field. Truly special athletes.

We hopped into the car and headed south toward Soldier Field. Entering the stadium, we made our way to the vendor's suite above the fifty-yard line. With plenty of time to spare before kickoff, I decided to take a walk. I excused myself and beat a path to a walkway that encircled the field. With an unobstructed view of the entire stadium, I casually lapped the field. I allowed the moment to sink in. "Wow, I'm in Soldier Field about to watch an NFL game," kept running through my head. It was a remarkable day. (Decades later I returned to Soldier Field to watch Mitchell in a preseason game against the Bears.)

I returned to the luxury suite and took a seat closest to the field. What a perspective. I can't remember much about the game, but I do recall the Bears beat the Rams, making me a very happy camper. I also have a very clear image all these years later of the mounds of shrimp made available to us that day. I might have consumed more shrimp during that three-hour period than I have cumulatively in my life otherwise. That day continues to bring back fond memories.

I have never connected the dots until writing this chapter that before Geoffrey and Mitchell started playing professionally, my attendance at NFL games was always connected to this one vendor in one way or another.

The sales reps who I accompanied to the Bears vs. Rams game were huge L.A. Rams fans. In 1980 the Rams moved from the Los Angeles Coliseum, their long-time home, to Anaheim Stadium in Orange County, home field for the Anaheim Angels, as they were then known, of Major League Baseball. With the move, the sales rep duo bought season tickets. Knowing I was a fan of the Rams archrival San Francisco 49ers, they graciously overlooked that conflict and invited me several times to take in a game between the Rams and Niners. Our second-deck end-zone seats provided a view down one of the sidelines. It didn't matter to me where we sat. Being in the stadium was all that was important.

Over time, the invites dried up. I have a clue as to why. In the 1990s, when I was invited, San Francisco beat the Rams seventeen straight times. It's highly likely that I did a very poor job of containing my enthusiasm. As nationally known sports jock Colin Cowherd is prone to remind his listeners, "fan" is just the first three letters of "fanatical," and I'll admit, I can get rather fanatical when my 49ers beat up the Rams. As part of this run, the Niners destroyed the Rams 35-10 in one of the games I attended. Their quarterback, Steve Young, threw for four touchdowns and 462 yards—at the time the second-highest total compiled by a QB against a Ram defense. I'm sure I gloated my way through those four quarters. I remember attending three S.F. versus L.A. games in Anaheim Stadium and was very grateful for having those opportunities.

At that point in my life, I'd venture to say that my in-person football viewing was not terribly out of the ordinary. Five NFL contests. Twenty-two UCLA games while a student and probably another eighty UCLA games as an alumni season-ticket holder.

Livie and I bought four tickets in 1978. Initially it was just us and a couple of friends attending games. But as the boys came along and got older, we'd make it a family outing. Geoffrey was five when he first joined us. Mitchell, being two, spent those Saturdays with a babysitter. When he turned five, it became a total family affair. Attending all Rose Bowl games became an annual routine, only rarely disrupted by the Jewish High Holidays or a conflict with a youth basketball or baseball game. We'd arrive early to tailgate and toss a football.

Dad and Coach

Fast forward to 2000. Geoffrey enters high school and joins the football team. Although he played little as a freshman, I attended every Friday game. My role model was my father. He didn't have a classic nine-to-five job. He was a butcher. Some days he was done by 6 p.m. Others not until 9 p.m. He worked every Saturday and some Sundays. He had no flexibility other than for sickness. He wouldn't dare ask his bosses for time off to watch his sons play ball. But, somehow, he managed to be at most of my games. I can't begin to count the number of times, after toiling on his feet for eight hours, he rolled up to a baseball field, the game already in the late innings, or entered the gymnasium to catch the final quarter of a basketball game. He came directly from work. No dinner. That could wait.

As a corporate executive, I was blessed with a more flexible work schedule when the boys began playing youth sports. Carving out time away from work was a no-brainer. From when Geoffrey was five until Mitchell was fifteen, a span of thirteen years, I was their baseball coach. For the first nine years I was the head coach for at least one of them. During several seasons I was head coach for both boys at the same time.

Besides games there were all the practices that required my attendance. Plus, Geoffrey played basketball at recreational centers before middle and high school. I don't believe I missed one of his tipoffs. That was easily done as I coached him there as well.

Our lives were shaped by the boys and their sports schedules. Beyond the games when school was in session, there seemingly was always a tournament during winter and spring breaks. And the summers were jam-packed with more basketball and baseball. We literally could never plan a true vacation during the boys' youth school years. Our travel was, in some fashion or another, associated with baseball or basketball tournaments. Livie, to this day, expresses her regrets about our family's inability to travel like "normal" people.

My father's influences have served me well and, I believe, have paid off in spades. I truly believe that my relationships with the boys were strengthened because of my involvement in their sporting activities. It gave us more time to be together and talk. It also gave me, as a parent, more opportunity to instill life lessons that became the foundation for the people they are today, of which Mom and Dad are quite proud. If done right, sports can guide impressionable youngsters in areas like life balance, teamwork, discipline, time management, commitment, relationships, handling of challenges and losses, communication and much more.

Raising Giants

I attended every one of Geoffrey's games during his four high school seasons. Nothing was allowed to get in the way. Mitchell's first year of football was Geoffrey's senior season. Fortunately, the junior varsity games were played on the same field immediately preceding Geoffrey's varsity tilts, so I was never forced to give up one for the other.

Once Geoffrey graduated high school and began his Oregon career, leaving Mitchell at Pali High, the specter of ongoing conflicts was very real. How would Livie and I be in the stands on Friday nights watching Mitchell and then attend Geoffrey's games on Saturday? Call us magicians, or simply give kudos to the scheduling G-ds, but we managed to be in the stands for both games almost every weekend. Thank goodness for early morning flights. And where Geoffrey's games were within driving distance, we packed the car and got on the road as early as needed Saturday morning. Mitchell would join us on most trips to watch Geoffrey.

Let's now do some math. Four years of high school football for each times nine games per season times two for both boys equals seventy-two. Let's remove a couple for a Jewish High Holiday and maybe a couple more when it was logistically impossible to be at two places at the same time, leaving a total of sixty-eight. Fortunately, neither missed a game to injury or illness during their respective four-year careers.

Geoffrey's freshman year at Oregon had eleven games on the schedule. The team needed six wins to qualify for a twelfth game, a bowl opportunity. Unfortunately, they came up one win short, so eleven was all they played. Big disappointment. At the time, every college player wanted to participate in a bowl game, for the experience, the exposure and, maybe more importantly, for the swag bag filled with gifts that are provided to each player.

At the outset, we were not sure of Oregon's plans for Geoffrey. He arrived on campus in shape and apparently accorded himself well enough in camp to suit up for the first game. We watched from our family room. He watched from the sideline, not getting on the field. That day was such a disappointment for the favored Ducks as they were upset by the Indiana Hoosiers. We also had quite a heart-palpitating moment during that game.

Trying to locate Geoffrey on the sidelines whenever the camera panned that direction, we thought we spotted him. But if that was him, he was sporting a tattoo around his bicep. What the f***!! "He left home about six weeks ago and now has a tattoo!" Livie and I were floored. Tattoos are forbidden in traditional Jewish faith. Calamity was averted when the camera once again picked up that same player. Upon a closer look, it was one of Geoffrey's linemates, not Geoffrey. Phew!!

The second game of the season was against Oklahoma in Norman. Although Geoffrey was unlikely to play, Livie and I decided to make the trip, leaving Mitchell in L.A., because of the legacy of Oklahoma football, plus Livie had a client in Kansas, which was not far from Norman. This trip afforded her a chance to visit the client. Although Oregon lost that day, we remember the visit for the respect shown us at the conclusion of the game.

It was very hot and humid that day. We sat in full sun on metal benches, sweating profusely the entire time. By game's end we were physically exhausted, and emotionally drained because of the game's outcome. But as we rose to leave, several of the Oklahoma fans sitting around us extended their hands and offered thank-yous for attending the game, for making the trip to Norman. That was the kindest expression we ever received from any fan base.

Too bad some Oregon fans weren't as kind. Two years later, Oregon hosted the Sooners at Autzen Stadium. That game will forever be remembered by Oklahoma fans for the officials robbing them of a "W." With seventy-two seconds to play, an onside kick was awarded to the Ducks. Later a video replay showed that OU actually recovered the kick. But replay review wasn't a thing back then. The call sealed the win for Oregon.

After the game I was walking in a parking lot adjacent to the stadium. I heard some commotion and looked over to see an Oregon mom and a Sooner fan screaming at each other. Apparently, the Oregon mom was talking sh&!, refusing to show the same kindness and consideration that Livie and I experienced in Norman. I walked over attempting to calm the combatants. Unfortunately, my efforts were fruitless. That was such an embarrassing moment.

The next couple of games after Oklahoma we again watched from home. We were not in a stadium for three out of Geoffrey's first four freshman games, all of which he observed from the sidelines. The fifth game was scheduled in Pullman, Washington, against the Washington State Cougars. Heading into the week, there was no indication that Geoffrey's playing status would change, so we prepared to watch from home again. That all changed mid-week.

Wednesday the phone rang. It was Geoffrey, somewhat out of breath. More likely due to excitement than exertion. "Dad, I'm playing this weekend!" Apparently a couple of his linemates were dinged up and unable to suit up. "Can you make it to the game?" he asked. "I'll see what I can do."

I went into scramble mode. Getting to Pullman from Los Angeles is, in the best of circumstances, a trip that requires some advanced planning. First leg is a flight from L.A. to Spokane, Washington. Then rent a car to drive two hours on a mostly two-lane highway in the middle of nowhere to arrive in Pullman. But to get all this done with only three days' notice, and do so while still attending Mitchell's game Friday night? I did. I knew that if Geoffrey was calling and asking, it was important to him, so it became a no-brainer for me.

I arrived in Pullman having no idea where to park. Google Maps and the like? Didn't exist back then. I located a Visitors Center in town. I was told I could park in their parking lot, take a bus to the stadium and then pick up another bus after the game for the return trip to the Center. (That returning bus never arrived. After waiting for the better part of an hour, with a chill wind howling, I had to taxi back to my car.) I jumped in the bus and departed for the stadium. Upon arrival, I located the Visiting Player Will Call, picked up my ticket and headed to my seat, located in the southern end zone.

The seat location wasn't ideal, but it sure ended up being a prime spot. Geoffrey first entered the game earlier but it was now the fourth quarter. Oregon was behind with possession of the ball. With 1:26 remaining on the clock, Ducks' quarterback Kellen Clemens brought the team to the line of scrimmage at the WSU eleven-yard line, the end zone in sight. He took the snap. The offensive line blew open a huge hole. Thank you, Geoffrey Schwartz.

Eleven yards later Clemens had scored the winning touchdown. As Clemens ran past Geoffrey toward pay dirt, my son immediately realized what he and his line mates had accomplished. He raised both arms to the sky to signal touchdown. An Associated Press photographer had trained his camera on Clemens. He snapped, just as Geoffrey's arms reached toward the heavens. That picture went viral, or as viral as possible for those days. And I had a front row seat for all this action!

From that Washington State game forward through Geoffrey's senior season I missed only one game. Coincidentally it was another game in Pullman against Washington State. The senior partner at Livie's law firm was being honored that same Saturday night in Los Angeles. How dare

Through the Turnstiles

they schedule such an event during football season. She wanted to attend the event. I, on the other hand, wanted to be in Pullman watching the game. What's that well-known adage, "Happy wife, happy life?" I suspect you can guess who won that disagreement.

As I recall, the event was quite nice, but my mind was 1,100 miles away the entire evening. I could not wait to return to the car to listen to the final minutes of the contest against Washington State. Fortunately, we turned on the car radio just in time to hear Oregon kick a last-minute field goal to earn a hard-fought win.

That evening was also memorable for something completely unassociated with the game itself. Once showered and packed up, the team boarded a bus in Pullman for a ten-mile journey to a small airport in Moscow, Idaho. Players, coaches and staff had boarded the airplane waiting to take off for the return trip to Eugene. Geoffrey heard the engines come to life as the plane backed away from the gate.

The pilot continued to thrust backward until the aircraft found itself with its back wheels off the tarmac in a patch of mud. All normal efforts to return the plane to the runway failed. Their only recourse at that time of night, because of the lack of resources at the smallish airport, was to fly in a crowbar from Spokane to Pullman that could be attached to a tug to pull the jet from the muck. It took about seven hours to get the plane airborne.

Players are typically fed after a game but the amount of food is planned, in part, based on the length of time to return to Eugene. The additional wasted hours in Pullman translated to all available food being consumed long before the flight departed. Being delayed at an airport is an annoying experience for us mere mortals. But to someone who has just beaten up their body over the course of three hours, sitting on an airplane made it a rough night.

🏈 🏈 🏈

Postgame for Geoffrey tended to be rather precarious for him. I clearly remember several worrisome instances while driving the two or three miles from Autzen Stadium to Geoffrey's apartment after a game. With both hands grasping the steering wheel, his forearms would begin to quiver. He was dehydrated. His muscles were seizing and cramping. I'd ask him to let me drive, but he stubbornly refused the offer.

Numerous times during his career Geoffrey needed IV (intravenous) fluids postgame to overcome dehydration and possible side effects. On days played in hot weather it wasn't uncommon for him to proactively receive IV fluids during halftime.

When all was said and done, I had attended forty-six of Geoffrey's college games. I will admit, without any hesitation, that it was extremely important for me to be at the boys' games, whether they played or not. My dad's influence. Apparently, it was important to Geoffrey as well, although communicated indirectly.

One day in either his sophomore or junior season Geoffrey approached Livie and me and asked if we would increase the allowance we were giving him. His scholarship covered most expenses and, of course, the cost of living in Eugene was quite reasonable, but he wanted more. Livie and I gave it some thought, discussed the alternatives and got back to him. We told him he had two options.

We could give him more allowance; however, it would mean fewer trips to games. It wasn't cheap to make the trips to Oregon. Airfare. Lodging. Food. Car rental. Our resources were not unlimited. Or we could leave the status quo and be able to continue our travels unimpeded. He thought for but a few seconds and wisely, at least to Livie and me, chose the status quo option. Without being direct, he was telling us that he wanted us around.

We had a similar experience with Mitchell during his first year at Cal. It was Geoffrey's senior season at Oregon. The schedule had Cal hosting the Trojans of USC on the same day as an Oregon bye. With Geoffrey not playing, Livie and I elected to drive to Berkeley to watch the game. Although Mitchell was redshirting and wouldn't be playing, this trip was a perfect chance to spend time with him. We made reservations at a bed & breakfast in Berkeley and headed up the coast.

We arranged to see Mitchell after the game. Pregame, we gathered our football gear and began our stroll to the stadium. Soon into our walk, I began to feel rain drops on my head. Usually vigilant about checking the weather, this time we neglected to do so before departing. As we walked, the rain intensified. Close to campus we ducked into a store to buy a hat. Found one I liked. Once purchased and outside, I placed the hat on my noggin, believing it would protect my head from the moisture. Yeah, right. I didn't bother looking before making the purchase. The hat

Through the Turnstiles

was made with a mesh upper. It was going to afford me zero protection. Dumb move.

Although we were without our usual wet-weather gear, we dutifully continued our trek to the stadium. The rain was strengthening. It continued to come down in sheets throughout the entire first half. Livie and I were drenched. So was Mitchell on the sidelines; however, he was this eighteen-year-old football stud. He could care less about getting wet. We, on the other hand, couldn't stand another moment of sitting in the downpour. We decided to leave at halftime, walking back to our B&B. Inside our room we removed our rain-soaked clothing, laying everything next to the fireplace to dry off. We left a message for Mitchell that we had departed the stadium and would see him in the morning.

The three of us gathered for breakfast the next morning. At some point I must have walked away because I wasn't privy to this conversation. Mitchell, seemingly upset about our leaving, said to his mom, "You never left any of Geoffrey's games." Oh my. That was true. But in bad-weather games, we almost always dressed in proper clothing. Plus, and more importantly, Geoffrey was on the field playing. Mitchell was a bystander that day. However, the message was abundantly clear. Like Geoffrey, it was important to Mitchell that his mother and father attend his games...in their entirety.

Spurred by this exchange, and my own desire to be present, I attended every one of Mitchell's fifty-one Cal games. Similar to Geoffrey's experience, one season Cal had a losing 5-6 record and therefore didn't qualify for a bowl game. Missing that game prevented Mitchell from tying a Cal record for most games started in a career: fifty-two. Home contests. Pac-10/12 away games. Non-conference foes across the country. Minnesota. Maryland. Reno, Nevada. I was at them all.

Between the two guys, I was in the stands for ninety-seven games. I believe Livie was with me for most of the West Coast–based contests and at least a couple of games beyond. Adding the ninety-seven to the sixty-eight high school games, plus the five pro contests, the tally at the end of their respective college careers was 170. Geoffrey and Mitchell had yet to play one NFL game. As a matter of fact, Geoffrey had yet to *attend* a professional game. For most of their formative years, L.A. did not have a home team. When the Raiders moved from Oakland to the Southland, I never bought tickets to those games. Go figure that the first professional game attended by Geoffrey was his first game as an NFL player.

Travel became progressively more challenging as the guys advanced from high school to college to the NFL, and we tried to accomplish the sometimes unachievable—seeing both in person each weekend. The simplest situation, of course, was the seven-mile trek from home to Pali High. Then Geoffrey headed to Oregon and things got a bit complicated.

For the three years with Geoffrey at Oregon and Mitchell at Pali, our goal was to attend both games during the same weekend. That would require a crack-of-dawn Saturday morning trip, whether by airplane or car, to arrive before Geoffrey's kickoff after watching Mitchell the night before. With usually all but one Oregon game on the West Coast, this was doable. However, there were instances, like the game in Oklahoma, where this pattern just wouldn't work, necessitating a Friday night liftoff. Regardless of a Friday night or Saturday morning departure, we always returned home Sunday.

Then Mitchell departed to Cal. The one year with both on college squads became a no-brainer with Mitchell redshirting, of course except for the "you never leave Geoffrey's games early" Cal/USC weekend.

Making Adjustments for NFL Games

Geoffrey landing in the NFL changed so much. The NFL schedule could include up to twenty games, as compared to the twelve-game college schedule, when accounting for pre-, regular and postseason contests, with games held from coast to coast. With college games at most a two-and-a-half-hour flight away, or a five-and-a-half-hour car journey to Cal, travel to NFL cities could consume up to eight hours door-to-door, including a five-and-a-half-hour airplane ride.

Home bases while in the NFL for both guys were as "close" as around 1,600 miles, and as far away as 2,700 miles or more, like in New Jersey when Geoffrey played for the New York Giants. If we wanted to spend any meaningful one-on-one time with the boys, we departed on Friday, returning Monday. It was virtually impossible to find a return flight to L.A. after the completion of a Sunday NFL contest other than a redeye, which, in our book, was a nonstarter. So, two days stretched to four.

Mitchell at Cal and Geoffrey in the NFL required the creative juices to flow. Given that I attended every one of Mitchell's games, it meant watching Geoffrey in person had to be on a Cal bye weekend or one of the NFL Monday night/Thursday night games. Otherwise, we spent Saturdays watching Mitchell live and then Sunday in the Berkeley area viewing Geoffrey on the tube. That was accomplished for kickoffs at 10 a.m. or 1 p.m. PST by locating a restaurant or bar televising Geoffrey's game and then taking custody of a table for the duration of the telecast. If Geoffrey's game was scheduled for the ESPN 5:15 p.m. slot, we'd breakfast with Mitchell, leaving Berkeley early enough to be home by kickoff.

Mitchell's away games posed a greater challenge to watching Geoffrey live. In Berkeley, we had our go-to restaurant. When in other cities, finding a local eatery was a chore, however, in most cases we were successful. For the exception, the game was being recorded at home. Upon arrival, I made a beeline to the TV.

The biggest change to our in-person viewing was triggered when both guys were on NFL rosters. No longer were most games local. The travel restrictions limited our in-person viewing to four or five games per season, typically including a preseason game. When the boys were in the league, the preseason schedule was consistent and uniform. Starters would be on the field for a quarter in the first game, a full half in the second, three quarters in the third and maybe one series in the final week of preseason. With this reliable cycle, I typically would attend game three when the guys started, knowing their field time would be greatest during that game. Before Geoffrey was a starter, I aimed for game four.

Preseason is a great example of how the NFL world has dramatically shifted. Preseason reliability no longer exists. In 2021 the regular season expanded to seventeen games. To compensate, one preseason game was sliced off the schedule. Now, with one fewer preseason game and concern about injury prevention and health, all the old customs have been tossed aside. Starters may not see even one snap in the preseason now. Others will play, but on a limited basis. It would be a real crapshoot in today's world as to which game to attend.

To map out our travel plans, I created an Excel spreadsheet listing the schedules of both guys, plus UCLA's schedule, since we still owned season tickets back then. From there we'd pick and choose which NFL games to attend. If lucky, we'd double dip by identifying a Sunday/Thursday combo in the same city.

We lucked out when the guys played for the Kansas City Chiefs, who are part of the West Division within the American Football Conference (AFC). The other teams in the Division were the Raiders, Chargers and Denver Broncos. When the boys played, the Raiders were based in

Raising Giants

Oakland. Today it's Las Vegas. Until the Chargers moved to Los Angeles in 2017, home was San Diego.

Schedules called for Division teams to play each other twice during a season, home and away, so we knew that, when the boys played for K.C., twice a season our travel remained within the state of California. As a matter of fact, the stadium where the Chargers first played in L.A. was only twenty miles from our house. When they moved to the newly built, over $5 billion SoFi Stadium in Inglewood, that was only ten miles away. That would be a short jaunt in most cities, but with L.A.'s infamous traffic...who knew.

Back to the game count. Geoffrey's NFL career spanned eight seasons; however, he lost the better part of two years because of injuries. That obviously limited our attendance. I'm thinking, or rather speculating, that with preseason games included, I conservatively attended twenty of his NFL games.

Mitchell, on the other hand, was a different story. He was blessed with health and longevity. Factoring in Mitchell's seven playoff games, including a winning Super Bowl appearance in 2020, he laced 'em up in 141 consecutive NFL games during his eight and a half years. Using a standard of four games a year and removing the COVID-impacted final season when fans were not permitted in the stands, I figure I attended thirty-two preseason and regular season games of his, plus a trio of postseason contests.

For ease of mathematics, let's assume thirty-five for Mitchell and twenty for Geoffrey for a total of fifty-five. Add this to the earlier subtotal of 170 and we arrive at 225. Yikes. That many games over two decades actually in the stands, fixated on the boys, regardless of weather, location or any other possible limiting factors. How blessed have I been?

But this doesn't tell the whole story as it relates to my football viewing. Remember I mentioned earlier in the chapter that Livie and I bought UCLA season tickets in 1978? Until Geoffrey began his high school football career in 2000, I would attend five or six Bruins games a season. That's twenty-two years and likely no less than 110 times I walked through the turnstiles. From 2000 until 2021, because of conflicts with the boys' schedules, I probably averaged no more than two, maybe three, games a season. Let's take the conservative approach and use two. That's another fortyish. Now I'm approaching 400 games total in my lifetime, based on conservative estimates.

Through the Turnstiles

Although our attendance was limited during their NFL careers, I never missed a game. DirecTV offered a package known as NFL Sunday Ticket, through which every single NFL game was available for viewing. And so we bought the package. The challenge would be watching both when their games in the NFL were on TV at the same time. I wasn't about to let that get in the way.

When Mitchell graduated Cal, he left us with a forty-two-inch flat-screen TV. It was being stored in the garage when I had an epiphany. On Sundays, when the two guys were playing concurrently, I would jury rig the "portable" TV to operate from the floor under the wall-mounted television already in our family room. And that's how we watched two games at the same time, at least in the beginning. But that setup was simply not acceptable long term.

So what did we do? We built that bonus room on our house. It wasn't a snap decision, as we had been contemplating this for several years, but could just never justify doing so. Now, needing to comfortably watch both Geoffrey and Mitchell, we had a "real" reason to build a new room above our garage. It is a bit less than 500 square feet, designed as a shrine to the boys. I would be inclined to refer to the room as a "Man Cave," but that won't fly. If you knew my wife, you'd know exactly why not.

With the two side-by-side sixty-inch flat-screen TVs, we'd fire up both when the boys' games overlapped. The one with Geoffrey or Mitchell on the field would be the TV with sound piped through the speakers. If they were on the field at the same time, we would pause one TV for as long as needed, watch the live game, then return to the other when the offense gave way to the defense. It took a bit of dexterity to shift from one to the other, but over time I became very skilled with the remote control.

We (well, more me than Livie) were very strict about outside interruptions during game watching. Phone calls were basically ignored. That's what voicemail was for. The only interruptions "allowed" were to the occasional text messages from a very short list of approved interlopers. But, truth be told, immediate responses were highly unlikely. It was all about timing and mood. Boys on the field. Not going to happen. Boys not playing well or team not playing well, equally likely to cause a delay. On the flip side, let one of the guys make a great play, and I'm likely to be the one reaching out. Or if I had a question about a specific play, I had Geoffrey when available or Duke Manyweather to query. (Much more about Duke throughout the book.)

Raising Giants

Beyond the trophies crowding the shelves, the Bonus Room (remember...happy wife, happy life) also displays six jerseys that I've collected from the boys over the years. Hung on a six-hook clothing rack, Mitchell's trio includes one from Cal, another from the Cleveland Browns and a third from Kansas City. Geoffrey's threesome are from his days with Oregon, Carolina and the New York Giants. Above the jerseys are ball caps from all the respective teams.

These were authentic jerseys, ones they once soiled while on the gridiron. When they were able to secure a jersey while still playing for that particular team, I wore it to every game I attended, home and away. The jersey was always the last layer worn, except in rainy conditions. I was awfully proud to walk the stadiums promoting the boys and the family name. I believe one time I saw a fan wearing a Geoffrey or Mitchell jersey, but that was the imitation store-bought variety.

And then there are the helmets that adorn the upper shelves of the wall unit surrounding the two large-screen TVs. One each from the Cleveland Browns, Oregon Ducks, Cal Bears and Kansas City Chiefs. Have you ever put on a football helmet? Heavy suckers. No wonder football players have awfully strong neck muscles. (In case it might have crossed your mind, I never wore helmets to games.)

I attended as many games as possible. I watched all the others through hook or crook. Maybe the most challenging was the game watched on my iPad while traveling to Israel or, during that same trip, waking up at 3:30 a.m., turning on my computer, and viewing Mitchell's game from my hotel room. (More details to come.) And yet that was not enough for me. I believe I can honestly say that every game they played has been recorded and then burned to a CD. I've stored the CDs in cases, segregated between Mitchell and Geoffrey. G-d forbid I need to flee the house quickly, these cases will be going with me. Hopefully through these CDs (or some other form of digital storage) my grandkids can actually see their daddy playing.

For games I attended in person, early on I would return home and view the recording in the days following. Never the full game though. Only plays with the boys on the field. I took advantage of the rewind, pause and slow-motion features on the recorder to give me a second and sometimes a third look at a play. I learned a whole lot about o-line play and Mitchell's and Geoffrey's approaches to the game by these quasi study sessions. In time, I no longer felt the need.

Through the Turnstiles

As I referenced a few pages earlier, I used an Excel spreadsheet—Livie has been known to boast about my Excel skills—to manage football schedules. At any point in time it included UCLA, Mitchell's and Geoffrey's current team, and Oregon. (I still follow the Ducks all these years after Geoffrey's departure.) I had a visual map to guide me through my/our decision-making regarding which games to attend, how many additional tickets might be needed, and when we might double dip and attend two games during one trip. It was an invaluable tool.

I've attended more games in my life than I ever could have imagined. High school. College. Professional. Rose Bowls and other bowl games. A national championship contest. Could the pace continue? That answer crystalized when attending the first game of UCLA's 2021 season. On paper it should have been a game of great interest. LSU, two years removed from winning the National Championship, was visiting the Rose Bowl. It was the first time these programs had ever faced each other. After a boring, scoreless first quarter, UCLA won rather easily that day. I should have been thrilled. In all candor, I spent a good part of the second half checking my watch. I was bored. Couldn't wait to head to the car.

The reality set in that day. Early on in my life, a game like this, a day at the Rose Bowl, would have set my juices flowing. That day didn't come close. I realized that I had reached a point of saturation. Whatever number I use, 220-plus games watching the boys from high school through the NFL or the 400 or so when including Saturdays at UCLA and the handful of other games I've attended, it's a whole, whole bunch. The appeal, the charm, the uniqueness, the cache of attending in person has vanished. It's an eight-hour day door-to-door attending a game at the Rose Bowl. With my side-by-side screens and channel surfing I can basically watch four games at a time versus the one in person.

Two seasons later I had confirmation of my saturation. In 1976 Livie and I attended the "Granddaddy of Them All," the Rose Bowl game pitting our UCLA Bruins against the undefeated and number-one-ranked Ohio State Buckeyes, led by cantankerous Coach Woody Hayes. It was a glorious day as my "gutsy" Bruins upset OSU 23-10. We literally were on our feet for three and a half quarters of that game.

In 2005 I attended that year's version of the Rose Bowl, invited by a Michigan alum. Texas versus the Wolverines. Some consider it the best Rose Bowl game ever played. What a special day. But then fast forward nineteen years later. My same buddy explored my interest in attending

Raising Giants

the 2024 Rose Bowl with eventual National Champions Michigan facing long-time stalwart Alabama. My *immediate* response was, "No thanks."

As the boys accepted the closure of their NFL careers and moved on to their next chapters, I too must accept this shift in my life. After forty-four years, I cancelled my UCLA season tickets. That was a very emotionally charged decision for me. If I want to attend a game or two, I can still buy tickets through UCLA or the secondary market, and likely do so for far less than what season tickets cost me, particularly when I factor in the annual donation required by UCLA just for the right to purchase the tickets.

However, with all this said, I still hold out a bucket-list wish. Geoffrey and I have, in limited fashion, discussed this idea. As grandson Alex gets older and more interested in football, I'd like nothing better than to have a guys' weekend once a year, where Geoffrey, Alex and I attend a game for a team I've never seen in person or a match-up between two storied rivals. Alabama. University of Texas. USC at Notre Dame. Michigan vs. Ohio State. I cannot think of any better way to add to my historical numbers...other than one day be in the stands watching my grandson.

9

THE MOST MEMORABLE GAMES

It was a question that in all the years had never been asked of me. It happened during a tailgate before that 2021 UCLA versus LSU football game at the Rose Bowl.

A good buddy of mine, Gary Saenger, one who has enthusiastically followed the guys and their careers, asked, "What are the most memorable games for each one of your boys?" My response was immediate, shocking Gary and, frankly, somewhat amazing me. The previous chapter outlined the number of Geoffrey's and Mitchell's games I attended spanning high school through the NFL—225! And yet my answer to this query was instantaneous and specific.

Geoffrey's Big Game

It was 2007. The Oregon Ducks were one of the best teams in the country. Heading into the first weekend of October, Oregon was 5-1 and ranked number five nationally. Their record included a thrashing of the perennial top-dog Michigan Wolverines in their Big House. The 39-7 final score was not indicative of the punishment handed out that day by the Ducks. I know because, of course, I was in the stands.

This particular autumn weekend the USC Trojans were visiting Autzen Stadium. They arrived ranked twelfth in the nation with a similar

Raising Giants

5-1 record, the only blemish a one-point loss to Stanford. The previous weekend they shellacked archrival Notre Dame 38-0.

The oddsmakers favored Oregon over USC, the first time since 2001 that the Trojans had not been favored over a Pac-10 opponent. The last time the Ducks had beaten USC was in 2001.

There was an uncharacteristic level of excitement in the air that day for this very important game. As you may have guessed by now, the Ducks beat the Trojans that afternoon—and they did it in front of an overflow crowd of 59,277 fanatical fans ("capacity" was 54,000), winning 24-17. That alone would have made for the most memorable game of Geoffrey's career. Being a UCLA alum added to the satisfaction of the final result. But there was more to the story.

It was the third quarter. Oregon was in possession of the football. Quarterback Dennis Dixon sat in shotgun behind the line of scrimmage. He motioned for the ball to be snapped. With football in hand, he looked downfield but saw no receiver open. What he saw, though, was a Trojan defensive end quickly beating a path toward him for a sack.

Instinctually, Dennis, through his peripheral vision, identified a fellow green-shirted teammate to his right. He lateraled the ball in that direction not knowing who it was. The teammate caught the ball and ran for a three-yard gain. Who was the teammate?

Yup, it was Geoffrey. He snatched the ball out of the air, cupped it into the crook of his elbow, and ran, until he felt the presence of the same defensive end who had hounded Dixon. In the open field, Geoffrey had visions of coughing up the ball while being tackled and giving USC possession, so instead of trying to gain more yards, he fell to the turf for a short gain. The ball was safe.

As Geoffrey walked back to the huddle, with one of his lineman teammates alongside stride for stride, he threw both arms in the air, palms to the sky, and shrugged his shoulders, as if to say, "What the f*** was that!" In the stands, fans throughout the stadium, including his father and mother, were in absolute disbelief, as was Geoffrey on the field. Did that really happen? Yes, amazingly, it did. Yet there was more.

But before going there, let me share this related story. It took place while Geoffrey was a Carolina Panther. He was part of the kick return team. (Since then, the rules have changed so dramatically that he wouldn't be on the field in today's world.) He was positioned at the twenty-yard line, with two kick returners at the goal line. He was their protector, but not an intended ball carrier.

Instead of the ball being kicked skyward with the expectation that it would land sixty yards later in the end zone, in this instance it was squibbed, meaning it bounced along the ground toward the goal line. Almost like a magnet attracting a piece of steel, the ball headed in Geoffrey's direction and then inexplicably leapt into his hands. Instinctively, Geoffrey somehow caught the ball in his arm (his hands were completely taped) and ran like crazy until he was tackled sixteen yards later.

When hit by the defender, he felt some pressure in his hip as the contact brought him to the turf. While Geoffrey walked away unscathed, the tackler remained on the field. That pressure Geoffrey felt was the tackler's helmet. For his effort, the tackler unfortunately suffered a concussion, the second one in a couple of weeks. I recall that ended that poor guy's season.

But here's the topper. As Geoffrey trotted off the field toward the Carolina sideline, Head Coach John Fox was waiting. He ripped into him, castigating Geoffrey for not holding the ball with two hands. Just what an offensive lineman is taught to do, right?

Now back to the USC game.

Phil Knight was in attendance that day. He had made his way to the field before the final whistle. Getting from the field to Oregon's locker room required walking through a tunnel. As Geoffrey marched up the tunnel, someone jumped on his back. Stunned, he twisted his head to find Phil catching a ride to the locker room.

I had already made my way into the Oregon locker room, awaiting Geoffrey's arrival for a big bear hug. Before he appeared, Phil bounded through the door. Our eyes met. He walked directly over to me and gave me one of the tightest hugs I've ever received. The Schwartz family was two for two.

Mitchell at Super Bowl LIV

If you have followed Mitchell's career, you might have already answered the "most memorable game" question. What else could the answer be other than the 2020 Super Bowl? Oh my goodness! The memories from that experience will remain with me for the rest of my life.

I'll be sharing more details about that glorious weekend in Miami in a separate chapter, but for now, here's the highlight of the highlight.

How many parents have been fortunate enough to attend a Super Bowl with their son in uniform on the field? And, of course, Mitchell was not just taking up space on the sideline. He was Kansas City's starting right tackle.

The pregame festivities were amazing. Chiefs' fans lucky enough to possess the magic pass were feted to all the food and drink that one could consume at a massive tailgate just inside the stadium. We then made our way to the stands through the throngs of K.C. fans. As game time approached, Livie and I looked at each other and simultaneously asked, "How surreal is this?" We pinched ourselves to make sure we were not dreaming.

Of course, it was very real. We watched the game full of anxiety and nervous energy. We so wanted K.C. to be victorious and for Mitchell to have a good game. As it turned out, "good" was an understatement. Mitchell had a historic game according to ProFootballFocus (PFF), an online grading service. Allow me the opportunity to gloat for a moment.

PFF evaluates and rates each and every play of each and every NFL game for all players who take a snap. When the postseason ended, PFF circulated a graphic that presented their findings for the highest-graded NFL players in all positions, complete with a photo of Mitchell.

To provide some statistical perspective, in the two playoff games leading up to the Super Bowl plus the game itself, Mitchell lined up for 142 pass-blocking snaps. He gave up *one* hurry. (A hurry is levied when the QB is forced to throw quicker than what the play calls for because of

pressure from a defensive player.) Better yet, he gave up *zero* sacks and *zero* hits in those 142 snaps.

Further, this is how Gordon McGuiness, Director of Media Strategy at PFF, described Mitchell's career:

> *Mitchell Schwartz was one of the NFL's most consistent pass blockers throughout his NFL career, both with the Cleveland Browns and then the Kansas City Chiefs. He had just two seasons in his career where he allowed more than forty pressures in the regular season and ranked inside the top ten among all offensive tackles in PFF pass blocking grade in his final two seasons in the league.*

So, yes, Mitchell had a phenomenal game. As ultimately did the Chiefs. And it was an extraordinary day for Livie and me. For all the wonderful stories from that day, of which there are many, stay tuned for Chapter 16, "Super Bowl LIV—A Dream Come True."

The Third Game

At this point the tally is one for Mitchell and one for Geoffrey. I suspect you might think that this third game would be a tiebreaker. Not the case. It involved both guys.

It was 2013. Geoffrey was a Kansas City Chief. Mitchell was in his second season as a Cleveland Brown. When Livie and I studied our trusty Excel spreadsheet before the season began, one game jumped off the page. October 27. Cleveland visiting Kansas City. You could imagine the excitement in the Schwartz household. And the angst.

Weeks before the game, Livie, the creative one in the family, came up with a brilliant idea. She bought two T-shirts, one from each team's website. Upon arrival, she located the scissors and cut each shirt in half, splitting the front and back sides. Having sewn as a teen, she knew how to carefully stitch the two different pieces together to form one shirt, the brown-colored half representing Cleveland, the other side Chiefs' bright gold. Geoffrey's number was added to the gold sleeve, Mitchell's to the brown sleeve. "Schwartz" was added on the back, half in each team's color. One for me. One for her. We wore these special T-shirts to the game.

As was our custom, we arrived at the stadium long before kickoff. My brother was also with us that day, albeit wearing a standard Chiefs' shirt.

He and I decided to take a lap around the stadium parking lot, walking through the throngs of tailgaters. What an experience that was.

The comments we received as we walked through the thousands of fans ran the gamut. Some of the more myopic Kansas City fans, seemingly seeing only the Browns' half of the T-shirt, wanted to run us out of town. Literally, "get the hell out of here." The limited number of Cleveland fans were ecstatic to see their brown and orange colors amid the sea of red and yellow and generally cheered us as we walked by.

Then there were the more inquisitive in the crowd. They stopped us to ask what was going on. After explaining, we typically received a high five, compliments to Livie on the idea, and good wishes for the game.

The contest itself was not very memorable. Geoffrey had not yet become a starter, so he saw very limited action. Mitchell, on the other hand, was on the field for all of Cleveland's offensive snaps.

Nonetheless, it was a very nervous time for Livie and me. How do we sit through a game without showing any favoritism? The answer would have been hard enough without the intrusion of CBS Sports, which televised the game that day.

Two brothers playing on the same field was unusual enough. The first Jewish brothers to play at the same time in the NFL in ninety years made it all the more rare. So there was a possible human-interest story here for CBS to explore.

Somehow, CBS discovered our seats. One of their people came to me before kickoff to share that we might find ourselves on TV at some point during the game. Oh my. That did not add to our nervousness, now, did it? Sure did.

So, with a chance that clapping for one son or the other would be captured on national television, Livie and I decided that we would watch the game with little to no outward emotion. We might as well have sat on our hands. The Chiefs scored. Did not clap. Mitchell made a good play. That was nice. But no visible demonstration. As it turned out, the camera never once panned to us. Oh well.

OK, if the game was not very remarkable, then what was so memorable, beyond the fact that both guys were on the field?

Geoffrey had told us before the game that he had arranged for a photo opportunity on the field immediately afterward. He directed us to be at a particular spot in the stands on field level right behind the end zone as the game ended. We got there and waited.

As players routinely do as the clock runs out, they gathered on the field for back slaps and congratulations. I don't remember it being a "thing" back then, but in years to come the players began exchanging jerseys postgame. Former teammates, competitors they respected. Mitchell must have at least a dozen jerseys, many personally autographed, hanging on his basement walls. From my vantage point, I saw Geoffrey and Mitchell approach one another. They embraced. They then turned in our direction and began walking the fifty or so yards to reach us. We jumped on the field and had pictures taken.

That was the most memorable moment of that day. It has always been rather surreal to have not one but two sons in the NFL. That vision of the two of them in their respective uniforms, heading our way with grins from ear to ear, made it all very real...and very unforgettable.

There it is. The top three out of 225. Are there other memorable games that do not rise to the level of this trio but deserve mention? Sure, unfortunately, not all for the right reasons.

Other Memorable Games

I have to mention the Oregon game in the Rose Bowl during Geoffrey's senior year. It was Geoffrey's first visit to a stadium where, growing up, he had watched the Bruins play every season since he was five. Because the Pac-10 schedule at that time did not include all conference opponents, Oregon did not play at UCLA until his fourth year of college.

The game itself was memorable for the wrong reasons. The Ducks came into the contest with two redshirt freshmen quarterbacks active because of injuries to their top-tier quarterbacks. The final score reflected the desperate situation as the Bruins blanked Oregon 16-0.

For Geoffrey, having grown up a fanatical UCLA fan, this was an extremely emotional game. Not only was he finally playing in the Rose Bowl, in front of a bit more than 72,000 fans, his grandfather was in the stands as well. My Dad was obviously a *huge* Geoffrey fan. This was to be the first college game of Geoffrey's that he attended, doing so in a wheelchair due to medical issues.

Geoffrey was absolutely devastated by the defeat. Years later he shared how he cried as he walked off the field. But his emotions were reset when he and my father connected after the game. The sadness washed away. It was Papa with unwavering love giving Geoffrey a bear hug. That was a memorable moment.

Raising Giants

As previously explained, Mitchell was rather highly recruited in high school. Apparently one game, one play, caught the eye of most recruiting coaches. I remember it so well.

Mitchell lined up at his usual left tackle position. At the snap he fired off the line to engage the defensive end in front of him. Seemingly before one could blink an eye, Mitchell had pancaked his opponent, leaving him lying flat on the ground.

Typically, a pancake will occur but one time per play for an offensive lineman. Not this time. After laying out the first guy, Mitchell returned to his feet and targeted a linebacker at the next level. Pancake number two. But Mitchell wasn't satisfied. He rose up again, this time setting his sights on a defensive back. After being bulldozed by Mitchell, the DB was staring at the stars. Quite an impressive show of Mitchell's ability.

When I learned that Oregon would be playing Michigan in the Big House in Geoffrey's senior season, I was so amped. Growing up, I watched every Michigan game I could. From college Hall of Fame coaches Bo Schembechler and Lloyd Carr to renowned players like Heisman Trophy winner Desmond Howard, former Michigan Head Coach Jim Harbaugh, and that guy some call the NFL G.O.A.T. (Greatest of All Time), Tom Brady, when they played it was must see TV. I also became very familiar with their famous fight song known as "The Victors."

I walked into the stadium awestruck. More than 100,000 people packed together like sardines, hoping Michigan could reverse their fortunes against Oregon. In a week-one contest the weekend prior against Appalachian State, a team oddsmakers described as "sacrificial lambs," the Wolverines were embarrassed in a loss that *Sports Illustrated* headlined as "The Greatest Upset of Them All."

I truly did not expect the Ducks to spank the Wolverines 39-7. And it was not that close. Plus, Geoffrey kicked off his revitalized year with a very solid game. It was a marvelous, and memorable, day.

Geoffrey's first college game in his hometown of Los Angeles happened during his junior season against the hated USC Trojans, played at the venerable Los Angeles Memorial Coliseum.

I knew that many of our friends and Geoffrey followers would have interest in attending the game, so I set out to get my hands on as many tickets as possible. Ended up with over forty. Unfortunately, I did not spend the time looking at the Coliseum layout to understand the ticket locations. Oh my, do I wish I had. I won't get into the specifics, but let me just say that sitting on Figueroa Avenue, a street bordering the Coliseum, might have provided a similar view to the ones we were given in the stadium.

They were, without a doubt, the worst family seats we ever received as a visiting collegiate team. Even with binoculars we were so far away from the action that the players looked like ants. Because of this, many of our friends, those who had paid good money for the tickets and excitedly awaited watching Geoffrey in person, left the stadium by halftime. I was embarrassed and quite unhappy. And this was the game where, hampered by his bad back, Geoffrey's performance was subpar.

Lastly, here's a story not about a football game but rather the tragedy of life and the good will of the human spirit. It happened in 2007, at the beginning of Geoffrey's senior season at Oregon. The venue was Reliant Stadium in Houston.

Days before a game scheduled between Oregon and the University of Houston, Hurricane Katrina thundered through New Orleans, causing great devastation and forcing thousands to relocate. Reliant was literally built in the shadows of the Houston Astrodome, known when first erected as the Eighth Wonder of the World. It was the very first domed stadium. In the aftermath of Katrina, the Astrodome became a temporary home for those displaced from the Big Easy.

As we waited to enter Reliant pregame, one school bus after another pulled into the Astrodome parking lot. Once parked, we watched the very distressing images of the hurricane refugees arriving, walking off the bus with nothing more than a pillowcase slung over their shoulders. The contents were the only possessions they could salvage after the impact of the hurricane. It hurt to watch.

The game that day took a back seat to what was happening outside in the adjacent parking lot and what ultimately emerged inside the stadium. Thanks to the kindness and unselfishness of the management of Reliant Stadium, in the stands that day were hundreds, if not thousands, of the displaced, who were allowed to attend the game free of charge, to hopefully provide some measure of pleasure during a time of extreme misery. That day was very sobering and has been indelibly imprinted in my mind. And thus, I felt the need to share.

Raising Giants

The memories are many. While a handful were not so pleasant, they were, without a doubt, the outliers. I have so many positive recollections from the two decades of Mitchell's and Geoffrey's football careers.

10

STADIUM HIGHLIGHTS

Having attended almost 400 games, I obviously have walked into dozens of stadiums along the way—thirty-eight at last count, including those for both college and the NFL. This chapter will share the good, the bad and the ugly (yes, I am a big Clint Eastwood fan) of my experiences at a number of these varied venues.

But before launching into stadium particulars, I thought I'd begin with a more routine narrative: the art and science of acquiring tickets, from the boys' high school days through the NFL. Each stage was different.

High School Seating

High school was the simplest. No season tickets. No assigned seating. Simply show up, buy a ticket and find a seat. I am neurotic about arriving early at a stadium, sometimes before the ticket booth is open for business. And such was the case at the boys' high school games. The cost of entry, as I recall, was a very reasonable $6.00 per person.

I had my preferred seating area: Pali High side of the stadium with the team directly in front of me. Typically fifty-yard line, toward the top of the section, on the aisle. I would save the aisle seat for Livie, who would typically arrive after me. If anyone else was joining us, I would lay out a jacket or blanket on the needed seats, awaiting their arrival.

Being a high school game with no broad fan interest, unlike Friday Night Lights in Texas, these contests were not televised. So I became a videographer, mimicking my buddy, Norm Beegun. Back in the day these cameras were heavy and bulky, unlike now, where our cell phones do a mighty fine job of recording the action. I bought my own hulking video camera. I schlepped it to every one of Geoffrey's and Mitchell's games, home and away, along with extra tapes. The recordings would come in handy in case the boys later wanted to study their on-field activity. I believe those archaic cassettes are still stored somewhere in my garage.

College Tickets

College was quite different. The NCAA made available four *free* tickets for each player for home and away games. By the Wednesday before a game, we would tell the boys how many tickets would be needed. They also knew to request aisle seats for Livie's benefit. Early in their tenure with each team it was more hit or miss as to whether we received the requested aisle seats. But as they became more vital to their respective teams, somehow the granting of aisle seats became a given. Imagine how that works!

If friends and/or family were joining us, resulting in our needing more tickets than the allotted four, the boys would barter with teammates. "If you give me X to this game, I'll give you X, or Y, or Z, to this other game." It always worked when the request was reasonable. When greater numbers were required, like the forty for that USC game, then I had to be more resourceful.

Both Oregon and Cal handled the logistics of entry to the stadium in very much the same way. One gate was set aside for family and friends to pass through. It was preferred that the entire group enter at one time, but if someone was tardy, they were on their own. I wasn't going to disrupt my routine for those who came late. Team staff were the gatekeepers, holding a list of approved names. Upon showing our IDs, we'd be given our ticket allotment. At this point, with tickets in hand, we were required by the NCAA to head directly into the stadium, passing through security along the way. Prior to this rule, tickets could be scalped. (I can't imagine why the NCAA would frown on such a practice. Haha.)

The location of family seats was different between Cal and Oregon and varied greatly when traveling. At Autzen Stadium in Eugene, there was essentially a caste system. Families of freshmen and sophomores were given end-zone seats. As our boys moved up the ladder as a junior or senior, we'd then sit along the Oregon sideline at about the twenty- to twenty-five-yard line—a great real-life example of the benefits that accrue with seniority.

My good buddy Mike Parr owns sixteen season tickets scattered throughout Autzen. Three of those were in a prime location. Oregon side. Forty-yard line. Higher up in the section for perfect viewing of the entire field. Sometimes, if I traveled alone, I would sit with Mike and forego the Oregon-supplied ticket.

The away games could be an adventure trying to locate the gate where visiting team families entered the stadium. Many times, we'd ask the security guards or the stadium staff for directions, only to be met with blank stares. They had no clue. But, because of my neurosis of having to arrive super early, we always got to our seats in time to enjoy pregame activities.

As with home games, Oregon and Cal staffed tables outside the stadium gates and provided us with the necessary allotment of tickets. Once inside, the task was finding our seats. Almost without exception, we could not go wrong by heading up the nearest stairs or escalator. Invariably the seats were higher up than closer to the field. Many times, top deck. Many times, in one of the two end zones. While not the most ideal, it was still far better than not being in the stadium.

As I recall, there was one time when at first blush the away game seats appeared ideal. Bulldog Stadium, home to the Fresno State Bulldogs, is a very intimate venue, with a total capacity of a touch under 41,000. It is basically one level from the bottom to the top of the bowl. We picked up our tickets and headed to our seats. Upon arrival, we looked around, questioning, "Could this be right?" It was the first row of seats at about the forty-yard line, about ten feet above field level, so the players on the sidelines could not obstruct our view. But there was a fundamental flaw that may have explained why we were seated there. Directly in front of us was a walkway that was in constant use as attendees visited the snack areas or other facilities. We often found ourselves dodging roving bodies to have a clear view of the activity on the field.

Tickets in the NFL

The NFL is a different animal when it comes to providing tickets, as compared to the NCAA. Each player is allotted only two per game. Home

Raising Giants

game tickets are free to the player, regardless of face value. However, the player must pay taxes on the face value of the two tickets. If we needed more than two, tickets were customarily available, but at face value. We had arranged with the boys before their entry into the NFL that Mom and Dad would never pay for tickets. (Thanks guys!) It was up to Mitchell or Geoffrey to determine if they would ask anyone else attending to pay. Livie and I stayed out of those conversations.

As for away games, the NFL deducts from their paychecks the face value of tickets for all those attending. When Livie and I attended away games, the boys kept to our "agreement" and kindly paid for our tickets. Anyone else wanting to attend, they were directed to the boys for "negotiation." Again, Livie and I were happy to not be in the middle.

Home family-seating sections varied. In Cleveland we might sit one time in an end-zone seat and the next along the Browns' sideline at about the ten- or fifteen-yard line. In New York, the family section was in the lower tier somewhere between the back of the end zone and the ten-yard line. Kansas City set aside two locations. Not sure to this day how the decision was made as to where they sat us. One was on field level in the corner of the end zone and was definitely the least desirable of the two.

It was impossible to sit comfortably in those seats. They were angled such that if sitting and looking straight ahead, line of sight would be from the end zone to about the ten-yard line. To see anything otherwise, we needed to twist our torso to the right, more and more so as play moved toward the opposite end zone.

This issue, however, was almost made moot by another circumstance. Those seated in the first few rows of the section at field level could not see through the players on the sidelines, so they stood to watch. If they stood, those behind had to stand. Like reverse dominos, one row after another rose up, ultimately reaching our family seats. So we either ended up on our feet for most of the game or were forced to watch the action via the big video boards positioned at either end of the field. Neither option was ideal.

The other seating location was preferred, and the one most frequently assigned to us during Mitchell's last two to three years with the Chiefs. The Club Level rests between field level and the top, third level. It has its own internal climate-controlled concession area, perfect during cold weather games for those fighting off the outside chill. Patrons had access to flat-screen TVs for game viewing and upscale food offerings. Ideal for us Schwartzes. The seats themselves were not angled much better than

Stadium Highlights

the ones below; however, we rarely had an obstructed view from those in front of us.

As for the stadiums themselves, no two are alike. Each one has a different atmosphere, a distinctive character to it. Some I walked away from extolling their virtues. Others were simply nondescript. And then there were the few I was very happy to leave in the rearview mirror.

The Rose Bowl

I will begin with the granddaddy of them all: The Rose Bowl in Pasadena, California, nestled into the Arroyo Seco, a dry riverbed, surrounded by a golf course that on game days becomes an extended parking lot for attendees. I suspect many of you have either attended a game in the Bowl or viewed one on your TV. It was first built in 1922, becoming the home of the annual New Year's Day Rose Bowl and since 1982 home base for the UCLA Bruins. Until 1997, seating capacity was second only to Michigan's "The Big House" at almost 105,000. Recognizing the reality that Los Angeles/UCLA were no longer capable of supporting six-figure crowds, the Bowl renovated and trimmed capacity to a touch over 91,000.

The entire environment, inside the Bowl and its surroundings, is very appealing to the eye. Our season seats offered spectacular views. Peeking over the east- and north-facing rims of the Bowl the beautiful, lush San Gabriel mountains captured our attention. It was a joy to watch a game at the Rose Bowl, especially when the Bruins were victorious.

Autzen Stadium in Eugene

Equally spectacular was Autzen Stadium, the off-campus venue of the Oregon Ducks. It was a twenty- to thirty-minute walk from our customary motel. About seven to eight minutes into our journey we would begin to hear the rush of water. Two or three minutes later we'd be standing on the bridge crossing the Willamette River. Absolutely gorgeous. Continuing on, we entered a wooded area, with lush vegetation on both sides of the path. And then, abruptly, the trees would end and there, a bit ahead, we would see Autzen Stadium, with a huge, Oregon styled "O" on the facade, announcing we had arrived. Inside Autzen, the student section spanned several aisles, helping to make it one of the loudest in the country. In that 2007 game against USC, the decibel level reached 127, ranking it as the fourth loudest in college football history. More specifically, Geoffrey has shared that the interception at the end of this game to seal the victory was the loudest moment he ever experienced in Autzen. Talk about home field advantage!

Autzen wasn't the only loud stadium that we encountered. Based on a report from FanBuzz.com, I've been inside seven of the top ten noisiest NFL stadiums, subjecting my ears to record-breaking decibel levels. Top on that list was Kansas City's Arrowhead Stadium. They hold the Guinness world record, yes, the entire world, for "loudest crowd roars" at a sports stadium at 142.2 decibels in a 2014 game. Next on the list was the home field of the Seattle Seahawks, another open-air stadium. In 2013 they laid claim to the Guinness record for the loudest crowd roar at an outdoor stadium, reaching levels of 136.6 and 137.6 decibels.

Lambeau Field

Number three on the list was Lambeau Field in Green Bay. What's interesting to me is that the top three are outdoor stadiums. I would have thought that indoor arenas would be louder, but that's not the case.

I grew up during the heyday of the Green Bay Packers, watching game after game played at legendary Lambeau Field. When I spotted a game versus Green Bay on the Carolina Panthers' schedule in 2008, it was circled immediately. Although that was Geoffrey's first year with the Panthers and he was on the practice squad, meaning he wasn't going to travel, I knew I still had to attend.

My decision was made all the easier because of the friendship I developed with another vendor of that distribution company I ran. He was a huge football fan and just happened to have Packers' season tickets. He invited me to join him and his friends for the game. I couldn't turn down the invite.

I was picked up by my buddy in a twelve-person van for the trip from Milwaukee, where I was staying, to Green Bay. As I recall, it was about a two-hour ride. Told that we were getting close to the stadium, something didn't add up. We were still traveling through a residential neighborhood. Most stadiums are located in more remote or industrial areas. Rather abruptly, it seemed, the bus turned into a church parking lot. "Why stop here?" I inquired.

Well, you see, that's the way it's done in Green Bay. The stadium was built among residential homes, churches and smaller industrial properties. Astonishingly, the homeowners allow game attendees to park on their properties, charging virtually nothing. (FYI, a parking spot in the neighborhood surrounding the Los Angeles Coliseum would cost nothing less than $70, and possibly into triple digits.) And, in a supreme example of neighborliness, especially through the lens of someone coming from the big city of Los Angeles, those parked on the property had free reign of the house for bathroom needs. No locked doors. Enter, do your business, and exit, with full trust.

We entered the stadium and found our seats. I was wearing Carolina garb and so obviously stood out among the green and yellow of Green Bay fans. A person sitting next to me began giving me some grief for "trespassing." As soon as I explained that my son played for Carolina, her entire attitude shifted. "Welcome, welcome, welcome." From that point on, those in the immediate vicinity acted like I was a long-lost friend.

Lambeau features a very special element within the stadium. It's known as the Ring of Honor. The Ring prominently displays the names of the best players and coaches in Green Bay franchise history on a facade that loops around the stadium. Imagine my excitement to see the names of the heroes from my youth—Bart Starr, Paul Hornung, Jim Taylor and Ray Nitschke—so honored. That alone made my day.

The Superdome in New Orleans: High Decibels

Number four is a stadium I did not visit, but Geoffrey did. Geoffrey once shared that Caesars Superdome in New Orleans was so loud that on a drive for a game winning field goal he had to stare directly at the ball the entire drive because he couldn't hear the snap count. The other loudest stadiums that I've encountered are those in Arizona, Pittsburgh, Minnesota and Dallas, three of the four indoor arenas. No wonder that Livie travels to all stadiums with ear plugs.

The racket is hard on one's ears, but the earsplitting commotion also greatly impacts the visiting team's performance. In Seattle particularly, the crowd noise is notorious for contributing to an increase in offensive players' false starts, that is, moving before the snap or causing delay-of-game penalties. As a matter of fact, their crowd is known as "the 12th man" because they have influenced games. On a stadium scoreboard, Seattle maintains a seasonal count of the number of false-start penalties flagged against the visiting offenses. The boys both talked about the difficulty of playing in Seattle. Their teams had to resort to silent counts, instead of relying on the bark of a quarterback's cadence. Obviously, that creates a tremendous home field advantage.

Back to Autzen. I also remember it for a very rare experience...that I enjoyed twice. *College GameDay* is a show broadcast by ESPN every Saturday morning during the college football season, airing before the day's games kick off. Typically, the location is on the campus where a high-profile game is being played that day. When home, I watch the show religiously.

Twice during Geoffrey's time at Oregon, *GameDay* built their set in Eugene near Autzen Stadium. Through Geoffrey's newly burgeoning contacts, he secured behind-the-scenes passes for my brother and me one time, and for me alone for a second bite of the apple. What a treat that was. I/we awoke well before the crack of dawn and, half asleep, trudged to the site of the set, located to the south of Autzen, just outside the timberline, with the big "O" on the stadium easily visible for the TV cameras to capture.

Passes allowed almost unfettered access to all the activity not shown on TV. How cool it was to be within arm's distance of the personalities, to be close enough to hear the director's commands. Of all that I witnessed those mornings, maybe the most unexpected, and humorous, was the attire of the hosts. When viewed through the TV lens, one sees formality with the guys in dress shirts, ties and jackets. Below the table was a completely different look. They were casually dressed in khakis, shorts and tennis shoes. OMG. What a treat those experiences were.

The Macy's Thanksgiving Day Parade

Speaking of unique experiences, I have watched the Macy's Thanksgiving Day Parade since my youth. My mother loved the televised spectacles and under her influence, so did I. (I'm excited to share that my grandkids now sit with me to watch.) One year, when Geoffrey played for the New York Giants, with a Thanksgiving weekend game on the docket, Livie and I made plans to be with the family. One thing led to another and before we knew it, my daughter-in-law, Meridith, had rented a Manhattan apartment that weekend for the four of us and grandson Alex. Looking through the floor-to-ceiling windows of the unit, it felt like we could reach out and touch the Empire State building.

One of Geoffrey's friends from Charlotte had a sister who lived in Jersey, who Geoffrey and Meridith got to know during their time there. Her husband had an office overlooking the parade route. We were invited to watch the parade from his office. My excitement was palpable thinking about getting a first-hand view of the parade. Aesop's Fables is the source of "be careful what you wish for, lest it come true." In this case, what I wished for resulted in a very disappointing experience.

I won't bore you with all the details. I'll simply share that what is shown on TV is but a glimpse of the totality of the parade. With the weather being mild for that late November day, I ventured outside to watch the parade from a sidewalk on 6th Avenue instead of being cooped up in the office above. I was expecting the procession to be fully active, with bands playing, performers performing, singers singing. That wasn't the case. From my vantage point, all I saw were participants queued up, restlessly waiting to make the right turn onto 34th Street and to march by Macy's iconic front entrance where all the live action takes place. It was such a disappointing experience that I would never return unless I had 34th Street tickets in hand.

Husky Stadium

The University of Washington's Husky Stadium offered another spectacular view. Seats for visiting-player families were in the west end zone. Positioned between us and the field was a track, a grassy area and an end zone. The other end zone seemed to exist in a different zip code. However, from our vantage point, we could look out onto Lake Washington, which lapped up against the stadium. Some fans would motor across the lake, tie up at the dock and then proceed into the stadium to watch the game. Others would drop anchor in the water and spend the afternoon lounging on their boat, enjoying the game on TV or radio.

I spoke about distance from the field at Washington. I shouldn't really complain. We attended Geoffrey's game against the Dallas Cowboys soon after Cowboys Stadium (now renamed AT&T Stadium) was built, called by some "Jerry's World" after owner Jerry Jones. It is a cavernous arena, and feels very cold and uninviting. Family tickets for this game found us sitting in rural San Antonio. (Well, it at least felt that way.) We were three rows from the very top, above an end zone. Ticket value was $75. They should have paid us to sit that high and far away from the field. Even with my binoculars, the players on the field looked almost microscopic. The only saving grace was that there were humongous video boards above the field. Viewing those allowed us to better keep track of the happenings on the field.

Our USC and Los Angeles Coliseum experience was a very, very close second for the remoteness of our seats. (I shared some of the details earlier.) Forty-plus of our closest family and friends joined Livie and me at the game, and many left at halftime. Shame on USC. There were 92,000 fans in attendance. USC could not have found more appropriate seats for the 400 or so visiting-player families and friends? Shameful!

The Big House and The Horseshoe

The University of Michigan and Ohio State University are two of the most popular football programs in the United States. Their respective stadiums are equally iconic. Just as I had been fortunate to watch Geoffrey in the Big House, a few years later, I found myself in The Horseshoe. What a thrill.

The Big House is aptly named. Huge. It officially seats 107,601 fans, and even crammed in over 115,000 for a game against Notre Dame. But, to me, it has little to no character. Awfully bland. Besides, The Horseshoe boasts a unique element that I have not encountered in any other stadium.

When Oregon played Michigan at The Big House, to shoehorn in the masses, every attendee was required, before entry, to pass their carry-in possessions through an approximate ten-inch-by-ten-inch wooden frame. Given it was early in the season, the weather was pleasant. All I carried with me that afternoon was some outerwear, which easily fit within the frame. The same could not be said for some of my fellow Oregon parents.

Several of the guys traveled with a full case of photographic equipment. There was no way the case would pass muster. The guys were directed to security stations to check in most of their gear. They were not thrilled. Hundreds, if not thousands, of dollars were tied up in that equipment. In the end, I'm happy to report that, after the shellacking in which Oregon beat Michigan 39-7, nothing was missing when the dads retrieved their possessions.

Stadium Highlights

The Horseshoe was a far more charming stadium. The year after Mitchell graduated, Cal had a game scheduled in The Horseshoe. Joined by the father of a former Cal teammate of Mitchell's, we journeyed to Columbus for that game. Unfortunately, Ohio State won, but not all was lost. The Ohio State marching band is known for spelling "Ohio" in cursive script during their pregame performance. As a capper, a third or fourth year sousaphone player peels off to dot the "i," considered a supreme honor and privilege. Seeing that in person made the trip totally worthwhile.

Some Trivia

Here's a trivia question. What players were on the field for the last game in old Giants Stadium and the very first game played in their newly constructed MetLife Stadium, completed in 2010 in the parking lot of its predecessor arena? The list included none other than Geoffrey Schwartz. And I was in attendance for both. The last game in the old stadium was a regular season tilt against the Giants while Geoffrey was on the roster of the Carolina Panthers. The first game in MetLife was a preseason game. Unfortunately, Geoffrey was injured in both. He pulled a groin muscle in the first. Continued playing. The second is where he gruesomely dislocated his big toe. (More details on that to come.)

The Immaculate Reception

I'm going to assume that many reading this book have never heard about this seminal moment in professional football, given it occurred in 1972. I grew up a big Oakland Raiders fan. (No longer, as they are divisional rivals to the Kansas City Chiefs.) That December day I was watching a playoff game pitting the visiting Raiders against the Pittsburgh Steelers. The Raiders had scored late in the final quarter to lead 7-6. Pittsburgh had one last desperate drive to change their fortunes.

Facing a fourth and ten from their own forty-yard line, sixty yards away from the goal line and pay dirt, with no timeouts left, Steelers' quarterback Terry Bradshaw launched a pass downfield. There was a violent collision between a Steelers' receiver and an Oakland defender at the Oakland thirty-five-yard line. The ball ricocheted backward off the players toward an astonished Steelers' Hall of Fame running back Franco Harris. In full gallop, Harris snatched the ball inches off the turf and ran untouched for a winning touchdown. What a blow to the gut for the Raiders and their fans, including me.

So why do I bring this up? The Cleveland Browns and Pittsburgh Steelers are both in the AFC North division. They play each other twice every season. In 2014, during Mitchell's time with the Browns, my brother and I decided to make a trip to Pittsburgh to take in the game. We found lodging at the team hotel, walking distance from Heinz Field.

Fred and I began our pregame trek to the stadium along a route that took us through a parking lot. As we walked closer, an out-of-place image came into sight. We were wondering, "What could that be?" It was a bronze statue of Franco Harris leaning forward to snatch a football, inches above the ground, on the exact physical spot where the catch was made.

The Immaculate Reception took place in Three Rivers Stadium, which began to show its age in the ensuing years. In 1999 ground was broken for Heinz Field, built literally in the shadow of Three Rivers. Three Rivers was then imploded, a parking lot was constructed on the site, and the monument to this thrilling moment in Steelers' history was erected. As I walked past the statue, it brought up that miserable memory from forty-plus years prior, but it was also very cool to relive a piece of history. (Sadly, Harris passed away on December 20, 2022.)

Dealing With the Elements

During the two decades of attending games, I experienced the full spectrum of climate conditions. I'm a West Coast guy. Extreme cold is just not in my DNA. As a matter of fact, I've never skied or even taken a vacation in a cold-weather climate. My first bone-chilling experience with frigid weather was truly a shock to the system.

It was the weekend before Thanksgiving in 2004, Geoffrey's freshman season. The Ducks were playing their in-state rival the Oregon State Beavers. I attended the game with Mike Parr. I remember checking the weather before heading up north, but either the forecast was off—way off—or I was just too naive to understand the implication.

It was a night game. I wore blue jeans, a cotton long-sleeve shirt and a bombardier-style leather jacket, without any lining. No hat. No gloves. No other cold-weather apparel. As the night wore on, the temps continued to drop. I buried my hands in my jacket pockets, attempting to keep them as warm as possible. I zippered the jacket tightly. But frankly, I was chilled to my bones. The temperature that evening dropped to forty-five degrees—but it felt like twenty-five. A real lesson learned. The night was made all the more frosty as Oregon State stomped all over Oregon, 50-21.

It's much easier to prepare for sitting in cold weather than extreme heat. Over the years I collected all sorts of cold-weather apparel and accessories. Knit beanies. Hand and foot warmers. Boots. Woolen underwear. Parkas. Gloves. Sweatshirts and sweatpants. The key was layers. Two pairs of socks with foot warmers. Two pairs of gloves with hand warmers. Undershirt, shirt, sweatshirt, jacket number one, jacket number two. You get the idea.

But then came the AFC Championship Game between the Kansas City Chiefs and the New England Patriots in K.C. in January 2019. The weather was predicted to be in single digits. Forty-five degrees was bad enough, but eight or nine degrees would be another story. So I went out and bought another layer for added protection. A jacket and overalls rated for below-zero weather. I felt like I was mummified that night but, on the other hand, I survived the evening...from a weather perspective. That was the game where Tom Brady drove the Patriots downfield for a game winning touchdown on the first series of overtime to prevent Kansas City from a trip to the Super Bowl. The Chiefs did not get their hands on the ball in that extra period. Since then, due to a similar circumstance, once again involving the Chiefs, the NFL has modified their overtime rules to allow both teams a possession in playoff games.

From sub-zero to 100-plus degrees. It was late September in Phoenix, Arizona. The Ducks were playing the Arizona State Sun Devils at Sun Devil Stadium on the ASU campus. Our tickets that day were in the nosebleed top deck. It was bad enough being so far from the field, but making matters worse, we were in complete sun. No overhang. No place to hide from the blazing desert 104-degree heat. As opposed to cold weather, where layers can be added to offset the chill, there are only so many layers that can be shed when it's hot before one's down to bare skin. We did our best to lather up with sunscreen to prevent sunburn, and sought out all the water we could find to keep hydrated. The only positive from that day was seeing Oregon demolish the Sun Devils, 48-13.

Raising Giants

At least the Arizona heat is dry. Sitting for a game with high temps and high humidity is more miserable. So was the experience on September 13, 2008, when Cal suited up against the Maryland Terrapins in College Park, Maryland. At the noontime kickoff, the ambient temperature was a tolerable eighty-four degrees, but the humidity was 68 percent. It was virtually unbearable. We were drenched in sweat the entire game.

I can't begin to imagine how the players on the field were impacted. Well, to some degree, I can. One or two of the Cal players vomited mid-field. Mitchell told me that his socks were so wet he was slipping and sliding inside his shoes, making blocking and pass protection even more difficult. One of his linemates, maybe the smartest of the bunch, replaced his drenched socks with dry ones during halftime. Apparently, that made a huge difference for him in the third and fourth quarters.

Another complication of that day's game was the 12 p.m. EST kickoff. Normal for the body clocks of the Maryland kids, it was 9 a.m. PST for the Cal team. Early on the Bears played like they had yet to wake up, falling behind 21-6 seconds into the second quarter. They fell behind by an additional seven points midway through the third quarter. A passionate comeback fell short. Cal lost the game 35-27.

I've now shared examples of the weather extremes. But what about sitting in the stands in pouring rain, or trying to watch through a blanket of thick fog? Three games in these conditions stood out, of which two occurred while Oregon lined up against Oregon State. Add the frigid game described earlier and that's a trio of games involving Oregon State. It's been eye-opening for me in writing this book to uncover trends and connections like this that previously went unrecognized.

Geoffrey was in his third year at Oregon in 2006, and I was still somewhat in my infancy when it came to proper attire for inclement-weather viewing. The Ducks were scheduled to play Oregon State in Corvallis the day after Thanksgiving. The game day forecast was for rain, so we brought with us whatever rain gear we accumulated. Deciding that it might not be enough, we bought plastic ponchos as an added layer.

We sat on hard, cold metal benches throughout the entire game, in driving rain that never let up. Making matters worse was the whipping wind that blew through the stadium for the entire three-plus hours. Oregon lost yet another game in foul weather conditions, another discovered trend.

Stadium Highlights

After waiting to talk with Geoffrey postgame, we all slogged back to our car, parked about a fifteen-minute walk from the stadium. It was me, Livie, Mitchell and Duke Manyweather. The thought of piling into the car drenched was so disgusting that, when we arrived at the car with rain still soaking us, I popped open the trunk. One by one we shed as many layers as possible into the trunk and then jumped inside the car. I think it took us the entire hour-long trip back to Eugene, with the heat on full blast, to begin to dry out and warm up.

In 2008 Mitchell's Cal schedule and Geoffrey's Carolina schedule synced up nicely. It was a bye weekend for Geoffrey, and Cal was hosting Oregon in a Saturday tilt. So Geoffrey made plans to jet across the country to watch the game, accompanied by his then-girlfriend Meridith. The forecast called for rain. Meridith was encouraged by Geoffrey to bring with her an almost ankle-length parka, or "puffer jacket" as she likes to call it. It served its purpose that day; however, Meridith was very unhappy sitting in the downpour. At some point early in the game, she disappeared into the depths of the stadium and, as I remember it, did not reappear until game's end.

The rain continued to worsen throughout the afternoon. The synthetic turf of Memorial Stadium became a marsh with huge puddles on the field toward the western end zone. It turned out to be Berkeley's worst game-day rainstorm in a decade. Cal won that game 26-16 so, for Mitchell, it was a joyful day. For Geoffrey, quite the contrary. Not only did his precious Ducks lose, but more importantly, he struck out with Meridith that day. We laugh about that experience today, but that afternoon we weren't quite sure whether Geoffrey and Meridith's relationship would survive. Thankfully, they recently celebrated their tenth wedding anniversary.

Remaining on the rain topic for one last story, I want to share the tale of "it never rains..." The rest of the sentence is "...in Autzen Stadium." It was first uttered at the beginning of the 1990 Oregon football season by Autzen Stadium public address announcer Don Essig, who's been at the microphone for over fifty-seven years. That season umbrellas were banned from the stadium because of fan complaints about obstructed views.

Maybe Don thought the weather gods would listen and erect a protective rain dome over the stadium. Ironically, that 1990 season and the two following did not have one rain game. I can attest to the fact that it does rain at Autzen Stadium but, really, not that frequently, especially considering that, on average, some precipitation falls on Eugene 151 days a year.

I lived with fog growing up. I'm used to it. Santa Rosa would get some serious spells during the year. Fog wasn't a stranger in Eugene. During football season, specifically September through November, the city averages eight days a month with some degree of fog. I suspect that on the night of November 19, 2005, the blanketing of Autzen Stadium that took place was excessive. As the game wore on, sitting in our end-zone seats, it became harder and harder to see the action on the field. Can't imagine how receivers could see a football on pass plays. It made for a very challenging night of football viewing. And guess the opponent? Indeed, the Oregon State Beavers.

Beyond the fog, that night is forever etched in Livie's mind, as well as mine. We wondered if we'd ever make it out of Autzen Stadium alive. Seriously. As parents of players, we were allowed onto the field after the final whistle. So with a few minutes left on the clock we left our seats and headed toward the gate where family would be funneled onto the field. We ultimately stopped in our tracks near the gate as we reached complete gridlock created by other attendees waiting for the gate to swing open.

We came to a halt immediately in front of several sections of Oregon students. For a reason still unknown to us, when the game ended, the students in those sections began a stampede toward the field. And they weren't waiting for any silly gate to open. They jumped from their seats onto the pathway where Livie and I were standing and then attempted to scale the five-foot wall separating us from the field.

I've never felt such a crush. Livie was panicking, spurred by her claustrophobia. Truth be told, I was beginning to feel some anxiety. I tried to create some distance between the wall and the throngs of people. It took a few minutes, but we did escape the crush and made it onto the field, relieved.

Mascots, Tailgating and Other Stories

If you follow college football at all, you know that each team has a mascot. It could be a two-legged variety wearing some form of costume. Or it could be a four-legged sort.

Ralphie the Buffalo is the mascot for the University of Colorado Buffaloes. Before the game, and again before the second half kickoff of every home game, Ralphie is trailered to one corner of the field and walked into a pen. At the appropriate time, a gate is opened. Ralphie bolts out of her pen with five handlers tethered to her (yes, Ralphie is a she) by rope in full sprint trying to keep pace (she can reach speeds of 25 mph) as they escort her in a horseshoe path around the field, ultimately guiding her back into her trailer.

This was our treat when visiting Boulder, Colorado, for the one game Mitchell and Cal played in Colorado. What a sight to see. A live buffalo racing around the field. Maybe more astonishing, though, was watching the five handlers trying to keep pace with this massive creature, knowing that as much as they tried, Ralphie would always be queen of the hill.

I've described earlier our experience attending the Oregon versus Oklahoma game in Geoffrey's freshman season. That day the Sooners scored four touchdowns and one field goal. After each, to the roar of the delighted crowd, the Oklahoma mascot appeared. Not a furry friend. Not a costumed human. Instead, it was the Sooner Schooner, the official mascot of the university. Over the years I had watched this scaled-down replica of an old-time wagon drive around the field in celebration of a score. Two ponies, named Boomer and Sooner, lead the wagon onto the field in an arc that almost reached the fifty-yard line. Although, from a Ducks perspective, it was for all the wrong reasons, I gotta admit I enjoyed watching the pageantry in person.

Of all the mascot characters I saw during the college years, one stood out. It was the Oregon Ducks' duck. It was the most active mascot. It was, to me, also the most attractive. Now, admittedly, I may be somewhat biased. I grew up a big Disney fan. I watched cartoon after cartoon featuring Mickey, Pluto and, of course, Donald Duck.

Though sometimes referred to as Puddles, the mascot is officially known as "The Duck." And it's no coincidence that the mascot reminds one of Disney's Donald Duck. There's such a resemblance that in 1947, then Oregon Athletic Director Les Harris met with Walt Disney and reached a handshake agreement granting Oregon permission to use The Duck as its mascot.

Decades later Disney lawyers questioned the earlier agreement. A university-produced photo showing Harris and Disney wearing matching jackets with an Oregon Donald Duck logo provided enough evidence for a formal agreement to be signed.

As I offered above, The Duck is mighty active during games. A pregame routine finds The Duck sitting on the back of a customized

Raising Giants

Harley-Davidson motorcycle, leading the team out of the tunnel onto the field. During the game, The Duck roams the field, sideline to sideline, encouraging cheers from the fans. And when Oregon scores, The Duck drops and performs one pushup for every point put up on the board. Imagine what that means. If the Ducks score, let's say, thirty-five points in a game, The Duck muscles up 7+14+21+28+35 pushups for a total of 105, in full costume. I understand that five students rotate being The Duck. This might help explain why.

Tailgating is a fact of life at football games—more prevalent than at any of the other major sporting events. Interestingly, there's quite a difference between college and the NFL when it comes to family-related pre- and postgame gatherings. (There's a later chapter focused on collegiate tailgating experiences.) In the NFL, family-oriented formal pre- and postgame get-togethers just don't exist. I do not believe in all the years of attending NFL games we established one relationship with the family of one of the boys' teammates. In college, we made several connections and are still in touch to this day. We might strike up casual conversation with some NFL family members who became familiar faces, but it was nothing like the relationships we developed with families during college.

Keep in mind that many players in the NFL have wives and kids. Their true interest after a game is to quickly shower, connect with their loved ones and head home. That was made crystal clear when I attended Geoffrey's first game with the Carolina Panthers. There was no pregame activity. Geoffrey told me to meet him in the lobby outside the team locker room after the game. When I arrived, plenty of people were milling around. Few talked to others. When players exited the locker room, those without families made a beeline out the door. Those with families collected their troops and headed outside. What a culture shock it was for me, coming from my college experiences. I was so accustomed to the gathering of players and families postgame.

Carolina wasn't unique. Once a Cleveland Browns' game came to an end, we found our way to the bowels of the stadium to stand in a smallish, cordoned-off area created especially for family members. There we waited for Mitchell. Our boys were invariably among the last to exit the locker room. Not exactly sure why. I suspect, at least with Mitchell, that he frequently had press duties. With Geoffrey, who often seemed to be the last one out, I think he just liked to socialize in the locker room. Sometimes waiting did result in a treat or two. Cleveland's Hall of Fame running back Jim Brown would walk by. The broadcast crews, including the likes of Michael Irvin and Deion "Prime Time" Sanders would pass by, waving in response to the calls of fans. For a super-fan like me, that was exciting. Once connected with Mitchell, we'd follow him to the valet to pick up his car and proceed home.

The New York Giants' routine was somewhat similar to Carolina's, in that postgame we were directed to a lobby area awaiting the players. From that lobby, we could have continued down a hallway, taken a right turn, and found a room set aside for families to meet the players. However, it was a very small, crowded room, so we waited in the lobby for Geoffrey's arrival. While waiting we'd receive a nod or fist bump from passing players who knew we were Geoffrey's parents. Hard to miss, given I was sporting Geoffrey's jersey. Haha.

Kansas City was, without question, the best of the bunch when it came to creating a family atmosphere. They made available a designated room in Arrowhead, accessible exclusively to player families and friends with proper identification. Inside were big, comfy chairs, big-screen TVs, a side room for the little tikes, chilled soft drinks and waters and an assortment of finger foods. That room remained open and accessible during the game for those who preferred being inside.

After the game, we'd make our way down three flights of stairs to a comfortably sized room, again only accessible to those with a proper wrist bracelet. To the left as we entered was a buffet of sandwiches, chips, fruits and desserts, including some mean chocolate chip cookies. Tables and chairs filled the room. A closed-circuit TV aired Coach Reid's postgame comments. One by one the players, showered and back in their civvies, would enter the room, locate their families, occasionally stop for conversation with their teammates, and then make their way to the outdoor parking lot.

We would patiently wait for Mitchell to pop his head into the room. That was the cue for us to approach, give him a big hug and congratulate him on his play. Then, like the Pied Piper, we'd follow him as he reversed course out of the room, through a hallway full of fans, press and security. Our ultimate destination was the field. We'd spend a few minutes there as Mitchell and Brooke interacted with fellow teammates and their families. It was the closest we would get to something approximating a college postgame tailgate.

Raising Giants

When attending an away game, whether college or pro, the process was quite different compared to home-game experiences. There was no lobby or family room waiting for us postgame, but rather an assigned area outside the stadium where the teams would exit their locker room. There we'd huddle, regardless of weather. I remember waiting for Mitchell in the horrible daytime Chicago humidity or Geoffrey in Denver at about midnight on an extremely cold November night.

Leaving a stadium for a visiting team was not as simple as just boarding a bus. Transportation Security Administration (TSA) was onsite. After a game, and before boarding their buses taking them directly to the airport, players are screened by TSA staff on the grounds of the stadium. A TSA screener accompanies the team on each police-escorted bus headed to the airport.

Once the bus leaves the stadium, it is not allowed to stop and board anyone else. Because they have already been screened, there's no reason to parade the players and staff through the airport and the internal security checkpoints. Instead, the buses are directed to the tarmac, where they pull up next to the plane and the team boards directly.

While writing this chapter, I marveled over the number of iconic, historical stadiums I visited because of the boys. I enjoyed Chamber of Commerce weather and survived frigid conditions. I sat through rain, wind and fog. Pretty much covered the gamut, with one exception, and that was snow. I was never at a game where any appreciable snow fell. Disappointing, in that I always loved watching football games with the white stuff on the field. I don't remember Geoffrey or Mitchell playing many games in snow, but they enjoyed the experience when they did. With one caveat. According to Geoffrey, when the soft snowflakes turned to hard pellets of sleet, that was miserable.

What I haven't addressed yet in this chapter is what I missed, by either choice or happenstance. In 2018 the Kansas City Chiefs were scheduled to play the Los Angeles Rams in Mexico City, Mexico. The NFL has, in recent years, extended their audience beyond the shores of the United States. There were three games scheduled for London, England, and two in Germany for the 2023 season. When we saw this Mexico City game on the schedule, it was an immediate "no." Livie and I have had unpleasant experiences in Mexico, so we decided to remain in L.A. and watch the game on TV.

Our decision was corroborated via a discussion we had with Mitchell. He told us that the Kansas City security staff had a talk with the team. They advised the players to suggest to family and friends to stay away. The high crime rate was one factor. The other was the distance from Mexico City to the stadium and the lack of reliable transportation at that time of night. So, home we'll stay.

The game was a Monday night affair three days before Thanksgiving. As has become our tradition, we spend Thanksgiving in Charlotte with Geoffrey, Meridith and the grandkids. This time we arranged our flight to Charlotte to arrive in time to watch Mitchell and the Chiefs on TV with Geoffrey.

So much for best laid plans. The game in Mexico City was moved. Too many soccer games in a short period of time, coupled with too much rain, and possibly the incompetence of the stadium groundskeepers, made the field unplayable, as determined by the NFL after a tour of the playing surface. What would the NFL do now?

In a tortuous reversal of fortunes, the game was shifted to the Coliseum in Los Angeles. What was a neutral-site game now would be a home game for the Rams. Thirteen miles east on the 10 freeway door-to-door from our house. And we were going to be in Charlotte. Imagine that. Livie and I debated changing our plans but opted to leave everything in place. But I gotta admit that sitting in Charlotte watching Mitchell on a field in our backyard was rather agonizing. Especially the way the game turned out.

The Rams won that night by a score of 54-51. It was, and continues to be, the highest-scoring contest in Monday Night Football history. (And recently selected by *Sports Illustrated* as the 39th best NFL game ever.) It's the only game in which both teams scored at least fifty points. The two quarterbacks, Jared Goff and Patrick Mahomes, threw for a combined 925 yards, including eleven touchdowns. It was an offensive explosion of epic proportions and, conversely, a complete defensive collapse. And I had to watch from afar.

Further to the scoring onslaught, Mitchell and Geoffrey have been part of a couple of auspicious games. They have both played on teams that scored the most points in a losing game. This one for Mitchell. Geoffrey as a member of the Giants losing to New Orleans 52-49.

So far, my stories have not really included details on fan behavior. Well, I can't very well leave out those stories. I've shared the very positive experience we had at Oklahoma. Most of our experiences ranged from neutral to positive. The exceptions centered on two teams, one collegiate and the other professional.

Raising Giants

The crowds at Arizona Stadium, home to University of Arizona football, won the prize for the most despicable fan base we encountered during our collegiate travels. I will share later in the book the details of Oregon quarterback Dennis Dixon's horrific knee injury in 2007. His season came to a disastrous conclusion during a game between the Ducks and the Wildcats at Arizona Stadium. You might imagine the anguish this caused the players and their families. It was the end of a dream. A healthy Dixon would have likely led Oregon to the national championship game at the end of that season.

After the game, Duck family members were congregating outside the team locker room. The Arizona fans passing us by were downright rude. One couple won the prize. They each had to be no less than seventy years old. Both walked with a cane. As they approached us, they raised their canes, shook them at us and began talking trash. It was everything I could do to not respond. Instead, I gave them the nastiest look I could muster as they limped by. (The lesson taught by my parents about respecting my elders won the day.) Don't think they cared.

Inside the stadium, younger fans were no different. At one game, from my seat, I witnessed an Oregon family in a heated argument with an Arizona fan on the field. One of the younger adults of this family jumped over a partition to physically confront this clown. We later learned that some casual trash talking escalated to the point where racist comments were being spewed forth at the Oregon family. I understand that fan bases can get very emotional, but there was absolutely no justification for what took place.

I'm not sure whether this next incident happened during this same game or not. Regardless, it involved Livie. Some big-mouth Arizona fan was walking up and down the aisle where we were sitting, and like his fellow fanatics, talking trash to the Oregon fans. One time, in doing so, he directed his vitriol toward Livie. She exploded and told him to get out of her face. Livie usually isn't this aggressive, and, frankly, I was concerned that this fool might physically accost her. I calmed her down, admonishing her for her reaction, as this guy walked away.

The NFL version of Arizona probably won't come as much of a surprise because of the reputation of this team's fan base. Yup, it's the Oakland Raiders' fans. While I don't believe all fans can be painted with a broad brush, there are certainly those who help to validate the impression. I can think of two instances when they lived up to their reputation.

Stadium Highlights

Kansas City was playing in Oakland. We were advised against wearing our Chiefs gear at the stadium. But stubborn me thought, "What the heck. What could happen?" So, getting out of the car parked in the stadium parking lot, I donned Mitchell's jersey. Our walk to the stadium really wasn't too bad. I actually saw several instances of Raiders' and Chiefs' fans happily coexisting over some bottles of suds. I do not recall anyone giving us any grief as we made our way through the lot.

But inside the stadium, the story was quite different. All along the path to our seats, we heard one derogatory comment after another aimed our way. I don't know why Livie seems to be such a target, but one Raiders' fan entered her personal space to offer his opinions about the Chiefs. Once again, she responded. Not sure if doing so chased the guy away or if he had simply completed his tirade, but off he went.

Verbal altercations are one thing. Putting our health in jeopardy elevates the "fun" to an entirely unacceptable level. One year Livie and I were making our way through horrible traffic trying to access a stadium parking lot. In the lane next to us was one of those large F-150-type trucks. Raider black in color—no surprise—with an Oakland flag flapping outside the driver's side window. As we pulled up next to him and he could see our Chiefs' gear, he gave us a one-finger salute. Classy.

As he edged ahead of us, he lurched in front, not with appropriate clearance and without offering a signal of any kind. I slammed on the brakes. Fortunately, no contact was made. But he couldn't resist flipping us off again as he cut in front.

In January 2012 Bleacher Report rated the rowdiest fans in the NFL. Raiders Nation found itself as number one. Years later nothing had changed. They were still over-the-top rowdy.

I realized, as I was reviewing the entirety of this chapter, that I've said very little about Memorial Stadium in Berkeley, home to the Cal Bears, and Mitchell's base of operations while at Cal. It deserves some attention.

Memorial Stadium was first built in 1923. In a curious move, given the earthquake activity that California, and particularly the San Francisco Bay Area, is deservedly famous for, the field is positioned directly atop the Hayward Fault. Fortunately, the fault's last major quake was 154 years ago, but that means it's long overdue for another shake. Recognizing the need for shoring up the stadium because of the seismic activity (the east half of the building has been shifting to the south at a rate of 1.2 millimeters each year) Cal began stadium renovations in 2010.

Raising Giants

The plans for the improvements were obviously hatched years before the actual construction began. How might we know the timetable of that? Geoffrey attended Cal's Junior Day in 2003. We were invited to spend time with Head Coach Jeff Tedford in his office. During the time together, he proudly pointed to a model of the stadium resting on the office floor and told us about the renovation plans.

Second Impressions

Speaking of Coach Tedford, four years later Mitchell and Livie dined with him during Mitchell's official recruiting trip to Cal. Livie mentioned to Coach Tedford the Geoffrey visit. Geoffrey, Livie and I obviously made zero impression on the Coach that day. He had absolutely no memory of ever having met with us. Fortunately he didn't let that stand in the way of recruiting and signing Mitchell and being a great coach for him.

Thank goodness impressions can be recast.

Fast forward to the fall of 2024. Cal is honoring Coach Tedford's 2004 team, the one with Aaron Rodgers at QB, at halftime of the Cal/Stanford game. In addition to teammates from that season, players from subsequent years were invited. That included Mitchell. Mitchell invited Livie and I to join him and Brooke. We accepted immediately.

The Friday evening before the big game, the players and their families, including Livie and me, were invited to a party held at Memorial Stadium. As we bounced around reconnecting with former players, Coach Tedford walked into the room. I gave him a moment or two to get his bearings before approaching.

I expected a warm handshake but instead received an enthusiastic bear hug. Why? Seeing us Coach was reminded of an experience we shared in the late summer heading into Mitchell's final season at Cal. Cal had exhausted their available scholarships. However there was a prized recruit that they coveted. The only way to secure his commitment was to have an existing scholarship released.

Stadium Highlights

Coach asked us if we'd be willing to pay for Mitchell's tuition that senior season so the team could make the scholarship offer. If so, Coach emphasized that doing so would not impact Mitchell's position on the team. Given the positive experience we all had with Cal, Coach Tedford and the team to that point, we unhesitatingly agreed.

As it turned out, it wasn't necessary. A scholarship opened up without our having to pony up. But Coach Tedford never forgot that discussion. During the embrace, he shared his sincere appreciation that he has carried with him ever since for our willingness to help.

The stadium pre-renovation was old and tired. Timeworn wooden benches made sitting for a game quite uncomfortable. I understand from Geoffrey, who visited the stadium twice while playing for Oregon, that the visiting team locker room was one of the worst in the country, at least prior to the improvements. Sardines in their cans had more room than did the players in the locker room. Even at full blast, the showers trickled. It was not a pleasant experience for any team playing the Bears.

But setting aside these less-desirable characteristics, the stadium offered some of the best views one could wish for. Sitting in the higher reaches of the stands on the Cal side, I was reminded of a song that was written in 1970 by a British jazz/soul group, The Peddlers, that contained the lyrics "on a clear day you can see forever." For on a clear Bay Area day, from our seats, we could cast our eyes on a spectacular view of the blue shimmering waters of San Francisco Bay. As the crow flies, about five miles. From those same seats, a look over our right shoulder would train our eyes on Tightwad Hill with the many freeloaders watching the game.

Many teams enjoy a tradition at their home stadium of having their players parade through a mass of fans as they exit their buses and head to the stadium. Cal was no different. I'll call it "The Walk." About ninety minutes prior to kickoff, the team buses would arrive at Memorial from the team's hotel. They would park about a football field away from the tunnel leading to their locker room. Throngs of fans would be lined up to see the players parade by. We were always part of that fandom.

Led by the Cal cheerleaders and band, the players walked to the tunnel. This was a great chance for Livie and me to give Mitchell a big pregame hug and wish him luck. It also gave us the opportunity to, as with many of the others standing shoulder to shoulder, high-five the players as they passed by. It really is a great tradition and a wonderful way to kick off game day.

In a previous paragraph I mentioned the closure of the stadium. As timing would have it, that shutdown occurred during Mitchell's final Cal season. Could it not have waited one more year? Talk about disruption. The team couldn't practice on the main field. They had to change gears to a makeshift practice field above the stadium. A temporary locker room was built adjacent to this field, but it didn't contain the creature comforts the players were accustomed to. This substitute field also meant trudging up a steep hill to access the area. Before practice, no big deal. They were fresh. But afterward, energy sapped from practice, the journey seemed so much longer, even if trudging downhill.

As much as practices were disrupted, home games were even worse. The closest stadium to Cal would have been the Oakland Coliseum, home base to the Oakland Raiders. It was only eleven and a half miles away. But, as I recall, there were some issues between Cal and the Raiders' organization and so a deal to allow the Bears to play there for that season couldn't be made. Instead, Cal was forced to play on the other side of the bay in what, at the time, was known as AT&T Park, home of the San Francisco Giants.

It's a baseball stadium. It wasn't configured for football. The end-zone corners were dangerously close to unforgiving brick walls. The atmosphere was completely different. Even though it was considered a home field, it did not have the feel of a home game. No real space for "The Walk." The locker rooms lacked the familiarity of a home stadium. Not nearly as many students traveled, either via school-sponsored buses or using their own transportation. Overall attendance was down compared to recent years at Memorial. And for us parents, it was a completely different vibe. I will detail the difference in Chapter 12, "Football and Food: A Special Combination."

Playing at AT&T, though, was not completely foreign to Mitchell. In 2008 Cal played a postseason bowl game at AT&T, known at the time as the Emerald Bowl. Cal beat the Miami Hurricanes that evening, 24-17.

Stadium Highlights

The win was awfully satisfying, but that wasn't the highlight of the day for Mitchell.

I've mentioned in other portions of the book that I'm an avid San Francisco Giants fan. I passed that enthusiasm on to both Mitchell and Geoffrey. That night at AT&T, the Bears were assigned the Giants' locker room. After the game, Mitchell walked out of the locker room, a leather lace in his hand. These laces are used to restring a baseball glove. The lace just happened to be on the floor immediately in front of Barry Bonds' locker. For the uninitiated, Bonds was the Giants' best player at the time, and one of the best performers in baseball history. (Let's leave the issue of his steroid use for another time, shall we?) Needless to say, being in the Giants locker room, seeing Barry Bonds' nameplate and his personalized rocker/recliner and walking away with the lace was quite the experience for Mitchell, one that I expect he'll never forget.

And so there you have it. Like I said at the beginning, the good, the bad and the ugly of it all. There's no debating that Livie and I have been very fortunate to have had such experiences...at least the positive ones.

11

THE MORE, THE MERRIER

There is a proverb attributed to African cultures that asserts "it takes a village to raise a child." While I didn't need a village to raise Geoffrey and Mitchell, I certainly benefited from the scores who joined me for the two-decade journey of my lifetime.

How lonely it would have been without the dozens and dozens of friends and family members who asked to be a part of what I affectionately dubbed "the fan club." That train left the station, in a manner of speaking, rather innocently. With both boys playing ball at Pali High, I would bend the ear of those closest to me, sharing my sons' latest on-field exploits. (Some might call it bragging.) It began with a small group, but as my universe expanded and the word spread, more and more friends, colleagues, associates and die-hard football fans wanted to be in the know. Far be it from me to ignore their requests and keep them in the dark!

Geoffrey's recruiting experience was the fuel for increased interest. The flame burned hotter once he enrolled at Oregon. Those already following him wanted more. Most were more familiar with the high school football landscape, but now that the ins and outs of the collegiate world were available, appetites grew. I could continue to piecemeal the information to these interested parties, or I could find a platform to communally reveal details of the boys' activities. I chose the latter, creating a website through GoDaddy that allowed me to share more broadly. I wrote updates as it seemed appropriate. I included photos that couldn't be shared during a strictly verbal exchange.

This method worked gloriously for a bit of time...until Geoffrey's Oregon teammates caught wind of the website. Let the teasing begin. I'm sure it was all in good fun, but Geoffrey wasn't keen on being the subject of any additional mockery, so I shut the site down. But what now? How could I continue sharing? Aha! There was an alternative, and one that prevented viewing from the unwanted roving eyes of his teammates.

The Fan Club Broadcast was born. I began collecting addresses from all those who would welcome email updates. Based on my archives, the first broadcast was distributed on October 30, 2007. It told the tale of the day Geoffrey was the third-leading rusher against USC. Initially the distribution list was probably two to three dozen. Today it's expanded to over 150 interested fans.

From that launch, I have distributed over 150 broadcasts, most during the season. Some have been specific to one or the other of the guys. Many spoke to the activities of both. And the interest has continued as the guys have transitioned to their post-playing careers. Here's one example of an early broadcast:

> *I am excited to report that Geoffrey signed a one-year contract this morning to play for the Kansas City Chiefs. A new coaching staff headed by Andy Reid. A chance to block for QB Alex Smith, another free agent signed by K.C. An o-line coach and GM who want Geoffrey to be part of their plans. Some reporters are already claiming that K.C.'s group of free agents signed thus far might be one of the top in the NFL.*
>
> *Mom and Dad are thrilled with the news. It means Geoffrey will play in San Diego, Oakland and Denver, plus somehow this team from Cleveland got on the schedule. Won't that be a kick to see both boys on the field at the same time?*
>
> *Health wise Geoffrey is probably in better shape than since his early days in college. No more hip problems. Surgeries behind him. Can't wait to see a perfectly healthy Geoffrey perform. Tomorrow he and Mitchell head to Scottsdale, Arizona, to begin some serious training before they both report for OTA's on April 1st.*
>
> *Speaking of Mitchell, he's recovered well from his last game injury. He'll be ready to rock 'n roll come April 1. The Browns also*

The More, the Merrier

begin the season with a new coaching staff...almost. The o-line coach from the previous regime was retained by the new head coach, making Mitchell a happy camper.

My last broadcast shared the accolades that Mitchell had received through the middle of December. To put icing on the cake, it was announced after the season that Mitchell made the NFL All-Rookie team for 2012. What a great way to begin his career.

Hard to believe that Geoffrey is entering his sixth NFL season and Mitchell his 2nd. My how time flies. We're looking forward to an exciting year for both Mitchell and Geoffrey.

I have always been very cautious sharing the existence of the list. I wait until someone has shown keen interest in the boys and only then open the door for inclusion. When I make the offer, it's always preceded with, "there's no obligation." Also, when sending the first email of each calendar year, I include in the broadcast an out, offering to remove anyone from the distribution list if they no longer wished to be involved. "No harm, no foul" is what I say. If memory serves me, only one person, in the fifteen or so years of the broadcast, has asked to be removed. Either people have been truly interested or have been too bashful/embarrassed to opt out!

These broadcasts almost never saw the light of day. As I've explained elsewhere in the book, Livie is not very keen on what she would consider self-promotion and thus was resistant to the broadcast idea. But I persevered. And then I discovered that she had, in essence, jumped on the bandwagon of spreading news about the guys without my knowledge.

Livie and I were members of a Los Angeles–based networking organization that ran dozens of meetings throughout a month. We were part of a "home" group but could also attend other meetings. We both actively "guested." If I visited another location and knew some of the attendees, those folks would invariably introduce me to people I hadn't met previously as the father of two football players. After sharing the details of where they had played/were currently playing, I would sometimes hear, "You know, I met someone else recently who also has a son playing for [fill in the blank]. Do you know her?" I belly-laughed. It was Livie. She uses Goodkin, not Schwartz, so the connection was initially impossible to make.

To have had this community with which to share so much of what transpired over the last twenty years has truly been heartwarming and has made this journey so much more enjoyable.

Interestingly, there's been a secondary benefit that I had not considered when I first began the broadcasts. Sure, I've appreciated the opportunity to be the disseminator of stories and updates. But more rewarding has been the volume of responses. They have been beyond expectation. There have been times when I received replies from upward of 50 percent of those who received the emails. This has allowed me to engage more personally with friends and family in a way that, likely, would not have occurred otherwise. I have truly loved reading the updates I receive from these folks. What a gift this has been!

Special Days for Papa

While the Fan Club Broadcasts provided me with connection to a broad cluster of followers, there have been so many opportunities over the course of the boys' careers to share more intimately. Earlier on I talked about the forty-plus enthusiasts who, in 2006, tolerated the unconscionable conditions at the Los Angeles Coliseum to watch Geoffrey play his first college football game in the L.A. area against USC. The next year, when Geoffrey played his one and only game while a Duck against UCLA in the Rose Bowl, we had no less than a dozen people show up, with one very special attendee.

As I shared previously, it was Geoffrey's wheelchair-bound Papa. My father's medical conditions at the time prevented him from any meaningful travel or attending stadiums that were not kind to those with challenges so, until his passing in October of 2011, he was glued to the tube for every televised game that involved Geoffrey and Mitchell...with just two exceptions.

The Oregon visit to the Rose Bowl in 2007 was one of those exceptions. For that I thank my brother, Fred. He handled all the logistics that day, driving my father the forty miles from his place to the Bowl, arranging for a handicapped parking pass and then wheeling Dad around the Bowl all day long. Dad fulfilled a dream come true that afternoon, personally watching his grandson on the football field. In researching the timeline for this section, Livie provided me a picture from that day. There's Dad proudly wearing a green Oregon sweatshirt with a smile planted on his face that signaled the pride he had in his grandson.

The More, the Merrier

Unfortunately, the Ducks lost that day, but no matter to Dad. Of course, he wanted Oregon to win, but seeing his grandson on the field brought him such joy. (In Yiddish the word is *naches*.) And for Geoffrey, having his proud Papa at the stadium for a big postgame hug and kiss helped to soften the blow of the loss.

We weren't sure if the ravages of time would prevent my father from attending another game, but he was an ornery fellow. This was a guy who repeatedly mocked that old adage of "the golden years," renaming them "the rusty years," yet, through all of his challenges, he never gave up. I firmly believe one reason he lived to eighty-four was his desire to see his two grandsons play collegiate and professional football. So when the opportunity presented itself to again visit the Rose Bowl, my father was eager for another outing.

This time it was Cal visiting. Game-time temps were forecasted to approach triple digits, even though the game was well into October, where the average daytime temperature in Pasadena, California, is about eighty degrees. In the days leading up to the Saturday contest, Fred and I heavily debated the wisdom of bringing my father to the Rose Bowl given the forecasted heat but, in the end, we did. Again, my brother was a tremendous help. Dad needed to be frequently removed from the blazing sun to shaded areas, which fell to Fred so that I could watch the game uninterrupted. Fortunately, at the end of the day, Dad was no worse for wear.

Similar to the experience with Geoffrey, Papa was beaming that day. After the game, I distinctly remember Dad giving Mitchell a huge Bear hug (pun intended) followed by the two of them engaging in a one-on-one about the game. It is a genuinely heartwarming memory. Actually, viewing the pictures for the first time in forever brought tears to my eyes.

One last Dad story. While with Carolina, Geoffrey was able to get his hands on several jerseys he wore during the season. I can't recall whether they were simply given to him or he had to pay, but one day he arrived in California with several in his suitcase. One was intended for me. Another for Papa. Oh my goodness, was my father pumped. From that point on, Dad wore that jersey every time he watched Geoffrey play, even though it wasn't so easy to put on.

You see, jerseys are purposely designed to be form-fitting to prevent the defense from latching on. Once the boys got into college, I learned that jerseys are pulled over pads by the equipment staff and then placed in the player's locker so when it came time to suit up, they pulled the pads over their head so as not to wrestle with the jerseys.

I wish Dad's health would have allowed him more opportunities to attend games in person, but we squeezed out what we could. He watched everything on television. And whenever the boys came to town for a visit, there was always a lunch with Papa. I watched in amazement how tolerant the guys were with all of Dad's questions. (The next generation exhibiting "respect for elders.") All were answered respectfully and thoroughly. If I had been the one inquiring, Mitchell and Geoffrey would have rolled their eyes, their patience quickly wearing thin. So I just sat back and listened, benefiting from Papa lobbing the questions I would have wanted to ask.

My Big Guest List

After that USC vs. Oregon game in 2006, I thought forty or so in-person enthusiasts would be a number never exceeded. I was wrong. In 2015, while Mitchell was with Cleveland, the Browns had a game on the schedule in San Diego. From the general Los Angeles area, San Diego is about one and three-quarters hours, in the best of conditions, directly south on the 405/5 freeways. I never imagined that over fifty people would express interest in making the trek that first weekend in October. But that was the case. Working with Fred again, he contacted the Chargers' ticket office to gauge availability for such a large group. Surprisingly, a block of seats that could accommodate such an assembly was available. End zone, first level. All together. Decent seats actually.

So I went about brokering tickets to family, fan-club members, and other interested parties. What a chore it turned out to be. While it was awesome being able to share the day with all of these people, the experience was bittersweet. I had people commit to buy tickets but then ghost me. Others made the commitment but just days before the game rather sheepishly advised me that they could no longer attend.

I had to pay for the tickets in advance to make them available to others. What was I now supposed to do at the last minute? If memory serves me, I believe I had to eat a few unused tickets. That hassle led to a decision for me. No longer would I attempt to satisfy such a large group. But for that day, it was a joyful afternoon with friends and family.

While I thoroughly enjoyed sharing game experiences with larger groups, I also loved the more intimate gatherings with smaller parties.

The More, the Merrier

It definitely allowed me more one-on-one time with these people—that is when I wasn't glued to my binoculars. I'd like to share several experiences that stand out.

Before the boys embarked on their football journeys, Livie's knowledge of the game of football was very limited. So it will likely come as no surprise that her friends were not football aficionados. Because it was her sons, she made the effort to learn the game, but we/she couldn't expect others to follow.

One season the Ducks were scheduled to play Arizona State in Tempe, Arizona, a suburb of Phoenix, at ASU's Sun Devil Stadium. We would be making the trip. It so happens that one of Livie's BFFs, Kathi, an Emmy-award winner for broadcast journalism, lives in the Phoenix area. Weeks before the game, Livie invited Kathi and her husband David to join us for the 7:15 p.m. kickoff. David jumped at the opportunity. Kathi needed some convincing, but ultimately agreed.

Fast forward to that weekend. It was Saturday afternoon. Livie and Kathi were sitting at the kitchen table in her home. Livie, feeling her oats now that she'd learned "so much" about football, was giving Kathi a football lesson. She drew out the field on a piece of paper and proceeded to explain its layout, first downs and a bevy of other insights. Livie thought it would be helpful for Kathi. Frankly, I'm not sure how much penetrated, but it was a gallant try.

The four of us hopped in the car about two hours before game time for the short trip to the stadium. We arrived around 5:30 p.m. It might have been the longest game of the season. Maybe ever. We remained after, as was our custom, to be with Geoffrey before the team departed for the airport. By the time we left the stadium, it was close to 1 a.m.

We were in the car headed back to the house. All of us were very tired, anxious to jump in bed for a good night's sleep. There was some casual conversation underway when Kathi declared, "Do you know that the first quarter took almost an hour!" I busted a gut laughing. Imagine for a moment the torture Kathi must have experienced sitting in the stadium watching a game that she knew nothing about, only to have it drag on, and on, and on. She was a trooper, but I dare say she's never attended another football contest since. And Livie never invited her again, knowing it would only be torture for her.

Raising Giants

Our dear, dear friend Karen Peterson, one of Livie's other BFFs, reacted differently during this journey. Karen, similar to Livie, knew *nothing* about football when this all began. But as time progressed, she amazingly became a student of the game, learning more and more as she read my broadcasts and as we talked about the guys and their careers. I was wonderfully surprised when my cell phone buzzed during a game, alerting me to an incoming text, and the sender would be Karen, asking me a question or commenting on a play. She was actually watching the game. And she was right on point with her question/comment. It really was touching that she had, without any encouragement, so thoroughly joined the journey.

While originally drafting this chapter I was at dinner with friends when my book project came up in conversation. It was perfect timing, as one of the dinner attendees was my dear friend Bob who once joined me for a game in Giants Stadium. Giants versus the New England Patriots. Bob was in New York to visit his son, Kyle, who had recently begun dating a deeply loyal Patriots' fan, Katie. All three joined me at the game.

Bob is one who, when told not to do something, would purposely be defiant, as he was that night. I told him in advance about my singular focus on Geoffrey during games and how I don't carry on conversation. That mattered not to him. During the entire game, particularly while I was fixated on Geoffrey through my trusty binoculars, Bob would attempt to engage. Several times, in a good-natured gesture, my response was a non-verbal, middle-finger salute. We would laugh, and he would continue to be a pest.

Katie was in somewhat of an awkward position. She and Kyle hadn't been dating very long, and now she was with what would be her future father-in-law and an absolute stranger, all rooting for the Giants to prevail, while she was a Patriots' fanatic...and sitting in the Giants' family section. Katie did a great job of swallowing her enthusiasm throughout the game, especially after a Tom Brady-esque drive at the end of the fourth quarter that led to a successful field goal with 0:01 remaining on the clock for a one-point New England win.

Afterward, all four of us walked to the area of the stadium where the players exited from their locker room and headed to the team parking lot. We saw Giants' quarterback Eli Manning walk past while awaiting the arrival of Geoffrey, who, consistent with past practice, was one of the last stragglers to leave. Bob, Kyle and Katie were able to spend a few minutes talking with Geoffrey before it was time for the two of us to head back to his home. It was a fun, fun night for me to be with friends and share the experience, but all the more exciting for the others, who got to view a football game much more up close and personal than ever before.

The "Code of Ethics"

There definitely was, shall we say, a "code of ethics" to follow for those joining us at games. Keep in mind that the seats, whether in college or the NFL, were located in the team's family section. With the tickets for college games free of charge, there was an expectation that guests would be properly attired and behave appropriately, as Katie demonstrated by tucking away her Patriots' hat and showing great restraint when New England outplayed the Giants. But that wasn't always the case.

Remember that Cal vs. University of Arizona game in Tucson? One of my dear friends, Neil, who formerly lived in Los Angeles and saw the boys grow up from birth, lived in Scottsdale, a 'burb of Phoenix. He had accompanied us to several of Geoffrey's and Mitchell's games against Arizona State, including that scorcher in Tempe, but never in Tucson. I asked him if he'd like to make the two-hour trek from Scottsdale to Tucson to join us. He jumped at the opportunity.

All plans for meeting up with him at the stadium were in place when he called several days before the game and asked if there was another ticket available. He wanted to bring a friend. Mitchell was able to secure a ticket.

I was already in our seats when Neil and his buddy arrived, having picked up their tickets at the Will Call window. Big hugs with Neil, and then the introduction to his friend. I couldn't believe my eyes. His tagalong was wearing a blue T-shirt emblazoned with "ARIZONA" across his chest. That wasn't kosher, but what could be done at that point? Unfortunately, it only got worse. The guy would demonstrably cheer for the Wildcats throughout the game. I asked Neil to muffle his buddy, but to no avail.

Fortunately, our friendship survived the evening, but the experience has not been forgotten. Whenever the opportunity presents itself, I will playfully remind Neil of that evening. And every time he profusely apologizes. I learned my lesson. Thereafter I assumed nothing. Anyone joining us was clearly told what attire could *not* be worn if they wanted to sit with us.

Raising Giants

There were a couple of other "dress code" experiences that bear sharing. First the one that could have been equally as inappropriate. It happened with a good buddy of mine and fellow author, Marc Isenberg, whom I invited to attend a USC vs. Oregon game in Autzen Stadium. We made plans to meet outside the stadium before the game. I hadn't shared "the code." As he approached at the prescribed time, my eyes seemed to deceive me.

First, Marc is a dyed-in-the-wool UCLA Bruins fan. Second, he knew he was attending a game with green and yellow home-team colors. What would possess him to put on a red shirt, one of USC's team colors, was beyond me. As he got closer, I gave him a very quizzical look, while at the same time swiping my shirt from chest to waist. The message? What the hell are you wearing?

It didn't take Marc but a couple of nanoseconds to recognize the error of his ways. After a big gulp, he conceded that he threw on the wrong T-shirt. "Is there a nearby student's store?" he inquired. Fortunately, one was within spittin' distance. We walked over, pushed our way through the pregame throngs and found him an appropriate shirt to wear. Crisis averted. And all accomplished in good spirits, consistent with my buddy's core character.

Speaking of character, here's a tale of the most humble man I know. Rich Jaroslovsky and I have been friends for more than six decades. Rich is more than a friend. Rather a brother from another mother. His accomplishments are extraordinary. Won a Pulitzer Prize for his efforts publishing a *Wall Street Journal* edition the day after the world went to hell on September 11, 2001. He traveled the globe with then President Ronald Reagan as the *Wall Street Journal* correspondent to the White House, and was responsible for creating WSJ.com. And this is a short list. Do you think I'm proud of my dear, dear friend?

He is also a Stanford alumnus. Cal was scheduled to play Stanford at a recently renovated Stanford Stadium. I asked Rich if he'd like to join us, though I wasn't sure whether he could handle being among the sea of blue-clad Bear fans. He was advised of the rules. No Cardinal-red attire. He not only accepted the invitation but also showed up that day dressed in California blue. How many would have suspended their loyalty in such a manner?

I wasn't so considerate. Mitchell and his Cal teammates had a game against USC on the schedule during his junior year. Based on my lousy experience when Geoffrey visited the Los Angeles Memorial Coliseum, I swore I'd never again sit in those distant family-designated seats. Livie had a former law partner, with whom I had become good friends, who was a forty-plus-year USC season-ticket holder. I asked if he had a couple of tickets available for that game.

He did. Great. I then asked if he would be so kind as to grant Livie and me special dispensation to wear our Cal gear. He graciously agreed. I proudly and boldly sported my Mitchell-worn Cal football jersey. You can imagine the looks I received sitting among USC's die-hard fans, but I've always been somewhat of a contrarian, so the stares troubled me not. I'm happy to report that Livie and I survived the day unscathed.

The funniest part of our experience that day had nothing to do with football. Besides Livie and me, the ticket holder had one more seat to fill. He invited a former colleague of his and Livie's to join us. The seats and rows surrounding us were occupied by those generally well on in years. We observed one or two walking up the stairs with oxygen tanks strapped to their bodies and what are called nasal cannulas embedded in their nostrils.

The fourth member of the quartet, observing those around us, quipped, "I'm bringing down the average age of the section." That was a mighty task as he himself was in his late seventies. The season-ticket holder was entering the second half of his eighties. This moment of levity was sorely needed as Cal was hammered by the Trojans that day, 48-14.

It's a Family Affair: Other Parents

Traveling weekend after weekend, and then year after year, to Mitchell's and Geoffrey's games routinely brought Livie and me together with other player families who shared the same commitment. Not surprisingly, the repeated connection led us to develop some very special relationships with a few of these other parents and extended families.

Geoffrey's time in Eugene spawned friendships with the parents of most of his linemates. Though we all lived in different cities/states, once onsite in Eugene, or wherever the game was played, the group was basically tied at the hip. We'd gather pregame to tailgate. After home games we'd assemble at a pizza joint for a meal. One of the dads was the team photographer. For every game, home and away, he would strap over his shoulder a case containing various cameras, lenses and related equipment. He typically was allowed access to the field at Autzen Stadium, so he was able to snap some close-range photos. For away games, where he wasn't a known commodity and didn't have proper credentials, he would act as if he were a member of the paparazzi and frequently found himself on the field. But not at Michigan's Big House. Since his camera case would not pass through the ten-inch-by-ten-inch wood-frame sentry heading into the stadium, his camera equipment instead took up residence in a security tent.

Another father developed a routine for away games that was most appreciated by his son and linemates. Although some food is provided to the players after a game, the chow is not plentiful and not always a palate favorite. To augment what the team provided, this father would somehow find a local In-N-Out Burger franchise and bring cheese-laden Double-Double burgers to the departure area for the guys to devour. The looks of pleasure on the faces of these teammates as the burger juices ran down their chins was a sight to see.

Like with all relationships, some become more deep-rooted than others. That was the case with one particular extended family. We hit it off from the get-go. Geoffrey and Max Unger were linemates during his four years at Oregon, developing a very strong bond, both on and off the field. That deep bond carried over with Livie and me and Max's parents, Keith and Cynda, and his grandparents, Cynnie and Ray. Geoffrey and Max had long professional careers, with Max on the field for two Super Bowls.

The two families enjoyed many pregame tailgates and postgame celebrations together. Over the years Keith and I had delighted in conversation about the guys' careers. Our relationship with the Ungers spanned the Pacific Ocean. On one trip to the Big Island of Hawaii, Livie and I visited the Ungers on their 10,000-acre ranch. Dinner was served on their outside patio where all meals were eaten. What a spectacular view as we watched the sun set in the west, causing the waves to sparkle. To this day, Geoffrey and Max are in contact, as are we with the Unger *ohana* (Hawaiian for family), typically through the broadcasts. Treasured relationships.

At Cal we similarly established relationships with two fellow Bear families. The genesis of one was the epitome of a small-world story. During Mitchell's recruiting period, we noticed that Cal was recruiting a Los Angeles–based high school offensive lineman with a familiar name. He was the son of a former UCLA Bruins offensive lineman who played during my tenure in Westwood. The dad coincidentally happened to be

The More, the Merrier

someone that my brother befriended while at UCLA, but had lost touch with after graduation.

When it became obvious that this was the very same Bruin from decades earlier, Fred found a phone number and called. Where one might expect a rather warm reconnection, my brother's recollection of that conversation suggested a coldness on this guy's part, to the effect of "why are you calling me?"

Fast forward about a year or so later. Mitchell was invited to attend the U.S. Army All-American all-star game for top national high school players held in the San Antonio, Texas, Alamodome. Concurrently, Mitchell was named to high school football recruiting analyst Tom Lemming's list of the top players in the country—a comprehensive catalog featuring his picks, complete with pictures. Knowing Mitchell was attending the All-American game, Lemming's staff invited Mitchell to a photo shoot, to be held at the remains of the historic Alamo in San Antonio.

We arrived at the Alamo at the prescribed time. Gotta say I was rather shocked with what I saw. I expected a much larger complex. The area was packed. Initially, we couldn't find the exact location for picture taking. And being of the male persuasion, we initially didn't ask anyone for help, instead just wandering around searching. Finally, I saw some yards ahead three rather tall individuals standing among a group of people. Believing they may have been there for the same reason, I approached.

"Excuse me, are you here for Lemming's pictures?" They responded affirmatively. We began chatting. Once we got past the pleasantries, the small-world coincidence struck us like a lightning bolt. I had stumbled upon my fellow Bruin, whom I had last seen decades earlier. His son, like Mitchell, had been chosen by Lemming. Joining him and his son, the third member of their trio, was his son's high school offensive line coach.

The irony of this chance meeting wasn't restricted to that moment. Both Mitchell and the other Bruins son were being recruited by Cal. They ended up being linemates. Additionally, the line coach...well, he became Mitchell's trainer during the summer leading up to his first Bears' preseason camp. He put both guys, plus a couple of others, through their paces at a park in L.A.'s Hollywood Hills. "Hills" was definitely the operative word here. The park was full of steep slopes for the guys to attack. I can assure you that the group was completely exhausted by the time their workout was over. But it all paid off. Mitchell arrived in Berkeley in awfully fine condition.

That opportunistic meeting at the Alamo (just think, I could have walked up to dozens of other people) was the beginning of a relationship that Livie and I enjoyed with him and his wife during Mitchell's time at Cal and thereafter. The four of us added another couple to the foursome early in Mitchell's first year. They also were Southern Californians. The six of us spent four years traveling to all games, lodged in the same hotels, attending games together (home and away), tailgating together, celebrating together and commiserating together.

We all got along so well. It was a blast. Beyond the games, several times a year the three dads would jump into one of our vehicles for the approximately five-and-a-half-hour trek up Interstate 5 through the guts of California to attend spring or summer camps at Memorial Stadium. It was a more up-close view of practices. We were allowed field access so long as we stayed clear of the action. Being so close meant we could hear the coaches provide direction, encouragement and the "occasional" rip for poor play.

We were able to interact with the coaches and staff, from Head Coach Jeff Tedford to Offensive Line Coach Jim Michalczik to some of the support staff like the head of operations or the recruiting director.

And then there was "Dog" (obviously a loving nickname for a forty-plus-year career Cal employee), who was the gatekeeper to the entire stadium. Getting to know him was a true benefit for us dads and family, as we sometimes were able to circumvent published stadium restrictions by knowing this man. Beyond attending practice, these trips also included meals together with the boys and chill time with the guys between their football activities. Wonderful, wonderful times.

One more very special relationship comes to mind. It had its roots in Mitchell's Little League years. The father of Mitchell's teammate, Zach, was very involved. Helped at all practices. Attended all games. We got to be friends. Then Cliff and Elana and Livie and I began to socialize. A few years after the conclusion of Little League, Cliff and Elana packed up and moved from the rat race to a more peaceful Bainbridge Island in Puget Sound off the coast of Washington state. Under most conditions, that move would have distanced the relationship. Not in this case.

Whether it was to attend a college game at the University of Washington or a pro contest against the Seattle Seahawks, the four of us managed to schedule time together. Cliff and Elana would board the ferry for the thirty-five-minute trip from the island to Pier 52 at the Seattle docks. From there, we'd meet them for a brunch or lunch depending on kickoff time. If prior to a U of W game, we'd bid our farewells and head to the game. But if for a Seahawks game, we'd walk together to the stadium. They were season-ticket holders. It all made for a great day.

Livie's dear cousin Karen grew up in the Seattle area. She now resides about ninety minutes north of Seattle. Karen and her husband Dan joined us for one of Mitchell's games at the University of Washington. When the guys played the Seahawks, Karen and Dan would join us at the game. Livie was in heaven, having a chance to spend time with this very special relative.

And that just scratches the surface. There are so many more relationships that were launched during the past couple of decades. Within my contact file are dozens of names that were added during this time. Past coaches, from high school and college. Though sporadically, I still have contact with some of these guys. I lunch with Coach Blatt. I text Jim Michalczik every time he moves up the ladder. Then there are the handful of reporters who covered the teams, from print to web media, whom I got to know and today am still in contact with. Demonstrating an ability to keep sensitive information confidential, these reporters trusted me with behind-the-scenes information about the teams and players. I felt like an insider.

It seems to me that the main theme of this chapter is sharing. The fan-club broadcasts. Attending games with others. The innumerable conversations along the way. I could try to express in my own words what all this has meant to me but I think I'll let these quotations do the talking:

- From actor Leonard Nimoy, Mr. Spock from the classic 1960s TV series *Star Trek*: "The miracle is this: The more we share the more we have."
- Linked to Margaret Mead, an American cultural anthropologist, speaker and author: "But for the full flowering of the human spirit we need groups, tribes."
- And maybe most fitting, attributed to Roman Stoic philosopher, statesman and dramatist Seneca: "There is no enjoying the possession of anything valuable unless one has someone to share it with."

There is no instrument available to gauge the level of enjoyment that I've experienced and the amount of enrichment I've received over the two decades through the ability to share this remarkable journey with others. To those who have been on board since the beginning, and equally to those who set sail at a later point in this journey, *thank you*!

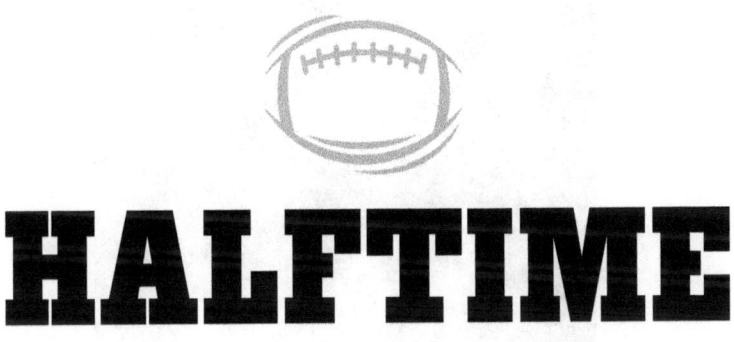

HALFTIME

MY JOURNEY THROUGH PHOTOS

Best Buddies . . . Then and Now

Me and the two blondies in our backyard.

Geoffrey and Mitchell with ear-to-ear grins.

My Journey Through Photos

The guys representing in their college gear.

Coming together after their teams battled in Arrowhead Stadium.

Raising Giants

Before There Was Football

Hoopster Geoffrey at one year old.

Mitchell preparing for his first at-bats.

My Journey Through Photos

Geoffrey was a monster on the mound at Pali High.

Mitchell was a standout first baseman and hitter on his Pali team.

The Football Journey

Exhausted after a high school practice session.

Mitchell in pregame warmups donning his Chiefs uniform.

Geoffrey after Oregon demolished Michigan.

My Journey Through Photos

Geoffrey's journey began at Pali High.

Mitchell standing tall in his Pali uniform.

It's a Family Affair

T-shirt created by Livie to wear at the Cleveland/KC game.

Geoffrey and Papa celebrating Geoffrey being drafted into the NFL.

My Journey Through Photos

Postgame gathering at Arrowhead: Me, Geoffrey, Meridith, Mitchell & Livie.

The Oregon tradition at Autzen Stadium: Me, Emmy, Alex & Geoffrey.

Pregame at MetLIfe: Geoffrey, me, Meridith, Livie and my brother Fred.

Mitchell with Brooke prior to his drum banging pregame at Arrowhead Stadium.

Mitchell sharing time with Papa postgame at the Rose Bowl.

Reached the Mountaintop—Super Bowl LIV

Yes, that's the Super Bowl Lombardi Trophy nestled between Mitchell and me.

Mitchell; hoists the Vince Lombardi Trophy at the Super Bowl Parade.

My Journey Through Photos

Super Bowl ring containing 10.85 carats of diamonds and rubies making my large hand seem small.

It was party time after the Super Bowl— me, Livie, Meridith and Geoffrey.

The Rest of the Story

Thirteen-year-old Bar Mitzvah Geoffrey almost eyeball to eyeball with me.

Geoffrey enjoying breakfast with legendary UCLA basketball coach John Wooden.

This is how I rolled at all games when watching the guys play.

THIRD QUARTER

12
FOOTBALL AND FOOD: A SPECIAL COMBINATION

As with most families, food holds a special place in the Schwartz/Goodkin household. I've included plenty of anecdotes related to our food and dining habits. Our celebrations involve food. Religious observations involve food. Football game days can include considerable consumption of food and drink. This chapter will take a broader look at the family connection between football and food.

You might assume that because of my boys' genetic mutations and careers in football, food has become even *more* essential to this particular generation of our family, but that's not so. Simply gaze in the rearview mirror to two generations prior. Geoffrey and Mitchell's grandparents were unfortunately voracious, unhealthy eaters, suffering the effects of overindulgence and zero exercise. My parents and Livie's father and stepmother were all overweight to morbidly obese. Three of the four died before their time of complications directly related to obesity.

Livie and I were intent on setting a better example. We have always eaten healthfully. We exercise. I believe I've been doing so in some form for close to fifty years now, without interruption. With the boys, from early on, we tried to balance their diet to prevent obesity. We pushed them outside the house for activity. Fortunately, when our kids were growing up, electronics, like PlayStation, Nintendo Switch, iPads and the like, were not as ubiquitous as they are today. I believe for the most part we accomplished our health goals. What couldn't be overcome was the boys' genetic makeup. They are simply huge human beings and have required a large caloric intake to fuel their physical activity.

Quantity and Quality

When dining out we needed to identify restaurants that served ample portions. Years before Mitchell ate so much that his stomach mutinied at that meal in Eugene, the family discovered a restaurant in Los Angeles that fit the quantity bill perfectly. Fortunately, the boys and I have also been fortunate to have in Livie a "good cooker," a fond description coined by my beloved grandmother. So with quantity always came quality. Yum, yum.

At the conclusion of Geoffrey's senior year at Pali High he was awarded the Palisades Post Cup Award, recognizing him as the top male senior athlete of his class. In another one of those small-world instances, the female winner of the Cup Award was the daughter of one of Livie's law firm partners. What were the chances? To celebrate, a family-style (in other words, large portions) Italian restaurant was chosen as the celebration site. Why had we not heard of this restaurant previously? Unfathomable! My oh my, did it fit the bill. The portions were enormous, yet tasty. Huge amounts of food were consumed that evening as both families toasted their high-performing offspring.

Speaking of food volume, here's a story for all time. Geoffrey was home visiting. Mitchell was still in high school. They were hungry and wanted to spend some time together, so plans were made to dine at a local Mexican restaurant. They were seated and spent a few minutes perusing the menu. The waiter arrived and asked for their order.

Geoffrey piped up first and ordered fajitas for two. The waiter jotted down the request, said "thank you," and began turning away from the table. One of the guys barked out, *"Wait!"* "We want *two* orders of fajitas for two." I suspect the waiter had never had two people placing *two* orders of fajitas for two. The order was adjusted accordingly. Not a morsel of food was left on either plate when the boys were done. Lesson learned? Don't ever underestimate a couple of famished ginormous men.

Like so many other tales in this book, this story had a postscript. Geoffrey participated in media week activities preceding the 2020 Super Bowl between the Chiefs and the Niners. Teams typically arrive the

Football and Food—A Special Combination

Monday before Super Bowl Sunday, usually attending a press conference that day to answer questions from the media.

Geoffrey knew that Mitchell would be one of the K.C. players designated to take the podium, given his stature with the team, so Geoffrey made plans to attend. He bought an ill-fitting blond wig and mustache to wear that night, in a satirical effort to disguise his six-foot, six-inch, 300-plus-pound identity.

Obviously, there was no way Geoffrey's costume would fool Mitchell. Mitchell spent most of his appearance at the podium trying to ignore his brother in order to avoid bursting into laughter. Finally, Mitchell called on his bro, who kept raising his hand to ask a question. Geoffrey blurted out, "Mr. Schwartz, there's been an allegation that when you ate at Don Antonio's restaurant on Pico Boulevard, you ordered fajitas for two, just for yourself. Is that true?" Mitchell answered quite succinctly, "Yes." And that was that.

Game-Day Feasting

Our appreciation of good food was kicked up a few notches while Geoffrey attended the University of Oregon in Eugene. Up to this point, our tailgating efforts were rather simplistic. Usually, in advance of heading to the Rose Bowl for Bruins games, we'd pack up some soft drinks, chips and munchies at home before landing at a local shop for the main course, some submarine-type sandwiches. Very, very basic. No firing up a grill for dogs and similar fare. I figured that heading up to Autzen Stadium would change that practice.

Interestingly, it didn't, at least for us. My buddy Mike Parr did tailgate before games in the stadium parking lot. We had an open invitation to join him and his family, which we enjoyed several times during Geoffrey's tenure in Eugene. For us the more common practice before games was to gather at the Moshofsky Center, affectionately known as the "Mo," rather than join the tailgaters outside. The Mo was built adjacent to Autzen Stadium, as an indoor practice facility, but on game days it was converted into a 117,000-square-foot party central. Row after row of tables and chairs were assembled. Food stations lined one side of the massive room. Livie and I would order our food, typically enjoying different cuisine, find our friends and chow down, waiting for the team to parade through the building.

As I talked about earlier as it related to Cal, many teams around the country have a formal arrival process, walking through throngs of adoring and animated fans on their way into their locker room. For Oregon, the team would drive from a nearby hotel to a parking lot immediately outside the Mo. Gathered before the team arrived would be the full complement of the band, the cheerleaders and song girls and "The Duck" team mascot. With everyone queued up outside, the Mo doors would fly open, the band would strike up the Oregon fight song and the pageant would begin.

With the music reverberating from wall to wall and floor to ceiling, those in attendance would, seemingly in unison, stand to clap and join in singing *Mighty Oregon*. First through the door was The Duck, followed closely by the band, the spirit squad, and then the players, coaches and staff. I didn't think the decibel levels could grow any louder, but as the players entered the building and marched through the swarm of fans, high-fiving along the way, the decibel level climbed. As Geoffrey would walk by, he'd stop for a big hug from both Livie and me, a wish of good luck and, with our pride oozing, "I love you."

Having played some ball myself, all the commotion pulsed through my body, reminding me of what it was like to run out onto my high school basketball court to cheering fans. In the Mo, with my adrenaline rush, I was ready to jump in line with the players and suit up.

My food consumption was limited to what I ordered while in the Mo. Once in the stadium, my back side was glued to my seat for the entirety of the contest. If I felt hungry during the game, I would piggyback on Livie's foray to the concession stands

Plentiful Postgame Provisions

When it came to eating, postgame was the opportunity to make up for lost time. There was a pizza joint no more than a handful of miles from Autzen Stadium. It became the go-to eatery for the linemen and their families to gather for an after-game meal, unless kickoff was 7 p.m. or later. By the time such a game would end, it was simply too late to assemble…and likely the restaurant had closed for the night. The volume of food consumed at the pizzeria was impressive. There was an all-you-can-eat salad bar. "All-you-can-eat" being the operative phrase. Perfect for famished offensive linemen. The profit from the number of pies ordered collectively by our group alone likely covered the days' operating expenses.

Football and Food—A Special Combination

And, of course, pizza can't be eaten without beer to wash it down. There typically was not a time during our stay at the pizzeria when someone from the group wasn't at the counter ordering more suds. Me? Diet coke, please. The one time in my life that I would have consumed a meaningful volume of alcohol, the first night of fraternity "Hell Weekend" during my freshman year at UCLA, my forehead was introduced to the metal track of a sliding door. Although the track suffered its own damage, my head was worse. After a trip to the ER, the doctors gave me firm instructions to abstain from drinking any alcohol during the weekend. Guess it set the stage for the rest of my life.

When on the road, there were few player-family gatherings. Postgame, after the players departed the stadium grounds headed for the airport, the families would bid each other adieu and scatter to their respective hotels...with one exception. And was that a doozy.

December 31, 2007, the Oregon Ducks played in the Sun Bowl in El Paso, Texas, against the South Florida Bulls, capping a most disappointing season. That was the year the Ducks were destined for the National Championship game, only to lose Heisman-candidate quarterback Dennis Dixon to that knee injury late in the season and plunge from an undefeated record to losing their final three. (I did ultimately attend a National Championship game. 2011. Auburn vs. Oregon with Geoffrey at the University of Phoenix Stadium in Glendale, Arizona. Cam Newton, 2010 Heisman winner, was Auburn's quarterback that year.) A heartbreaking conclusion as Auburn kicked a field goal with 0:01 on the clock to walk away as 22-19 champions. Obviously Geoffrey was crushed.

Since it was the final collegiate game for Geoffrey and many of his offensive linemates, families were undeterred by the late-season collapse and made plans to be in El Paso. One family was intent on making this last experience one for the books. They lived in the Midwest. Their offensive lineman son hardly saw action on the field during his four years at Oregon, yet the family could be found at numerous games during his career. As a going away present to him, his teammates and their families, his parents that night booked an entire Mexican restaurant in town for dinner and the beginning of a New Year's Eve celebration.

The restaurant was transformed into a flock of Ducks. Everyone was in remarkable spirits as the non-web-footed counterparts annihilated South Florida 56-14 that afternoon behind the unexpected leadership of a fifth-string quarterback who was making his first collegiate start and who threw for four touchdowns, tying a Sun Bowl record.

To say the food was plentiful would have been an understatement. The staff had not a moment to relax, having to constantly restock the buffet line of fajitas, enchiladas, tacos, burritos, beans, rice, guac and all the other trimmings. And, of course, the pitchers of beer flowed along with unending alcoholic beverages, all without my support. Other than being in New Orleans for the National Championship game, I can't imagine a better way to end a marvelous four-year run at the University of Oregon for Geoffrey and his parents. I was so stuffed that a gurney was a consideration for transit back to our car.

You might have noticed the absence of any Autzen Stadium stories related to food. There's a very good reason for the omission. The food inside Autzen was lackluster, at best. The usual nondescript run-of-the-mill stadium fare of hotdogs, popcorn, pretzels and sodas. Thank goodness the choices in the Mo were much more appealing, and so that's where I ate. Cal's Memorial Stadium, although a crumbling mess structurally, especially as compared to the more recently renovated Autzen Stadium, could at least boast one advantage over their Pac-12 rival. A much better assortment of pleasing concessions.

For those who have seen the front jacket of the boys' book, *Eat My Schwartz*, once one gets past the shock of seeing the guys in their boxer shorts, one might notice Geoffrey, with mouth agape, gripping a turkey drumstick seemingly headed for a first bite. He and I are both big fans of these turkey parts, being my first go-to piece on Thanksgiving. Cal's Memorial Stadium offered one of the two best turkey drumsticks at a stadium/arena that I ever wolfed down.

The turkey-leg concession stand was at the opposite end of the stadium from where we sat. Normally I would resist making a trek for any food, but this was an exception. Upon entry to the stadium, I would head directly to our seats. After offloading the seat cushions and whatever outerwear was required for the day/night, I'd hike back up the dozens of stairs and briskly walk to the concession stand.

With a huge turkey leg in hand, bigger than the one pictured on the book cover, I'd retrace my steps back to the seats, albeit stopping to buy a soft pretzel—no salt, please—and a large diet soda. I could have bought the soda with the turkey leg, but then I would have had to schlep it all the way back. Another soda stand was literally at the top of the steps leading

Football and Food—A Special Combination

to our seats. I now had all I needed for nourishment that would last me the entire game.

I have no idea whether the concessionaire who sold the turkey legs at Cal's Memorial Stadium was the same vendor who peddled turkey legs at AT&T Park during Mitchell's senior year when Cal played their games across the Bay, but it could have been. If memory serves me, the legs were of similar size and just as scrumptious. But if the mood struck me, AT&T Park offered much better food options than did Memorial Stadium. There were hand-carved tri-tip sandwiches available at the Baby Bull stand, named after former San Francisco Giants' great Orlando Cepeda, whose nickname was "The Baby Bull." Large, delicious sausages smothered with grilled peppers and onions could be found at Say Hey! Willie Mays Sausages, honoring the Giants' icon and Hall of Famer "The Say Hey Kid." Plenty of tasty options.

Some Serious Tailgating

The real story associated with Cal was the tailgating before and after games. Livie and I learned very quickly how committed the Bears parents were to the tailgating experience. The term "Bearents,"—the creative blending of "Bears" and "parents" (Merging two words to create an original third is known as a *portmanteau* word. Who knew...until I watched Jeopardy!)—was, from what I understand, the brainchild of a husband-and-wife team who graduated from Cal decades earlier but maintained their fanaticism through the years for all things Bears, especially when it came to football.

This couple wore every hat imaginable to ensure that they, along with Cal parents, current and past, could assemble before games, for sure, and after, as kickoff time allowed, to party, create lifelong relationships, celebrate, commiserate and generally produce lasting memories of our time at Berkeley.

Clark Kerr is a residence hall situated about one-half mile directly south of Memorial Stadium. It was the residence hall that most freshman football players called home during their first year. The southwest corner of the property offered a two-level parking lot for students and guests. On game days, the upper tier was reserved for football-player families holding a special pass, sold by the Bearents. At the beginning of each season, we paid, as I recall, a very nominal fee to secure a parking spot for each home game.

That's how game day started. At least a couple of hours before kickoff—and maybe more like three knowing my tendencies—we'd depart the "parental hotel," so phrased because so many of us parents stayed the weekend at this hotel across the bay in Emeryville, destined for the Clark Kerr parking lot. Although there were no assigned spaces, it was funny how human nature took hold and, by habit, we pulled into the same spot, or maybe one adjoining, again and again. If they were not already there, we waited for our friends to show up before unloading our gear from the car.

Too bad I didn't, using some form of time-lapse photography, chronicle the arrival of cars and the production of everyone setting up their tailgating environment. It was an eclectic approach. Some arrived in their sports cars. Others in SUVs filled to the brim. Occasionally, we'd see a small trailer hitched to the rear of a vehicle. Some were minimalists, like us, who brought little to the fair, while others were quite unrestrained, bringing Hibachis, tables and chairs, coolers, container after container of prepared and to-be cooked foods and more. It was an example of human nature at its best because the general attitude was share and share alike. Nothing felt off limits.

We didn't bring much with us, as the turkey legs at the stadium were beckoning. We also didn't stay very long. Getting to the stadium to see the players make their walk from their buses to the stadium, being able to hug Mitchell and wish him "good luck," and observing his pregame ritual on the field were far more appealing to us. Some of the parents would trek the fifteen to twenty minutes to Memorial for the walk and then return to the parking lot to resume tailgating. Others would depart the stadium to join another tailgate party in session.

After the players disappeared into the stadium, I would head directly to the entry gate to await the opening of the stadium so I could watch the players warm up. Typically, I was joined by the dad of one of Mitchell's teammates. Livie, not fully appreciating the pregame activities and not desiring to enter the stadium as early as I, would occasionally opt for a walk around campus or the nearby streets of Berkeley rather than entering so early.

The postgame tailgating, presuming the kickoff was no later than midafternoon, was far more involved. Players would join the party. A food box was awaiting each player as they left the locker room, but the assortment and tastiness of that sampling paled in comparison to what

Football and Food—A Special Combination

was waiting in the parking lot. The band, arranged by the two Bearents organizers, would visit once or twice a year to serenade the families with the Cal fight song and other tunes they played during the game. Their reward? The food! They were welcome to stop at any table and consume as much as their hearts desired.

Inclement weather would never prevent the festivities from occurring. We'd all put on our rain gear and let the water run off our backs, or unfurl an umbrella in the worst of conditions. Some people brought with them those portable tents that would be quickly assembled if the downpour became too severe. But in all cases, the interaction among families and the ingestion of food and drink never wavered.

Once or twice a year, a buffet was planned for everyone in attendance. Tables abutted each other down the middle of the upper parking lot, spanning about fifty yards. Everyone, and truly it was *everyone*, would bring a dish or two or three, and would barbecue meats on site to contribute. It was a feast of massive proportions, scrumptious and palate pleasing. No one ever went away hungry, I'm sure. And the bonus? I met parents with whom I had not spoken previously, or was able to spend more time with casual acquaintances because of the camaraderie and sociability of those present—all drawn together by food.

One tailgating experience has stood out over time for me. As with Geoffrey's Oregon teams, the Cal roster was comprised of many Polynesians. Because of the bonds developed on teams, the "Polys" would refer to their teammates as an *uso,* meaning "brother." I often heard Geoffrey's teammates fondly refer to him as an *uso.* Anyway, on one Saturday afternoon late in the season, it might have been the last career home game for several of the Poly players, their families decided to share a delicacy of their culture.

Early that Saturday morning, a very large barbecue rotisserie grill hitched to the back of a four-wheeler drove to the upper parking lot level. It was larger than what one would need in normal circumstances. We all had no idea why it was there. In short order we knew.

The grill was backed into a corner of the lot and unhitched. As numbers of us gawked, we saw the Polynesian families gather around the grill to begin preparations. The coals were loaded. And then the guest of honor appeared. A pig. It was to be dressed for roasting but first needed to be mounted on a spit. Once in place, the pig was then braced and balanced before being secured on the rotisserie. What a sight! With the coals lit, that damn pig rotated throughout the day while most of us attended the game. Several people remained behind to provide the TLC necessary to produce a scrumptious outcome. By the time we returned to the dorm lot, the swine had been sliced and diced and was ready for consumption.

Tailgating with Cal family was not just reserved for home games. The Cal alums who founded the Bearents were quite committed to ensuring that tailgating was available at away games. From their Northern California home, depending on distance to cover, the couple would depart one, two, maybe three days in advance of a game in their fully stocked RV, adorned from bumper to bumper with Cal trappings, to arrive on site by game day. Whether it was Pac-12 contests across San Francisco Bay or 800-plus miles to Pullman, Washington, or Tucson, Arizona, or even more than half-way across the country to Minneapolis, Minnesota, these dear people were always awaiting our arrival. They would blast out via email where they would be setting up, with an advisory to be on the lookout for a Cal flag flapping in the wind about ten feet above the RV roofline. It was always easy to spot.

Being away from home, these tailgates were obviously much more limited in what food was offered but, nonetheless, served a great purpose, providing an anchor location for the visiting parents and families to gather before heading into the stadium. The RV was open to anyone who wanted to take a load off or use the facilities. Tables outside featured whatever food was available. Additional seating was provided. On warm days, the awning would be extended for shade. Since basically all food was provided for us, each family would happily place money into a Cal Bears' jar to help offset what was spent by these generous folks for nourishment and gas.

Regardless of whether it was at a home game or at a competitor's stadium, the true treasure of these tailgating experiences was the human element. In a world with so much hate, divisiveness, acrimony and downright meanness, these gatherings reflected the inherent good nature of people. We shared without a second thought. We bridged cultures without thinking of ethnicity, religion, age, class, wealth or any characteristic that might divide people. Football brought us together, but our basic, fundamental character kept us together.

Now for the granddaddy of all tailgates, at least in my experience. If there was a Seven Wonders of the World list for food, this tailgate would have been included. It likely would also have qualified for the Mount Rushmore of tailgates. It was quite literally everything one could ask for in such a gathering.

As I've shared already, Oregon visited Michigan at the beginning of Geoffrey's senior season in 2007. Livie's friend Kathi's husband, David, is a Michigan alum and a big Wolverine fan. So is his stepbrother, who happens to live in the Ann Arbor, Michigan, area, home of the University of Michigan, and from what we have heard attends all home games.

I had met the stepbrother at family events, where we would always engage in football talk, particularly Michigan, UCLA and wherever the boys were playing. David informed him that I, along with my brother and a friend, would be traveling to Ann Arbor for the Oregon game. He generously offered to meet us pregame and guide us to a tailgate that he described as special. How could we turn down such an offer?

We met at a designated location and were then escorted to a grassy knoll situated about fifteen to twenty feet above the entrance where the Michigan players exit their buses for entry to the stadium. The tailgate was thirty-three years in the making. It was thrown by two U of M alums, one a doctor, the other a lawyer, at every home game except for those that fell on a Jewish holiday. Apparently, it all started very modestly, originally by invitation. But it then grew year after year to where up to a thousand people would stroll through the party, all welcomed with open arms and no expectation of feeding the piggy bank, no invitation required.

I wish I had a picture to show because words alone can't convey the majesty of this food orgy. Under a tent, the size of which seemed to approximate a small banquet room, there was food and drink of every kind, apportioned as though one was in a supermarket. There was a section of cold foods next to tables of hot foods. Some of the hot grub was catered while some was cooked on site. Reports suggest 300 pieces of fried chicken could be served in a day, along with 40 salamis and 60 dozen bagels. Seemingly every kind of dessert imaginable was available, from cakes to cookies to frozen pops. Coolers and coolers of ice-cold soft drinks ringed the tent. An extended bar with everything from beer to wine to all sorts of liquors and spirits was there for the taking. One would have to work very hard to walk away hungry or thirsty.

My understanding was that one of these tailgate parties would cost north of five figures. Talk about generosity. Similar to Cal, away games were not ignored. The traveling tailgate was about half the size, and half

Raising Giants

the cost, of the home-field variety. That still translates to a rather large footprint. It's also not surprising that such a large space is necessary for away games.

Michigan visited the Rose Bowl three times between 1982 and 2000 to play UCLA, all of which I attended. They have played in seventeen Rose Bowls in Pasadena since 1970, one being the exhilarating game I witnessed between Texas and Michigan. So I can tell you from personal experience, as well as watching from the comforts of my couch, that Wolverines travel extremely well to away games. The West Coast forays might be due to the allure of the weather, huh? The average high temps in Ann Arbor in December and January are thirty-six and thirty-one degrees, respectively, while in Pasadena the like temps are sixty-six and sixty-seven degrees. The Rose Bowl was awash in maize and blue, Michigan's school colors. When playing UCLA, I would swear Wolverine fans outnumbered their Bruin counterparts.

Food and football. Football and food. From my vantage point, they will always be interconnected. It's a perfect example to me of the phrase attributed to Aristotle, the ancient Greek philosopher: "the whole is greater than the sum of its parts." Football, and all its inherent aspects, by its lonesome, can bring extreme joy to those engaged. Food can also hold the same attraction. But in combination, my oh my.

13
FOOTBALL INTELLIGENCE

Ever heard of the book *Football For Dummies*? It actually is the title of one of the 2,500 *For Dummies* books that have been published since their first release in 1991, *DOS For Dummies*. While the title refers to the readers, there was a time decades ago when this was a commonly expressed characterization of the players themselves! I'm here to say, not just anecdotally but from real-life experience, that, as a whole, players are far from dummies.

I had no clue about football's complexity when my journey first began. Most other major sports have a limited number of players on the field, court, pitch, etc. or are completely individualistic, like tennis, golf and so many of the Olympic sports. Although baseball has nine players on the field, when it comes to catching a fly ball or hitting a 100-mph fastball, it's all about one. Shooting a free throw or boxing out for a rebound in basketball is a one-person affair. But then there's football, a completely different animal.

I have many stories to share about the complexity and interdependency of the game of football. Let me set the foundation with this one particular account. It occurred during Mitchell's tenure at Cal. Because I was so in the know when it came to football—NOT—I was kvetching to Mitchell about an interception thrown by a Cal quarterback that stymied a come-from-behind effort to win a game.

Raising Giants

Late in the contest, the Bears were marching toward a game-winning touchdown. A pass play was called. The quarterback dropped back and fired a pass toward the sideline. Instead of the receiver making the catch, the defensive back jumped in front of the wide out, intercepted the pass and ran it back some seventy yards for a game-clinching final touchdown. I bellyached to Mitchell, "What kind of throw was that?" blaming the QB for a poor pass.

Didn't take but a second or two for Mitchell to set his old man straight. It was the receiver's fault, dummy. (He didn't use that word, but I got the message. Haha.) He ran the wrong route. When the receiver came out of his break running toward the sidelines, he was to intersect, for the purposes of this story, the thirty-yard line. The QB threw to that spot, as the two had practiced time and again. However, the receiver had lazily extended the route and, instead of being at the thirty, was at the twenty-nine. One yard was the difference between a catch, and a possible win, and an intercepted pass. This one exchange jolted my eyes open to the intricacies of the game of football and has given me cause to resist playing the blame game, although that effort isn't always successful.

Being a right tackle definitely has its challenges. I will explain later in the chapter why right tackles do not enjoy the same level of respect as their left tackle counterparts. But first, consider this aspect of the intricacies of the game...and how easy it would be to point a finger in the wrong direction.

Offensive linemen are schooled to hold their blocks for the better part of seven to eight seconds. That's an awfully tough task. They are disadvantaged. As opposed to defensive linemen, who charge off the line of scrimmage with full forward momentum, offensive linemen are routinely backtracking. Try stopping, for instance, the forward pursuit of a muscle-bound 280-pound defender, hell-bent on sacking the quarterback, while pedaling backward. And, obviously, the game for defensive linemen is in front of them. For offensive linemen, they have no clue what's happening behind them.

Let's say the right tackle does his job and prevents his defender from gaining ground toward the quarterback. However, let's say the left guard has been beaten by his defensive counterpart, who's now in a full sprint to tackle the QB. What's the natural tendency for the quarterback? Run away from the pursuit, which would be, in this case, toward the right side of the offensive line. And who's watching? The defense. So as they see the

QB heading in that direction, they try to disengage from the o-lineman's block to chase the QB. Bad things are about to happen for the right tackle.

First, though one might believe otherwise, holding happens on every single play. If the o-lineman has a grasp of the defensive player's jersey, his hands are inside the shoulders and he continues to move his feet, it's generally considered an acceptable move, or at least won't usually be flagged by an official. But if they're engaged and the defender sees the QB leak outside the pocket (remember, the o-lineman has no clue this is happening) the defender will try to run in the direction of the QB. If the o-lineman remains engaged too long, to where the referee can see his extended arms and his hands clutching a jersey, or sees the forward progress of the defender obstructed, a yellow hanky will certainly fly from the referee, calling an offensive holding penalty. Fifteen yards in the wrong direction.

The other possible outcome? No holding penalty but the disengaged defender will either sack the QB, run him out of bounds or cause the ball to be thrown away. In so many cases, I have observed the right tackle being blamed in these circumstances. Not the left guard whose matador protection initially allowed the defense to seep into the backfield. Not the running back who may have missed a blocking assignment intended to pick up an oncoming rusher. Not the QB who should have released the ball long before the pressure got to him. But the right tackle.

I offer these two examples as just a foreshadowing of the bigger picture. Some reckon that 95 percent of people who use Microsoft's Excel spreadsheet program only use about 5 percent of the available functionality. Others believe the ratio is more like 80 percent of people only use 20 percent of the functionality. In either case, it's not much. The more I've learned about football, the more I find myself believing the same ratios are applicable to football. Outside of those who have played the game, I suspect most have little clue about the intricacies and interdependencies of the sport.

My earliest football teachers were the talking heads inside that black-and-white screen that presented games in a very simplistic manner back in the day. No replays. No telestrator, as made famous by commentator and coach, John Madden. No "Up Close and Personal" segments as introduced by ABC's Jim McKay. No *Hard Knocks*, the Emmy-winning series that exposes some of the secrets of NFL training camp. So I learned accordingly.

Livie, on the other hand, was clueless when it came to sports in general, but most certainly with football. Imagine, then, the conundrum she faced as her boys began playing and climbing the ladder of the sport. For someone as bright as she it was awfully frustrating. What was she to do? As much as they loved their mother, the boys were not going to become football instructors. Her friends, like Kathi, were useless for this purpose. I knew enough to be dangerous but not enough to really make a dent. Observing over time would fill in some holes, but who had the patience?

One day Mitchell, Geoffrey, Livie and I were wandering around a bookstore. We strolled over to the sports section. There it was. Blending the eye-catching hues of yellow balanced by a more somber and sophisticated black was the cover of *Football for Dummies*. Four hundred and eight pages of text, illustrations, charts and pictures intended to make the novice more knowledgeable. Livie snatched the book from the shelf. But wait, there was more as we further surveyed the section.

Holly Robinson Peete, wife of former University of Southern California quarterback Rodney Peete, who enjoyed a fifteen-year career in the NFL, wrote a book entitled *Get Your Own Damn Beer, I'm Watching the Game!*, intended to "take the complexity out of the game by breaking it down to its component parts." Bullseye. Maybe between the two books Livie could construct a foundation of understanding. Frankly, I'm not sure how much of either book she read, but to her credit she has learned a bunch.

To truly understand the game of football, having never played the sport, is a daunting task. As the boys progressed through their respective careers, I tried to be a sponge to improve my base of knowledge. I would ask them questions until I was sure I had overstayed my welcome. I have listened to most of their podcasts and interviews and read virtually everything written by them to enhance my knowledge. I watch with keen interest Geoffrey breaking down plays on his X (Twitter) page or YouTube. I intently listen to Geoffrey's various podcasts or Mitchell's radio appearances. And yet, I know that my overall knowledge of how the game is played is quite deficient, more specifically when it comes to activity outside the offensive line.

The Bull Rush

Livie and I have a picture mounted on our Bonus Room wall that is a visual demonstration of the nuances of this crazy game. It's a snapshot

Football Intelligence

of Mitchell defending likely future Hall of Famer Kalil Mack when Mack was an Oakland Raider and Mitchell was with the Chiefs. Mack was trying to bull rush Mitchell, that is, by pure brute strength, attempting to drive Mitchell backward so Mack would have a path to the quarterback. Remember, a defender has all the leverage as he's moving forward, not backpedaling. What did Mitchell do to stymie Mack's attack?

He employed what's known as the Hamilton technique, a move that he didn't consciously use until year four, and one that he applied every practice in the week leading up to the game. The picture shows Mitchell with his hand under Mack's forearm, pushing the arm skyward and thus removing Mack's forward energy. A very purposeful and ideal counter-move to the potentially problematic bull rush. The casual observer would be clueless, but to an All-Pro lineman a resourceful application of a valuable technique. (For Mitchell's detailed explanation, link to this url: https://tinyurl.com/34nc2452.)

Here's another example of the subtleties of the game and of Mitchell's resourcefulness and nuanced play. J.J. Watt is another defensive end who will one day have his bust in the NFL Hall of Fame. Truth be told, Watt gave Mitchell fits when lined up against him. Was he stronger? Likely. Was he quicker? No question. But according to Mitchell the real challenge with Watt was his unconventionality. When an o-lineman expected him to bull rush, he'd spin. When Watt would be expected to charge up field and around the corner, he'd twist with another defensive lineman and try to advance through the middle of the line. He was very resourceful. But so was Mitchell.

I've shared throughout the book how smart a football player Mitchell was. (His intellect is quite evident outside the confines of a football field as well.) With a game upcoming against the Houston Texans and J.J. Watt, Mitchell devoted much of the week leading up to the game to film study. Could he unearth a weakness to exploit? Leave it to Mitchell.

The timing had to be right, and likely only doable once, but Mitchell found the weakness. If Watt saw an o-lineman extend his arms in a punching motion intended to create distance between him and Watt, Watt would raise his arms above his opponent's arm level and then, in a violent motion, swipe his arms downward toward the field. The purpose? If successful, doing so forces the o-lineman's arms toward the turf, throwing the lineman off balance and giving Watt the advantage in his battle to get by.

So how did Mitchell respond? On one particular play, Mitchell began his punching motion, a severe thrust forward with his arms. The typical intention of this move is to land both hands on the opponent's chest. Watt, sensing Mitchell's movement, reacted. As Watt began his swipe, Mitchell swiftly retracted his arms as Watt thrust his downward. Advantage now to Mitchell. With Watt's momentum now earthbound, Mitchell helped complete the process by lifting his arms above Watt's and pushed downward on Watt's extended arms, a move I'll label as the "Schwartz Swipe." The ultimate result had Watt sprawled full body on the turf, offering no threat of disrupting the quarterback. And having done it once, Watt now was on notice that it could happen again. How might that have changed his approach during the rest of the game?

All-Pro Disrespect

Since I've provided two examples of Mitchell getting the best of his defensive end opponents, this might be the best opportunity to address possibly my biggest gripe with the NFL. Simply stated, the NFL as a league, and those within it, have disrespected offensive right tackles for the longest time.

It all began in the 1980s when New York Giants' linebacker Lawrence Taylor terrorized offensive lines. He simply couldn't be stopped. So, to try to limit the damage he inflicted, offenses began to counter by placing their most talented offensive lineman at left tackle (the impetus for the book *The Blind Side*), as Taylor typically lined up on that side of the defense. They also resorted to double-teaming Taylor with a tight end. That cat and mouse game between the offense and defense has lasted for decades.

Once the o-line stacked their left side, the defense responded by moving their best d-end to the opposite side, the offensive right. Instead of the right tackles opposing the weaker of the defensive ends, it was quite the contrary. Just look at list of the guys Mitchell confronted late in his career: J.J. Watt, Kalil Mack, Von Miller, Joey Bosa and Melvin Ingram. I dare say that one day this entire group will be enshrined in the Hall of Fame.

Yet, admittedly, except for Watt, who seemed to usually get the better of Mitchell, the other four, in my humble opinion, he consistently bested. Those, except for Watt, were also the Murderers' Row of the Western Conference, the same division in which Kansas City played, so Mitchell lined up against each one of them twice within a season.

Football Intelligence

Mitchell thought highly of all these guys, as I believe they did of him. Specifically, here are Von Miller's own words when asked about Mitchell:

He's dynamic, strong, he's got everything you want from a tackle, Miller said of his infamous opponent. I'm a fan of the game and I know great players. Mitch is a great player. It's funny how you get three All-Pros and no Pro Bowls. I've got a lot of respect for him and whenever I get the opportunity to switch jerseys with him you know I'm gonna.
—"Kansas City Chiefs vs. Denver Broncos: What they're saying" Arrowhead Pride, Vox Media (September 29, 2018)

Schwartz is the gold standard for tackles, Miller said. And not just for right tackles. He's the gold standard for tackles—he plays every game. It doesn't matter what pass rusher he goes against, he's going to be solid. He was great in Cleveland and he's even better in Kansas City.
—"Von Miller on playing Mahomes, Chiefs on Monday night: 'I have an opportunity to be great'" KUSA-TV (September 20, 2018)

And there you have it. My biggest gripe, confirmed by Von Miller. Mitchell was ultimately named to four consecutive Associated Press (AP) All-Pro teams as voted by a national panel of fifty NFL-focused AP writers and broadcasters. First team in 2018. Second team in '16, '17 and '19. That means four years running he was considered the first- or second-best right tackle out of thirty-two in the league. However, as Miller alluded to, not once in Mitchell's career was he named to the NFL's Pro Bowl team as selected by players, coaches and fans. How's that possible? It's called respect, or lack thereof. And a result of the selection system.

The AP designates the best player at each position during a given season. Right tackles receive their own recognition separate from left tackles. That's the fair approach in my opinion. But the NFL's Pro Bowl is nothing more than a beauty contest. They cluster the left and right tackles and so, with left tackles more highly valued, unfairly so, than their right-side counterparts, the tackles named to the year-end Pro Bowl have, with less than a handful of exceptions in recent years, been those who line up on the left side. A total of six tackles are named each year to both the NFC and AFC rosters. Hard for anyone to convince me that Mitchell wasn't one of the top six tackles in the AFC during that four-year stretch, especially considering his AP All-Pro recognition.

Not only have right tackles been undervalued when considered for postseason honors, that same attitude prevails when it comes to contracts. I looked up the average yearly contract for left and right tackles based on what appear to be 2021 numbers. The top left-side tackle earned $23 million. The right-side counterpart almost 20 percent less at $19 million. The top six salaries for right tackles all exceed $17 million. Number seven drops precipitously to less than $10 million. There are twenty left tackles who make more than $10 million annually. This disparity can't be rationally explained in my world.

Further to the unwarranted disparity are these numbers, based on the average cap hit per player. Since NFL contracts have so many bonuses and other elements beyond base salaries, the cap hit is seen as possibly the best indicator of contract values. Left tackle's average cap hit: $6,624,676. Right tackle: $3,154,705. In what universe is that justifiable?

The Pro Bowl roster selection process is determined by the consensus votes of fans, players and coaches. Each group's vote counts for one-third. The fans? Do they really vote with their gray matter rather than their hearts? The coaches? Do we think the coaches spend time during the season evaluating players throughout the league? Hardly a chance. And the players? Would an offensive lineman know anything about a cornerback, for instance? Doubtful as well. So how reliable is the entire process?

To support my premise, I offer these comments from Geoffrey. They were in response to the NFL publicizing their list of the 100 top players in the league heading into the 2022 season. He tweeted, "Yearly reminder the NFL Top 100 list is voted on by players and should not be taken seriously. It's excellent content for debate." He went on to explain, "It's been many years since I filled these out. I wrote down my brother's name, then my favorite teammates, then my offensive lineman friends and turned it in. That's how most of us voted. I don't care enough to sit down and write out a serious top 100 list." Yikes. What more is there to say?

Brawn vs. Brain in the NFL

Growing up watching the game, I thought that physicality in football was much more important than intellect. Brawn versus brains. I'd be hard-pressed to recall a time when a commentator or reporter plugged the intelligence of a football player. Conversely, it was not unusual to hear demeaning commentary. Take Hall of Fame and four-time Super Bowl champion quarterback Terry Bradshaw of the Pittsburgh Steelers. He was constantly criticized during his career for being "the dumbest quarterback in the league." How's that possible given his accomplishments?

If one has followed the NFL over the decades, as I have, it was exceedingly obvious that the quarterback position was dominated by white players. Why? Candidly, Blacks weren't thought to have the intellect to play the position. Thank goodness there's been a dramatic shift in attitudes in recent years. The 2018–2019 playoffs featured five African American starting quarterbacks. Heading into the 2024 season, fifteen of the thirty-two opening weekend starting quarterbacks were Black.

I offer these examples not to address intellectual inequality or racism but rather to accentuate the notion that dummies can't play football, especially in today's iteration. I am overwhelmed when I listen to and/or watch Mitchell or Geoffrey break down a play on film, knowing that they've likely only scratched the surface of what's truly involved in a play.

I'm sure it was more than a decade ago when I read an article having to do with intelligence levels of NFL players by position. I believe it was published by *Sports Illustrated*. The reporter, based upon their research, identified the top two most-intelligent position groups as being the quarterbacks and the offensive linemen. He attempted to offer an explanation as to what made the hogs a smarter collection of athletes.

Envision a cinder-block wall. They are obviously very strong, and seemingly impenetrable. Imagine being told to *run through* such a barrier in order to get to the other side. Well, imagine one position group, when hearing a coach's directive, would, without hesitation, try to crash through the wall with helmets as battering rams. About all that could be accomplished would be, at best, a headache, or at worst, a concussion.

The offensive line group would instead use their gray matter. "Coach, can we jump on shoulders to scale the wall?" "Coach, what about digging a trench underneath?" They would explore options to achieve the stated goal without causing bodily damage to themselves. They were using their noggins.

Mitchell has always been known for his intelligence. He achieved a 4.3 GPA in high school and earned an impressive 3.4 GPA at Cal Berkeley, consistently ranked as a top public university in the United States by *U.S. News and World Report*, while devoting countless hours per week to football. In elementary school, Mitchell missed but one spelling word on his weekly tests. (Not on "porpoise!" This was the word misspelled.) Being the perfectionist he was, and still is, as demonstrated routinely on the football field and his *Mitch in the Kitch* podcasts, that was a catastrophic event for him but, fortunately, it didn't scar him for life. His coaches and teammates all recognized his smarts.

- A head coach once offered that Mitchell might have been the smartest player he's coached.
- One former teammate commented that Mitchell might be the smartest he's played with.
- A former linemate nicknamed Mitchell "The Oracle" because of his football smarts.
- And coincidentally, while penning the first draft of this chapter, I received a Google Alert that included this—"Michalczik [that's Jim Michalczik, Mitchell's line coach at Cal and current offensive line coach for the Michigan State Spartans] calls Mitchell Schwartz, a three-star prospect who played at Cal from 2008 through 2011, the smartest player he has ever coached."

In my opinion, both Geoffrey and Mitchell flourished on the field, not because of their athletic talents, but rather because of what's between their ears. Obviously, they could not have played professional ball if not athletically gifted. However, they were not in the same rarified air as many of their counterparts.

Mark Madsen played basketball for Stanford University and then spent nine years in the NBA. He was not the most athletically gifted, often referred to as a "banger," one who used his brains and brawn to overachieve. Kinda like Geoffrey.

One day I made the connection and then thought, "How can I get the two together?" Turns out I had a resource. I reached out and asked if a connection was doable. It was not only doable; it came to pass. One day, early in Mark's career while playing for the Los Angeles Lakers, found him and his long limbs sprawled on our couch for a visit with Geoffrey. The two talked and talked, Mark encouraging Geoffrey to work hard and use his innate talents to, like Mark, achieve his athletic goals. That day made a lasting impression on Geoffrey that carried forth ever since.

I know that Geoffrey and Mitchell were students not only of their positions but also of those around them. They studied voraciously. They took volumes of notes. They meticulously examined film. They knew their responsibilities plus those of their neighboring linemen. I remember Geoffrey telling me a story that demonstrated the chemistry that existed between him, while lining up at right tackle, and the right guard. They both approached the line of scrimmage with a play call and its requirements in mind. They scanned the defense and realized that the defensive alignment required an adjustment to the offense's original approach. No words were spoken between teammates other than "Got it?" from Geoffrey, followed by a grunt of "Yep." That was it. Their role in the play was handled flawlessly.

The more that I have learned about the game of football, the more I realize what I don't know. The terminology is overwhelming. Vertical set. Zone blocking. Aiming points. Landmarks. And these are just a sampling of offensive line terms. The precision required has been shocking to me. I figured if an offensive lineman punched a defensive counterpart anywhere in the chest area, that would be good enough. Not the case. Sometimes the block requires the hands to strike the center of the chest. Other times the strike might be one-handed and must land on one side of the chest or the other, or to either shoulder area, guiding the defensive player against their will in a direction they don't want to go.

For those who watch football, you've heard the term "man in motion" used repeatedly by the announcers/commentators. Ever wonder why a wide receiver, for instance, runs pre-snap along the line of scrimmage from one side of the formation to the other? One purpose is to determine the defense's intent. If a defender follows the wide receiver across the field, then schematically the defense is probably in a man-to-man coverage. Lack of movement would suggest a zone coverage, in which defensive backs cover a specific area on the field. With this knowledge the quarterback will either run the play called or audible to an alternative play.

How'd I learn this? I read an article by a former NFL lineman entitled *Learn How to Watch an NFL Game Like an Expert* (https://tinyurl.com/4cahxwcr). That former lineman was none other than Geoffrey. He described, in ample detail, assisted by film clips, some of the questions a viewer might have. However, the five sections he addressed are just a drop in the proverbial bucket.

Imagine this for a moment. You are a baseball player, on the mound preparing to make your next pitch. The catcher fingers the sign. You nod in approval. From that point on, nothing changes. The pitch is thrown as called by the catcher. Or it better be. Crossing up the catcher by throwing a curve rather than a fastball will only lead to trouble. Both catcher and pitcher must be on the same page from the moment the pitch is confirmed.

Now imagine you're an offensive lineman. Your quarterback has just called a play. (Keep in mind that in today's world of football, the play call was made by the offensive coordinator or head coach and relayed to the QB through a speaker built into the helmet. Decades ago, QBs generally called their own plays.) You break the huddle and trot to the line of scrimmage. As opposed to the pitcher, who will do nothing different than what was called by the catcher, the offensive line's choreography is just beginning. They need to scan the defense. Is the linebacker, who they may need to block, in the position they initially anticipated? Has the safety cheated closer to the line of scrimmage than expected? Has the defensive end positioned himself further outside the tackle along the line of scrimmage?

It's a chess game of major proportions, more resembling the three-tiered version that my favorite, pointed-ear Vulcan, Mr. Spock of *Star Trek* fame, exposed. It's said that an individual who plays the three-level version of chess has a "higher order of understanding and mastery of the system" beyond the comprehension of their peers.

Based on what I've learned over the years, I firmly believe that some position groups are more akin to the three-tiered chess players. Besides the quarterback, the offensive line must master much more information than anyone else on the field and must apply their knowledge instantaneously and continuously, from pre-snap almost to a play's conclusion. The constant need to modify and adapt their actions is, to me, a perfect real-world example of the Third Law of Motion from Sir Isaac Newton (one of the greatest mathematicians, physicists and scientists of all time): "For every action, there is an equal and opposite reaction." Offensive linemen *must* continuously adjust.

To see this in action, not only watch a game but also listen intently. Take note of the center as he positions himself over the ball. With one hand on the ball, he will, with his free hand, point toward the defense and yell out a number. It's not just a random number. It's the jersey number of the middle linebacker, otherwise known as the "Mike" linebacker. The offensive line blocking scheme is predicated on the positioning of the Mike. If not where expected, blocking schemes will need to be adjusted. (The weak side, meaning the side opposite the tight end, is referred to as the "Will" linebacker, while the strong side LB, on the tight end side, is known as the "Sam" linebacker.)

Have you ever seen an offensive lineman slap his backside pre-snap while on the line of scrimmage? I can assure you he's not shooing away a nagging creepy-crawly. They have seen something in the alignment of the defense that might necessitate an adjustment in blocking requirements for the running back. The slap brings this to the attention of the running back and, maybe more importantly, also to the quarterback.

While watching future Hall of Fame quarterback Peyton Manning it was almost impossible not to hear him barking out the word "Omaha" as he scanned the defense pre-snap. Viewers have scratched their heads wondering the exact meaning of "Omaha." One year after his retirement, Manning came clean.

"Omaha was just an indicator word. It was a trigger word that meant we had changed the play, there was low time on the clock and the ball needed to be snapped right now to kind of let my offensive lineman know that 'Hey, we'd gone to Plan B, there's low time on the clock.' It's a rhythmic three-syllable word, 'O-ma-ha, set hut.'"

Last second, time running out, and the play is changed. Nanoseconds for the offensive line to make their mental and physical adjustments. Tell me it doesn't take a special person and an elite level of intellect to execute.

When It Gets Loud

Here's one last example of the discipline necessary to play the game of football. I've been in several stadiums where I was hard-pressed to hear the person next to me. That's how deafeningly loud some of these stadiums are. Imagine being on the field that day in Arrowhead Stadium when the decibel level reached a record level of 142. To put that into perspective, jet planes measure between 120 and 140 decibels. (Any sound above 85 has the potential to cause hearing damage, especially with prolonged exposure.)

In this environment, there's absolutely no way a quarterback can yell loud enough at the line of scrimmage for his team to hear the snap count. What's a team to do? Shift to a silent count, like is done routinely in Seattle. Not a word is spoken. The timing of the snap is based on a movement from an interior lineman, such as a head bob from the center or the guard tapping the center. This orchestrated dance is done with such proficiency that illegal motion penalties are few and far between.

Masterminds and Other Delights

The preceding has provided but a minimal sampling of the complexities involved in playing football, especially from an offensive lineman's perspective. This is a sport that requires a collection of the best minds to achieve success on the field.

Speaking of best minds. Not only do those outside the sport have an appetite to learn, so do those who play the game. Geoffrey's high school teammate, and one of his besties, has become the recognized guru for training offensive linemen. His accession is a source of great pride for Livie and me, as we have gotten to know Duke Manyweather very well. Duke was one of the few with whom I spoke to/texted during games involving the boys. "Was that G's fault?" and Duke would explain, in some detail, why it was or was not. He was my football professor.

Believing that there's an appetite for learning and a want to be better, Duke created *OL Masterminds*. With a modest kickoff of twenty-seven people in 2018, the three-day 2024 summit, held in Texas, had grown to over 325 attendees. It features current NFL linemen and dozens of top-tier college prospects, along with coaches and former offensive linemen, some of whom are in the Hall of Fame. I believe Geoffrey has attended all but one of these gatherings, offering his insights, and has worked with Duke behind the scenes in the development of the program. Mitchell has also been in attendance a couple of times to provide his wealth of knowledge.

The main purpose of the event is to assemble the best and brightest, upcoming rookies and veterans, of this position group to share their secrets, discuss their preparation and together watch film of the best pass rushers in the league. Imagine that. These guys play for different teams. On Sundays they are competitors. However, for the days together at this summit, they forget about what separates them. Instead, through fellowship and a desire to "pay it forward," they give of their time to learn and teach, both for self-improvement and team advancement.

Post career, both Mitchell and Geoffrey have taken to analyzing offensive line play and are apparently doing well.

- "Schwartz is so good at analysis. I love the way he breaks things down with no need for hype or hyperbole."
- "Love this breakdown of Outside Zone. If you're looking to learn a little O-line play this is a MUST WATCH."

Both guys use their Twitter accounts to comment and break down plays. They offer great detail explaining a play from the perspective of both sides of the ball, pinpointing the rights and wrongs, but always in a way that is uncomplicated to those thirsting to learn. Humorously, Geoffrey has come up with a unique method for focusing one's attention. Instead of using a standard laser pointer, which he claims "are useless on computer screens," he employs the handle-end of a spoon to guide a viewer's attention. I have routinely suggested that he locate a utensil manufacturer or supplier for an endorsement opportunity, but that apparently has not gained any traction.

In addition to using Twitter as a vehicle of learning, both guys actively appear on podcasts or are interviewed for their football insights. Mitchell, since his retirement, has routinely been a guest on *The Athletic Football Show* hosted by Robert Mays, where Robert picks his brain about all things NFL football. Geoffrey, on the other hand, hosts his own podcast, *Geoff Schwartz Is Smarter Than You*, attempting to make his listeners smarter football spectators. The podcast drops once a week but then expands to two or three times per week during the season.

Truth be told, when I first heard the podcast title, I was rather shocked. I have adopted the Barry Sanders approach to success and tried to convey the same to Geoffrey and Mitchell. Sanders, a former Detroit Lion and Hall of Famer, and considered one of the best running backs ever to lace up cleats, after scoring a touchdown, would give the ball to the referee, and then head to the sidelines. No dancing. No gyrations. No boasting. He didn't even flip the ball to the ref. Just a simple handoff. Crossing the goal line is what he got paid to do, right?

I believe my efforts to instill modesty in the guys was successful. They both played their careers humbly. Attention was not their aim. Yet here was this seemingly boastful title. But then I started listening. The content wasn't about Geoffrey at all. I learned about the game. With over 350 episodes in the can, I trust that others have become smarter as well. While Geoffrey is no savant, there are times when his football intelligence really shines.

Take the unusual hiatus that former Tampa Bay Buccaneers' quarterback Tom Brady took during training camp leading up to the 2022 season. After two weeks of camp, it was announced that Brady was taking a break. Highly unusual. It was not medically related but rather he would be dealing "with some personal things." Speculation ran rampant.

On his podcast, his daily *Pac-12 Today* Sirius radio show and during several interviews, Geoffrey offered his perspective. He believed the absence was nothing more than keeping a promise. After concluding the preceding season, Brady announced his retirement. Then he reversed course and committed to return in 2022. Geoffrey believed that with the retirement announcement came a promise by Brady to his wife that the family would take a vacation during August, because now they could.

After returning to camp, the speculation was put to rest. Numerous sources reported that Brady's absence was indeed tied to a previously planned vacation in the Bahamas to be with family.

With as much objectivity as I can muster, I am convinced that offensive linemen are very bright individuals and see the game through a broad lens. So explain this: Why do football telecasts not include an o-lineman as part of the broadcast team rather than field goal kickers? Kickers are on the field for maybe an average of six plays a game. And all they need to know is how to toe the ball through the goalposts. Yet they are featured. How about an offensive lineman? Would I love to see Geoffrey or Mitchell assume such a position? Sure, but any o-lineman, in my opinion, would be a huge upgrade over a place kicker. As I've attempted to address in this chapter, beside the QBs, offensive linemen have the best grasp of the overall game of football. Networks, are you listening?

Before putting this chapter to bed, let me offer a story that, I believe, demonstrates my progress toward understanding the game of football and possibly the prejudices that exist in favor of the more well-known stars in the NFL.

I so clearly remember the night Mitchell and K.C. faced the Denver Broncos in a Sunday night game televised on NBC. Chris Collinsworth was the commentator. Mitchell was lined up against Von Miller. A screen pass was called. Mitchell's role was to take Miller up field and beyond the quarterback so the pass could be thrown in the area he vacated. The Broncos sniffed out the play and moved a defender toward the intended receiver. That caused QB Patrick Mahomes to abort the play. He began scrambling, to his comfortable right side. And who was waiting there?

Von Miller chased after Mahomes. The pass was thrown away as a result. And then Collinsworth started his rant, giving all the credit to Miller for being in position and destroying the play. Really? Chris, you played the game. You know that the right tackle's role was to push Miller up field on a screen pass. Yet you were effusive in praise for Miller while laying blame upon Mitchell for being derelict in his protection. I came unglued, screaming at the tube. I knew better...and had never played the game. If someone who laced 'em up for eight seasons can't accurately describe the play and the inherent responsibilities, then who can.

The bottom line in all of this? Football players are not "dummies." On the contrary, as a whole, they are bright people who are also athletically gifted. Brains *and* brawn. The combination of the two makes them very special individuals. Maybe it's us uninitiated who are more deserving of the moniker.

14
"DO YOU CELEBRATE THANKSGIVING?"—SPORTS AND BEING JEWISH

Mitchell and Geoffrey were brought up in a Jewish household in a part of Los Angeles highly populated with Jews. West L.A., the neighboring cities of Santa Monica and Beverly Hills, plus the Pico Robertson area, are densely Jewish. The boys at two years old were enrolled in a pre-school on the campus of our local synagogue. So being around Jews and immersed in Jewish culture has always been part of the fabric of their lives.

The world in general though, as we know, finds Jews in the minority. We only represent 2.4 percent of the United States population as of 2020. As confirmation of the concentration in Los Angeles, 17.5 percent of the L.A. metro population are Jews. The specific areas I mentioned above are even more densely populated with Jews.

When the boys were younger, if the Jewish High Holidays of Rosh Hashanah, the New Year, or Yom Kippur, the Day of Atonement and the holiest day of the Jewish calendar, fell on a school day, the boys missed school so the family could be together in synagogue. Eventually though, maybe about the time they entered high school, the L.A. School District decided to close school on the Jewish holidays. Student absences were high and apparently a consequential number of teachers were observing the holidays. There weren't enough to staff classes.

I'm happy to share that neither Geoffrey nor Mitchell experienced any direct, obvious antisemitism growing up. Livie and I are extremely thankful for that. Apparently, as a Little Leaguer, I experienced some religious bias, at least according to my father. He claimed I was once excluded from an all-star team because the commissioner of the league was antisemitic. I never quite bought into that view, but my father was convinced. I think it was rather my father's baggage. He, and my mother, based on their experiences growing up in New York with parents who emigrated from Europe in the early twentieth century, lived with a ghetto mentality. I cannot recall them ever socializing with anyone not Jewish. Fortunately, I did not carry this bias forward.

The boys attended Jewish pre-school and Hebrew school, and both were called to the Torah as a Bar Mitzvah. They have a strong Jewish identity. To my knowledge they never had an issue when required to miss school or were unable to play ball because of the High Holidays, although I'd bet my bottom dollar that they were far more disappointed by the latter. So when it came time for them to leave the roost for college, Livie and I wondered how they would fare outside of their cocoon, and wondered if being on their own would, in any way, cause them to be less connected to their Jewishness.

During Geoffrey's recruiting process, it was made clear to all coaches of the possibility of conflict with football games falling on a Jewish Holiday. The offensive line coach for the Oregon Ducks, Neal Zoumboukos, was especially sensitive to this. He was a devoted, practicing Greek Orthodox. He declared that the team, if Geoffrey were to choose the Ducks, would be respectful of his beliefs and work with him if playing on a holiday would be problematic. That declaration was put to the test his very first season.

Yom Kippur fell on a Saturday during the fall of 2004. Recognizing that to be the case, Geoffrey approached Coach early in the week leading up to the game and told him that he couldn't play that Saturday. Coach approved Geoffrey's absence. We were later told about the "behind the scenes" conversation that took place between Coach Z. and Oregon's head coach Mike Bellotti. Frankly, a head scratcher for me.

Geoffrey's absence needed to be signed off on by Bellotti. Thankfully he did so without hesitation. However, let's look at the broader picture. It was Geoffrey's first season. He was a bench warmer at the time. So giving him the day off was no sweat off of anyone's back. The team wasn't going to miss him, and Geoffrey could observe the holiday without missing any playing time.

"Do You Celebrate Thanksgiving?"—Sports and Being Jewish

I do wonder to this day what might have been said, how the decision might have been different, if Geoffrey was a starter and more integral to the team. But that's not the head scratcher. That moment arose when Coach Bellotti asked Coach Z., "Does this happen every year?" Surprising to me that a coach of a major D1 college football program was so unaware that the Jewish holidays shift year to year. (The Jewish calendar is lunar based, not solar.)

In 2007, Geoffrey's senior season, we had another instance when Yom Kippur conflicted with one of his games. It was to be a 7 p.m. kickoff on the day of Yom Kippur. He approached Livie and me with a strategy for the day. "How about I fast until game time (fasting begins no later than sundown the night before and concludes at sundown on the day of the holiday)," he offers, "and then play?" WHAT?!? Did we hear you correctly? You want to starve your body for twenty-plus hours and then place extreme stress and strain on your personal temple by playing? NO! Not a chance! Not going to happen. By this time in his life, he was a twenty-one-year-old adult, making his own decisions. However, in this particular case, Mom and Dad couldn't remain silent. He didn't fast that day and suited up that night.

This was always a struggle for the boys. How should they handle the scheduling conflict, being true to their religious upbringing while also satisfying their commitment to their team? It wasn't always easy.

Koufax, Drysdale and Geoffrey

If you are a baseball fan of a more mature generation, you might remember the story of Sandy Koufax, who is Jewish. He was a pitcher for the Los Angeles Dodgers from 1955 through 1966. To say he was great is to dramatically understate his contributions to his team and to baseball as a whole. He ultimately became the youngest player ever selected to the Baseball Hall of Fame. In my book, none better.

The year 1965 found the Dodgers in the World Series against the Minnesota Twins. The first game of the series fell on Yom Kippur. Normally, Koufax would have been on the mound that first night; however, because it was the holiest day of the Jewish year, he chose to forego the start to observe the holiday. I was ten years old back then and can remember, like it was yesterday, falling in love with Koufax—remember I'm a dyed-in-the-wool San Francisco Giants fan—because of his conviction to his Judaism.

Raising Giants

This story has been a shining example passed along from one Jewish generation to the next ever since.

Now, as an adult, I still very much appreciate Koufax's devotion to his Judaism; however I'm now more keenly aware of some of the realities related to this situation. Koufax was the best of the best. No manager or organization would dare tell him he had to pitch. The World Series is a four-game minimum, potentially a seven-game affair. If Koufax misses the first game, the next contest is the following day. While in baseball there are games on consecutive days, in football it's but once a week. Missing just one game a year of the seventeen scheduled means a player loses out on 6 percent of the season. And then there's the potential to lose one's starting position.

We learned about that firsthand with Geoffrey. During his one year in Kansas City, he began the season on second string. An injury around game four or five to a starter on the line gave Geoffrey a chance. He never surrendered the starting role the rest of the season, even when, several games later, the starter was healthy enough to return. It is somewhat of an unwritten rule in football that starters return to the lineup once healthy. The fact that Geoffrey retained his starting status clearly spoke to how well he was playing. And that nine-game (or so) stretch is what ultimately earned him his big contract with the New York Giants the following season.

So there is danger missing a football game, for any reason. A player may never regain their first-string status. Skipping a game could be construed by coaches and ownership as not being committed to the team, the organization. That could have a huge impact on longevity with a team as the roster is reevaluated each year. This particular time it worked to Geoffrey's benefit. But there's no guarantee that at another time an absence could have altered the course of Geoffrey's and/or Mitchell's careers.

Back to the Koufax situation for a bit of levity. He did not pitch that first game. Instead, Don Drysdale took the mound. Statistically speaking, Drysdale was only the second-best pitcher in baseball in 1965. So, really, the Dodgers shouldn't have skipped a beat. Let's compare that with football. If Mitchell or Geoffrey were to miss a game, their replacement would be less talented. Whereas the Dodgers were basically replacing one first-string pitcher with another, the boys' football teams would have replaced them with a true second-stringer.

"Do You Celebrate Thanksgiving?"—Sports and Being Jewish

And there's this additional factor: Baseball is much more an individual sport than football. Replacing Koufax with Drysdale would not impact anyone else on the field. However, replacing just one offensive lineman will create the distinct possibility that the chemistry along the entire line is damaged. The linemen work in concert with one another on every play. All it takes is one wrong move by one player and a quarterback is sacked or a running back is tackled behind the line of scrimmage.

So Drysdale replaces Koufax, and he blows up. Maybe his worst outing of the season. Dodger manager Walter Alston is forced to make a pitching change. He slowly walks to the mound to lift Drysdale. Once on the hill, as the story goes, Drysdale looks at Alston and, with the most serious face he could muster, says to Alston, "Bet you wish I was Jewish." Every time I hear that story, I split a gut laughing.

To conclude the Koufax story, and to add some important context, the Dodgers not only lost the first game but also went down in defeat to the Twins in game two with Koufax on the mound. Yet the Dodgers came back and won the series, thanks to none other than Sandy Koufax, who pitched and won game five and then, with only two days of rest, and with an ailing, arthritic elbow, was the victorious pitcher in the clinching game seven. A win-win scenario. Koufax was able to observe the High Holy Day and the Dodgers were able to hoist the championship trophy.

The Rabbi's Gripe

Sandy Koufax, by skipping that first Series game, provided such positive inspiration for Jewish kids, like me, and Jewish families. It emboldened Jews to be more comfortable with their religion and religious choices. His action garnered national attention. However, inadvertently, he also placed some pressure on youngsters and others wishing to follow in his footsteps.

Geoffrey experienced that firsthand. It was his second year with the New York Giants. The schedule published in April showed the Giants playing on a Sunday night against the Dallas Cowboys. It was Erev Rosh Hashanah ("Erev" is the Hebrew word for "evening before" a Jewish holiday). It being New York, with the obvious concentration of Jews living in the area, it didn't take long for Geoffrey to be asked by the press about playing that evening. He affirmed he would, for many of the reasons I outlined in the preceding paragraphs.

Then one day in May, before the season, I received a Google Alert. Opening the link, I see a letter entitled, "An open letter to NY Giant Geoff Schwartz," authored by a Rabbi from the New Jersey area. The first paragraph ends with "I have to admit that I was a bit crestfallen" when he learned of Geoffrey's plans to play. He went on to bring up Sandy Koufax, writing, "I was hoping for another Sandy Koufax-like headline that I could show to my kids."

This pulpit-less Rabbi decided to take Geoffrey to task for his decision. That didn't sit well with me. For the first and only time related to a negative article about my sons, I reacted and reached out. I had gotten to know a sports reporter in the Jersey area. I explained what had happened and asked if he could help me locate an email address for this Rabbi. He was kind enough to help and found me an address. I reached out to the Rabbi. We talked. He ultimately made a few changes to the online letter but left most of the content intact, including a most fundamentally absurd suggestion.

He compared this situation to one involving the late, great football coach and commentator John Madden. Madden became famous for his turducken on his Thanksgiving Day telecast and for handing out a turkey leg to the game's most valuable player. To quote verbatim, this Rabbi thought it would be "great...if during a national broadcast the players might take a break from their bitter rivalry to dip apples and honey and wish their Jewish fans" a happy holiday. The Rabbi offered to "send a crate of apples and some local honey." What? Seriously?

When Geoffrey first arrived in the NFL, I believe there were a total of eleven Jews on NFL rosters. During Mitchell's time that number dwindled to five. (At the time of this publication, there were ten Jewish owners in the league.) And all of those players weren't Jewish in the biblical sense. For most branches of Judaism, one is officially Jewish only if born of a Jewish mother. The father has no bearing. I know that of the original eleven, some were not born to Jewish mothers but rather had Jewish fathers. Some had not had a Bar Mitzvah. And one, who was a teammate of Geoffrey's at one point, said neither parent was Jewish, but he was listed because his name sounded like he was. Apparently, those keeping track of these statistics were eager to bloat the numbers.

When the boys played there were fifty-three guys allowed each week on game day rosters. Forty-six were eligible to dress out and were considered active. Let's do some quick math. Using the full fifty-three times thirty-two teams equals 1,696 total players in the league. Using the high-water mark of eleven Jews in the league at one time, that translates to 0.6 percent of the entire league. Look carefully. See the decimal point preceding the "6?" We're talking about less than 1 percent. Geoffrey was the only Jewish player on the Giants. (His owner was one of the eleven Jewish owners at the time.)

Just for a moment consider how outlandish the apples and honey suggestion truly was. A team was to disrupt their regular pregame, halftime or postgame routine, or a TV broadcast was to be interrupted to insert a segment meaningful only to Jews, for such a disproportional audience? It was simply never going to happen. Not because of any religious bias but because it wasn't practical.

That letter, to me, could have painted Geoffrey in a negative light. Maybe it did to a few, but I doubt it had that effect on the masses. It did, alternatively, display the ignorance of this Rabbi who, in my opinion, was looking to gild his own lily, seeking a broader social media audience. The letter also served to corroborate my thoughts about how the Sandy Koufax decision back in 1965 still echoes today and how, if taken out of context, it can trigger some unrealistic expectations and give license for some to judge others who might not align with their religious practices.

Honoring Their Religion

Sadly, the Rabbi spent no time seeking to uncover all the examples of how Geoffrey, specifically, since the article was addressed to him, and Mitchell, have honored their religion, given of their time and become role models to the next generation of Jewish youth. Following are some of those activities.

- **Chai Lifeline.** In 2015, Geoffrey and Mitchell were honored by Chai Lifeline. As we have learned, this remarkable organization was founded in 1987 to "help families with children battling a deadly disease." As a way of giving back and showing their appreciation for the honor, Mitchell and Geoffrey have returned to Los Angeles several times to interact with the children, their families and their siblings. They answered questions from these newly minted wide-eyed fans. They threw Nerf footballs around the gym with the boys and girls. During the time spent, all that ailed these families seemed to melt away. Very, very heartwarming to see the smiles of joy on the faces of the kids and their parents. Chai offers the children within their program a chance to attend a camp in New York State's scenic Catskill Mountains. Known as Camp Simcha (Simcha is a Hebrew word that means "gladness" or "joy"), it was created "to bring childhood back to children who lost it when they were diagnosed with their serious illness." Geoffrey was invited to spend a day at one of these camps. It was an extraordinary day for him, in which he was able to fully engage with the kids.

- **Sunday School appearances in Kansas City.** During Geoffrey's one year in Kansas City he was invited to attend a gathering of Sunday School classes at a local synagogue. Several years later, during Mitchell's time with the Chiefs, he was invited to the same synagogue. Both spoke about being Jewish and playing in the NFL, especially for the Chiefs. The kids, dressed in K.C. red and yellow, gathered around their local heroes, presenting the guys with colorful posters adorned with their names and jersey numbers. The photos memorializing the events displayed the sheer joy of those in attendance, from the kids to their parents.
- **High Holidays in other cities.** The Jewish High Holidays seemed to land on an NFL game day more times than I would have thought throughout the boys' careers. When that did occur, and when Geoffrey could break away from team activities, he would find a local synagogue and attend services on the day preceding a game. As would Livie and I. We attended services in Charlotte, North Carolina; Reno, Nevada; Minneapolis, Minnesota; Dallas, Texas; and Paramus, New Jersey. If Geoffrey was able to join us, he would. It was a fascinating experience. Although we were in cities far from our home synagogue, once we walked through the doors, although architecturally different, we felt so at home. We learned that there exists a very comforting familiarity synagogue to synagogue, regardless of location.
- **Sharing holidays.** Geoffrey is always ready for a good conversation. He enjoyed talking religion with his non-Jewish teammates to learn about their practices and to be able to share his beliefs. To help advance that dialogue and exploration, Geoffrey and Meridith would occasionally invite teammates and their families to their home for Passover Seder, or to break the Yom Kippur fast.
- **Celebrating Chanukah.** Chanukah always takes place during football season. When the team played in another city, Geoffrey

was known to "smuggle" a menorah and candles into the hotel—something I'm sure the hotel staff would have frowned upon—and invite his teammates and staff to his room for the candle-lighting ceremony. Mitchell, on the other hand, was known to bring a menorah into the locker room. Great ways for the guys to bond with their buddies. During his stops in Cleveland and Kansas City, Mitchell was invited by local synagogues to attend public lighting of candles during the eight-day period of Chanukah. In his warm overcoat and trading his football helmet for a kippa (skull cap), we enjoyed seeing him pictured with the youngsters thrilled to engage with their local Jewish sports hero.

- **Speaking to Holocaust survivors.** The Holocaust may be the single most gruesome event in the history of mankind. Certainly in the annals of Jewish history. Over six million lives needlessly and criminally taken during World War II. In 2015, there were over twenty living Holocaust survivors in the greater Mercer County of New Jersey (home of Princeton University) area. To recognize the extraordinary heroism of these survivors and their lifetime of accomplishments, the Jewish Family and Children's Service (JFCS) of Greater Mercer County planned a gala. Because he was "very clear and outspoken about his Judaism," Geoffrey was invited to be the celebrity guest for this special event. Interviewed at some point after his appearance, Geoffrey shared how "unbelievable" it was to "see these people, their strength and will." The Executive Director of the JFCS said of Geoffrey, "he brought the event to an exciting new level and continued the theme of heritage paving the way for the future."

- **A chance meeting at the NFL Hall of Fame.** One day during Mitchell's time in Cleveland, he visited the NFL Hall of Fame in Canton, Ohio. As he walked to the front entrance, he spotted a group of teenagers. They happened to be observant Jews, all of them wearing kippas on their heads. As Mitchell approached, one of the boys glanced his way and recognized him. It caused a stir. They became giddy and began peppering him with questions. It's moments like these when the boys realize how much of a role model they are to Jewish youth, regardless of whether the youngsters play sports or not.

Standing Up Against Antisemitism

I mentioned earlier in the chapter how my father claimed I was the subject of an overt act of antisemitism. Geoffrey was involved in an incident which could lead one to the same conclusion.

College football officially begins each year with a summer camp to prepare the team for the rigors of their upcoming season. It's a grueling several weeks. As camp ends, to mark the transition between camp and the official start of season practices, teams traditionally schedule something akin to an amateur night, where the incoming freshmen are expected to perform. They sing. Usually not that well. They sometimes dance. Some have moves. They prepare skits. Typically, these are done at the expense of the coaches. And then there are the neophyte comedians.

During Geoffrey's senior season, a freshman lineman walked to the microphone. For some background, the player was from a city in the deep south with a population a touch above 18,000 according to a 2010 census. The town had no Jews according to the census. In the entire state of Georgia, Jews only represent 0.4 percent of the total population.

His joke that night had to do with Adolf Hitler and the concentration camps. He dared to mention Geoffrey in connection with the ovens that killed the Jews in these camps. There is *never* a time or place when this topic is funny. In any context. NEVER! As the words rolled out of his mouth, one could hear an audible rumble through the room. The players and coaches were aghast. Like owls, heads swiveled in Geoffrey's direction. Coach Z. came running over to Geoffrey out of concern.

Of course, Geoffrey couldn't, and didn't, let this go unaddressed. He approached his teammate and basically said, "Bro, that wasn't cool," and explained why. The teammate claimed he was clueless, that he had no idea the joke, or anything related to Hitler, was offensive. They talked it through. Geoffrey has told us that this teammate never made another inappropriate comment or joke.

Geoffrey accepted his teammate's explanation and moved on, although his Mom will tell you that she's hardly ever heard such distress in his voice as the day he called to share this story with us. Is it possible that this teammate was so oblivious to one of history's worst events? Some with whom I've shared this story believe it's impossible. "Wasn't this taught in school?" they would counter. Since I personally have no clue if, or how, this subject is taught in Georgia schools, I'm in no position to render a judgment on that specifically. His being so insensitive might be more the result of his upbringing and/or the influences surrounding him while growing up rather than what was learned, or not, in school.

This experience for Geoffrey somewhat repeated itself years later. DeSean Jackson, an NFL wide receiver at the time for the Philadelphia Eagles shared antisemitic quotes attributed to Adolf Hitler on Jackson's Instagram page over the July 4th weekend in 2020. (I will not get into the nitty-gritty details of what took place. If you wish to learn more, you're welcome to research the event yourself.) You can imagine the uproar that it caused in the Jewish community. Geoffrey was one of the first to tweet his thoughts about Jackson's highly controversial and, by all accounts, completely inaccurate posts. For Geoffrey, it was déjà vu. Jackson, like the Oregon freshman, claimed innocence for the insensitivity.

However, this case was a bit harder to swallow. Jackson grew up in Southern California, attending a high school in Long Beach. Upon graduation he attended the University of California, Berkeley on a football scholarship. It's rather hard to accept, from my perspective, that Jackson could have been so clueless having attended these academic institutions, but that was his contention, just like Geoffrey's teammate. Geoffrey and Mitchell both denounced Jackson for his tweets. Mitchell appeared on CNN, interviewed by host Don Lemon, to share his thoughts on the controversy.

But Geoffrey, while denouncing the comments, also offered his opinions through the lens of his college experience. He gave Jackson a bit of latitude, even though that elicited some negative commentary aimed at Geoffrey. How could he give Jackson any type of pass? Similar to Geoffrey's teammate, Jackson apologized. He put actions behind his words. It was reported that soon thereafter Jackson met with a group formed to fight antisemitism and spent time with a ninety-four-year-old Holocaust survivor, attempting to educate himself further. The survivor subsequently invited Jackson to visit one of the former concentration camps in Germany. I'm not sure if he ever made the trip.

Livie and I were so proud of the boys for standing up against antisemitism and making their feelings about religious intolerance known. Personally, I was also super proud of Geoffrey for not being so absolute in his reaction. He could have castigated Jackson, showing no mercy for his truly thoughtless and irresponsible posts. Instead, he allowed his personal experience from college to shape his reaction and demonstrate some tolerance for others with different ways of thinking.

Geoffrey has always been open to engaging his non-Jewish teammates in religious conversations. The intent was not to proselytize or attempt to convert anyone to Judaism, but rather to learn. Geoffrey has numerous times shared with us personally, shared with his radio listeners and shared in his written material how frustrated he is by the inability in today's world for people with different beliefs to engage in conversation about potentially highly charged subjects, particularly when it comes to politics and religion. Just look to Washington, D.C. as proof positive that an aisle can prevent mature adults, owning different opinions, from engaging in rational, sensible and balanced discourse.

Passing It On

Livie and I have often spoken about passing the torch of our Jewish faith from one generation to the next. We tried our best to do so with our offspring. I think we fared well. The question for us then became, "What will happen when, G-d willing, Mitchell and Geoffrey have children?"

Geoffrey met Meridith a few weeks after first arriving in Charlotte. Their relationship moved along very quickly. In short order Geoffrey had the idea that Meridith could be the one. (Meridith was Geoffrey's first real relationship. Interestingly, Livie was my first.) It might have been as early as their second date when Geoffrey engaged Mer in a conversation about the future.

Meridith is not Jewish. Geoffrey explained that raising his children in a Jewish home was vitally important to him and that, if their relationship were to continue, he needed to know that she would be willing to raise their children Jewish. Mer didn't hesitate for a moment. If indeed their relationship progressed to marriage, the kids would be brought up in a Jewish household. And she's been good to her word ever since.

Both kids were enrolled in daycare at the local Jewish Community Center since they were three years old. Upon entry into elementary school, they both attended Sunday School at the local synagogue. They observe all of the Jewish holidays. The kids from time to time attend Friday night and Saturday morning services. Friday night in their house sees Geoffrey, Mer and the kids lighting the Shabbat candles and offering traditional blessings over bread and wine. Livie affectionately jokes that her Southern daughter-in-law is a better Hebrew speaker than she is, a lifelong Jew.

As I mentioned elsewhere in the book, to be recognized as Jewish one's mother needs to be Jewish. Of course, that wasn't the case in Geoffrey's family. But there is a remedy. A conversion. Under Jewish law, the kids could be immersed in a bath, known as a mikveh, as part of the conversion process. And that's what happened. Geoffrey joined them in the bath at their synagogue. The appropriate blessings were offered. Upon exiting the mikveh, Alex and Emmy were Jewish in the eyes of their religion.

The Chanukah Bush

As Jewishly oriented as the family is, there's one non-Jewish practice that Meridith holds on to. It has no religious connotation. It's purely symbolic. Us Jews respectfully refer to it as a Chanukah Bush.

I became fed up with spending Thanksgiving in Los Angeles, where temperatures hovered around seventy to seventy-five degrees. That's simply not holiday weather to me. So, to rectify the situation, beginning in 2016, Livie and I have visited Charlotte for Turkey Day. (Sometimes our extended stay allows us to celebrate Chanukah while in North Carolina. An added benefit.) And a family tradition has been established.

Livie and I typically arrive days before Thanksgiving. Wednesday night, Thanksgiving eve, the entire family piles into a couple of cars headed to dinner at Geoffrey and Meridith's favorite sushi restaurant. Once gorged, we jump back into our vehicles for the next stop—a local Christmas tree lot. That's right. It initially felt like I was in a foreign country. In six-plus decades of life leading up to this newfound practice, I had never stepped into such a place.

Now it's an annual ritual and, truth be told, it's fun. The smell of the pines is refreshing. To see the excitement on the faces of Alex and Emmy is delightful. We've gotten to know the owners, who are very cordial and welcoming. After wandering the lot, sometimes repeatedly, Meridith picks out her tree. Because their house will allow, the selected tree is ten to eleven feet tall and maybe six feet wide at its base. It takes four of the lot's staff to load the tree onto the bed of Geoffrey's truck.

Next stop, home. While it took four strapping guys to load the tree onto the truck, getting it into the house rests with just Geoffrey and me. We've developed our routine to schlep that monstrous tree from the front driveway, along the walkway leading to the house, up the three steps to the front porch, and then through the double doors opened to the max. From there we secure the tree stand and wrestle with the tree until it's standing tall, making sure it won't topple. All this completed without breaking our backs. And then the real fun begins.

Meridith scurries around the house gathering all the stored Christmas tree decorations. In boxes of various shapes and sizes, the collection is spread around the base of the tree. With the help of the kids, Meridith begins the joyful process of decorating the tree with lights, tinsel and ornaments. In Meridith's world, it all needs to be completed before she goes to bed. And it always is.

There's one more piece to this story, which may validate that the Christmas tree is purely ceremonial to Meridith. From what I understand, trees are often not removed from households until at least New Year's Day. In the Geoffrey Schwartz home, that's a week too late. Christmas morning, after the last of the gifts are distributed, will find Meridith removing all decorations and, by her lonesome, dragging the tree out the door to the curb. Yes, Meridith by herself. The Grinch has surfaced. She's done with it. Geoffrey now regularly tweets a video of Meridith hauling the tree to the front curb. It has become a highly anticipated annual rite of passage for his tens of thousands of Twitter followers. "Savage," they say.

"Will You Convert?" and Other Awkward Moments

Through his engagement with teammates, Geoffrey has received inquiries about his willingness to convert from Judaism. Most were innocuous, but one was rather egregious. One day during his time with the Giants, Geoffrey and a teammate, while having a meal in the cafeteria, got into a conversation about religion. As the exchange continued, the teammate asked Geoffrey if he'd be willing to convert to Christianity. "No," was Geoffrey's immediate response. But that wasn't satisfactory for the teammate. A follow-up question by this insistent teammate inquired about having my grandson converted. What? When Geoffrey, once again, rather emphatically, replied, "NO," the teammate suggested that Geoffrey and his family would, by not converting, be sent to the underworld at the end of their lives. Geoffrey had had enough. He picked up his food and walked away.

Fortunately, this was an isolated incident and, I believe, the most grievous display of religious insensitivity that Geoffrey ever faced. I am pleased to report that he and Mitchell have had many more positive experiences, including some that I would describe as lighthearted, maybe even comical.

"Do You Celebrate Thanksgiving?"—Sports and Being Jewish

The first story that comes to mind occurred during a welcome-back gathering at our home synagogue. Our Rabbi, a huge sports fan himself, invited Mitchell and Geoffrey to visit the synagogue to spend a morning with the Sunday School children and congregants talking about being Jewish in the world of professional football. The room was full. Almost standing room only. After some opening words from Geoffrey and Mitchell, a Q & A session followed, facilitated by the Rabbi. Most questions were very thoughtful, but there was this one: "Being Jewish, how can you touch pigskin?"

Mitchell and Geoffrey were flummoxed. They weren't quite sure how to answer without embarrassing this senior gentleman. They tried evasion, but the questioner wouldn't let it go that easily. Without a response, he repeated the question. Fortunately, the Rabbi stepped in, sensing the awkward moment and, in a way that only a Rabbi could, deflected the conversation in another direction. A direct answer was never offered. It was an uncomfortable few minutes, but it didn't diminish the overall enjoyment that the audience seemed to experience during the couple of hours of give and take.

The irony of that question is that footballs are not made from pigskin. Never were. Originally the balls were made from pig bladders. Maybe that's splitting hairs. Regardless, in 1872, new rules were implemented by The Football Association requiring footballs to be "made of leather or suitable material." Cow leather is what's been used ever since.

Final word. I truly thought the question was bizarre. But maybe not so. I conducted some research and discovered that in Deuteronomy, chapter 14:8–10, it reads, "And the pig, because it has a split hoof, but does not chew the cud; it is unclean for you. You shall neither eat of their flesh nor touch their carcass." I've known about the former restriction but was clueless about the latter. So, for observant Jews, touching a football made from a pig bladder would have been restricted. You can learn something new all the time.

Years before our lives ever connected seriously with football, something interesting took place at Geoffrey's Bar Mitzvah. There comes a time in the service when the Rabbi offers a special prayer to the boy or girl being Bar/Bat Mitzvahed. This is done on the bima, a raised platform in the synagogue where the service is conducted. It was just the two of them. As the Rabbi brought Geoffrey toward the front of the bima, they faced each other. The Rabbi stopped in his tracks. We heard, "Wait a minute." The Rabbi disappeared to an adjacent anteroom, only to quickly return with a small stool in his grasp.

It wasn't very tall; however, it served the Rabbi's purpose. The stool was planted firmly on the ground in front of Geoffrey. The Rabbi ascended, steadied himself and then announced, "I will not look up to a thirteen-year-old Bar Mitzvah." The congregation broke into laughter. The Rabbi wasn't short himself, but his vanity—or attempt at humor—would just not allow Geoffrey to stand taller than him.

Lastly is the question for all times, asked of Geoffrey. He was having one of his pow-wows with a teammate about their respective religious beliefs. Apparently, the conversation swung toward holidays. In what appeared to be an honest question directed at Geoffrey, he heard, "Do you celebrate Thanksgiving?" For real? Although the question surely demonstrated a naivete and was rather absurd, Geoffrey calmly reminded this person that Thanksgiving is an American holiday, not a Jewish one.

Visiting Israel

Visiting Israel was always a bucket-list item for me. Being of such importance, Livie and I talked with the boys about making the journey a family affair. We targeted May of 2015 to celebrate my sixtieth birthday. That would have been the present of all presents to be able to share the experience with the entire family. But it wasn't meant to be. Something more joyful occurred a year earlier that made visiting Israel unattainable. A precious bundle of joy was born in July of 2014. Norman Alexander Schwartz, named after my father Norman, came into the world on July 11. Remarkably, Alex shares the same birthday with his old man.

Fortunately for Mitchell and Geoffrey, all was not lost. They found themselves headed to Israel in 2018. Organized by America's Voices in Israel, both guys and their wives were invited to join a group of five other current and former professional football players to tour the country. (As Livie and I found out one year later, when we finally made our pilgrimage to Israel, visiting the country is a moving and inspiring experience.) The guys were escorted to the usual sites like the Western Wall and Masada, and also were granted audience with the highest level of Israel's leadership. We have a picture prominently displayed on a wall in our house of Geoffrey and Mitchell flanking Prime Minister Benjamin Netanyahu as they presented him with Giants' and Chiefs' football jerseys, bearing his nickname "Bibi" above the boys' respective numbers on the back side of the jerseys.

Ten Random Facts About Being a Jewish Athlete
(Prepared by Geoffrey in 2012.)

1. Along with my brother, Mitchell, who is on the Browns, we represented more than 20 percent of the Jews in the NFL in 2012. I'm proud to be a role model to young Jewish kids and athletes, letting them know it's possible for them to reach their goals.
2. We are also the first Jewish brothers to play in the NFL since 1923.
3. No, I don't keep kosher. I love bacon, cheeseburgers, and pork chops.
4. My agent is *not* Jewish, nor is my financial adviser, but my CPA is.
5. I carry my personal Menorah and have lit Chanukah candles in the hotel rooms the night before games. Last season when in St. Louis my Jewish coach joined me for the lighting.
6. Most of my peers are knowledgeable about the religion. However, I have gotten some interesting questions, such as, "Do you celebrate Thanksgiving?" Yes, we do. It's an American holiday.
7. There is a lack of Jewish groupies. Where are all the tall Jewish blonde women?
8. *Latkes* are the most delicious treat ever, especially when homemade. If you've never had one before, head over to your local deli for some.
9. People are often shocked to learn that I don't miss Santa Claus or having a Christmas tree. How can you miss something you've never had? However ...
10. I love Christmas when it falls on a Wednesday or Thursday (our heavy workdays). It changes a full day of practice to a half day. I'm all about the Christmas spirit then!

A bit of related background regarding number two in the list. Indeed, Jewish brothers Ralph and Arnold Horween had preceded Geoffrey and Mitchell in the NFL by ninety years. Their parents immigrated to the United States with a family name of either Horwitz or Horowitz, then changed to Horween when the brothers were in their youth. To protect against antisemitism? Ashamed of their name? It seems that nobody knows for sure.

But that wasn't the last name change for Ralph and Arnold. Remember earlier in the book when I wrote about my Jewish mother preventing me from playing football? Seems like the Horweens' mother carried the same concerns. So, as the story is told, to deceive their mother, thus allowing the boys to become NFLers, the guys assumed the last name of McMahon as they entered the NFL. I guess I wasn't that smart.

The On-Air Accusation

This is a story that I've wanted to address since it took place but haven't found the right forum to do so. It's been burning a hole in my gut. Now is the time to spill the beans.

I've chosen inclusion in this chapter because to me it is tinged with antisemitic overtones, but also to me rings true of reverse racism. Let me set the foundation.

The summer of 2022 found the Los Angeles Rams conducting preseason practices with the Cincinnati Bengals. During one of the practices multiple fights broke out. One incident involved the Rams' all-star defense tackle Aaron Donald. In retaliation for a punch thrown, he removed his helmet and swung it repeatedly at one of the opposing team aggressors. The NFL is quite explicit about this type of action. Quoting from their rule book, "A player must not use a helmet that is no longer worn by anyone as a weapon to strike, swing at, or throw at an opponent." There's no question per available video that Donald swung his helmet...several times.

In response to this brawl, Geoffrey went to Twitter to express his thoughts. He wrote, "Fights happen. We know that and accept it. However, swinging a helmet is out of control and dangerous. He should be suspended." As objectively as you can assess, do you detect any racism in his comments? I can't. Yet others tried to make that connection, and did so very publicly.

"Do You Celebrate Thanksgiving?"—Sports and Being Jewish

Stephen A. Smith is a sports television personality who appears regularly on ESPN. In the days after Geoffrey posted his tweet, Stephen A. was a panelist on *First Take*, a sports talk television show appearing on ESPN. The topic of the brawl was front and center on that episode. After some preliminary comments by Smith, he launched into this diatribe about Geoffrey and his tweet. This is what Smith said:

> *When you got white analysts talking that way and using that language about Black dudes, that's another level. And that's why I appreciate RC [Ryan Clark, his fellow panelist] bringing that up. I'm not accusing any analyst of racism or anything like that, I'm just telling them how we take it. Now what I want to do, if I'm looking at whoever sent that tweet out, I forgot his name, it was Schwartz or whomever, but it doesn't matter. Whoever sent that tweet out and whoever thinks like that, now I want to see you say that about the white dude that does it. Because if I don't hear the same verbiage, if I don't hear the same language if something like that happens with somebody white, now I'm looking at you with a raised eyebrow and saying, "what the hell you trying to say?"*

Now that I've completed typing this prattle, let me take a breath before offering my retort.

First, I refer you back to my original question from above. Is there anything remotely racist about any words used by Geoffrey? NO. NOT IN THE LEAST. Granted, Smith offered, "I'm not accusing any analyst of racism," however, it was, at least to me, definitely implied, especially when beginning with "When you got white analysts talking that way..." That, again to me, sets the tone that this will be a race-colored conversation.

Why was it necessary to highlight Geoffrey's race? Oh, the answer isn't hard to come by. I believe Smith had an agenda to serve, plus, what better way to generate social media clicks?

Geoffrey doesn't have a racist bone in his body. Ask anyone who knows him. If the roles were reversed, as Stephen A. had suggested, there is *no* doubt in my mind that Geoffrey's public reaction would be identical. Did Stephen A. have the decency to call Geoffrey directly to discuss Geoffrey's comments before airing his "grievances?" You know the answer to that one. I believe it would be considered professional courtesy, which wasn't demonstrated.

Raising Giants

Let's reverse the scenario for a moment. Referring to Geoffrey simply by his last name of Schwartz, an obvious Jewish name, could be construed by some as being antisemitic. Why not refer to him by his full name? Why just his last Jewish-sounding name? I guess the answer to that would have to come from Stephen A.

My blood still boils whenever this story surfaces. To some this experience might be seen as the "cost" to Geoffrey or anyone else in the public domain rendering an opinion to an ever more gluttonous click-bait society. White, Black, Brown, Yellow. Christian, Jewish, Protestant, Muslim. It doesn't matter the skin color or the religious orientation, especially when the messaging is not inflammatory. It should not be a focus of the discourse.

Geoffrey, in his inimitable way, let this story die, not responding, knowing it would only inflame the embers. For me, I'm now closer to putting this episode in the rearview mirror.

* * *

Writing this chapter has given me great clarity. Livie and I tried our best to instill in the boys an appreciation for their heritage and hoped that our efforts would provide a life-long commitment to Judaism. I believe we succeeded in raising two mensches (Yiddish for a person of integrity and honor). We are extraordinarily proud of the boys for becoming role models to all the youths who have followed their football journeys. It's not so easy to stand up and be counted. It takes immense courage to be public with religious views, particularly in today's world of escalating antisemitism. And yet Mitchell and Geoffrey have done just that. It makes us kvell. ("Kvell" is a Yiddish word meaning "to be delighted, feel happy and proud.")

15

SHOE DOG—MY INTERACTIONS WITH PHIL KNIGHT

By nature, I'm a shy guy. An introvert. Just ask Livie. Maybe that's why our marriage has lasted this long—forty-seven years as of September 2024. She's the ultimate extrovert.

I have been a management consultant since 2000. It was excruciating for me to attend networking events that were a must if I were to find gigs, particularly in the beginning. But I worked through it. I generated business and made life-long friends because I stretched my comfort zone at these gatherings.

Those who have come to know me well would likely be hard pressed to describe me as a shy, introverted person. Once I get to know someone, and especially if a friendship has been struck up, I somehow lose the shyness. Whereas most of us have heard the expression "familiarity breeds contempt," in my world, familiarity is the elixir to overcoming my shyness.

So, help me explain this conundrum. How does a person like me, who is naturally reserved and timid, become emboldened in the presence of those of notoriety, like famous actors and athletes? Inexplicably, I'm a completely different person. The shyness melts away. I have no clue why and frankly, at this point in my life, you won't find me getting shrunk to unlock the reason(s). It is what it is.

Raising Giants

At the venerable Hollywood Bowl amphitheater located in the Hollywood Hills neighborhood of Los Angeles, I once looked up from my seat to spot Kareem Abdul-Jabbar. At seven feet, two inches, he's not hard to spot. My heart began to pitter patter. I have followed Abdul-Jabbar since I was a teenager, when he was Lew Alcindor, before I attended his, and my, alma mater, UCLA. I followed him closely during his NBA career as he became the career scoring leader at 38,387 points until LeBron James shot past him in February of 2023.

He took a seat a few aisles in front of me and a few rows to the left. I figured that was the end of that. But it wasn't. After just a brief few minutes, he rose in unison with his party and exited the original box. Guided by a Bowl employee, he walked across several aisles, then made a hard right turn. Several rows later another hard right. And then they stopped...in front of the box immediately to the right of mine. Ultimately, he was literally sitting right next to me, separated only by the barrier between boxes. I could have reached out and touched him.

I sat there for a moment or two to fashion a question to possibly initiate a conversation. My question landed like a dud. He responded with a one-word answer, "No." And that was that. But here I was trying to strike up a conversation with a stranger, albeit a very famous one. My only hesitation was to formulate the question. It was not about whether to ask.

I've done the same with several actors. A couple of them responded very warmly. Others not so much. Decades ago I sat next to Tom Selleck of *Magnum, P.I.* and *Blue Bloods* fame in a sauna at a local gym after a workout. I wanted to catch his eye to tell him I was a big *Magnum, P.I.* fan. Unlike an owl that can rotate its neck 270 degrees, it was as if Selleck's neck was fused in place. He stared straight ahead. But again, there I was ready to behave beyond my normally introverted character.

* * *

As I shared earlier in the book, Livie and I attended Geoffrey's second game of his first season at Oregon, against Oklahoma. When I was growing up watching college football, there was cachet associated with Oklahoma. They always seemed to be battling for the National Championship. As a matter of fact, heading into this game they were ranked number two in the country. Bud Wilkinson and Barry Switzer were two renowned head coaches at Oklahoma. Adrian Peterson (AP) was on the team. As a freshman that season, he finished the year leading the nation in total rushing and became the first freshman in college football history to be a runner-up in the Heisman Trophy balloting. Who wouldn't want to see him play?

Ironically, AP, who some think will be a future NFL Hall of Fame inductee, and Geoffrey were teammates in 2012 during Geoffrey's only season with the Vikings. AP rushed for 2,097 yards that year, eight short of Eric Dickerson's all-time record for one season. Geoffrey was used sparingly that campaign, but I do recall him opening holes for at least two of AP's seventy-plus-yard runs that season.

Not only did Geoffrey carve holes for AP's almost record year, he was also an offensive-line mainstay for three other running backs who had extraordinary seasons. In 2009, while with the Carolina Panthers, the combo of Jonathan Stewart and DeAngelo Williams became the first running back teammates to both rush for over 1,110 yards in the same season. And when he played for Kansas City in 2013, running back Jamal Charles gained almost 2000 yards between rushing and receiving, with a league-leading nineteen touchdowns, earning him All-Pro honors.

We made our flight arrangements and booked a hotel in Norman for the game. I can't recall whether staying at the team hotel was simply prohibited or just strongly discouraged, but we booked a room at a hotel separate from where the Ducks were spending the night. I suspect the separation was to eliminate distractions for the players. Once in the NFL, it was different. We were able to have the boys book us a room in the team hotel. That made spending time with them the day before a game a whole lot easier. We would invariably meet them during a two-to-three-hour window in their late afternoon schedule. They would come to our room to hang out, as it was strictly prohibited for us to enter their rooms. Or we'd find a restaurant in the hotel or nearby to grab a bite to eat.

Given this was our first away-game experience, we had no idea what to expect. With games almost always on a Saturday, the team would arrive Friday late afternoon. At the airport they would hop on charter buses and be escorted by police to the home-team stadium for a walk-through to familiarize themselves with the surroundings. From there the team headed to the hotel, where they would check in, grab some dinner and attend meetings. By approximately 9 p.m. they had completed all the obligatory activities and had a couple of free hours before bed check.

Raising Giants

Yes, bed check. Coaches at the prescribed time would go room to room to ensure that players were ready for a good night's sleep.

Geoffrey told us it was OK to visit the team hotel that night and spend a few minutes with him before he headed upstairs. This became a staple of our travel experience during Geoffrey's and Mitchell's college days. So that Friday evening in Norman, we jumped in the car and headed to the team hotel.

The lobby was a madhouse. We were among dozens of Oregon fans who descended upon the team hotel. I imagine some had booked rooms in the hotel. Being our first away-game experience, we knew not another soul in the lobby. Well, maybe that wasn't exactly true. There was one person who I recognized, albeit I had never met him.

Remember my dear friend Mike Parr? Oregon alumnus, one of their most devoted fans and the person who was instrumental in getting Geoffrey on Oregon's radar screen during high school. Ironically our relationship almost didn't happen. Mike and I met when both of us were industry competitors. When I returned from an industry conference telling my staff of our newfound relationship, they were aghast. "You can't be friends with the adversary." I chuckled and basically said, "Watch me." The rest, as it's said, is history.

Mike attends every home game. He bleeds Oregon green and yellow. He also has extremely strong ties with the team. His company is a sponsor of the Oregon Ducks football program. They are the lead sponsor for the annual extravaganza that announces the year's recruiting class. (The last few years Geoffrey has served as cohost of this event.) Mike has sat at the head table with other boosters, the head coach and one other very key Oregon supporter.

I've referenced Phil Knight, of Nike fame, several times previously. Phil ran track at Oregon and then, six years after graduating with a bachelor's degree in business, he cofounded Nike. Over the course of time, Phil has demonstrated his love of the university by donating over a billion dollars to Oregon. Oregon's overall sports programs have benefited from Phil's seemingly boundless generosity, including Autzen Stadium improvements; the 12,634 seat, multi-purpose Matthew Knight Arena (named after Knight's son, who unfortunately passed away at age thirty-four after a scuba diving accident), where Ducks' basketball is played; and multiple state-of-the-art athletic facilities, such as the recently renovated

Hayward Field, now considered a world-class track and field stadium. His impact runs deep.

There are some who do not appreciate all that Phil has done for Oregon, complaining that his focus is too myopic, spending all his money on sports. Well, that's just not the case. His kindness extends to the Knight Law Center housing the Oregon School of Law. There's the recently funded Phil and Penny Knight Campus for Accelerating Scientific Impact, a 175,000-square-foot building focusing on bioengineering and applied science research. He has endowed chairs and professorships in other academic disciplines. His reach is well beyond athletics. Whether by intent or simply by circumstance, incoming GPA of Oregon students rose as much as a full point since Phil began his donation spree.

Mike and I, even before Geoffrey attended Oregon, frequently talked about Phil. Through those conversations and the pictures Mike shared with me, I kinda knew what Phil looked like. So, getting back to that Friday night in Norman at the team hotel, it wasn't that odd for me to have spotted his somewhat familiar face across the lobby, surrounded by a throng of Oregon fans.

I tapped Livie on the shoulder, pointed and said, "Look, there's Phil Knight." She scanned the lobby to see where I was pointing. For her, that would have been the end of that. Not for me. I declared, "I'm going over to introduce myself." "You're doing what?" "Yup, I'm going to say hello." She tried to convince me that it was a poor idea. What did I have to lose? Would I be turned away by his security detail, or "goon squad," as I affectionately call these protective services? I wanted to find out, so I got up and started walking in his direction.

I truly did expect him to be surrounded by security. Not the case. His "detail" was made up of Oregon's five-feet-seven-inch, or thereabouts, associate athletic director. Not another soul. And, actually, this was the case wherever I saw Phil. At Autzen Stadium. At the Big House on the campus of the University of Michigan. Watching Oregon take on UCLA in Pauley Pavilion. It was always Phil, dressed in his usual garb of blue jeans, blue sports coat and some version of an Oregon baseball cap, accompanied by the assistant A.D. or, in his absence, only one other person associated with Oregon.

I walked up to where Phil was standing. I waited for what I thought was an appropriate moment to interject, said "Excuse me," and then asked, "Are you Phil Knight?" He obviously answered in the affirmative. "I'm Geoff Schwartz's father, Lee," as I extended my hand. I figured he'd have no idea who the hell I was if I didn't tie it to Geoffrey. Once he made the connection, a nice, warm smile came to his face. I fully expected that, after a quick acknowledgement, he would then turn back to those around him. Not the case. He told me how happy he was that Geoffrey chose Oregon. And, as with a number of other stories in this book, there's a back story to this one.

The Baseball Backstory

As I have shared, Geoffrey was a multiple-sport high school athlete through his senior year. We clearly knew that college basketball wasn't in the cards for him. Football obviously was. Baseball? Well, not one college team came knocking on the door. He couldn't hit a lick, other than a very occasional long ball that appeared to be shot out of a cannon. It was all or nothing for him.

Pitching-wise he was much more accomplished. Except he didn't throw hard enough. Unless freakishly talented otherwise, Major League Baseball (MLB) expects guys standing six-feet, six-inches-tall to throw fastballs no less than ninety miles an hour. That was never in Geoffrey's repertoire, so colleges never came looking. But he had shared his baseball aspirations with Oregon during his recruitment. Unfortunately, Oregon was the only Pac-10 school at the time without a varsity baseball program. But another option did exist.

The Aloha Knights, now known as the Corvallis Knights, are a collegiate summer baseball program featuring players primarily from the West Coast who have attended at least one year of college and have at least one more year of eligibility remaining. Unlike college baseball, where only aluminum or other composite bats are used, players in these leagues only use wooden bats. These summer leagues allow college baseball players to compete using professional rules and equipment so MLB scouts can observe them under big-league conditions.

The Knights are Oregon based. They were founded in Beaverton but then moved to Corvallis in 2007, the home of Oregon's in-state rival the Oregon State Beavers. The team's primary sponsor is Phil Knight's wife Penny. I suspect it was that connection that was the impetus for Geoffrey being offered a chance to play for the Knights the summer before his freshman football season. He was so excited. He didn't see much field time, but what he did was memorable.

That year the Knights had a spectacular season. They won the Pacific International League title, qualifying them for the National Baseball Congress (NBC) World Series, which they won. Geoffrey was not part of the World Series team (football came calling), but in a league game prior he was given his chance.

Late in this game Geoffrey was called out of the bullpen for a relief appearance. His heart was racing far beyond what would be normal for that trot to the mound. He completed his eight warmup pitches and readied himself for the first batter. He was so amped up that he launched several pitches exceeding that critical ninety-miles-per-hour threshold. The first two batters went down swinging. He only needed one more out to complete a spotless inning.

The next three batters walked. He could no longer find the strike zone. Maybe his adrenaline rush just wore out. Ultimately, all three runners scored on a subsequent double. An inning-ending ground out finally put Geoffrey's misery to an end. What initially looked to be a flawless inning did not end up that way. For those who follow baseball, Geoffrey's earned run average (ERA) for the game, and for the season, was an astronomical 27.00. To the uninitiated, these days an ERA of 4.00 or below is considered good. Alas, he went from the summit to the bottom of the gorge in just one short inning.

In the end, the Knights overcame the three runs and won that game on their way to the World Series title. Months later, Geoffrey unexpectedly received a package from the Knights. "Did I leave something behind in the locker room?" he wondered. Geoffrey ripped open the box, exposing what seemed like a very nice jewelry case, but that made no sense to Geoffrey. He lifted the top. Keep in mind that his sole contribution to that team was that forgettable three-run inning. Yet, in a demonstration that he was considered a part of the team, even with only one inning's worth of contribution, the organization had sent him a World Series ring. How generous and honorable.

Back to Phil Knight

Getting back to my initial contact with Phil Knight, as he and I were talking, Livie walked over and I introduced the two of them. Then Knight swiveled to look behind him and waved someone over. It was Penny.

He explained Geoffrey's involvement with the Knights. The four of us stood there for what seemed like fifteen minutes engaged in a delightful conversation. This was far more than I ever anticipated and became the foundation for my further interactions with this famous entrepreneur and philanthropist.

Oregon, different from Cal, allowed parents—yes, only the dads—to enter the team locker room after all games. What a kick that was, especially following winning contests. As you might imagine, the atmosphere after wins was noisy, sometimes bordering on rowdiness. That definitely described the mood after that glorious triumph over USC in 2007.

During Geoffrey's time in Eugene, Oregon built the most advanced locker room in all of college football. For instance, the lockers were individually air filtered to rid each one, and the entire room, of the nasty smell of old sweat. Knight provided most, if not all, of the money for the locker room upgrade. He directed those in the athletic department responsible for the project to visit other campuses around the country to learn what they were doing, and then demanded Oregon do better. And that they did. What an amazing facility.

Whether by Knight's request or an expression of appreciation for his generosity, as one walked into the locker room, there it was: his personal locker. Obviously, it didn't house any football gear. I frankly don't remember if anything was stored in the locker. In plain sight was a nameplate engraved with Knight's name. And that's basically the exact location where I ran into him after the USC game. He and I had had several rather nondescript, but very cordial, interactions up to that point, but nothing to suggest he would apply that bone-crushing bear hug.

The following week Oregon laced 'em up against Arizona State. The game was telecast on one of the major networks. Somehow, that network was able to secure Knight's presence to introduce the players preceding the game. Most intros are short and sweet. "Starting at right tackle, number 75, Geoff Schwartz." But this day was to be different.

To highlight Geoffrey's three-yard gain the previous week, Knight embellished the introduction. "Starting at right tackle, the third-leading rusher from last week's triumph over USC, number 75, Geoff Schwartz." I suspect that was a complete ad-lib by Knight, but who was going to stop him? I actually didn't hear the intro until we returned home from the Arizona State contest. Once back, anxious to hear the unfiltered words,

Shoe Dog—My Interactions with Phil Knight

I turned on the tube, accessed the game's recording and listened to Knight's intro. Music to my ears.

Throughout Geoffrey's time at Oregon, and even thereafter, I'd run into Knight...or sometimes catch his attention from afar. I remember that magnificent day in Ann Arbor when Oregon spanked Michigan. I was indulging at that monster tailgate party that overlooked the drop-off point for the teams. Apparently, that was also where dignitaries found entry, for there was Knight, with Oregon's assistant A.D. in tow, striding toward the entry. He spotted me. (Maybe it was my Oregon jersey amid a sea of Michigan blue.) He briefly paused and gave me a big old wave.

Running into Knight at home or away football games was not very surprising. He didn't miss too many games. At Autzen, it was customary to see him on the sideline holding audience pregame while the Ducks were going through their warmups. Prior to the kickoff, Knight would head up to his personal suite to watch the game, located smack dab above the fifty-yard line.

When sitting in the stands with a sight line to Phil's box, I would sometimes train my binoculars on him in the suite. Early on I noticed him watching the game wearing headphones. I came to learn that he was listening to the coaches calling plays from the booth upstairs to the sidelines down below. When you're Phil Knight and have made the impact on all things Oregon that he has, why not?

Several years after Geoffrey's graduation, I attended a UCLA basketball game at Pauley Pavilion on the Bruins' campus. By pure happenstance, they were playing Oregon that night. I was sitting in the second level of seats. At some point during the game, I looked to the lower level and spotted someone I met and got to know during Geoffrey's time in Eugene. As I glanced down, he coincidentally stood up and looked upward. We waved to each other. He then pointed to someone sitting next to him.

It was Knight. This newfound friend was besties with Phil. He must have mentioned to Knight that I was sitting above, because seconds later Knight rose, looked to my location, and waved with one of those big smiles I was accustomed to seeing.

I have spent some time in this chapter sharing my experiences with someone that I never could have dreamed about knowing, in any capacity. He was part of my Oregon experience and so, to me, qualifies inclusion. But I also include him for a more personal reason.

I had always thought that people of Knight's stature, prominence, and wealth were unapproachable. As I alluded to earlier in the chapter, I expected all such people to be surrounded by their "squad," preventing access. Maybe my bias was borne as an impressionable twelve-year-old.

My family was not at all wealthy. Middle class might have been a reach. So for my father to take me to a professional basketball game was a real stretch. San Francisco Warriors versus the New York Knicks. The day after St. Patrick's Day. Bill Bradley, who ultimately became Senator Bill Bradley of New Jersey, was in the Knicks' lineup, playing his first NBA season after a two-year Rhodes Scholarship program in Oxford, England. The Cow Palace was packed for Bradley's second visit to the West Coast that season. Our seats were in the nosebleed section. We were joined by a friend of my father's and his son, who was my friend. At halftime, my buddy and I decided to wander down to the court. Fifty years ago, that was an OK thing to do.

To our surprise, there on the hardwood was the Warriors' starting center Nate Thurmond. I recognize that to many these names mean nothing, but in that era, Bradley and Thurmond were among the best in the NBA. Why wasn't Thurmond with his team in the locker room? Unfortunately, he had been injured and was on crutches. I thought his misfortune would translate to our good fortune. With each of us carrying an autograph book, we attempted to approach Thurmond. Didn't get within spitting distance of him. Security stepped in and shooed us away. That experience has stuck with me ever since, coloring my view of Thurmond, and, subsequently, probably people like Knight. In my adolescent mind, Thurmond's stature was no different than my adult view of Phil.

But as I've described, Knight was different. Approachable. Always ready to have his picture taken with his fans. Generous. Getting to know him, even in the limited fashion I did, helped me shift my paradigm of people like him toward a more positive image.

By the way, for the curious, the term Shoe Dog is used to describe people who devote themselves wholly to the making, selling, buying and/or designing of shoes. Sound like Phil Knight?

16
SUPER BOWL LIV—
A DREAM COME TRUE

My first Super Bowl recollection dates back to January 12, 1969 (about a month earlier than when the game is played these days). I was all of thirteen years old. It was the first such game to carry the trademark "Super Bowl." I honestly cannot recall whether I watched the first two contests that carried the title of AFL-NFL Championship Game. I suspect I did, but I wouldn't bet the house on it. However, that '69 game is etched in my memory like it was yesterday.

I wasn't at home in front of the television that afternoon. It was basketball season for me. I was a trailblazer in my hometown of Santa Rosa, being the first Jew on a roster of our local Christian Youth Organization (CYO)-sponsored league and team. I can only imagine the thoughts going through the minds of the nuns in the stands when they saw me jog onto the court with my Mezuzah draped around my jersey's shoulder strap.

Typically, the games were played on the campus of a Santa Rosa–area Catholic high school. On this Sunday, the schedule had us traveling to the San Francisco Bay Area, preventing my viewing of the Super Bowl. Instead, my father and I found a radio station in the car that was broadcasting the game. We caught the beginning and then the end. It was a game that many believe forever changed the landscape of the NFL.

In 1966 the NFL and the American Football League (AFL) merged into one, creating the National Football Conference (NFC) and the American

Football Conference (AFC) under the umbrella of the NFL. Although, on the surface, it might have appeared that the two conferences were now to be equals, the powers-that-be of the former NFL considered the former AFL a stepchild.

Possibly this notion of the AFL being a lower-quality league was confirmed by the results of the first two encounters between the AFL and NFL in the AFL-NFL World Championship Game. Both games were won by the NFC representative by margins of 25 and 19, eclipsing the pregame odds of 14 and 13.5, respectively, favoring the NFC team. It was no surprise, then, that the odds heading into Super Bowl III, the first game played under the Super Bowl moniker, greatly favored the NFC team. I've read that number to be either 18 or 19.5 points, greater than any odds on an NFL football game before or since.

Super Bowl III (yes, the league established the Roman numeral at this point and called the game "III" even though it was the first contest under the new name) pitted the upstart New York Jets from the AFC against the heavily favored Baltimore Colts of the NFC. The Jets had won eleven games that season; the Colts were almost perfect at 13-1. New York was led by quarterback Joe Willie (Broadway Joe) Namath, a future Hall of Famer who, up to that point in his career, had modest success with an overall 27-19 win-loss record in games he started. In a brazen act about three days prior to the actual game, reportedly spurred on by some degree of intoxication, Broadway Joe boastfully, arrogantly, predicted, "We're gonna win the game. I guarantee it." His coach, Wilbur Charles "Weeb" Ewbank, later stated that he "could have shot" Namath for making that statement.

Namath made good on his prediction. The final score was 16-7 in favor of the Jets, and it wasn't that close. The Colts' second-string quarterback at the time, Hall of Famer-to-be, Johnny Unitas, entered the game in the fourth quarter and led the Colts to a meaningless touchdown that made the game appear closer than the final score would indicate. As Namath ran off the field to the deafening cheers of Jets fans, seen in an iconic photo of the moment, he raised his right hand and pointed his index finger to the sky. The message was clear. At least for that one day, the New York Jets, and the AFC, were number one in the world of professional football.

From that point on, demonstrating that Mitchell wasn't the only Schwartz able to string consecutive events together, I have not missed

Super Bowl LIV—A Dream Come True

viewing a Super Bowl. The streak is alive in the mid-fifties and counting. Then, in 1980, a concurrent string was launched, one much more meaningful than the Super Bowl viewing streak.

Livie entered law school in the fall of 1978. I soon learned that it's customary for first-year law students to form study groups for support through the rigorous demands of learning the course materials. Livie joined a group with six of her classmates. Given the amount of time they spent with one another, the pod developed a camaraderie that morphed into personal friendships and social interactions outside of law school.

Fast forward to the very beginning of 1980. One of the guys from the study group invited all members plus wives and significant others to his condominium for a Super Bowl viewing party. We all enjoyed the time together. I was overjoyed with the game's outcome. My San Francisco 49ers soundly defeated the Pittsburgh Steelers.

The following year we received another invitation. And the following year, and every year until 2020. As couples grew into families, the kids were also included. Not wanting to sound sexist—lord knows that would never fly with Livie—however, the reality was the women looked after the youngsters while the guys watched the game. Geoffrey and Mitchell were always with us.

The composition of the group changed with time. Some dropped off, newbies were invited. The location must have changed four or five times as our dear, dear friend Dave and his wife Phyllis moved about Southern California. Sadly, Dave passed in early 2004 from eye cancer but Phyl carried the torch. The annual Super Bowl party continued uninterrupted until COVID put an end to the streak. Phyl and I withstood the test of time as the only two constants throughout all the years.

As time passed, Phyl and her two children, David Jr. and Sydney, who refer to Livie and me as Aunt and Uncle, were adamant that I could not miss a party. The streak had to survive. Plus, I was the one who Phyl relied upon to sound the alert to warm up the lasagna that would be served during halftime. She would have been lost without that direction. Haha. But as the boys began their NFL journeys, talk would shift to "what if?" During one of these conversations, in a Pope-like act, I was granted special dispensation by Phyl, David Jr. and Sydney. If one of the boys played in a Super Bowl, I would be excused from attending their Super Bowl party.

Unfortunately for Geoffrey, his teams never made it past the first round of the playoffs. But in 2019, the tides turned for Mitchell. At the conclusion of week eight, the Kansas City Chiefs had a very pedestrian 5-3 record. The next couple of weeks found them winning one game and losing the other, leaving them 6-4. At that point in the season, expectations for a Super Bowl run were not very high.

But then something clicked for K.C. Led by 2018 MVP Patrick Mahomes, the Chiefs caught fire. They won their final six games to finish first in the AFC West. That standing and their overall record earned them a bye in the Wild Card weekend of the playoffs. First up for Kansas City in the Division Playoffs were the Houston Texans, winners of a Wild Card weekend contest. The game started badly for the Chiefs. They fell behind 21-0 by the end of the first quarter. Sitting there watching I'm thinking that any chance at a Super Bowl was rapidly slipping away. But then, in pure Chiefs' manner, they flipped the switch. In the final three quarters Kansas City outscored Houston 51-10. Hope had been restored.

Next up was the Conference Championship game pitting the Chiefs against the Tennessee Titans. As was becoming a common practice, K.C. fell behind and trailed the Titans 17-7 with about six minutes left in the first half. And then it happened again. In quick fashion the Chiefs scored two touchdowns in the final four minutes of the half to take a four-point lead heading into halftime.

That score held until the opening seconds of the fourth quarter, when the Chiefs crossed the goal line for another seven points. They were now up by eleven. As Livie and I watched, we both started to believe. Another touchdown at the midpoint of the fourth quarter put K.C. up by eighteen points. Overcoming such a deficit with but 7:30 left in a game would have been a monumental undertaking. Livie and I tried to hold our excitement in check.

There's a word that we Jews use in this situation. *Keinehora,* or alternatively *kaynahora*. It's basically a concept that causes us to exert some caution in these situations. Don't get overly excited, otherwise we might jinx the good vibes and cause a reversal in fortune. So we tried to patiently await the ultimate outcome before expressing our overwhelming joy.

Tick tock. Tick tock. Ten, nine, eight and so on until the clock struck 0:00. Livie and I looked at each other and yelled, "We're going to a Super Bowl!" We jumped for joy. (Writing this raised goosebumps on my arms, just like that Sunday afternoon.)

Super Bowl LIV—A Dream Come True

We're Going to the Super Bowl!

Mitchell would be playing in a Super Bowl. For real. It was no longer a dream. We could now set our sights on making plans to be in Miami on February 2, 2020. (Incidentally, one of my most-prized photos of Mitchell is him pictured on the field after the AFC Championship game, confetti raining down around him, with a grin that clearly conveyed his jubilation for what he and his team had accomplished.)

Super Bowls are planned years in advance. Most attendees buy tickets long before anyone knows who will be playing. So available flights to the game locale are not plentiful two weeks prior, nor are hotel rooms. We began looking at flight availability and, as we presumed, there weren't many options. Time for plan B. Might this be a chance to kill two birds with one stone? We dialed Geoffrey.

The thought was for us to first fly to Charlotte—there were plenty of available flights—on Thursday before the Super Bowl, rent a car Friday morning and then drive the ten and a half hours to Miami. Monday after the game we'd drive back to North Carolina and remain for ten days to two weeks to be with Geoffrey, Meridith and, of course, our two wonderful grandkids. Geoffrey didn't hesitate. "Sure." We immediately booked our flights.

Next was the lodging. With over 62,000 people attending the game, most probably not locals, hotel availability had to be very limited. We contacted Mitchell. Was it possible to stay at the team hotel? Indeed, it was. He would book us a room with the block set aside for the Chiefs. The plan was to arrive Friday, depart on Monday. The two potentially biggest travel hurdles had been solved.

I can't begin to adequately convey the excitement that Livie and I lived with during those two weeks leading up to the game. We were not only attending a Super Bowl, but one of our sons would be playing. What seemed like a pipe dream up until the boys entered the NFL, and then a limited opportunity once in the league, this surreal experience was now to be a reality. Maybe this wasn't completely coincidental.

Super Bowl number fifty-four. In Roman numerals that's LIV. Livie's full name is Olivia. All those in her work circle refer to her as such. Me? I was introduced to her as "Livie" and have called her that ever since, as do all those outside of her law practice. LIV. Livie. Meant to be?

The trip to Charlotte couldn't come soon enough. The day arrived. We hopped on the plane. Couldn't wait to see Alex and Emmy. Went to bed that night with great anticipation for our journey to Miami. The trip was expected to take ten and a half hours. While on the surface that might sound daunting, it really wasn't to me. I was used to being in a car for seven and a half hours trekking from Los Angeles to Santa Rosa or five and a half hours to Berkeley during Mitchell's college years. What's another few hours?

It never dawned on us that we were traveling on a Friday into a metropolis that was expecting tens of thousands of visitors for the weekend. That ten and a half hours stretched to twelve. I've gotta admit the extra ninety minutes was stressful. The additional time was also the result of our dinner plans for the evening. Instead of going directly to the hotel, which would have reduced the total time, we headed to South Beach, the southern portion of Miami Beach. Getting to South Beach on a Friday evening with all the Super Bowl congestion was like traveling the San Diego Fwy (405) in West Los Angeles on a typical evening commute. Agonizing.

Geoffrey and Meridith flew into Miami that afternoon. They joined Livie and me and two other couples as guests of Deryk Gilmore and his wife Camille. While this wasn't Deryk's first Super Bowl involving one of his clients, he acted like it was. He was so excited and, of course, proud of Mitchell and his accomplishments. We had a marvelous evening. At the conclusion, it was time to head to the team hotel.

Though we arrived late, the JW Marriott Spa and Resort was buzzing with activity. We drove up the driveway toward the hotel only to be stopped midway. As one might imagine, security was extremely tight. We had to state our purpose and allow a guard dog to sniff the car, from front to back and side to side, before the gate would open. We dropped the car at the valet, collected our luggage and proceeded to the front desk to check in. My, oh, my. Dozens of Chiefs' fans in Chiefs' jerseys, T-shirts and hats packed the reception area. Reminded me of the hotel lobby in Oklahoma. And Chiefs' players were out in force, casually walking about.

We got to our room and crashed after a long day. I don't think either one of us stirred the entire night. We awoke, got dressed and checked in with the Chiefs. They had an envelope for us containing various passes and the all-important game tickets. There was a Starbucks on site for breakfast. From there we walked the property. It was absolutely gorgeous. One of the passes allowed us access to a Chiefs-only banquet room.

Super Bowl LIV—A Dream Come True

The room was comfortably large. It contained tables offering a huge variety of candies and treats, cooler after cooler of non-alcoholic drinks, plus a popcorn machine. We could indulge while there or load up our pockets, bags or whatever and take as much as we'd like to our rooms. There were chairs aplenty to take a load off. I recall there being a pool table and a foosball table for some recreational activity. The room was open most of the day. Very nice touch.

After breakfast and our tour, Livie and I joined Geoffrey and Meridith poolside in a cabana they had rented. The day was on the cool side, so no one jumped into the pool or the lounging canal that snaked its way through the area. We ordered lunch and enjoyed other snacks while poolside. Once again, a pass allowed us access to the area. Otherwise, we would have been charged to gain entry. We topped off the day with a delightful seafood dinner accompanied by Geoffrey and Meridith plus Duke and his girlfriend. Sitting at the table, those of us who had lived the football journey were expressing our amazement that we had come to this point. Geoffrey was so proud of his bro. Attending a Super Bowl with Mitchell on the field was about to become a reality.

On game days I'm typically a nervous Nellie anyway. On Super Bowl Sunday my anxiety level was through the roof. We got up, once again had breakfast at Starbucks and once again wandered the grounds, anxiously awaiting the prescribed time for boarding the buses destined for the stadium. Transportation was provided for the families of the players. Another one of those passes in the welcome envelope.

We gathered our trappings for the day. Passes, tickets, my all-important binoculars. I laugh now, but those damn binoculars could have been the ruin of Geoffrey's relationship with Meridith. Geoffrey's first preseason I attended one of his games. It wasn't that long after he and Meridith began dating. As is my usual custom, I had the binoculars trained on Geoffrey for basically the entire time. Didn't engage Meridith in much conversation during the three hours of the game.

I came to find out, years later, that I didn't make much of an impression with Meridith that day. As a matter of fact, she thought she had erred in some way. She asked Geoffrey, "Did I do something wrong to upset your father?" He inquired why this was coming up. Since I wasn't present, I have no clue as to her attitude or tone of voice at that time, but she "complained" about my always peering through the binoculars at Geoffrey, "even when he wasn't in the game." Geoffrey assured her that she had done nothing wrong. He explained that's my M.O. Nothing personal. And, if they were to be together long term, it was best to just accept the reality. Thankfully, it all worked out.

Beyond gathering all the game day essentials, Livie and I also donned our respective uniforms. Livie wore a Kansas City Chiefs T-shirt decorated with a special pin given to her by Brooke and Mitchell which read, "NFL Mom." I pulled on my authentic Chiefs' jersey, the one that is otherwise prominently hung in the "shrine" room upstairs.

Trying to abate our collective restlessness (OK, truth be told, maybe mine more than hers) Livie and I headed downstairs to get in line for the buses. I was shocked at how long the line already was. Oh well, I presumed that there would be enough buses for everyone with passes, so I tried to patiently wait as the line didn't move forward but grew longer behind us. We had arranged to meet Geoffrey and Meridith in line but, initially, they were nowhere to be found.

We noticed the line up front beginning to move and then saw the first bus depart. But still no Geoffrey and Meridith. My anxiety level, having calmed a bit while waiting in line, once again spiked. "Where the hell are they?" I questioned. Geoffrey in a crowd is not hard to spot, being six-feet-six-inches tall and as wide as a front door. I finally caught a glimpse of his head bobbing as he walked toward us. What a relief.

We boarded a bus. We were told it was about a thirty-minute drive from the hotel to Miami's Hard Rock Stadium, home of the Miami Dolphins. I took a window seat. Partly because I wanted to watch the scenery but also because Livie's claustrophobia prevents her from sitting up against the cabin wall. I spent almost the entire half-hour trek just staring at the view. There were times I just surveyed the surroundings. However, there were stretches where I was consumed with, "Is this for real? Are we really headed to watch our son in a Super Bowl?"

The Super Tailgate and Game

We arrived at the stadium. The bus was directed to the drop-off zone. We were given instructions on how to find a bus after the game and then freed to make the ten-minute walk to the appropriate stadium entrance. You see, we weren't to enter through any gate. The Chiefs had assembled the largest, by sheer size, tailgate party I've ever seen. (The one in Michigan had, by far, much more food available.) I understand 3,000 folks held passes for that area. It was adorned with all sorts of Chiefs' banners and signage. And then there were the food and drink tables. Nothing too elaborate, but we never felt deprived of food or beverages, alcoholic or otherwise, during the ninety or so minutes we spent at the tailgate.

The clock kept ticking toward the 6:30 p.m. EST kickoff. I believe it was around 5 p.m. when Livie and I said enough with the tailgate, it was time to enter the stadium proper. Now, in all fairness, it was again likely more me than Livie that spurred the move. As I've shared, it was my practice to enter games at the earliest possible moment. I wanted to take in all the pregame activities and cast my eyes on Mitchell as much as possible.

At Cal, getting to our seats so early had its reward. As I've mentioned, Mitchell initially had grand plans of being a quarterback. I don't believe that basic desire ever really left him, so to scratch that itch, he established a pregame ritual with one of his teammates. Mitchell would stand on the twenty-yard line, with his teammate positioned around the goal line, and begin firing passes to him. As his arm loosened up, Mitchell would stretch the distance to the thirty-yard line, then the forty. At this distance the routine shifted. It wasn't just about how far he could throw the ball; it was now a matter of tossing the pigskin so that it hit the vertical bar on the goal post.

For those less familiar with the positioning of a goal post, or as a reminder otherwise, it sits at the back of the ten-yard deep end zone. So, if Mitchell is standing at the forty-yard line, he's heaving the ball fifty yards in the air to hit the crossbar. I sat in the stands in amazement one day when, standing at the forty-yard line, he successfully bounced the football off the crossbar. Fifty bloody yards on a fly. And that wasn't the only time. There are not many who possess the arm strength to accomplish this feat, especially an offensive lineman.

Livie and I asked Geoffrey and Meridith if they'd like to join us on our way from the tailgate into the stadium. They were ready as well. Time to begin focusing on the real reason we were in Miami that day. We got through the turnstiles and proceeded to our seats. Even though we had consumed plenty of food during the tailgate, we stopped along the way to buy some additional nourishment—Geoffrey typically isn't one to turn down such an opportunity—to bring to our seats. As I've explained, once a game starts, my butt is glued to the seat. I was not going to miss one down of the boys playing. I even trained my body, or just had the perfect bladder, to be able to sit through an entire game without having to make a pit stop.

Raising Giants

We found some chow and walked down to our seats. We were at the fifteen-yard line, sixteen rows up from the field, right on the aisle. Super seats. Apparently, Mitchell had three options where to seat us in the stadium. Very graciously, as he paid for our two tickets, he sat us in the best of the three. Face value of each ticket was $3,300. Geoffrey was strategically positioned behind us. If someone had to sit behind this behemoth, it wasn't going to be Livie or me. We took in the on-field festivities. After their normal pregame routine, the Chiefs headed back to the locker room for a chance to take a deep breath and for any last-minute words of wisdom from the coaching staff.

Obviously being at a Super Bowl is so much different than watching on TV. The excitement in the stadium is palpable. There was a buzz throughout. Our necks were on a swivel trying to take in all the activity. And then the Chiefs reappeared from their locker room. I immediately pulled up the binoculars attempting to find Mitchell. I did and pointed him out to Livie. At that moment, time kinda froze. We looked at each other and almost simultaneously uttered, "Is this real?" (Yeah, I know, we sound like a broken record.)

In a twist of fate, the team opposing the Chiefs in Super Bowl LIV was the very team I grew up rooting for, the San Francisco 49ers. In "normal" times, I would be rooting for the '9ers—but obviously not this time, although I guess I could have taken the position of my favorite cashier, Jean, at our local supermarket.

Jean's a huge sports fan. Her favorite football team? The 49ers. Since she's gotten to know me, her second favorite became the Chiefs. As we were talking the Sunday before my departure for Miami, Jean tells me, "I'm in the best situation." I looked at her quizzically. She went on to explain that if San Francisco were to win, she's thrilled. But if Kansas City wins, she would feel like she also won, given our relationship. I couldn't adopt that approach.

I don't want to spend much time here discussing the game itself. There are plenty of written reports, YouTube videos and other commentary to access. Instead, let me draw attention to the Chiefs' proclivity throughout the playoffs to fall behind. It played out in front of more than 62,000 fans in the stadium and 112 million viewers watching throughout the world on television. Kansas City's first-half performance was disappointing. The half ended with the Chiefs tied with the 49ers 10-10 after gaining a paltry 150 yards.

Super Bowl LIV—A Dream Come True

The third quarter added to the stress. With 8:12 remaining in the third stanza, Kansas City had fallen behind 20-10. The teams traded possessions for the remainder of that quarter. Mahomes uncharacteristically threw two interceptions and was very pedestrian to that point. Nothing changed through the first half of the fourth quarter. In the stands, the four of us were feeling as though the game was slipping away. And then it happened... again. Magically, the "real" Mahomes surfaced. The Chiefs scored three consecutive touchdowns in a span of five minutes to jump ahead by 11 points, highlighted by one of those special Mahomes moments.

It was third down and fifteen yards to go with about 7:15 remaining on the fourth-quarter clock. He took the snap from the shotgun and began backpedaling. Quarterbacks are trained to retreat no more than nine yards behind the line of scrimmage. The offensive linemen train for that level of drop. On this particular play, because of defensive line pressure up the middle (no, not from Mitchell's side) Mahomes continued to retreat. At the twenty-one-yard line, fourteen yards behind the line of scrimmage, Mahomes stopped, planted his front left foot into the ground, and, somewhat sidearm, flung the ball downfield.

We watched the flight of the ball as it traveled almost sixty yards downfield into the waiting hands of a wide-open wide receiver Tyreek Hill, who, by almost all accounts, was considered the fastest person in pads in the NFL. He pulled the ball into his chest, giving it a bear hug as a trio of 49ers' defensive backs tried to wrestle the ball from him. At that moment the entire momentum of the game shifted. It was unmistakable. Our confidence level did an immediate about face. We started to believe that a third miraculous comeback was in the works.

As the Chiefs marched down the field for the first of three TDs, then followed by the second and the third, San Francisco had no counter. While the Chiefs amassed 190 yards in those three fourth-quarter drives, more than what they gained in the entire first half, the 49ers could only advance the ball an anemic fifty-nine yards.

With the momentum, the score 24-20 in the Chiefs favor, Kansas City in possession of the ball and driving once again toward their end zone, the outcome of the game seemed secure. This was to be the Chiefs second Super Bowl victory, the last one having taken place fifty years prior in 1970.

With about one minute left on the clock, we heard Meridith from behind us, "Let's go. Hurry!" At that instant, we knew not why. We tried to question because the game was seconds away from a wild on-field Chiefs' celebration that we wanted to take in. But Meridith had no intention of wasting a moment, and we were not about to cross her. People were already leaving their seats. She didn't want us to get caught in the mass of humanity about to exit via the aisle. So dutifully we followed. And thank goodness we did. It led to one of the most extraordinary experiences of my life.

As the three of us followed Meridith, funneling out the aisle and then dodging the masses heading to the exits, we finally caught wind of why we were almost in a sprint instead of celebrating a win at our seats. Meridith wanted to locate the area in the stadium where people were being let onto the field at the game's conclusion.

Sunday morning after breakfast we had a conversation about field access after the game. We learned that each player would be given two field passes. That was it. One ticket was to be used by Mitchell's wife Brooke. That made complete sense. But what about the second ticket? That was going to Mitchell's best friend. "What?" was my immediate reaction. But then as I thought about the situation, it made perfect sense. If the ticket went to me, Livie would not be happy. If it went to her, I certainly wouldn't be a happy camper. If to Geoffrey, we'd both probably be disappointed. So in this King Solomon-esque moment (the Israeli king who helped resolve a dispute between two woman both claiming to be the rightful mother of a young offspring), the best decision as to the second ticket was made.

Meridith was fully aware that I didn't possess a postgame field pass. But, love her, she wasn't going to accept that eventuality without an effort. We finally arrived at the field access gate. People were lined up waiting to pass through the multiple levels of security. We jumped in. When we got to the front, we were asked for our pass. We pulled out every single pass we possessed, but none were the right ones. We were denied access. We walked away dispirited.

My Jewish upbringing instilled in me a belief in a higher being. However, I'm not one to live my life attributing my actions or successes to a higher power. But what was about to happen seemingly could not have occurred without divine intervention.

After being denied, the four of us huddled together to assess our situation. About the time we finally reconciled that getting on the field wasn't meant to be, we spotted one of Kansas City's staff walking our way.

Meridith got to know him the year Geoffrey played for the Chiefs. Livie and I had gotten to know him during Mitchell's time with K.C. Meridith stopped him in his tracks, and then proceeded to share our plight. "Is there any way to get Mitchell's dad on the field?" she asked, basically pleading. He thought for a few seconds and said he couldn't think of a way. I was ready to walk away, finally defeated, when he made the most incredibly generous offer I've ever received.

Around his neck was his personal, magical field pass. He was carrying some papers in one hand. He tucked those documents under his arm, grabbed the lanyard draped around his neck and simply said, "Take mine." Let's put this in perspective. That might have been the only chance that a team he worked for wins a Super Bowl, and therefore possibly a once-in-a-lifetime opportunity to celebrate with the team on the field. "Are you sure?" I asked somewhat sympathetically. He confirmed his intentions without any hesitation. I placed the pass around my neck, returned to the security line and waited to be granted permission to proceed to the field.

I finally passed through the last checkpoint and entered the tunnel to the field. Several steps later I came to an abrupt stop. No one was being allowed field access. I had no idea why not. I immediately got to thinking. What if the players were not on the field when the line was finally released? Was this effort all for naught? It was not.

The line began to move. I exited the tunnel to a wild scene. Confetti from the stadium roof was still raining down onto the field. I bent over, picked up several strands and stuffed them into a pants pocket as a souvenir of the occasion. Now it was time to find Mitchell. It wasn't necessarily going to be easy. The field in front of me was a mass of humanity. Players, family, team personnel, press and camera crews. I continued forward, step by step, scanning the horizon hoping to locate Mitchell. And then there he was.

I quickened my pace as I marched toward him. At some point he swiveled his head and noticed me. First, he had a kinda perplexed look on his face. I suspect going through his mind was, "How in the heck did you make it on the field?" Without him having to ask, I quickly shared the story of acquiring my pass. But before those words came out of my mouth, I jumped up to hug him and plant a kiss on his cheek. Of course, that was accompanied by "Congratulations!!" I then hung on to him, like a little puppy dog, mirroring his every step. I did not want to miss a precious moment.

As he walked around, congratulations came from every direction. Teammates. Coaches. Fans. Several well-known actors with ties to the Kansas City area and the Chiefs were on the field. At one point through the din I heard, "Are you Mitchell's father?" from one of these well-known entertainers. Guess my number 71 Chiefs jersey might have been a clue. Once I confirmed I was, we ended up talking for a few minutes. Mitchell was interviewed several times. I hung on to every word. All this time, the stage for the Lombardi Trophy presentation was being wheeled out and assembled.

The Lombardi Trophy is named after the legendary coach of the Green Bay Packers, Vince Lombardi. It was first presented after the 1967 game in which his Packers won the first AFL-NFL World Championship. The Packers also won installment number two of the Championship game before the Super Bowl moniker was adopted in 1969. Since then, the trophy is presented to the winning team's ownership and head coach by the NFL Commissioner. For the Chiefs in 2020, that was Clark Hunt, CEO and owner, and Head Coach Andy Reid. Clark Hunt is the son of Lamar Hunt, one of the founders of the original American Football League, and one of the AFL owners instrumental in the merger of the NFL and AFL.

I followed Mitchell onto the stage for the presentation. I had goosebumps then watching the ceremony, just as I have now recalling that magical moment. Once the official presentation was complete, the trophy was then passed from owners, to coaches, to players. Ultimately this twenty-two-inch tall, seven-pound treasure landed in Mitchell's arms. As with most players, he planted a huge kiss on the trophy. And then a moment I will cherish forever.

The Photo

I have the photo, and the memory etched in my mind, to confirm this once-in-a-lifetime moment. Mitchell and I standing side by side on the stage with the trophy, held by Mitchell, nestled between the two of us. Whoever took the picture was able to frame us under signage in the background erected on the stage that displayed an artful "LIV" logo with an image of the trophy inserted between the "L" and the "I", all positioned above "Super Bowl." It's the perfect photo. Mitchell beaming, wearing a hat and T-shirt emblazoned with "Champions." Me, wearing a Mitchell

Super Bowl LIV—A Dream Come True

jersey, with all of the day's passes around my neck, and with a smile that I probably haven't replicated much in my lifetime.

Ultimately it was time to let Mitchell get to his locker room. I said my goodbyes and then headed out of the stadium. I ran into Geoffrey waiting for me. Whereas the bus dropped us off near the tailgate party, I exited the stadium at the opposite end of where the buses were staged for pick up. By that time, I was completely drained from all the excitement and emotion of the day. The walk to the bus was pure drudgery. It seemed to take forever. We finally arrived at the staging area, found Meridith and Livie, and boarded the bus for the return trip to the hotel. In most instances that would be the end of the day. But not this night. There was still a party to attend.

It's a Super Bowl tradition for both teams to plan an after-game party, win or lose. Based on this sole experience, I can't imagine being on the losing end and wanting to party afterward. Fortunately, that was not to be my experience. All I needed to do was catch a second wind once we arrived back at the hotel. By that time though, it was well past my bedtime. I hadn't been up this late in forever. But this was a special night. Time to soldier on.

The bus dropped us off in front of the hotel. We marched up the driveway to the hotel entrance and then to our room. We sat down for a few minutes...but not too many, fearful that any prolonged respite might find us asleep for the night. We changed clothes to feel refreshed and then began our trek to the ballroom for the big bash. After such a long day, the hall couldn't have been any further away from our room.

But once we arrived, I caught a second wind. The area was buzzing. The hallway leading to the ballroom hall was packed with fans. The hall itself was crammed with wall-to-wall celebrants. We tried to find Mitchell but initially could not spot him. Usually that's a simple task, but in the darkened room and with many more people of his stature wandering about, it was a more challenging task. When it was obvious that Mitchell had not yet arrived, Livie and I continued to weave our way through the hall and hallway. We ran into family and friends.

In the hallway, I spotted Clark Hunt, the Chiefs' CEO. As I've explained otherwise, I find myself very comfortable approaching someone so notable, so I did just that. Walked up, introduced myself as Mitchell's father and congratulated him on the magnificent win. He was so gracious.

Spent a few minutes with me, mostly singing the praises of Mitchell and sharing how fortunate the Chiefs were to have him on their team.

Finally, we spotted Mitchell. Curiously, he was lugging a plastic bag with him. We walked alongside as he made a round of the banquet hall. After completing his first pass, he began gathering friends and family, kind of like the Pied Piper. We all followed, exiting the ballroom and making a path toward a less crowded area in the hallway. Mitchell was able to find a table on which he set the plastic bag. We soon discovered the contents. Authentic Super Bowl LIV Champion T-shirts distributed by the team in the locker room. The players were given permission to grab what they needed. Didn't take but a minute before I yanked that T-shirt over my head. Pictures were taken. We then headed back to the ballroom.

By that time, the room was even more crowded than before. Someone was on stage singing. The music wasn't familiar, and the acoustics, with all those people singing, talking, dancing, was rather overwhelming. Being well past our witching hour, and maybe having to accept we were no longer spring chickens, Livie and I decided to head back to our room. We said our goodbyes.

The Morning After and Beyond

In the morning we caught up with Geoffrey and Meridith and discovered what we missed out by leaving so "early," at 2 a.m. Haha. The act on stage when we left was internationally acclaimed American rapper Flo Rida. After he completed his set, a second act was scheduled to appear. It was rumored that Pitbull, another rapper, who has sold over 100 million singles worldwide and has been honored with thirty-five Billboard Latin Music awards, was booked to perform. Sure enough, soon after Flo Rida concluded his performance, Pitbull made his way on stage for an hour set. Livie and I were disappointed. Oh well.

What an incredible day. What an incredible experience. One that is forever etched in our memories and hearts and will never be repeated. As fate would have it, the very next season Mitchell walked off the field bothered by a bad back. He never returned to the game he loved. His remarkable career had come to an end. But what an amazing conclusion. He will forever be able to proudly boast that he is a Super Bowl champion, and will also be remembered for the sparkling three postseason games.

There's also an irony to this game. More than 62,000 people crowded the stadium that day. Probably over a thousand people were in very close

Super Bowl LIV—A Dream Come True

proximity to each other in that crowded ballroom. Forty-one calendar days later the country was virtually shut down because of COVID. We wonder if SB54 was one of the first super spreaders of the disease. We'll never know. Thankfully none of the people that we knew at the game became ill afterward.

Monday morning we awoke, had breakfast, packed, checked out, said our final goodbyes and began our long journey back to Charlotte. I think both Livie and I were emotionally drained and physically tired, and anxious to see our grandkids. This glorious weekend had come to an end. But it was not the end of Super Bowl-related activities.

Three days later, on February 5, a blustery, chilly morning, with temperatures in the twenties and wind chill in the teens, maybe one million people gathered in the streets of Kansas City for a celebratory parade. A string of double-decker buses carried the players through several miles of downtown. Fortunately, the event was streamed so we were able to watch it in its entirety from Charlotte. "There's Mitchell," Livie and I would point out to each other whenever his face appeared on the screen. He waved to the adoring fans. He took his turn clutching the Lombardi Trophy. At one point he exited the bus and walked alongside, high fiving all those standing close. It was cold but that really didn't register. The excitement of the moment overshadowed all else.

There was still one more event to take place to put a bow on Mitchell's Super Bowl experience. On September 1, under COVID restrictions, the Chiefs gathered in Arrowhead Stadium to receive their championship rings. My, oh, my. I've never seen a ring with so many jewels. My understanding is that each year the winning team tries to outdo all those who came before. I think the Chiefs succeeded. The ring featured 255 diamonds and 36 rubies for a total gem carat weight of 10.85 carats. There must be at least a dozen different symbols adorning the ring: reference to the two Super Bowls played during K.C.'s history; each player's signature engraved on the inside; the score of SB54 and on and on. Once travel resumed after COVID, we took a trip to Kansas City to visit Mitchell and Brooke. Livie and I were able to slip the ring onto our fingers. With my fat fingers the ring fit well. We took the requisite pictures and then handed this treasured piece of jewelry back to Mitchell.

I've been asked about the financial rewards that come to the players for their participation in postseason games. For many the money will not be life-changing, given the millions they make each season from their standard contracts. But it's surely enough to fund a trip, some house improvements, the cost of parent tickets, etc. In Mitchell's year, he would have pocketed approximately $222,000 from postseason games, $130,000 of that resulting from winning the Super Bowl. So, again, not chump change.

However, it does cause some of the players to question their involvement in postseason games. Those who played in a 2020 Divisional Playoff game would have earned $33,000. Given by that time they would have played in preseason games, a rigorous sixteen-game schedule, and all the practices throughout, is it worth potential injury or, if nothing else, more blows to the body, for such a "small" amount of financial reward? One very prominent teammate of Mitchell's once told him that he'd rather his team not make the playoffs for just this very reason.

Thinking back on the whole Super Bowl experience is somewhat bittersweet. Much sweeter than bitter, though. If my words in this chapter have not conveyed that message, then I've really missed the mark. The bitter is confined to one singular aspect. Super Bowl LIV was the last of the boys' games Livie and I attended. Intellectually we know that all good things must come to an end, but the emotional side is where the struggle exists. We had an incredible run. Hundreds of games. What better way to close the chapter than with a Super Bowl win? Nonetheless, a chapter closed.

I could not conclude this chapter without one more mention of the tremendously generous act by the Chiefs' staff member. It took a very special person to surrender his opportunity for possibly a once-in-a-lifetime experience to someone he truly hardly knew. I will forever be indebted and truly prayed that his gesture would be rewarded one day. Thankfully it has, as the Chiefs, with him still on staff, have returned to the Super Bowl twice since. To acknowledge his selfless deed, we sent him a gift certificate so that he, his wife and son could enjoy some of the better fare that Kansas City could offer. And, of course, whenever we've communicated since, I have reiterated my heartfelt appreciation for a gesture that will always be a part of our dream-come-true Super Bowl adventure.

FOURTH QUARTER

17
INEVITABLE: FOOTBALL AND INJURIES

Since I began putting pen to paper for this book, or more accurately fingers to a keyboard, this is a chapter that I've dreaded writing. Kept putting it off while I drafted other chapters. Then I peered up at a message that rests above my desk. It was extracted from a business magazine article I read on the topic of procrastination and reads, "DO THE WORST FIRST." Well, at least this wasn't the last chapter written.

Emotionally, this chapter dredges up the most agonizing experiences of my twenty-year football journey. I wasn't naive. I knew that injuries go hand in hand with playing football. I've heard Geoffrey and other players declare that the only day they are fully healthy is the day *before* summer camp begins. A sprained ankle here, a pulled hamstring there. I never, though, would have believed that Mitchell and Geoffrey would collectively suffer double-digit injuries, many of which were quite significant.

Maybe my naivete was the result of the overall good health the boys experienced from birth through high school. If my recollection is accurate, the boys collectively might have missed a handful of school days during that period. Thankfully, they just did not get sick. And if they did, the severity didn't justify a school absence.

The Early Injuries

There was one particular day when Geoffrey was in high school that really tested his resilience. He wasn't feeling well one morning but didn't want to stay home. He had a big basketball game on the docket that afternoon, tipping off against a team with one player who would ultimately play in the NBA. As the day progressed, Geoffrey's condition worsened, but he didn't share that with his parents or coaches.

He took the court that evening, battling a temperature and likely a touch of the flu. It wasn't his best high school performance. But it did demonstrate the grit and fortitude that would epitomize his and Mitchell's approach to dealing with injuries, regardless of their magnitude.

Unfortunately for Geoffrey, injuries and surgeries did not begin with football. He was two years old when his grandmother discovered a bulge in his lower stomach area. A trip to the doctor confirmed what we all suspected. He had developed a hernia requiring surgical repair. What parent doesn't struggle with the notion of their toddler undergoing an operation at such an early age?

With anxiety on overdrive, we took him to a local hospital. The surgeon spent some time with us to ease our angst and assure us that all would be well. Soon thereafter the anesthesiologist parted the double doors that would lead to the surgical area. I couldn't believe my eyes. It was a fraternity brother of mine who I had not seen in eleven years.

Truth be told, I was completely taken aback. This bro spent many a college day in an altered state. He didn't impress me as the sharpest knife in the drawer. Much more of a goofball. Our personalities were 180 degrees apart. But on this day, my preconceived notions melted away. He obviously went through all the proper schooling and training to become an anesthesiologist and be hired by a prestigious hospital.

After some pleasantries, he caressed Geoffrey into his arms. He assured Livie and me that all would be well, that he would take especially good care of Geoffrey. He and all the doctors involved did just that. Geoffrey sailed through the surgery and recovered quickly. While not everyone is cut out for fraternity life, this experience just affirmed to me the value of such a brotherhood. The outcome would likely have been the same without my bro involved, but him being part of the surgical team greatly eased my concerns that day.

Unfortunately, doctors and a hospital were not a one-time childhood experience for Geoffrey. At some point when he was twelve, he began complaining about pain in his shin. We thought it was nothing more than growing pains. No alarm bells went off. But the pain persisted, so we scheduled an appointment with our pediatrician. His diagnosis led him to suggest we visit a pediatric orthopedist for further evaluation.

X-rays identified what appeared to be a cyst growing in Geoffrey's tibia, the larger of the two shin bones. His doctor recommended surgery. Until he could visually see the growth and have it pathologically studied, the doctor would not offer an opinion as to the possibility of the cyst being cancerous. Once removed and tested, we breathed a sigh of relief. Thankfully, it was benign. Geoffrey healed and returned to full activity, albeit to this day a hole remains in his tibia where the cyst was removed, and will be there forever.

That was the extent of Geoffrey's childhood surgical experiences, but it does not exhaust the list of medical maladies he suffered during high school. Osgood Schlatter's Disease is an inflammation of the growth plate at the top front portion of the tibia. Shin splints, medically known as medial tibial stress syndrome, refers to pain along the front of the tibia that typically occurs in athletes who have "intensified or changed their training routines." Geoffrey suffered from both disorders during two different basketball seasons, causing him to miss games and practices. Not too surprising given he played ball year-round, but likely more a result of his growing so rapidly when he was a teenager.

Twelve years old and already two surgeries. Who would have guessed that these two were precursors to the many additional operations that Geoffrey would endure?

As the Years Wore On

By now you may have noticed a theme of disparity between Geoffrey's and Mitchell's experiences. Here, once again, it's repeated. Mitchell glided through his childhood and teenage years unscathed, with one exception that comes to mind.

I've talked about our family's ritual of attending UCLA football games at the Rose Bowl in Pasadena. Our practice was to arrive at the Bowl two hours before game time. The lot where we parked was immediately adjacent to a large expanse of lawn where early arrivals would tailgate before kickoff. Many would settle in lounge chairs, enjoy some nourishment and chill until heading to the Bowl. Others, like us, would bring a football to toss around while waiting.

Raising Giants

On this particular eighty-five degree balmy day in 1998, UCLA was hosting crosstown archrival USC. Big-time game. We were excited. Mitchell, Geoffrey and I began to toss the football. We started within yards of each other but purposefully lengthened the distance as time passed. Mitchell must have been at least twenty-five to thirty yards across the lawn when I chucked the ball in his direction. Like a receiver tracking a throw, he began running toward the ball, with eyes glued to the flight. At the same time, unbeknownst to me, another father had heaved a football to his son headed in the same general area. I can see the convergence today in my mind as if it happened yesterday. The two kids, running close to full speed, ran into each other. And down went Mitchell.

I was never the fastest sprinter in my day, but that afternoon I might have broken the land speed record...or at least it felt that way. I raced to Mitchell. Blood was gushing from his mouth. I took a closer look. One of his front teeth had chipped. He was missing the bottom half of the tooth. He was in obvious pain. I addressed the wound where the impact cut his inner mouth as best I could. There was no option other than to jump back into the car and head home. He ultimately needed the dentist to place a temporary cap on the tooth until he matured.

Looking back, what a game to have missed. The Bruins notched their tenth consecutive win of that season, a 34-17 drubbing of their archrival. The contest was over at halftime with UCLA enjoying a seventeen-point lead. But in the end, Mitchell's well-being far outweighed any college football game.

Other than this one incident, Mitchell was a healthy specimen through his high school years. Geoffrey, on the other hand, obviously couldn't lay claim to the same. In addition to the shin area flare-ups, there was also a badly sprained ankle during his senior football season. Looking back, he probably should have been taken for a doctor's consult on whether to continue playing or take time off, but that wasn't done. Instead, he had the ankle heavily taped each day and lumbered through practices and games, never missing a day or a snap. Was it the wisest approach? Probably not. But it might have further set the tone for later in his life having to deal with the myriad of injuries he would suffer.

I've now served up the injury appetizers. Nothing too terribly alarming. Nothing that would really predict the breadth of injuries the boys would experience later in life. Here's an itemized summary of their injury history, to be followed by some of the agonizing details.

Inevitable: Football and Injuries

Injury	Year	Team	Notes
MITCHELL			
Back surgery #1	1/2011	Cal	After junior season
Back surgery #2	2/2021	Kansas City	End of his career
MCL strain #1	1/2012	Cleveland	End of season injury
MCL strain #2	12/2018	Kansas City	Mid-season; continued playing
MCL strain #3	10/2019	Kansas City	Broke consecutive snap streak
High ankle sprain	12/16/2016	Kansas City	Skipped mid-week practices but didn't miss a game
GEOFFREY			
MCL strain	2004	Oregon	No lost field time
Back surgery	1/2007	Oregon	
Chest injury	9/2007	Oregon	Dropped bar during bench press
Groin/abductor tear	12/2009	Carolina	Played through injury
Hip impingement surgeries	8/2011 & 12/2011	Carolina	Cost him entire season
Sports Hernia surgery	8/2012	Minnesota	Impacted seasonal playing time
Dislocated toe	8/2014	New York	Missed eleven games
Broken ankle #1	11/2014	New York	Lost remainder of season
C. diff	11/2015	New York	Fortunately recovered
Broken ankle #2	11/2015	New York	Basically end of his career

** Disclaimer: This list is based on what I'm aware of. I learned my lesson with Geoffrey's chest injury that I wasn't always privy to this info but at this point I believe it's complete.

Raising Giants

My oh my. My body hurts just reading the lists. But more so, my soul aches. As a parent, we never want to see our children, as toddlers, youngsters or adults, uncomfortable or in pain. If I ache, I can only imagine what they experienced physically, mentally, emotionally.

As I recorded each entry in the tables, my mind shifted to the moment(s) when the injury actually occurred. I was in the stadium when Geoffrey's toe was gruesomely dislocated. Livie and I were in the hospital room where, prepping for Mitchell's first back surgery, the nurse missed the vein in Mitchell's hand when inserting the IV needle. As he lay in the hospital bed, Mitchell immediately turned chalk white and became lightheaded.

On other occasions Livie and I watched from our couch as Geoffrey twice broke his ankle/leg. We both screamed in horror, "NO!!!"

Of course, not all injuries are equal. And not are all specifically football related. As I gaze at the injury lists above, several could be associated with genetics, rather than the ravages of the gridiron. Both boys had their backs repaired...and rather early in their football careers. Bulging and herniated discs created the need to operate. Was it the football pounding? Or was it genetic? My nonprofessional opinion is that the die was cast at birth.

My mother was diagnosed in midlife with stenosis, the narrowing of the spinal canal. Obviously, she was not a football player. As a matter of fact, the closest she got to being an athlete was her weekly bowling leagues. Then there's me. Yes, while I didn't play football, I've been very engaged in sports my entire life. So, to receive a diagnosis of stenosis⊘, scoliosis⊘ and compressed discs⊘ in later life may ultimately be the result of long-term wear and tear. Or maybe it was genetically handed down from my mother. Then again, maybe it's the result of my being run down by a car in 1984, which blew up my knee, tearing my PCL, MCL and meniscus. The postoperative rehabilitation left my knee forever unable to fully bend or extend, leaving me with an uneven gait.

Fortunately, medical procedures have continued to advance to the extent that the repairs on the boys' backs were almost routine. The relief was immediate. They had the best care post-op. No time on the field was missed after Geoffrey's surgery and Mitchell's first operation. However, that wasn't the case after Mitchell's second bout with back issues. That one ended his career.

Mitchell's Final Injury

Livie and I were unaware that Mitchell was experiencing back issues until days before he walked off the field for the last time on October 19, 2020. As with past flare-ups, he believed he could work through any discomfort, but when he took the field that Sunday, believing he could bull his way through the problem, he realized after a couple of series he may have confronted his kryptonite.

While I won't specifically blame football for Geoffrey's only and Mitchell's first of two surgeries, because of the genetic implications I shared, I do believe that Mitchell's reoccurrence directly resulted from having missed but one game snap during the twelve-plus-year span of his football career, from college through the NFL. Four seasons at Cal only missing one snap. 7,894 regular season consecutive snaps in the NFL over the course of eight seasons and 121 starts. Mitchell's former Cleveland teammate, Joe Thomas, holds the record for consecutive snaps at 10,363. When Joe's streak was snapped, Mitchell assumed the honor as the NFL's "Iron Man" for about two and a half years. Rarified air. The constant banging during games, practices, camps, training, etc. would compromise the basic structure of John Q. Public's back, much less a spine that formerly experienced damage and repair.

I don't believe that anyone—Mitchell, Livie or me, his coaches or his team trainers/doctors—thought that his gingerly stroll from the sidelines to the locker room that day would be his final appearance on an NFL field. I suspect the consensus was that he might be out for the short term but would return to the field, certainly before year's end. However, no matter the course of physical therapy attempted or the amount of effort exerted, his back continued to foil any return.

Ultimately, the only chance for Mitchell to resume his career was a second back surgery. The hope was that such a procedure would finally correct any impairment and lead to familiar number 71 once again lining up at right tackle. As we came to learn, that wasn't to be the case. He had played his last snap. As I write this section the vision of his final walk is as clear and upsetting as it was the day it happened.

Throughout the book I've commented about previously undetected themes that surfaced as my thoughts were penned. Here we have another example. Amazingly, all three of the back surgeries had a common thread.

It all began the day that Geoffrey and his Oregon team played USC in Los Angeles during his junior season. My brother and I wanted to beat the crowd, so we hopped in the car headed for the Los Angeles Coliseum in the late morning for a 7:15 p.m. kickoff. The Coliseum itself does not provide ample parking for the expected 92,000 fans that were to fill the stadium that evening. Once the lots are jam-packed, the only options are street parking in questionable neighborhoods, or paying exorbitant rates ($70–$100) to park on the front lawns or driveways of those who live nearby.

We arrived at a parking lot immediately west of the Coliseum. It was so early in the day it was basically empty. The attendants directed us to a spot along the southern border of the lot. One by one other cars entering were pointed to the same general area. We exited our car at the same time the space next to us was being filled. Once parked, a father and son began removing their tailgating gear from the bed of their truck. We struck up a conversation.

By this time in the season, November and the tenth game of the campaign, we knew that Geoffrey's back was problematic and likely in need of surgical repair. So how ironic, a conspicuous demonstration of how small the world really is, to ultimately discover that the senior gentleman parked next to us was the preeminent back surgeon in the country. He was the go-to guy for the NFL. He has operated on the most well-known athletes and entertainers. I was in no position to explain Geoffrey's plight to a man who was the head orthopedic doctor on USC's staff, but I did collect his business card. When the time came for Geoffrey to explore his surgical options, this doctor was a must-see.

Before Geoffrey made an appointment to see the guru, he consulted first with a Eugene-based back surgeon who treated Oregon athletes. His recommendation was surgery. Next in order was a trip to Los Angeles for a second opinion. Upon arrival at the office of the specialist we had met previously in the parking lot, Geoffrey was escorted through a private back door and down a hallway to an office to await the doctor. I learned that athletes and those of renown qualified for this special treatment.

"Commoners" had a different experience. Some years later, I was having back issues. I made an appointment to see this same surgeon. I waited almost three, yes, that's right, three hours to finally be examined. But it was worth the wait. This surgeon wasn't cut happy. He explained that he could operate but thought the best path for me would be physical therapy. He recommended a therapist he relied upon for his clients. It was the best medical advice I may have ever received. While my back will forever be damaged goods, I have not needed surgery.

Back to Geoffrey. After a thorough evaluation, the L.A. surgeon subsequently agreed with the first opinion. He then told Geoffrey that he was in superb hands. The Eugene-based doctor had been trained by and practiced with this distinguished L.A.-based surgeon. All turned out well.

But that wasn't the extent of the connection to this world-renowned doctor. Both of Mitchell's back surgeries were performed by doctors who had studied under and/or worked with this guy. It seemed as though every back surgeon was linked to this superstar. Our family was extremely fortunate to be connected with those who were part of his "family" tree.

As I suggested earlier, I believe genetics had some bearing on the back issues suffered by both Mitchell and Geoffrey. I also believe that genetics were at the root of two other medical problems. Geoffrey had established himself with Carolina, starting all thirty-two regular season games in 2009 and 2010, his second and third campaigns with the Panthers. His final contract year, 2011, was setting up to be a transformative season. If he entrenched himself as a three-year starter, the prospects of him signing a lucrative second contract with the Panthers would be almost assured.

Geoffrey arrived at summer camp with great anticipation. Locked into a starting role, he knew his standing on the team. But in the first few days of camp, something was amiss. He was struggling with discomfort in his hip area. He couldn't freely fire off when run blocking or pass protecting. Before the boys got into football, I always believed that the power of linemen was a result of upper body strength. Chest. Biceps. Triceps. What I learned is that the power to exert their will on defensive foes comes from their core. Abdominal muscles. Gluts. Hip flexors. Psoas muscles. Weakness in any of these areas compromises a lineman's ability to perform at peak level.

Initially, Geoffrey's concerns fell on deaf ears. It was as if the coaches and medical staff believed he was making things up or, at the very least, being rather wimpy about his condition. But why would he feign injury, or embellish the discomfort he was feeling? It made no sense. He was a starter. Why jeopardize his starting position? He couldn't handle pain? He demonstrated his ability to grind through pain during his junior season at Oregon. And would he put at risk a second, potentially life-altering, contract that was a forgone conclusion should he start for three years? Frankly, it pissed me off...and still does. But it was a reality check. (In a separate chapter I will speak to football being an emotionless, heartless business, not the game, as the word might suggest, that most believe it is.)

Ultimately, the team's doctors finally put Geoffrey through a series of tests. He wasn't crying wolf. As a matter of fact, it was quite the opposite. He once again demonstrated that he possessed a high degree of pain tolerance. He was diagnosed with impingements in both hips. In layperson terms, he had developed bone spurs at the top of both femurs that rest in the cups of the hip socket. The spurs were tearing the cartilage in his hip.

No wonder he couldn't perform. Impingements can cause groin stiffness, pain in the front of the thigh or down the buttocks and/or loss of a hip's full range of motion. While it is possible to treat nonsurgically, given Geoffrey's profession and the size of the spur, the Panthers' medical staff recommended a surgical repair of the more pronounced left side. That surgery took place in August of 2011. Before the left side could adequately heal to return to the field, the team elected to surgically repair the right side a few months later. The entire season was lost, and so was the opportunity for a second contract with Carolina.

FYI, research shows that hip impingements appear to be caused by a combination of genetic and environmental factors. Genetically speaking, a misshapen femoral head, a deformed femoral neck or a hip socket that covers too much of the femoral head can lead to the condition. On the flip side, researchers believe that significant athletic activity before a child's bones are mature or repetitive "bumping" from contact sports can also be the culprit. We'll never know the balance between the two in Geoffrey's case.

And we'll never know whether the hip impingement triggered Geoffrey's next injury, which occurred in 2012. Carolina elected to not offer Geoffrey that second contract, ignoring his performance during his two healthy years. As a free agent, he evaluated his options for the 2012 season and signed with the Minnesota Vikings, in large part spurred by his familiarity with the Vikings' offensive line coach, who was Carolina's offensive coordinator during Geoffrey's first three years with the Panthers.

Coming off a season lost to injuries and carrying the burden of having his contract not renewed by Carolina, Geoffrey entered 2012 needing to prove himself to his new team. It's awfully challenging to differentiate oneself if not completely healthy. Geoffrey wasn't. For a second consecutive year, his body betrayed him as camp got underway. Once again, his hip/abdominal area was giving him problems. Once again, the team expressed skepticism. The offender this time? A sports hernia. The condition is not a hernia in the traditional sense. Medically it's known as *athletic pubalgia*.

Regardless how one wishes to label the condition, it can be a debilitating injury. Basically, the soft tissues found in the lower abdomen and groin area that are responsible for repetitive and/or explosive motions, especially those motions that require twisting of the pelvis such as in football, tear. In Geoffrey's case specifically, a muscle had literally torn off a bone in his pubic area. The only course of action at that point was surgery to reattach the muscle to the bone.

With post-surgery physical therapy and rehabilitation, people with a sports hernia can usually fully return to their sport or activities between six and twelve weeks later. That timetable would have significantly bit into Geoffrey's season. Twenty-one days after surgery, Geoffrey was back on the field. But now he was behind. And in the eyes of his coaches, he never caught up. He spent the season as a second-string substitute who received limited playing opportunities.

A second consecutive season lost to injury. Were the hip impingement condition and the sports hernia somehow connected? The answer is...possibly. As I researched for this chapter section, I came across the following statement from the National Library of Medicine: "Impingement is proposed to lead to increased symphyseal motion with overload on the surrounding extra-articular structures and muscle, which can result in the development of sports hernia and athletic pubalgia."

The Injury Trifecta

Two injuries with a likelihood of connection. How about a trifecta? In 2009, two years prior to the onset of the hip impingement ailment, Geoffrey was playing for Carolina in the second-to-last game of the season. The opponent was the team he would play for several years later, the New York Giants. I was in the stands. I believe it was the fourth quarter, though it may have been the third stanza. Definitely in the second half. Geoffrey completed a play and immediately began to hobble.

Of course, from the stands, I had no idea what was happening. He had torn the adductor muscle in his groin. Once again demonstrating his grit and determination, he remained on the field. The injury, however uncomfortable/painful it was, did not cause him to miss a snap that game nor the Panther's season finale the following week. He played through this injury, even though rest and home care are typically prescribed, taking up to three weeks to heal, but when it came to his hip impingement, he was accused of being weak. Looking back, might the groin tear have been the harbinger of the injuries he was to experience in 2011 and 2012?

Quiz time. What is the most common football injury? Certainly, chronic traumatic encephalopathy (CTE) has been highly publicized over the last decade. But that's not the correct answer. Ankle sprains seem rather common, but again, not the answer. According to OrthoCarolina Sports Medicine Center, "the official team physician of the Carolina Panthers," most football injuries occur to the knees.

The most well-known knee injury is the tear of the anterior cruciate ligament, commonly referred to by its acronym, ACL. It is a horribly debilitating injury. Recovery and rehabilitation can take eight to nine months. Unless the damage occurs in camp or very early in a season, the player will need to set their sights on the following year for a return to the field. But most well-known does not translate to most frequent.

The most common knee injury in football players, at any level, particularly in offensive and defensive linemen, is a sprain of the MCL (medial collateral ligament). This strong ligament, located on the "inside" portion of the knee, connects the femur and tibia bones, with the job of preventing side-to-side motion of the knee. Between Geoffrey and Mitchell, they have experienced four MCL strains, at least that I'm aware of.

Geoffrey's occurred in 2004 while playing for Oregon. "Friendly fire" was the cause. It's not uncommon to have a teammate fall on their mate's knee after a scuffle with a defender. That happened with Geoffrey. During a practice. Fortunately, Geoffrey was wearing a brace on the knee when it was rolled on. Thank goodness that, while not mandated by the NCAA, collegiate teams make it a requirement for all offensive linemen to be equipped with heavy duty, metallic braces. After the injury, Geoffrey was told by his offensive line coach, who witnessed the injury in real time, that had he not been wearing the brace, what was only an MCL strain could have been much worse, like a torn ACL.

I have always found it curious that many NFL linemen don't wear these knee protectors. I've heard explanations ranging from "they're too cumbersome" to "they slow me down" to not wanting to show up at practice ten minutes early to put them on. Mitchell, as he's prone to be, can be an outlier. After injuring his MCL at the end of his rookie season, he wore a knee brace off and on, more for "mental peace" than anything else. After tearing his MCL twice during his stay at K.C., he wore a brace for the rest of his career, explaining that the pro version "was sleeker and lighter than the big college ones."

Unfortunately, at least in my opinion, the NFL does very little to overcome resistance to certain protective equipment, as in this case. Their collective bargaining agreement makes it difficult for teams to impose blanket equipment requirements, even if it makes perfect sense to do so. I can't help but wonder how many devastating knee injuries requiring starters to miss significant field time could be prevented by their mandated use. If it's unfair for only offensive linemen to wear, then even the playing field by requiring their defensive counterparts to also strap 'em on.

Often, MCL strains do not lead to missed playing time. Some additional tape, a brace and physical therapy by team trainers allow players to suit up. That was the case with Geoffrey. He didn't miss a snap. Mitchell's first two MCL strains did not disrupt his play, as evidenced by his iron-man consecutive snap string. The third instance broke that streak.

Mitchell's first MCL injury occurred during the final game of his rookie year in 2012. He was playing for the Browns in Pittsburgh's Heinz Field against the Steelers. Livie and I watched the entire game. Although my binoculars remained in their case in a separate room, I was still riveted on Mitchell while watching from the couch. The game ended without a hint of injury. So imagine our surprise when Mitchell phoned postgame to tell us that he had strained his MCL. It apparently wasn't consequential, as he played most of the game without showing any signs of damage to the knee. Being the final game of the season, no future games were at risk. However, the season wasn't truly over for him. He was required to report to the facility for a few weeks of recovery rehab.

The second tweak occurred while playing for the Chiefs in 2018. This time, though, my Sherlock Holmes instincts detected a slight change in Mitchell's gait. As "Dandy" Don Meredith, quarterback in the '60s for the Dallas Cowboys and network color analyst alongside blustery commentator Howard Cosell from 1970 through 1984, famously added to the lexicon of sports commentating, Mitchell had a slight "hitch in his get-along." Once again, fortunately, it wasn't severe enough to have him yanked from the game or pulled from any future start. Would a brace have prevented either injury? We'll never know.

Self-Infliction

Thus far the injuries chronicled in this chapter are what I would call incidental. All were a result of either a genetic malady or simply playing the game of football. There was likely nothing that Geoffrey or Mitchell could have done to prevent the occurrence. But then there was that one instance that was self-inflicted.

Since I've addressed this incident in the chapter about Geoffrey's draft journey, I won't spend much more time here. As a reminder, Geoffrey, to protect an injured wrist, employed an alternative grip known as a "suicide" grip when bench pressing. The bar slipped off his palms, the full brunt of 225 pounds crashing onto his chest. Create an image? He suffered the consequences of the action for the remainder of the football season through his Combine visit. This was the one injury that was completely avoidable.

The Scourge of C. Diff

If you study the injury list above, you will likely notice that all but one of the ailments occurred to the physical structure of the body. Bones. Ligaments. Muscles. Soft tissue. But one stands out: C. diff.

What in the world is C. diff? Its full medical name is *Clostridoioides difficile* or *C. difficile*. (No wonder it's mostly referred to as "C. diff.") It's a germ (bacterium) that causes inflammation of the colon and severe diarrhea. Nothing to be taken lightly as the severity of the diarrhea could lead to risky complications such as dehydration, electrolyte imbalance, kidney failure or other organ damage.

One day nurse Meridith (she really is a nurse) observed a rash on Geoffrey's arm. With a black marker in hand, she outlined the area to later gauge whether the rash was spreading. It did expand. So Geoffrey alerted the team. Believing it was an infection, Geoffrey received two bags of antibiotics plus some oral medication. Within a couple of days, Geoffrey found himself needing a bathroom. Horrible diarrhea. It persisted. Mer was convinced that he'd contracted C. diff caused by an excess of antibiotics.

Geoffrey advised the Giants of Meridith's diagnosis. They didn't initially agree (sound familiar?) and therefore didn't test or provide him with curative medication. They finally relented and referred him to a specialist. The doctor listened to the symptoms and reacted immediately.

Inevitable: Football and Injuries

To paraphrase, "I don't need to test you. You have C. diff." The doctor prescribed medication.

I just don't get these NFL teams. Do they really think players want to be ill or injured? What's the benefit of acting like an ostrich with their head in the sand ignoring what's obvious? But that's the culture that exists. In this case it could have been catastrophic, both to Geoffrey and the team. I understand that C. diff is highly contagious and, without proper steps taken, could have infected a broad swath of the team.

To patients heading toward surgery, back operations are not viewed lightly. But as medical techniques have advanced, these surgeries are rather run of the mill, at least to those with scalpel in hand. For the moment, let's accept that as a matter of being. So, if one evaluates the injuries thus far described, separate from C. diff, almost all could be grouped within a "run of the mill" category.

What follows shifts this theme. It all began in August of 2014. *ProFootballFocus* and *Rotoworld®* had rated Geoffrey as the number-one free-agent guard heading into the season.

The Beginning of the End

In March 2014, after a thorough evaluation of teams and offers, Geoffrey had signed as a free agent with the New York Giants for what he hoped would be "the" contract of his football career. It was a four-year deal worth $16.8 million with a guarantee of $6.2 million. One other team had offered him a similar contract, but the lure of playing in New York for the Giants was too strong.

Geoffrey arrived at the Giants' facility ready for summer workouts. Until this time in his football career, including college and the NFL, he anchored the right side of the offensive line. An occasional snap on the left, but they were very few and far between. Remember the reference I made earlier to Malcolm Gladwell and his rule of 10,000 hours required to achieve true expertise in any activity? Accepting this premise, Geoffrey's body was accustomed to, possibly hard-wired for, the stance and mechanics of a right-side-oriented lineman.

Unfortunately, the Giants either didn't do their homework before signing Geoffrey or were just stubborn. He arrived in New York after playing a full season with the Kansas City Chiefs. At what position? Right guard. The year before he was on the Minnesota Vikings roster. At what position? Right guard. Looking back further, what side did he play for

Carolina? Of course, the right. So we all presumed that Geoffrey would occupy a right-side position. Didn't happen. His first Giants workouts found him at left guard.

Maybe this was because when Geoffrey initially signed with the Giants, they had a ten-year incumbent at right guard who had played exclusively with the team, earning two Super Bowl rings. This person also was selected to the Pro Bowl in 2013, which recognized play during the 2012 season...and who happened to be the son-in-law of the head coach. So what chance did Geoffrey have of unseating him? Virtually none.

However, after suiting up for the Pro Bowl, this right guard underwent hip surgery soon after the game. He seemingly recovered enough to begin the 2013 season on the active roster, but the repair was not long-lasting. In October he was placed on the injured reserve list, otherwise known as "IR," and was on the shelf for the rest of the season. So when Geoffrey signed in March of 2014, maybe the Giants had some inkling that the career of this offensive line mainstay was over, and a replacement was in order. On July 21, 2014, the right guard's retirement was officially announced.

What followed made no sense. Geoffrey approached his line coach after the retirement was official to ask why he was positioned on the left side versus the right. The first response suggested a lack of awareness on the coach's part, and possibly the Giants as a team. "Oh, you played on the right?" My goodness. Really? A rather implausible answer. How could the coach not know? You mean he hadn't watched any tape of Geoffrey from the years before? Hard to understand.

It was explained to me at some point that position coaches are not consulted with or kept in the loop when it comes to player evaluations and/or signing of free agents. OK. But to not take the initiative to learn what's coming your way?

I can't remember whether it was further into this initial conversation or at some later date, but Geoffrey asked again. The o-line coach offered another outrageous response to the request to play the right side. "When you become an All-Pro on the left side, we can consider moving you to the right." Holy s***!! How ridiculous is that?

For the NFL's 2014 preseason, four games were on tap. For two teams, however, there was a fifth contest, played before the official onset of preseason games: the Pro Football Hall of Fame Game. It's an annual exhibition held during the weekend of the Hall of Fame induction ceremonies in a 23,000-seat stadium located adjacent to the Hall of Fame building in Canton, Ohio. (I've been to the Hall. It was an extraordinary experience for someone who has intimately followed professional football since childhood. If you have a chance to visit, I'd highly recommend doing so.) The Giants lined up against the Buffalo Bills that day and won, 27-13.

With five preseason games, I decided to attend the Giants' fourth contest. It was against the New York Jets in MetLife Stadium, home to both New York teams. This day found the Giants occupying the visiting-team locker room. Interestingly, the stadium is physically located in New Jersey, not in the state of New York.

Sitting among more green-clad Jets fans than those rooting for the Giants, I watched the game as was my custom, binoculars trained on Geoffrey. It was the second half. Geoffrey was on the field at his foreign left-guard position. A play was called. Geoffrey trotted to the line of scrimmage. The ball was snapped. I initially watched Geoffrey but then briefly directed my attention away to follow the play's progress. When I turned back toward Geoffrey, he was lying on the ground. At first, I figured it was nothing more than him taking a moment to get to his feet.

He rose but then crumbled back to the turf...and remained there. The head trainer and a couple of his staff, seeing Geoffrey was unable to stand, jogged his way. My heart was beating through my chest. I continued to watch intently. They were looking at his foot. In due course, I saw the trainer gesture to the sideline, a motion that imitated the turning of a car steering wheel. It was a signal I'd never seen before but, unfortunately, have come to know all too well. Bring out the cart.

Every stadium has what is commonly referred to as an injury cart sitting in waiting should a player need to be transported off the field. A moment or two after the request, the cart appeared on the field, headed toward Geoffrey. He was helped onto the rear bed of the cart, the training staff placing a towel over his foot. I'm thinking, "that can't be good."

As Geoffrey was about to be carted off, he looked in my direction. Since college, he had maintained a wonderful pregame habit of scanning the stands looking for where Livie and I were seated. This night we connected pregame so he knew where to look. In a gesture I'm sure was intended to put my mind at ease, I saw him make a fist and then raise his thumb to the sky, as if to say, "Dad, I'm OK." But I knew better.

Raising Giants

As he was led off the field toward the locker room, I hurriedly gathered all my possessions and looked for a stadium attendant. I explained I was the father of the injured player who was just carted off and asked if he could help me get to the locker room. He couldn't help, but he did direct me to someone who could. (I must share that the staff that night were extremely helpful.) I was escorted from my seating area down to the bowels of the stadium and into the Giants locker room area.

There I was met by the Giants' head orthopedic surgeon. The entire medical staff were very accommodating, allowing me full access to Geoffrey and the related activity as Geoffrey's injury was diagnosed. He had gruesomely dislocated his right big toe. A Giants staff doctor with over thirty years of experience with the team told Geoffrey that his dislocation was the most severe he had seen in his career. Geoffrey was seemingly in good spirits, but I was a mess. I knew what this meant. I suspect Geoffrey did as well. A long, arduous recovery. Unable to play for weeks and weeks. A horrible beginning to Geoffrey's tenure with the Giants. To this day, I question, "Did it have to happen?"

NO! Had Geoffrey been in his usual right-guard position, this injury would *not* have happened. How do I know that? As referenced earlier in this section and elsewhere in the book, Geoffrey's body was trained for the right side. What does that mean? When in his pre-snap stance on the right side, his right foot is further back than his left foot. At the snap in pass protection, otherwise referred to as "pass pro," the first movement is backward with the right leg.

When Geoffrey lined up for that ultimately debilitating snap, his stance required the opposite alignment. Left foot back. Ideally, at the snap, his first movement would have been backward with his left foot; however, because his body was so accustomed to the opposite, he began by drawing his right leg backward. In so doing, he firmly planted the right foot, particularly the ball of the foot, that soft pad located between the big toe and the arch, in the turf.

He immediately realized this was wrong. What's the big deal? The misstep places him in a compromised position when trying to offset the rush of an oncoming defensive lineman. The force of the plant and his attempt to correct his stance caused his big toe to dislocate. The toe, as opposed to its normal position lying flat on the ground and pointing forward, was standing in salute toward the heavens.

Inevitable: Football and Injuries

Growing up I was a big fan of the fictional detective Sherlock Holmes, whose books were authored by Sir Arthur Conan Doyle. A quote widely associated with this series of tomes is one uttered by Holmes to his sidekick Watson as he explains his reasoning for solving a crime: "Elementary, my dear Watson." The fact that Geoffrey should have been playing on the right side, to me, was simply elementary.

The dislocation caused Geoffrey to be placed on IR and miss the first eleven games of that season. In years prior, being on IR would have meant the end of his season. But in 2012, the NFL altered a condition of IR. One player per team could be activated off the reserved list to return to the active roster before season end. The player had to be immediately "designated for return" at the time he was placed on the list and had to wait a minimum of eight games to return to active duty.

Apparently, the Giants thought Geoffrey's recovery would likely be completed by week eight. That proved to be a bit optimistic. He returned to the field in game twelve as a starter playing the entire game. Week thirteen found the Giants lining up against the Jacksonville Jaguars. I have, since my early baseball and basketball days, always requested "lucky" number 13 for my game jerseys. I'm not a superstitious type. Unfortunately for Geoffrey, this thirteenth game was far from lucky for him.

Livie and I were home watching the game. The Giants' offense was on the field. A play concluded and there was Geoffrey sprawled on the turf. He wasn't getting up. I remember audibly screaming. I couldn't believe my eyes. He had basically just recovered from the toe dislocation, working his tail off for several months to return and now he apparently was injured again. Once again, the training staff jogged toward Geoffrey. Once again, the cart was requested. An air cast, which is typically affixed to immobilize a broken bone, was inflated over his leg. And, once again, off the field he went with what appeared to be another extreme injury.

We waited for the phone to ring with a status report. Deryk. Meridith. Geoffrey himself. Anyone! Finally, we received the official word. He had indeed severely injured himself. I understand technically it's called a fracture dislocation of the ankle. In layperson's terms, he broke his ankle, but unfortunately that wasn't the extent of the damage. He also tore the deltoid ligament. A crucial component of the ankle's anatomy.

If only it was a broken bone, recovery would have been about six weeks. The complication of the ligament tear extended that period several more weeks. Given the time of the season, the result was another trip to injured reserve, out for the season. The damage would require a surgical procedure to affix a metal plate to the fractured tibia to encourage proper healing. More months of pain, mental stress, emotional anguish...and rehabilitation.

Once again, Geoffrey worked fiendishly to be ready for the opening whistle of 2015. He was ready for camp to open when the trajectory of his career changed. I remember the day so vividly. Geoffrey, Meridith and Alex, as has become an annual tradition now with Emmy as well, traveled across country in the early summer to join Livie and me at our time-share in Northern San Diego County. One afternoon we were spending a few hours at a local outlet mall enjoying the outdoor climes and browsing the shops when Geoffrey's cell phone began to buzz. It was Deryk. He stepped aside to answer.

What in the world would warrant a call from his agent during Geoffrey's vacation? It must have been important. And, indeed, it was. Geoffrey's face had lost its color when he walked back to us. The Giants had called Deryk, telling him that if Geoffrey were to remain a Giant, his contract would need to be "restructured." That was team-speak for cutting his pay. The injuries apparently led the Giants to believe that Geoffrey's value was no longer consistent with the money owed on the remaining three years of his contract. So a contract really isn't a contract, a document binding the parties, as most of us might believe. That's the way it is in the world of professional football. (More thoughts on that later.)

After consulting with Mer, Livie and me, and more conversation with Deryk, Geoffrey decided that it was best for him to accept the restructuring (in other words, take less money) to remain with the team rather than be released and become a free agent once again. He directed Deryk to get him the best deal possible. The contract was modified in time for Geoffrey to report to camp. When he arrived, his broken leg had healed. He occupied his rightful place as the starting right guard.

The 2015 season proceeded as everyone had anticipated when he first signed the four-year deal with the Giants. He was a starter blowing open holes for his running backs and providing unflinching protection for quarterback Eli Manning. Week eleven's contest had the Giants playing division rival Washington Redskins, now known as the Commanders, in their home stadium, FedEx Field.

The play I'm about to describe seemed to happen in slow motion. I was sitting on my couch, fixated on Geoffrey as he engaged a Redskins' defender. Behind him activity swirled. One of his linemates was attempting to block another defender. The running back was trying to locate a hole to run through. The three players all came together as if choreographing a dance move when, as a trio, they fell toward the ground. Instead of landing directly on the turf, all 800 pounds of human being landed on Geoffrey's previously broken leg.

Geoffrey was once again sprawled on the turf. I intuitively knew what had happened. I screamed, louder than while watching the first break, "NO! NO! NO!" I'll spare you any further details. It was indeed another broken bone, immediately above the plate that was still affixed to his tibia, which was intended to be removed after the season. Did that compromise or cause any weakness to the area above? Geoffrey was told no, but who knows.

Three major, catastrophic injuries in the span of sixteen months. None of which were self-inflicted. All resulting from circumstances outside his control. It wasn't like he didn't work hard enough, wasn't in tip-top shape, didn't take care of his body. I cringe thinking about what he went through during those sixteen and a half months. The physical agony of the injuries and surgeries is hard enough to deal with but, beyond the physical, there is the emotional and psychological anguish.

Here's a guy who was as strong as a bull, at one point holding the Oregon squat record at 505 pounds, but for each injury spent weeks having others cater to his needs. He was either crutch-bound or required a scooter to get around. In either case, he couldn't carry a thing. He couldn't pick up or play with toddler Alex. Meridith, who is a nurse, couldn't leave her day job behind as Geoffrey needed care when she returned home from work.

Former Indianapolis Colts' quarterback Andrew Luck, who some believed to be one of the league's brightest stars during his career, retired from professional football earlier than what one would have expected. Luck, in candor not always associated with professional athletes, explained that he could no longer take the years of pain and rehab from his string of injuries. He lost one whole season to an injury and another nine games three seasons earlier. As with Geoffrey and many others similarly pained, the arduous task of rehabilitation takes a toll. Geoffrey has publicly spoken, with complete candor, about the daily grind necessary to recover. Never a day off. The loneliness of being away from his teammates. The doubt created. "Will I be able to return? If so, will I be a shell of my former self?" Days of having to convince himself to not walk away.

A week after this second break, the Giants placed Geoffrey, once again (how many times have I had to write that) on the IR. This was the final straw with the Giants. They released Geoffrey in February of 2016. The release voided the two remaining years of the contract as the money was not guaranteed. Geoffrey pocketed but a bit over one-half of the original contract.

Geoffrey's Final Stand

Hoping to continue his career, Geoffrey diligently rehabbed once again through the first half of 2016. Deryk believed he could find him another team. And he did. Geoffrey signed a free agent contract with the Detroit Lions to attend summer camp. On the surface, the marriage seemed to be a good fit for all. Detroit entered camp with a young offensive line. Geoffrey could provide the senior leadership. But it ultimately wasn't meant to be.

I believe it was the third preseason game. Geoffrey was expecting to play a good portion of the contest. When it seemed like the time for him to enter the fray, nothing was happening. He approached his offensive line coach to inquire. He was told he wasn't going to play. One didn't need to be a genius to understand the writing on the wall. The next morning after arriving at the facility, Geoffrey was summoned to the head coach's office. There he was told that he was being released. It was the end of his career.

Incidentally, when Geoffrey signed with the Lions in that preseason, he wanted to retain the jersey number that followed him throughout his career, but it was in use by another player. So he negotiated a deal whereby he paid about $2,000 to the guy who already laid claim to that number. The irony, of course, is that Geoffrey was cut and never used the number.

We all were heartbroken. I truly believed at the time that Geoffrey was given a raw deal by the Lions. He was told he had a chance to fight for playing time—that he could be a needed mentor to the young bucks on the line. It all seemed rather disingenuous back then.

Livie was relieved. It was always hard for her to watch the boys play, anxious that the next play would result in injury. I can't tell you how many times she would turn to me during a game, whether in the stands or while watching TV, to ask, "Is he OK?"

Inevitable: Football and Injuries

For Geoffrey, while having to accept the finality of a football career that began fourteen years previously as a high school freshman, he knew the true story. Although he had wanted to retire on his own terms, he knew the trio of horrific injuries had taken their toll. He couldn't move like he once was capable of. His ankle no longer had the flexibility required to perform at the highest levels. He couldn't handle consecutive days of practice. He knew. One thing about Geoffrey that's always been true, he could be honest with himself. And, ultimately, I came to accept the reality that Detroit had seen in Geoffrey what Geoffrey already knew.

Unfortunately, circumstances robbed him of the robust career that could have been his if only he had the health and good fortune of Mitchell. But it was what it was. He was a consummate professional. He worked vigorously to hone his craft to be the best football player he could be. And the other thing for sure? He *did not* "rob" from, or put another way "steal from," the Giants as Twitter trolls have asserted. I can't begin to fully articulate how galling it is to me to see the tweets claiming that the money he was paid during the two years with the team was "stolen" from the Giants.

I could probably write an entire separate book to share my thoughts about social media and how it has negatively contributed to some of the ills we see in today's society, but that's for another day. I am, without a doubt, sure that if any one of these trolls, who invariably hide behind avatars and phony names, ever came across Geoffrey on a city street, they wouldn't have the guts to repeat their tweets but, rather, would more likely excitedly approach and ask for an autograph. I know that Geoffrey simply ignores the gibberish and, consistent with his collegiate roots, lets it all run down his back like water off a duck's back. He's a better man than I.

Here's a perfect example. Found this one day while eyeballing Geoffrey's Twitter page. This is what prompted a lengthy exchange:

Somebody1 @Somebody1
First real fight of #giants training camp. Shane Lemieux, obviously unhappy with something Dexter Lawrence did, comes out of nowhere and tackles Dex. Leonard Williams immediately comes to Lawrence's defense and pummels/pins Lemieux to the ground.

Geoff Schwartz @geoffschwartz
Did they run their laps yet?

Raising Giants

A rather innocuous response by Geoffrey having to do with the attitude and disciplinary approach of the New York Giants' former coach who was handed his pink slip at the conclusion of the prior season.

Then, unsolicited, this troll responded with:

Somebody2 @Somebody2

Don't forget you were top 3 worst signings the giants made during the worst decade of team history. You definitely needed a few more laps.

He further offered:

Somebody2 @Somebody2

Geoff let's not exaggerate for the twitter idiots. Year 1 you didn't break your leg. You dislocated a toe in August and played 1.5 games the entire season.
That sound like a guy dying to get on the field?

Geoffrey followed, attempting to set straight the facts of the case:

Geoff Schwartz @geoffschwartz

Only on this app do people attempt to mansplain your career to you.

And I'll give you credit. You're right. I didn't just break my ankle.
I also blew out my deltoid ligament.

A reasonable attempt, but it's impossible to set the record straight with such trolls and with those who aren't the sharpest blades in the drawer. This person began Twittering in 2018 and up until the time of this tweet had only sixty-seven followers. That's a paltry number. The avatar used is of a current or former Giants' player, trying to imply that this numbskull is a professional football player. NOT! Wonder if this troll got permission to use the image of such a public persona.

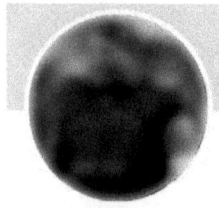

Somebody2@Somebody2
📅 Joined August 2018
67 Following **19** Followers

Inevitable: Football and Injuries

In the whole scheme of things, this exchange is rather tame, but I hope it provides some indication of what Geoffrey, Mitchell and others on social media are forced to put up with. Fortunately Geoffrey is unfazed by all this nonsense.

Brain Injuries

Injuries are inevitable. They come in, shall we say, all shapes and sizes. Some relatively minor, others more consequential, like back surgeries, dislocated toes and broken bones. But, thank goodness, all of the injuries that have beset the boys have impacted areas of the body *below* the neck. In today's world, where CTE is an ever-growing concern for football players, where we see retired guys showing signs of cognitive degeneration, where former players are taking their lives, and where careers are intentionally cut short out of concern for possible future impairment, I am so grateful to share that, to the best of my knowledge, neither Mitchell nor Geoffrey have ever been concussed, lost consciousness on the field or simply had their bell rung. Nor do they exhibit the early signs of the effects of CTE.

There is still so much unknown about CTE and how it impacts the brain. One train of thought is that it's due to the violent interactions between players when one or both are running at full speed and their helmets collide. Offensive linemen are typically immune from this type of collision, since they most frequently play in a "telephone booth." The other side of the coin suggests that the accumulation of small but repetitive helmet clanking is the culprit. To this, Mitchell has said, "no, no." Watching Mitchell, one would observe that he does not allow the head slapping and helmet butting frequently seen between teammates as an atta-boy for a good play. He has made it very clear that doing so with him is verboten.

Technique, or lack thereof, could be a contributor to the accumulation-of-small-hits theory. Linemen, as best I'm aware, are taught to keep their heads up and out of the way in pass protection. They never want their heads to drop. That provides an opening for the defender to use the downward momentum created and push the o-lineman to the ground. Keeping one's head out of harm's way during run blocking is more challenging but, again, the use of the helmet is not the technique taught.

And thankfully the head slap that once was regularly employed by defensive linemen—a move where a defensive player hits an opponent on the side of the head, rattling their helmet—was completely outlawed in 1977. Made famous by the Los Angeles Rams' All-Star and Hall of Famer David "Deacon" Jones, that move was a brutal, and accepted, part of defensive line moves. I can only speculate that the trauma caused by such vicious activity was a contributor to the initial onset of CTE, especially considering that many of the early sufferers were offensive linemen.

When Geoffrey and Mitchell began their football journeys, CTE was not on the radar screen. As it became more pronounced, both guys continued to play, knowing what might befall them. As I mentioned, to date there have been no signs of any complications. I can only pray to G-d that it will remain so during the rest of their lives.

The NFL and its competition committee, and entrepreneurs wishing to find a solution, are spending time and money to identify ways to minimize the impact of violent hits to the head. Several years ago I attended a football-related symposium where one exhibitor was demonstrating a helmet prototype claiming to reduce the impact of concussive helmet-to-helmet contact. But they were struggling to gain any momentum in the football world. The helmet was perceived as too big and bulky to wear. So comfort, and maybe vanity, topped safety.

Fast forward several years. A news report crossed my desk. The NFL mandated for the beginning of the 2022 season the use of what is being called "Guardian Caps." They fit over standard helmets and must be worn by offensive and defensive linemen, linebackers and tight ends throughout training camps and during the first two preseason games—the time when the league says head injuries are most prevalent. The claim is that these caps will result in at least a 10 percent reduction in severity of impact to a player's brain, 20 percent if both involved players are wearing a cap. It seems like a small percentage of improvement; however, it does suggest progress.

Unfortunately, many players are not on board. One called the caps "silly." Another player claimed to be "aggravated" by the caps, making him feel like a "bobblehead on the field." Another player complained that the extra twelve ounces made the helmet feel "heavy." Not surprising. Most helmets with a face mask weigh between three to five pounds. It's suggested that even the difference of an ounce can drastically change performance on the field. So adding another three-quarters of a pound is consequential. It'll be interesting to follow the use of the caps. Sometimes, regardless of the perceived benefits, change is hard to come by.

Inevitable: Football and Injuries

Key Injuries to Other Players

All football players experience injuries, of course. Over the years, I witnessed a number of unfortunate injuries to teammates and others that tugged at my heart. I thought I would share three of them, all of which had some level of impact on the players' future careers.

I've previously made mention of Geoffrey's teammate, Dennis Dixon, who suffered a tragic season-ending, Heisman Trophy–depriving injury during his senior season at Oregon. The original diagnosis was a torn ACL. Apparently, the tear did not warrant immediate surgery. As a matter of fact, Dixon rested during the week of practice and was in the starting lineup for the next weekend's game against Arizona.

I believe only an intimate few really knew the severity of the injury, but suit up Dennis did. In the first quarter, he was healthy enough to scramble for a touchdown. The key here was that his path was a straight line from behind the line of scrimmage to the end zone. But on the next series, a play was called that required Dixon to run parallel to the line of scrimmage, plant the injured leg and then cut up field. That was that. With the abrupt change in direction, he dropped to the turf like he'd been shot. The tear was now complete. His season was over. And so was his candidacy for the Heisman. Such a disappointment.

Launched in late 2000s, continuing through the early 2010s, collegiate and NFL running backs began a practice of trying to hurdle oncoming defenders who were trying to tackle them below the waist. It was a precarious practice, proven so the night of November 7, 2009. Mitchell and his Cal team had a game in Memorial Stadium. In the second quarter, a Cal running back was darting toward the end zone to score a touchdown when a defender approached. As had become his habit, the running back leaped into the air trying to clear the tackler. A second defender was on scene and pushed the runner further into the air.

With the push, the ball carrier had to be at least five feet above ground, maybe six, horizontal to the field and rotating like a whirlybird. He returned to earth landing on the back of his head. His helmet popped off. Mitchell ran over to see how he was doing, only to see his eyes rolling back into his forehead. After thirteen minutes the running back was stretchered off the field to a local hospital. He was diagnosed with a concussion, his second in two weeks, and never returned to play that season.

He skipped his following senior season and entered the draft. Although he posted the fastest forty-yard time in his Combine and had a brilliant career at Cal, he was the third running back selected, and thirtieth player overall. Injuries tend to cause players to drop in the draft. I believe this was another example of a player dropping because of an injury.

His professional career was short-lived. In his second year, he suffered two more concussions. He was placed on IR and never saw the field again, being ultimately released two years later. What a shame! That evening at Cal he made what, I believe, proved to be a dreadful decision, trying to hurdle himself into the end zone, and paid dearly for doing so.

A close friend of mine has been following Geoffrey and Mitchell since this journey first began. I, in turn, have been excitedly watching his son progress from a scrawny high school freshman, who timidly assumed his position on kickoff returns, to a college wide receiver, playing for a top program. He ran like the wind at six feet, four inches tall and over 200 pounds. Finally ascending to a starting position, he was snagging balls all over the field that were later in the day shown on ESPN's nationally televised *SportsCenter's* "Top Ten" segment.

One afternoon in 2021, I was channel surfing and came upon a game in which he was playing. I happened to see a pass thrown his way. As he caught the ball, he was tackled. Similar to Geoffrey's experiences, he laid prone on the ground. The camera panned to his ankle. It so reminded me of Geoffrey's dislocated toe. His leg was broken, his foot gruesomely pointing in an unnatural direction. I gasped. I knew all too well what he could expect in his immediate future.

Fast forward, his recovery was a complete success. His post-recovery forty-yard times were faster than before the injury. He finished his college career and became a free agent signee. Did his injury impact his draft experience?

Some Final Thoughts

Before wrapping up this chapter, I'd like to share some thoughts, maybe more hypotheses, related to injuries in football. Admittedly, I haven't spent much time researching. Most of this is anecdotal.

First, let's look back to when I was a kid. Professional players focused on football during the season. There were few offseason workouts and little offseason conditioning. This was due in part to the financial realities

Inevitable: Football and Injuries

at that time. Salaries, paid only during the season (as is done today), were not sufficient to support a family year-round. I've heard stories of professional footballers taking part-time or interim jobs during the offseason at furniture stores and car dealerships to make ends meet.

In today's world, players are likely training, to some degree, at least ten months out of twelve. They are punishing their bodies most of the year. Some have been reported to begin working out mere days after a season has concluded. What does that mean for the body? Little to no rest. Little time for recovery. Does the lack of downtime lead to more injuries over the course of a season, a career? Or does the longer training regimen prevent injuries? I would speculate that the answer is the former.

The NFL and the NFL Players Association, which exists to protect player safety, have addressed the amount of physical contact over the last couple of collective bargaining agreements (CBAs). No longer are two practices allowed in one day during preseason camp, as was the case when Geoffrey first arrived in the league. Overall, there are fewer practices during camp. And midweek in-season workouts have been trimmed back as well. Less stress and strain on, what I believe to be, overtaxed bodies. However, I don't believe the CBA has any influence over offseason activities.

The players today are simply bigger, faster and stronger. I think back to that time in Chicago when I saw the Rams team exit their hotel. When I compare those images with the ones I've seen during the boys' careers, it's like comparing night and day, apples to oranges. The guys are generally taller. Most are buff, that is, with recognizable muscle definition. Many have limited fat. The model of Adonis comes to mind. And they are, without a doubt, faster and quicker. Imagine the concussive forces exerted on the body in today's environment when two or more players ram into each other, especially if they have a running start. I did spend a few moments Googling the physics of football impacts. It's rather mind boggling to read the numbers. I'm very happy that Mitchell and Geoffrey played on the line of scrimmage in a "telephone booth." Doing so greatly minimized those concussive forces experienced, for instance, when a linebacker has a fifteen-yard head start zeroing in on a running back to bring him to the turf.

Lastly, in my humble opinion, our bodies, regardless of level of conditioning, are simply not built to withstand these enormous forces on such a consistent basis. The overall skeletal makeup of a human being has not changed over time and is generally the same one to another. Sure, some folks are bigger boned, like Geoffrey and Mitchell. Having larger bones didn't prevent Geoffrey from breaking his tibia twice though, did it?

And what about soft tissues, like ligaments, tendons and muscles? It seems to me, anecdotally, that we see far more soft-tissue injuries than previously. Pectoral muscle tears come to mind immediately. How about Achilles tendons snapping, without any real stress on the area? A player is routinely running and then collapses as if they were gunned down. Unfortunately, I've seen enough to know right away when the tendon has torn.

I truly believe that these factors are contributing to a rise in overall injuries below the neck, irrespective of the efforts of the NFL and NFLPA to reduce such occurrences. I further assert that the trend is on an upward trajectory. Genetics will continue to produce bigger, faster and stronger players. The laws of physics are unbending. More injuries will occur.

🏈 🏈 🏈

Writing this chapter has unleashed so many emotions for me. Sadness. Anger. Frustration. Injuries have been part of my twenty-year journey, so I needed to include an account of them. But with all the anguish and heartbreak, the experiences have also been the source of great pride. At any time, Mitchell or Geoffrey, particularly Geoffrey, could have raised the white flag and said "no more." But through pure grit and determination, and constitutions that were forged as youngsters, they did their best with the cards dealt to them.

They not only persevered, they achieved great success in their chosen field and set the foundation for the next chapters in their lives. I can only hope that through their actions others can find the fortitude to overcome life challenges that seem insurmountable.

18

DON'T BE FOOLED—
IT *IS* A BUSINESS

I grew up watching professional sports, believing I was simply enjoying a game. As Wikipedia defines it, a game is "a structured form of play, usually undertaken for entertainment or fun, and sometimes used as an educational tool." The definition went on to distinguish "game" from "work," offering that "games are different from work, which is usually carried out for remuneration." Talk about being naive.

My experience with the boys clearly shined light on a simple and indisputable fact. *Football is a business*. Decision-making involves little to no emotion. While traits such as character, leadership and the ability to blend into team chemistry are considered in roster-building, the process overall is strictly an intellectual exercise, not softened by a tug at the heartstrings. And unfortunately candor and transparency are seemingly not valued. Overall it can be a ruthless process.

Geoffrey's Perspective

I was prepared to offer my thoughts on the business of football until I read a piece authored by someone I know quite well and trust absolutely, and who has a more personal perspective from which to share. In an article penned for FoxSports.com titled "NFL Cutdown Day Is Here. A Former Lineman Tells You What It's Like," Geoffrey made it crystal clear how football is a business. Here's a summary of what he said.

Geoffrey played eight full seasons in the NFL as an offensive lineman. He was released four times. Each instance, he explained in the article, was different, and yet so similar. One minute he had a job and then, via one phone call, or one conversation, it was all gone.

Geoffrey was drafted by the Carolina Panthers in the seventh round in 2008. At the end of preseason, Geoffrey was released but immediately reclaimed by the Panthers and signed onto the practice squad. He was ultimately elevated to the regular roster. Because he was on the practice squad in year one, he was considered a free agent after his fourth year. The Panthers at that point had the right to offer him a tender, which he believed they'd do.

That turned out to be a naive impression, as the general manager (GM) told Geoffrey's agent, Deryk Gilmore, at the Combine that the Panthers weren't offering him a tender and he was being let go. He wrote, "that one stung," as he realized for the first time that the NFL is a business.

Next up, the New York Giants. Geoffrey signed a four-year contract with the team. After experiencing a second devastating ankle injury, surgery, and months of rehab, he planned on returning fully recovered for a third season. But that wasn't part of the Giants' plans. Instead, Geoffrey received a call in early February from the Giants GM telling him to hop on a plane to New York for his official release.

This one "stung" for a couple of reasons. He fully believed he would be there for the term of his contract, especially after showing his commitment rehabbing through two grueling years. But secondly, and more in line with the notion that the NFL is a business, Geoffrey was very bothered by the Giants' lack of transparency. As a seven-year vet, he felt he deserved a reason for the release. Although he asked multiple times, the team—specifically coaches and front office staff—refused to talk with him, which he shared was rare when being released.

After being released by the Giants Geoffrey signed with the Detroit Lions.

Heading into a preseason game against the Baltimore Ravens, Geoffrey was told he would play in the second half. Instead, during halftime his offensive line coach pulled him aside and said he was "down" for the second half, that is, he wasn't going to see any action.

After getting settled on the sidelines to begin the second half, he approached his offensive line coach and asked him directly, "Am I being

Don't Be Fooled—It *Is* a Business

cut tomorrow?" His answer: "It doesn't look good." The handwriting was on the wall. He was being cut. Once again transparency was absent.

At this point in Geoffrey's career, he could read the tea leaves. He was done. His career had come to an end. He wanted so desperately to end his career on the field but, like so many of his NFL brethren, it ended with "a quick phone call, turn in your playbook and move on to the rest of your life." He concluded the article with "this is a zero-sum game."

(If you'd like to read the article in its entirety, here's a link: https://tinyurl.com/2ajpuvaw.)

Geoffrey's Fox article was written after his time in the NFL. Our first experience with the business of professional football took place during the draft process. I shared earlier how Geoffrey plummeted to selection number 241 in his draft as a result of the back surgery between his junior and senior collegiate seasons. After having a noteworthy senior year in which he exhibited zero evidence of a back problem, there was no logical reason to have been red-flagged and dropped to the point of almost not being drafted.

The league as a whole made a business decision. Let me be clear. I'm not suggesting they all huddled together and colluded, that is, all agreed to not select Geoffrey until the later rounds. But it seems to me to be a very understood "unwritten rule." There's so much evidence to support my contention.

The "business" approach I speak of can also be seen in the double standards at play. Remember the story I shared about Geoffrey being interviewed during his Combine visit? He was caught on film during a college game atypically giving less than full effort on the field. One play among hundreds of others throughout his career, and yet that's the one brought to his attention. What happened with all the holes he opened for his running backs? What about the pancakes? What about safe pockets for his quarterbacks? His coaches would have attested to his character. It just seemed to be a double standard made to fit a narrative. I'm sure that coaches are all perfect. NOT!

Geoffrey talked about the sting of the Carolina Panthers not tendering him after his fourth season with them. What Geoffrey did not share was the conversation he had with the general manager prior to his second hip surgery. After the first operation, the surgeon suggested undergoing the second. The team was all in favor, telling Geoffrey that doing so would be advisable, as they considered him part of their future plans. Seems they had a different definition of "future" than I do.

The stop at Minnesota was agonizing. I've talked about Geoffrey's sports hernia and subsequent surgery leading into the campaign with the Vikings. I'll concede that the injury contributed to his slow start that season. However, once healed, although provided with numerous indications that playing time would increase, that never materialized. What ever happened to the notions of truth and transparency?

Geoffrey's experience with Kansas City is a real head-scratcher, especially now, knowing the organization through our experience with Mitchell.

I've not found records, if such records exist, as to how many NFL players replacing a starter during a season remained a starter when the injured position mate was healthy enough to resume playing. Geoffrey held that distinction. He replaced a starter in the fourth or fifth game of his only season with Kansas City and didn't return to second-string status for the remainder of the year. We all figured that would translate into a new contract acknowledging his value heading into the next season. Didn't happen.

Geoffrey's attitude throughout his NFL career was one of betting on himself. After leaving Carolina, he refused to sign any contract that would not recognize his self-determined value. That's why he accepted one-year deals with Minnesota and Kansas City. He wanted to prove his worth to a team such that a more lucrative, longer-term deal could be reached. Offered by Gordon McGuiness, Chief of Media Strategy for PFF: "Geoff Schwartz was underrated throughout his NFL career and we highlighted him as part of our Secret Superstars series after an impressive 2010 season with the Carolina Panthers."

He truly thought he had achieved this goal during that season in Kansas City, however the Chiefs' brass didn't come to the same conclusion, even though ProFootballFocus sang his praises. PFF's Gordon McGuiness explained, "In terms of a PFF grade, the best season of his career came in 2013 with the Kansas City Chiefs, when he played three spots along the offensive line and finished as PFF's fifth-highest graded guard in the league."

Geoffrey easily was the highest-rated Chiefs' offensive lineman that season and was recognized as the top free-agent guard in the league. Others at PFF demonstrated their admiration of Geoffrey by saying

Don't Be Fooled—It *Is* a Business

"Schwartz has played as well as any [guard] not named Evan Mathis on a per-snap basis the last two years."

And yet, when it came time to discuss a new contract, all the Chiefs were willing to offer was a paltry (by NFL standards) one-year deal at $1.4 million. It just didn't make sense. I wonder if there was something unspoken that led to K.C.'s approach. It wouldn't at all surprise me if they were not being candid, that there was more to their decision than they shared. It remains a head-scratcher for me. Thank goodness that at least one other team, that being the New York Giants, recognized his value, offering him a four-year contract worth $16.8 million with $6.2 million guaranteed.

However, as discussed previously in the book, Geoffrey's experience with the Giants wasn't as rosy as anticipated when he proudly and excitedly signed that free agent contract. After one injury-plagued year, the Giants ultimately took a machete to his agreement. Take it or leave it. While I'm not privy to such contract activity, I am hard-pressed to remember hearing or reading about other similar "adjustments" of this nature. Then they unceremoniously axed him completely after the second season of what was to be a four-year contract. In my corporate world, contracts are much more binding, but in the NFL they are not. Maybe they should be reclassified as "understandings," far less legally binding.

And, as Geoffrey described in his Fox article, when he was let go the Giants didn't have the decency to share their reasons face-to-face. I've been in corporate leadership for decades. Even when an action was unpleasant, I never shirked my responsibility of meeting in person to convey the news. Yes, it's a business, but whether it be football or the corporate world in general, there are still certain civilities expected.

I've already shared some of my thoughts related to Geoffrey's experience with Detroit. While I may need to accept the notion that Geoffrey's body could no longer handle the rigors of football, and that prompted the Lions' decision to release him, I still find fault with how they handled the communications during his last preseason contest.

Heading into the game, they told Geoffrey to be ready to play in the second half. When it seemed to be that time, Geoffrey began loosening up. Then the offensive line coach approached and told Geoffrey he was "down" for the second half. Am I to understand that during the thirty-minute first half the Lions' staff huddled and determined that Geoffrey's time with the team was over. Hard for me to fathom.

Raising Giants

And then when probed about the longer-term prospects, Geoffrey hears, "It doesn't look good." My oh my. Twice, with Geoffrey's career apparently on the line, honesty was absent. I don't understand why decency and civility can't be more the norm.

Mitchell didn't move around as much as Geoffrey, and so there's less of this behavior associated with him. But he did have one doozy of an experience at the end of his contract with Cleveland that epitomizes this "it's a business" reality.

As was his purpose, Deryk Gilmore was having conversations with multiple teams about a free agent contract for Mitchell. Although throughout his four years with the team Cleveland was not competitive and rarely won, Mitchell had connected with his teammates and the city of Cleveland, the latter I've gotta believe enhanced by meeting his wife-to-be, Brooke, along the way. He was quite open to signing a new deal with the Browns.

The negotiations continued fast and furious as the free-agent period was headed toward a close. At the eleventh hour, late one evening, Deryk thought he had a deal that would benefit both the Browns and Mitchell. The Browns would retain a valued member of their offensive line and Mitchell would be paid more akin to his league value. It might have been one of those win-win arrangements. Deryk requested that Cleveland give him until the morning to consult with Mitchell and finalize the deal. That request was approved. Everyone in Mitchell's camp thought his future would be in Cleveland. It was not to be.

Deryk received the go-ahead from Mitchell to complete the deal the following morning. With that in hand, he made the call. There was no longer a deal on the table. The Browns informed Deryk that they had no interest in signing Mitchell and were moving on. Mitchell was basically cast adrift.

I will never be able to validate this hypothesis, however, I believe that, soon after hanging up with Deryk the evening before, the Browns called some of their counterparts in the league, those teams publicly associated with negotiations with/interest in Mitchell, to probe the temperature of what was being offered. I further believe that, in so doing, they discovered that their last offer exceeded any numbers being offered otherwise. So they pretended the verbal agreement never happened. I've known Deryk long enough and well enough to absolutely believe that what he shared with us that night was not fabrication.

Subsequently, an article was published that concluded, "The front office came back and said Schwartz left on his own, but there's no reason for him to lie when he ended up taking less money in Kansas City. The Browns also lost star center Alex Mack in the same offseason and the new strategy in place was doomed from the start. A line that took years to build was dismantled in a day for no reason other than incompetence." Of course, the Browns exec had a different perspective: "I've seen a lot of their agents mouth off in the media, and I'll just leave it at that." Quite a professional response, huh? I welcome you to come to your own conclusion.

It was a devastating blow to Mitchell. I know, as he and Brooke were with us in L.A. during this period. Mentally and emotionally he had made peace with the fact that Cleveland would be his home for the foreseeable future. Plus, at that moment in the timeline, teams had mostly filled their rosters through the draft and free agency. There was serious concern as to what opportunities still existed. Deryk and his colleagues at the agency went to work.

Kansas City was in play. By the end of the day, Mitchell was a Chief, having signed a five-year deal. It wasn't for the same money as discussed with the Browns, but it wasn't going to make him a pauper either. Some people are completely driven by money. That's not Mitchell.

Many of you may have heard the old adage about "things work out for a reason." For Mitchell, although the journey that agonizing day was stressful, it all worked out for the best. He was paid handsomely to start for a team that appreciated him as a football player. In his first two years with K.C., the Chiefs had a combined record of 22-10, leading their division each year, and making the playoffs. Cleveland, on the other hand, was a woeful 1-31 during those two seasons. Dead last in their division. Karma?

From 2016 through 2019, the Chiefs had an aggregate record of 46-18, first in their division each year, culminating with that Super Bowl LIV win. During that same three-year period the Browns had an embarrassing 14-49-1 record, never climbing higher than third position in their division. And, of course, Mitchell found himself on AP's All-Pro first or second team in all four years. Is there any question about how things worked out?

The Numbers Game

To provide some perspective, allow me to offer some of the numbers and economics related to running the NFL. First, though, a disclaimer. Although I graduated from UCLA with an economics degree, I do not claim to be an expert in any fashion as it relates to the economics of the NFL or the collective bargaining agreement (CBA). This is just one person's perspective, based on a closer look than most.

If a widget cost $1.00 in 1984, that same widget would cost $2.85 in 2022 due to inflation, according to the Bureau of Labor Statistics consumer price index. In 1984, the Bowlen family bought the Denver Broncos for $78,000,000. In June of 2022, the Bowlens sold the team to a group led by an heir to the Walmart fortune for $4.65 billion. I'll help with the mathematics.

Instead of a multiplier of 2.85, the Bowlen's investment grew sixty times during that period of time. Where else can one invest and see such a return? To demonstrate that it's not an outlier, the Dallas Cowboys were purchased by Jerry Jones in 1989 for a "paltry" sum of $150 million. Today, Dallas is the world's most valuable sports property, estimated to be worth $9.2 billion. Oh, poor Jerry, his investment has "only" appreciated sixty-one times.

In case you might be wondering, the average NFL team value in 2008 was "only" $1 billion dollars. In 2022, that number had vaulted to $4.47 billion, a gain of almost 400 percent. Imagine for a moment going to sleep and waking up richer, much richer, in the morning, day after day, year after year. That is, in effect, what's happening. And values will only continue their climb. More and more money will come into the NFL coffers in the coming years through expansion, particularly overseas, more lucrative media deals and bloated marketing contracts.

In the end, this is all about money. And the owners are in the driver's seat. I remember, during the lead-up to the new CBA in 2006, watching a news conference during which league ownership, represented by the Carolina Panthers' owner, tried to make a case as to why they couldn't agree to the proposed agreement on the table. It was reported at the time that the whole disagreement between the parties was mostly over revenue sharing. During the segment, the Panthers' owner drew a pie chart on a piece of paper. He attempted to demonstrate how much of the total revenue received by the league went to owners and how much to the players.

As drawn, players were to receive more than owners. However, there was an important element missing. He didn't include in his explanation that, as part of the current CBA, teams received $1 billion "off the top" before any other distributions were made. That "oversight" skewed the

Don't Be Fooled—It *Is* a Business

numbers, attempting to portray the players as having the advantage. Add that billion back in and the advantage swung to the owners.

Don't get me wrong. I understand capitalism. The owners are the ones who put their fortunes on the line. However, the basic construct of the league is so financially sound that the downside that most business owners face, like failure, losses or bankruptcy, has really been eliminated. The United States government has more of a chance to go into default than any NFL team.

Fortunately, the players are progressively benefiting from the escalation in values and the income being realized by the NFL. The contracts being signed by quarterbacks since 2021 are mind-boggling. Mitchell's former Chiefs teammate, Patrick Mahomes, signed an extension with an all-in value of $450 million! He's now part-owner of the Kansas City Royals baseball team as well as two local professional soccer teams plus a Miami-based pickleball team. Astonishingly, heading into the 2024 season, four QBs will earn a base salary of over $50 million, part of a total of eight who are getting paid at least $40 million. Staggering.

I've engaged in conversation with friends who are as fanatical about sports as I am, but who possess greater all-around knowledge of the history of its collective bargaining agreements between owners and players. One of these friends, Marc Isenberg, who has read and studied extensively on the subject, has a theory as to why football's CBA is the least favorable to their players compared to the other major professional sports leagues.

In a few words, the players' union lacks solidarity and commitment. Marc points to Major League Baseball as the shining example of how the strength of a players' union acting as one can shift the balance between ownership and the players. During a sixteen-year tenure as executive director of the Major League Baseball Players Association (MLBPA), Marvin Miller has been credited with teaching MLB players the basics of human capital as a commodity they were selling to club owners. While he ran MLBPA, the average player's annual salary rose from $19,000 in 1966 to $326,000 in 1982. Upon learning of Miller's death in 2012, former MLB Commissioner Fay Vincent stated, "He changed not just the sport but the business of the sport permanently, and he truly emancipated the baseball player—and in the process all professional athletes."

The National Football League Players Association (NFLPA) seemingly has not had an executive director with the same fortitude and determination as Marvin Miller. Miller basically broke the backs of the owners during his tenure, leading his constituents to several work stoppages. The first, in 1972, made MLB history. Player reps voted 47-0 in favor of a strike (with one abstention), which spoke to the solidarity built within the player ranks.

Conversely, let's peek at the most recent vote for the NFL CBA. It was 1,019 to 959. A majority of only 60 out of almost 2,000 votes. And this is the issue. NFL players have not spoken with one voice, which is necessary to break the stranglehold the owners possess over the players.

To be fair, beyond the extraordinary shift in amounts to be paid to players, guaranteed contracts are also changing. Of the nearly 2,000 players under contract in 2022, 112 had fully guaranteed deals. But that's only a touch over 0.5 percent. One quarterback in 2022 signed a fully guaranteed contract of $230 million. Outlandish! It's my understanding that most people associated with the NFL have excoriated this deal.

One of the most contentious points of a contract negotiation is the amount guaranteed, struggling to agree upon an amount meaningful to the player. Remember, Geoffrey's guarantee was only $41,000. Compare that with other professional leagues. Major League Baseball contracts are fully guaranteed. If, for example, a player signs a $200 million dollar deal and then five days later is involved in a tragic automobile accident that ends his career, he will still receive the full amount of the contract. Same applies with the NBA.

This has never made sense to me. I understand that football is a violent game and prone to injury that can impact longevity (don't we know), but it's not like baseball or hoops players have demonstrably longer careers. The averages for both respectively are 2.7 and 4.5 years, as compared with the NFL's 3.3.

While the financial landscape is evolving to where player compensation packages are improving, let's not lose sight of the fact that football is a business run by astute businesspeople who are first and foremost concerned with the protection of their assets. Although it's the players who day in and day out put their short- and long-term health in jeopardy (yes, for a sport they love and one in which they chose to play) it has been the owners who have enjoyed the greater financial benefit. Those who watch and those who play must understand that, at the end of the day, football is a game within a business. Buyer beware.

Before one concludes that I lack appreciation for the amazing opportunities both my sons were afforded, let me dispel such thoughts. There

Don't Be Fooled—It *Is* a Business

are few life-changing experiences that can compare to what Geoffrey and Mitchell have lived. The people they have met along the way. The chance to play a game they love...and were extremely good at. The financial security, possibly for generations to come, that resulted. The doors that have opened and will continue to open because of their NFL association. They have and will continue to reap the benefits. But the bottom line is that there is a bottom line, as for any business entity.

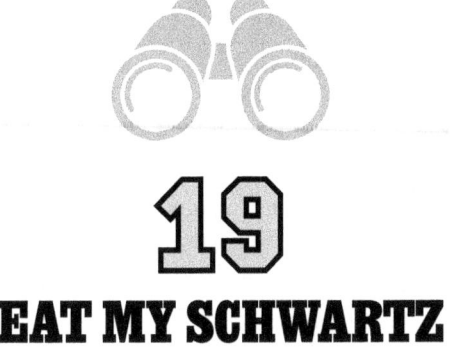

19
EAT MY SCHWARTZ

Bookstores, at least the ones that still exist, all contain a section labeled "Sports." Shelves in these sections are crammed with autobiographies, biographies and general stories of athletes. Some of the book subjects are very well-known, while others are more obscure. Indeed, some are authored by the greatest of all time (GOATs) in their respective sports. Others have a meaningful story to share. My bookshelves contain many of these works.

Imagine, then, my astonishment when (to the best of my recollection) in 2015 Deryk Gilmore floated the idea for a book with a subject matter very dear to my heart. It was a Geoffrey and Mitchell project that ultimately resulted in the publication of their book *Eat My Schwartz: Our Story of NFL Football, Food, Family, and Faith*, in 2016. "How do they qualify to have a book written about them?" I thought to myself. They weren't famous. At the time neither was considered elite in their profession. I didn't think either had much of a compelling story to share. Yet the idea was hatched.

I continued to search for a rhyme or reason that would justify such an endeavor. Sure, they are good people, but is that reason enough? They are brothers who had ascended to the highest levels of their profession. There are more brothers playing in the NFL than you might imagine. Nothing special. They were the first pair of Jewish brothers

Raising Giants

to have played in the NFL in ninety years. I'm sure that could provide a human-interest twist, but primarily to the 2.4 percent of the United States population who are Jewish. What was I missing? As I subsequently learned with many aspects of the *Eat My Schwartz* journey, it really didn't matter what I thought.

Once again Deryk Gilmore's name comes to the fore. I described in previous pages his creative bent when working for Oregon. Here was another example. Through his many contacts, Deryk had gotten to know a television and publishing veteran, a celebrity ghostwriter, novelist and children's book author, who has written about or collaborated with a couple of NFL superstars. It's fair to say this person had a bit of street cred when it came to publishing a book.

The pair huddled and, I suspect, debated the pros and cons of launching such a project. They advanced the idea to Geoffrey and Mitchell. I sure hope they asked the guys to sit before presenting what seemed, to me at least, this improbable idea. I was not a participant in any of the initial conversations among the four of them, so I can't speak to the give and take, but in the end, the project was given a thumbs up to proceed. I wonder if the guys were as skeptical as I was. (I asked and they don't remember.)

Maybe it was a great idea, but there was one critical element missing at that point. Who was going to write the book? It certainly wasn't going to be Mitchell or Geoffrey. Book writing was not a skill set that either possessed. Plus, they were still playing football. No time. However, as in so many cases, it's not necessarily what one knows but who one knows. Deryk's associate knew a writer with whom they had previously worked. The project idea was brought to Seth Kaufman's attention.

Seth enjoyed a career in e-commerce before calling an audible and hanging out his own shingle. He has ghostwritten twelve books, with several landing on the Amazon Top 10 and the *New York Times* nonfiction lists. One of his collaborations was with well-known NCAA and NBA head coach Rick Pitino on his book, *Pitino, My Story*. With a testimonial like this from Rick—"Seth was a total professional. He did the scouting work, helped me game plan and delivered a book that truly captured my journey"—there seemed to be little doubt that an outstanding team had been recruited. Seth agreed to be part of the project.

The ball was now in Seth's court. He had to translate an idea into words on paper to pages in a book to a book on a bookstore's shelves...

or availability through Amazon. Not an everyday task, but something that he was highly qualified to accomplish. His first step was to learn the story. That began with interviewing the key participants—Mitchell, Geoffrey and their mother and father. We each initially spent between ninety minutes to two hours downloading our memories and perspectives. Seth was very adept at asking the right questions to bring the stories to light. There were then plenty of follow-up calls to fill in blanks and to provide greater clarity. From this Seth stitched together all the input to produce the first manuscript.

As my experience in writing this book has confirmed for me, I have a very full memory for all that took place over the twenty years of my sons' careers. So I offered to read the manuscript, from first word to last, to see what might have been missing, to add context and content to incomplete tales, to identify passages that might have best been conveyed differently. I didn't realize what I was walking into by volunteering my services. That initial interview with Seth morphed into significant additional hours of review. But, like the writing of this book, it was a labor of love. I enjoyed *every* minute of it.

First, there was a constant give and take between Seth and me, as well as between Seth and the guys. Phone calls and emails flew between us. More changes were made to the manuscript. More stories buttoned up. If I recall correctly, Seth presented two additional manuscript drafts before Geoffrey and Mitchell gave their approval for the next step. This teamwork spanned weeks before it was time to hand the manuscript off to the publisher.

Seth had acquitted himself quite well. So much so that Geoffrey wrote this testimonial that resides on Seth's website:

> *Seth Kaufman's vision and creativity were critical in shaping Eat My Schwartz from a germ of an idea to a full-fledged book. His guidance helped us sell the proposal. And his writing helped craft a memoir that one football scribe called "easily, one of the most unique and well-done books about NFL life I've ever read."*

Seth is an All-Pro collaborator.

I'm not sure when in the timeline a publisher was selected, but one had been chosen. I believe it was once again the result of who knew whom. St. Martin's Press, headquartered in New York City, bought the rights to publish the book. Now they had to perform their magic. Get the written words into final publishable form, make sure the format was appropriate, eliminate all grammatical and punctuation boo-boos and ensure that the design, from cover to cover, was appealing. To some degree I was actively involved with the publishing team.

Before they could schedule a production run, two critical elements had to be finalized. Coin a catchy title and design an attention-getting cover. As I suspect happens on a regular basis, getting from a first-thought title idea to the final is an iterative process. *Eat My Schwartz* was no different. I understand it began with "Livin' the Dream." From there it morphed to "May the Schwartz Be With You." Sound familiar?

Spaceballs first found its way to the big screen in 1987. Cowritten, produced and directed by American actor, comedian and filmmaker Mel Brooks, the movie was a hilarious parody of the highly successful Star Wars franchise. In the movie, Brooks, parodying the Star Wars' Yoda character, is the wise and powerful keeper of the Schwartz, a metaphysical power. In what some consider one of the best quotes from the film, attempting to mimic the popular Star Wars directive, "May the Force be with you," Brooks' character is heard saying, "May the Schwartz be with you."

And therein might have been the problem with using any portion of this phrase as the name of the boys' book. I'm no legal expert, however, my rudimentary understanding would suggest that there might have been some copyright infringement at play. So, scrap that idea. Someone from the publishing team then creatively arrived at *Eat My Schwartz*, with the subtitle of *Our Story of NFL Football, Food, Family, and Faith*. I thought this was perfect. It captured all that was important in the lives of Geoffrey and Mitchell while, at the same time, wittily connecting the boys to the fuel that sustains them.

With the title wrapped up, the one remaining big-picture effort before the book could be published was the front cover design. This is one area of the book's production for which I basically sat on the sidelines. One day one of the guys sent me the first proofs from a cover photo shoot. I kinda rubbed my eyes to be sure they weren't deceiving me. "Yikes" was my first response. The juxtaposition of two very distinct impressions created by the one photo was rather mind-numbing for me.

From the waist up was mostly a conventional look. Geoffrey and Mitchell wearing sports coats, dress shirts and ties. They looked like they

Eat My Schwartz

were headed to synagogue. But then the eye shifts to what's in Geoffrey's hand. Remember, the book's title is *Eat My Schwartz*, with emphasis on "eat." He's grasping a sizable turkey leg, inches from his mouth, seemingly about ready to wolf down his first bite. Mitchell, on the other hand, clutching a football, is peering at Geoffrey with a look like, "Are you crazy?!?"

Enough for conventionality. At some point one's eyes are drawn to what's below the belt. My first reaction was "you gotta be kidding me!" No way, in my mind, did I think a photo of my two boys in plaid boxer underwear would/should ever pass muster for a cover photo. But that's indeed what adorns the front cover of their book. My, oh, my.

The back cover photo sheds the formality of dress clothes but maintains the theme from the front side. Dressed in white T-shirts, one with a traditional crew style collar while the other fashions a V-neck style, Geoffrey is once again clutching a turkey leg. Mitchell is cradling a football. Both are smiling brightly. These photos were not my first choice, nor probably my tenth, but over time I've come to appreciate the creativity and boldness.

Having a book published is much more of a collaborative effort than I ever knew. So many different parties involved. In the end, 5,000 books were printed on the first run in September of 2016. Copies were distributed to bookstores around the country. What a thrill to walk into a Barnes and Noble, whether in Los Angeles, California, or Kansas City, Kansas, and stumble upon a prominent display of *Eat My Schwartz*. The books were also available through Amazon.

Once in circulation, the next step was a promotional tour, with the boys traveling about the country for book-signing opportunities. They hit the airwaves hard and were heard on dozens and dozens of radio shows and podcasts promoting the book. The Jewish press from around the world caught wind of the book and wrote numerous articles. Our home synagogue and another local shul hosted book-signing events that were very well attended.

What an incredible experience. Another part of this journey that Livie and I never envisioned. Of course, we have our own copies as do almost 5,000 others. One copy resides in a very special place, among twenty million—this isn't a typo—other books, serials, manuscripts, maps, music, recordings, images and electronic resources. The Library of Congress, located in Washington, D.C., is the research library that officially serves the

Raising Giants

United States Congress and is the de facto national library of the United States. It has, within its catacombs, a first edition of *Eat My Schwartz*. It's so bizarre for me to think that a book about my sons takes up a microscopic sliver of space in this special library.

The journey I've described in the pages of this book is packed with first-time experiences. Seeing how a book morphs from concept to reality is one of those experiences. Maybe that was the impetus for me to think about writing my own tale. Possibly one day *Raising Giants* will sit aside *Eat My Schwartz: Our Story of NFL Football, Food, Family, and Faith* in the Library of Congress.

20
WHAT'S NEXT?

My father toiled behind the meat counter of a grocery store for over three decades. He was on his feet eight hours a day before automation was a thing. The beef arrived in quarter panels. From there, my father would produce hamburger meat, steaks and roasts. Thirty-plus years.

My first job out of college lasted twenty-plus years. I began as a stock boy in a warehouse and ultimately ascended to company president. Until unpleasant circumstances with owner family members arose toward the later years, I hadn't entertained leaving. And at the time, a two-decade tenure was not uncommon. As a matter of fact, when hiring, if I reviewed a resume indicating that the candidate frequently moved from job to job, the resume was tossed in the round file.

I come from the Baby Boomer generation. Gen X followed. Somewhere in the early to mid-1980s (depending upon what report/article one reads), the Millennial generation was born. And they have completely changed how long one remains at any one company. As a matter of fact, studies have revealed that 21 percent of Millennials will change jobs within a year, which is three times the number of non-Millennials. It's no longer unusual to see a Millennial generation employee jump ship every eighteen months to two years. And interestingly, it's not always for upward advancement. Sometimes it's a lateral move with the hope of the grass being greener at the new company. The grass is not always greener, not unlike the transfer portal.

Geoffrey and Mitchell are both Millennials—Geoffrey right at the dawn of the generation. So it would not have been implausible to suggest, before he or Mitchell launched their post-college journeys, that they would be short-termers at whatever profession caught their attention. But who would have thought that they would stumble upon a profession with a *built-in* short-term duration?

The average career of a football player is 3.3/3.4 years, with offensive linemen enjoying a slight uptick at 3.5/3.6 years. In other words, a player entering the NFL is best advised to begin thinking about what comes after football almost immediately upon being drafted. Both Geoffrey and Mitchell experienced a reprieve in this regard. They both lasted almost a decade, although the ravages of multiple injuries constantly had Geoffrey wondering about his longevity.

Being a "single-shingle" consultant (in other words, it was me, myself and I), I would only succeed if I generated business. "Eat what you kill" is the expression. I learned from the get-go that networking, "the action or process of interacting with others to exchange information and develop professional or social contacts," was imperative. Though far from a natural activity for me, being the introvert that I am, it seems that I was good enough at creating relationships, as I enjoyed a successful twenty-plus-year consulting career.

Having learned the benefits of reaching out to others, I was hell-bent on persuading the boys to adopt the same approach, regardless of what their future held. I started with Geoffrey, since he's three years ahead of Mitchell. I encouraged Geoffrey to proactively meet people or, at the very least, take advantage of chance meetings. He wasn't an eager adaptor.

Geoffrey, Jerry Rice and Networking

As I've shared, I grew up a huge San Francisco 49ers fan. I was able to instill that same love in the boys. Jerry Rice spent sixteen years with the 49ers, beginning the year before Geoffrey was born. He is a Hall of Famer, where his biography names him "the most prolific wide receiver in NFL history." Geoffrey grew up watching and admiring Rice.

One day Geoffrey is sitting at an airport gate awaiting his plane's departure. Who's there? Yes, Jerry Rice. Apparently, Rice was booked on the same flight. Geoffrey excitedly texted me. Since he now was part of the NFL fraternity, Geoffrey had something in common with Rice. I suggested to Geoffrey that he approach Rice and introduce himself. Fellow NFLers. Long-time 49ers fan. Nothing happened, either in the gate area or while passing each other on the airplane. Geoffrey was just not comfortable connecting.

A few years later, Geoffrey had plans to visit L.A. I had a conflict one of the nights he was to be in town, scheduled to attend a networking event specific to my industry focus. Turns out there was another networking event happening at the same time as mine and just across the street from my meeting. But this one had a different orientation. Members/attendees had to be former athletes who played collegiately or professionally at some point in their lives. And I knew the group founder. I inquired whether Geoffrey could attend their meeting as a guest. "Of course."

I thought it would be a superb opportunity for Geoffrey, so I encouraged him to attend. At first, Geoffrey's reaction had a similar resistance. "No." We talked further. Ultimately, he conceded. He first joined me for a few minutes at my meeting, where I could introduce him to so many who had followed his journey but had never had occasion to meet him. He was a "big" hit, especially when seen in the flesh. I'm generally considered to be a good-sized person at six feet, one-and-a-half inches tall—that is, unless I'm standing next to either of my sons.

Geoffrey ultimately excused himself for the walk across the street to this other meeting.

I can't be sure, but I think his attendance at his first networking event was a game changer. When we met up after our respective meetings had concluded, he was almost giddy. "Dad, guess who was there?" Obviously I had no clue. "Tell me."

First, he mentions that Jason Blatt, his Pali high school football coach, was in attendance. Remember, Jason had made a lasting impression on Geoffrey with the advice, "Don't lie to yourself." Own your mistakes. Be honest as to ability and work ethic.

Jason had left coaching and transitioned to selling real estate and insurance. The athlete-focused networking group was a perfect venue for him, given his four-year career at Colorado and his National Championship ring.

Coach Blatt wasn't the only person at the meeting that Geoffrey knew. Through Deryk, Geoffrey was hooked up with an insurance agent whose roster of clients was heavily populated by football players and other athletes. I want to say that his primary office at the time was in Chicago. Currently it's New York, best I know. In either case, it was thousands of miles away from Los Angeles, yet there he was at this meeting doing his networking thing.

I truly believe that this one experience opened Geoffrey's eyes to the critical importance of networking and may have helped him connect the dots for what would be needed to transition from football to whatever would be next. And what would that be? He talked about possibly following in his mother's footsteps to become an attorney. Given his gift of gab, like his mother, and his natural intelligence, also like his mother, he could be a fine advocate for clients, but there was one huge obstacle.

While Geoffrey is very intelligent, his commitment to study was always lacking. Maybe it was some form of attention deficit disorder (ADD). We never had him tested for it, but we've always speculated that he might have a mild form. To become an attorney, one must first attend three years of law school and then pass the bar exam. Doing so requires an extreme commitment to paying attention in class, and then applying oneself to the hours and hours of required homework. Not Geoffrey's strong suit. Cross this off the list.

It was also hard to see Geoffrey in a job that would require him to sit at a desk all day long. Wasn't going to happen. He doesn't have the ability to remain focused for any length of time. Even today, in his current activities, Livie and I can always tell when he's multitasking. So what could Geoffrey undertake that would take advantage of his inherent attributes?

I harken back to a reference made a few paragraphs above to answer this question. Geoffrey loves to talk. My goodness, it would likely take two hands to count the number of times we received teacher calls about his penchant for speaking out of turn, or talking loudly, the latter genetically passed down from his Papa. Couple this with his love of sports and the answer quickly comes into focus. But that would-be career path was not smoothly paved.

When Geoffrey was a young tyke of two or three years old, Livie and I recognized that he was stuttering. As time passed, it was getting no better. Most apparent when he was tired, anxious or nervous. We first attempted to address his speech using therapists at his elementary school but, unfortunately, that paid no tangible benefit. Classmates made fun of him. His school yearbooks include several passages where the author mimicked

What's Next?

his stuttering in words, like "Hope you have a h-a-a-a-p-p-p-y summer." Can't imagine how difficult that was for Geoffrey to see.

But then, through what I would claim to be another example of divine intervention, we were provided with a referral to a world-renowned speech therapist, Suzi Fosnot. Fortunately, Suzi's schedule allowed for time to see Geoffrey. Once or twice a week, for years, we trekked the thirty miles each way in Los Angeles traffic for sessions with Suzi. Her original diagnosis was not very encouraging.

Geoffrey was in fifth or sixth grade when the referral was first made. According to Suzi, it would have been much better to have begun the process years earlier. She wasn't sure if, at this later stage, her efforts could make much of a difference. But that didn't stop any of us. Visits continued. Geoffrey diligently completed his exercises and, slowly but surely, began making strides. Against all odds, while the stuttering has never fully disappeared, it has dissipated to where, as an adult, if one didn't know, they would be hard-pressed to hear Geoffrey stutter. The true test was at his Bar Mitzvah.

Part of a Bar Mitzvah service includes the teenager or teenager-to-be offering their thoughts about this Jewish rite of passage via a speech to those assembled in synagogue. Imagine for a moment the thoughts running through the young mind of a stutterer having to "perform" in front of a crowd of approximately 150 people. Anxiety off the charts.

Suzi knew this could be a huge challenge for Geoffrey, so she spent time preparing him. The outcome was flawless. Livie and I were so proud of him that day. That was July of 1999.

One year later, the movie *The King's Speech* was released on the silver screen. It's a British historical drama telling the story of how future King George VI coped with stammering. At the end of the movie, King George, having just ascended to the throne, must broadcast to his subjects a message about the recent declaration of war against Nazi Germany. His speech therapist was called in to prepare the King.

What one sees in the movie is his therapist notating the written speech. What to emphasize. Where to pause. The pages were full of pencil marks. Geoffrey and Mitchell joined us one day at a theater to catch the movie. Almost immediately after its conclusion, Geoffrey excitedly shared with us, "That was me!" He went on to explain that Suzi went through the same treatment to prepare him for his Bar Mitzvah speech.

A New Journey into Broadcasting

The boys have, obviously, accomplished much during their relatively short time on this earth. Livie and I are extremely proud of what they have achieved. With regard to Geoffrey, I hear from others frequently enough, "I bet you're proud of Geoffrey." Of course, but my follow-on explanation sometimes catches people off guard.

How could I/we not be proud of Geoffrey's football accomplishments? Geoffrey was genetically blessed, as was Mitchell, with exceptional athletic ability. With hard work, commitment and tenacity, they have been able to take advantage of and build upon G-d's gifts.

With Geoffrey's stuttering, here he had to overcome rather than build upon. This challenge could have been a debilitating disorder, one that could have impacted his life's path. But he didn't allow that to happen. So, without hesitation or equivocation, I explain that what I'm most proud of with Geoffrey is his overcoming his stuttering challenges. In so doing, he set the stage for his transition from football to his post-NFL career, which will extend much longer than his playing days.

For someone who loves to talk and is a subject-matter expert in his chosen field, Geoffrey's next chapter was rather obvious to him. Media and broadcasting. So he set his sights on this track. But, like most professions, this one is full of wannabes. It's a steep climb for someone like Geoffrey. One day, after appearing on a syndicated sports talk show on the NFL Network, I asked Geoffrey about his chances to secure more appearances on NFL Network shows. His reply, as was typical, was quite direct. "Not a chance, Dad!" I was a bit taken aback by his tone.

But his explanation made sense. "Dad, the only people seen on NFL Network are those with a yellow jacket or a ring." I knew immediately what he was alluding to. A yellow sports coat is presented to those enshrined in the NFL Hall of Fame. And the ring? Presented to players who have won a Super Bowl. Geoffrey didn't qualify for either. And the more I thought about those who appear on the Network, the more it jumped out at me. He was, as he is many times, right on point.

Geoffrey had his work cut out for him to carve a media path. He would always be swimming upstream, not having a jacket or ring and being an offensive lineman. There was a day when linemen, offensive or defensive, were part of announcing teams. Not in today's world. Plus, no matter how much progress he could make, each and every season a batch of prominent NFLers, some who one day would wear a yellow jacket, others with rings already on their fingers and some with just more cachet than Geoffrey, would retire and leapfrog Geoffrey directly into a booth, whether radio or TV. Or the offspring of fathers who enjoyed more notoriety than Geoffrey would dip their toes in the waters. Did they have the experience or qualifications Geoffrey possessed? Not necessarily, but there they were. This is not sour grapes. It's just reality.

Undaunted, Geoffrey began his media and broadcast journey when in New York playing for the Giants. New York is considered by many as "the media capital of the world," so what better place to kick off his efforts? SNY, SportsNet New York, is a regional sports network available on cable to those residing in the New York City metropolitan area and beyond, throughout the state. Through contacts within the Giants' organization, Geoffrey was given opportunities to appear on late afternoon football-related show segments.

I once was visiting for a game when one of these opportunities presented itself, so I jumped in the car with him for the trip from New Jersey to Manhattan for the broadcast. How odd in some ways. The only makeup I ever saw applied up to this point was by Livie, to herself, yet Geoffrey's face was caked with the stuff prior to his appearance. And while Geoffrey appeared as calm as a day without wind on a football Sunday, it was obvious, to me at least, that his nerves were in high gear.

Once in front of the camera, though, Geoffrey was in his comfort zone. At ease. Thoughtful. Articulate. And *no* stuttering. It was apparent to his old man that he had found his calling. But, as I alluded to on the previous page, this was no slam dunk. Much work was required and, even then, there were no guarantees.

The NFL, as part of its player benefits, offers aspiring broadcasters a chance to attend a four-day Broadcast Boot Camp. Now bitten by the bug, Geoffrey applied and was accepted to the tenth annual Camp at NFL Films. Sessions included hands-on work in areas such as tape study, editing, radio production, field reporting and studio and show preparation. Top talent was on hand to assist. That year included James Brown of CBS, Ron Jaworski of ESPN and Curt Menafee of Fox.

With a certificate of completion from the Boot Camp in hand, Geoffrey began expanding his networking efforts. Once again living in Charlotte, he reached out to one of the local TV stations to explore opportunities. He became somewhat of a regular, albeit at non-football wages. But he realized that his march toward brighter days would require him giving of his time for little to no recompense. He was OK with that. Thank goodness the money he made while playing football allowed him this freedom.

The path has never been a straight line and not always on an upward trajectory. Somewhat like his football career, there have been ups and downs. And, there were days of doubt. "Can I make this happen?" "Why are things not moving along more quickly?"

Doubt can be debilitating and can stymie progress. About four years or so into this new chapter of Geoffrey's life, I felt him entering a trough of doubt. A thought came to mind. He had elevated himself to a level where some of the top radio sports disc jockeys would invite him to appear on their shows. He developed a closer relationship with one or two. I went to Geoffrey with an idea. Contact one or both and ask them if, on his next visit to Los Angeles, they'd be willing to break bread with him to talk about his career. He wasn't to ask for anything other than "what more could I do to advance myself?"

In typical Geoffrey fashion, he first resisted. But then soon enough thereafter he committed to reaching out. He asked to meet with one of the two and that media VIP accepted without hesitation. They met for dinner at a nearby restaurant, spending the evening talking all things sports until the conversation got a bit more serious. Geoffrey popped the question. "What more could I do?"

The personality looked at Geoffrey and asked, "How old are you?" If I recall correctly, Geoffrey was in his early thirties at the time. Hearing that, the response was something resembling, "Why are you in such a hurry?" At the same age in his career, this person, who had climbed to the top of his hill, who has achieved huge success in his field, was no different than Geoffrey. He was working in a smaller market. He was hustling for everything he could land. His words of wisdom that night were quite enlightening for Geoffrey. You're on a good path. Continue. Continue to network. Continue to explore. Continue to learn and hone your craft.

I can't leave the story at this point before sharing the more humorous element of that evening. For those who have never dined with Geoffrey, and as I've tried to convey in this book, it would not be an inappropriate presumption to believe that he could consume huge amounts of food. When the two were done with dinner, Geoffrey's colleague was almost incredulous. "That's all?" They had feasted on crab legs, and the number of shells on Geoffrey's plate were not piled as high as anticipated.

What's Next?

In essence, Geoffrey now had his marching orders. And so, with a mission to accomplish, he has soldiered on. I won't document all the details of his ascension, but I proudly will share his current lineup of gigs.

- Depending on the time of year, his podcast, *Geoff Schwartz Is Smarter Than You*, will drop one to two times a week. Want to be a more educated football fan, tune in.
- For five years he co-hosted *Pac-12 Today* on SiriusXM; however, with the demise of the Pac-12 that gig disappeared. But the magic between Geoffrey and Sean O'Connell continues as Geoffrey appears weekly on Sean's new radio show.
- Geoffrey is one of a trio of hosts on Fox Sports Radio's *Countdown to Kickoff* show airing Sunday mornings from 7 a.m. to 10 a.m. PST, leading into the day's games with a betting orientation. So successful has the show become that it will now be heard year-round rather than just during the football season.
- He writes two to three articles a week for Fox Sports covering both the NCAA and the NFL, furthering his betting perspective. (In this regard, he's taking after Livie's father, who was an avid gambler. We've been assured by Geoffrey that his bets, individually as well as in the aggregate, are modest, not financially harmful—we sure hope so—and being tracked.)
- He is a periodic guest/cohost on sports talk shows airing on Fox Sports 1 and various SiriusXM radio stations.
- He is now a regular personality on VSiN, the Vegas Sports Information Network, appearing three times a week on *Money Talks* and weekends on *Live Bets*.
- On top of all this, I receive handfuls of Google Alerts each week providing links to articles in which Geoffrey has been quoted/has written and links to podcasts and interviews. (Being the obsessive dad, I probably spend an hour a week archiving all of his articles and appearances.)
- Geoffrey is hugely active on social media, particularly Twitter (150,000-plus followers) and Instagram.
- And last, but certainly not least, for the second year in a row, Geoffrey joins betting expert Chris "The Bear" Fallica as they cohost *Bear Bets*, a Fox Sports podcast that dives into the action-packed realm of NFL and college football betting. The podcasts drop every Thursday and Friday during football season.

A number of Geoffrey's colleagues have publicly asserted that he may be "the busiest guy on the radio." I think it's safe to say he's found his niche and has built a solid and, hopefully, long-standing foundation for a successful future.

Mitchell's New Chapter

Since you've gotten to this point in my story, it won't be a surprise for you to learn that Mitchell's path to his next chapter has been quite dissimilar to Geoffrey's. The boys are simply different.

Mitchell started his first game in the NFL. Couple that with being blessed with extraordinary health during his career, and maybe he developed a confidence that his career would be long-term, and thus the need to plan for the future wasn't as acute as with Geoffrey. Although there are no guarantees of longevity, and careers can end abruptly, Mitchell rarely engaged in conversations about "What's next?"

If anything, ideas began to germinate toward the middle of his stay in Kansas City. Not surprisingly, those centered around (what else) food. Mitchell is a foodie. Has been for years and years. I remember him in his younger days before college parked in front of the TV watching food shows long before it was cool to do so. He was an ardent follower of celebrity chef Emeril Lagasse, whose food shows were ever-present on the Food Network.

Never one to just consume information without attempting application, Mitchell was often found in the kitchen practicing. One of his early specialties was pizza. He'd prepare his own dough and then build from there. Mitchell would invite friends to the house for a pizza party. He would serve each friend their own individual-sized pie with their preferred ingredients layered on top. It was just the beginning.

So maybe a career as a restaurateur was in his future. But what a steep climb. Sixty percent of new restaurants fail within the first year. And nearly 80 percent shutter by year five. That was demonstrated to Mitchell during his time in Kansas City. He met someone with plans of opening a deli. They talked about Mitchell becoming an investor. Good thing he didn't sign on the dotted line. The deli collapsed before it reached its first anniversary. And why? Apparently the number-one reason restaurants fail is wrong choice of location.

But he did succeed in one aspect. How many of us have a sandwich named after us? Very few. As one review described, "The Mitchell Schwartz Tailgate" was "the most outrageous specialty sandwich" on the deli's menu. Not surprising, it was a double decker with a layer of hot pastrami topped with corned beef separated by Thousand Island dressing. A dollop of hot mustard added some flavor. As if that wasn't enough, the Tailgate also included a cup of matzah ball soup and a plate of pickles. My stomach is growling just writing about this food orgy.

Chef Schwartz

Mitchell, though, was undaunted by this restaurant experience. Food was still tugging at him. So this time he took things into his own hands. *Mitch in the Kitch* was born. Combining his love of food and recipe creativity, Mitchell has evolved from a food hobbyist to his alter ego, Chef Schwartz. Employing characteristics that made him a standout in the NFL, Mitchell, through his website www.mitchinthekitch.blog, plus his YouTube videos, provides his fans with detailed recipe lists, meticulous instructions and step-by-step cooking videos to produce scrumptious briskets, banana French toast and other cuisine to satisfy the palate. The remodeled kitchen in his new home was designed for optimal layout to film more episodes.

Geoffrey in his own right is a foodie as well. In 2023 an opportunity presented itself for the two brothers to film a food show that was to appear on a cable network. Ten episodes were planned for the guys to battle for food supremacy. After filming seven of the ten in cities around the country, the plug was unfortunately pulled.

The only other tangible idea articulated by Mitchell was somewhat off-the-wall yet, in some ways, it made perfect sense. Imagine an ex-NFL offensive lineman with Mitchell's pedigree on the field wearing a striped shirt. (For those needing a connection, that's the jersey referees wear.) It would keep him connected to football. He knows the game from the inside, so maybe some of the bogus offensive line holding calls would not be flagged. Running up and down the field might help his conditioning. So why not?

Soon after he expressed this path as a possibility, I had occasion to meet a former head of NFL referees. Who better to ask about what it would take to be a ref? The first requirement was likely a deal breaker from the outset. NFL referees toil through ten years of on-field training before being considered for a top slot. For someone who played in the NFL, that time frame might be trimmed in half. But that would still mean five years of weekend travel to high school, lower-level NCAA and then top-tier collegiate games. That wasn't going to happen.

Raising Giants

Now that Mitchell has formally retired, he's in a great place. Physically his body is no longer being punished. He has freedom to choose his daily routine. And financially, he's on very solid ground. With his funds well-managed, he, my grandchildren, and maybe generations beyond, will live comfortably. This gives him some runway before deciding what's next.

In recent years Mitchell has dabbled in the broadcasting world. During football season he's a weekly guest on a local Kansas City radio sports show and has been a guest contributor on a weekly football-centric podcast with Robert Mays of *The Athletic*. For a season he joined his former teammate Joe Thomas on the roster of the 33rd Team, described by the NFL as "the premier football think tank" for fans, with contributors who are former NFL executives, coaches and players with over 2,000 combined years of experience. There the two teamed up on the *Grumpy OL Show*. Maybe media is also in his future.

Those who follow professional football are likely familiar with *Monday Night Football* with Peyton and Eli, where the Manning brothers join forces to provide commentary and analysis during MNF. And then there's *New Heights*, the weekly podcast by Travis and Jason Kelce that drops weekly insights about trending NFL news and highlights. (As of this writing the Kelce brothers have signed a $100 million contract with Amazon's podcast studio, Wondery.) I will fully admit that the Kelces and Mannings are much more high profile than the Schwartzes, but it would be very difficult for anyone to convince me that Geoffrey and Mitchell could not have been the first brother duo to team up and lend their perspectives on all things football, given their tremendous knowledge of the game. Unfortunately, this never occurred and likely the cow is already out of the barn, so to speak.

It's been an interesting transition for Livie and me. We never envisioned having one son in the NFL, much less two. And now, we're equally blown away that they both have transitioned, to one degree or another, into satisfying and rewarding media careers. Plus, as an added benefit to their parents, their new professions allow us to hear their comforting voices and see their handsome faces on a regular basis, although Geoffrey will say that he has a face for radio. Haha. I typically spend a couple of hours a day enjoying some newfound hobbies with a bud in my ear. It's also a delight to watch the pure thrill of our grandchildren when they see daddy on TV. Studies suggest that parents are only as happy as their least happy child. Seems to me our family is overflowing with joy.

21
THE CHANGING LANDSCAPE OF COLLEGIATE FOOTBALL

I spent my professional career working with manufacturing and distribution companies, both as an employee and later as a consultant, driven by the principle of change. There are numerous maxims that address this concept, but the one I favor is, "If you're standing still, you're falling behind."

The other philosophy I advanced had to do with being on time. "If you're on time, you're late," is what I'd tell my staffers/clients...and children. I remember the grousing that would ensue when I told Geoffrey and Mitchell that we had to leave for the airport two hours in advance of our flight. My oh my, you'd think I had just grounded them.

Fast forward to them as adults. Maybe it's true that as kids age their parents become smarter, because now the guys arrive at the airport sufficiently early, without any encouragement. Geoffrey had the timing lesson underscored when he joined the New York Giants. If a meeting was called for, let's say, 8:30 a.m., the players knew they had better have their butts in their seats at that time. What Geoffrey quickly learned was that, although the clocks displayed 8:30, the actual time was 8:25. The head coach had ordered all clocks to be set five minutes ahead of the actual time to ensure timeliness. I laughed with great satisfaction when Geoffrey shared this story.

Raising Giants

Compared with the environment when Mitchell and Geoffrey played college football, much has changed in the last few years. Not marginally, but titanically. Recruiting. The infusion of lucrative endorsement deals for student-athletes. Collectives. Conference realignment. It's amazing to me how quickly this has all happened; however, I do not believe it has been triggered by the NCAA's altruistic desire to be a "good Samaritan."

The NCAA has typically been slow to make any meaningful change. And why should it? Its annual revenue exceeds $1 billion. Just like the NFL, the NCAA is a business. Although it wishes to portray the organization as being the protector of students who happen to be athletes, that's not the case in my opinion. It's athletes first, students second, and what revenue can be created through the most popular sports.

It's jokingly been said that the compliance manual governing recruiting activity rivals the U.S. federal tax code books in thickness. In fact, it's "only" about one-sixth the size, coming in at a hefty 450 pages, give or take. Much of what exists in the NCAA's bible of rules is antiquated and no longer relevant. Here are a couple of personal examples that highlight this reality.

When Geoffrey and Mitchell were being recruited the mailbox would regularly be stuffed with brochures and other marketing materials from interested schools, especially Oregon and Cal. (I have saved in a file cabinet located in the garage every last piece of promotional material received along the way.) What I remember most about the Oregon material specifically is how creative and eye-catching it was, thanks to Deryk Gilmore's handiwork. Many pieces were in four-color as opposed to simple, mundane black, white and gray tones. Then, one day, the colorful pieces were no more.

Given my relationship with Deryk, I asked why. The NCAA compliance office scolded Oregon for distributing the four-color material. There was, and may still be, a rule preventing the multiple-color application. Why? When the rule was originally written, four-color printing was expensive and not available to all NCAA institutions. But this was the 2000s. Four-color printers were very affordable, especially for a football program. Instead of reevaluating the rule, the NCAA thought it better to prevent Oregon, and I suspect other schools, from being creative.

I imagine that many of you reading this book are familiar with a vehicle once built by General Motors known as a "Hummer." It was the civilian version of a military Humvee. They were not inexpensive. In

2008/2009 the base model was priced at $30,000. Fully loaded was about $43,000. Maybe a bit too rich as, in 2010, GM shut down production. But while available, the University of Oregon bought one. It was painted dark green with a yellow "O" logo adorning both the driver's and passenger's side doors. Very eye-catching. The vehicle was paraded in front of recruits as they visited Eugene. Though we never enjoyed a ride in the Hummer, I believe it was used to transport recruits on visits.

Once again, Oregon received notice from the NCAA to cease and desist. Why? Because not all schools under the NCAA's umbrella had the resources to purchase such a vehicle. OK, I get it...kinda. So, basically, the message was that those who had the ability to make such a purchase were being held back by those who couldn't, or chose not to. Life isn't fair. Was there some compromise, rather than an absolute "no?" Apparently not. And since the NCAA had a stranglehold on member institutions, Oregon, in this case, had no choice but to suspend the Hummer's use.

Breaking the Stranglehold: NIL and the Transfer Portal

The headlock that seemed to give the NCAA absolute control over the student-athletes appeared to be almost impossible to break. Then, one day, the suffocating stranglehold was broken, thanks to a lawsuit.

Ed O'Bannon played basketball for the UCLA Bruins in the mid-1990s. After his career as a Bruin, O'Bannon sued the NCAA in an antitrust class action, arguing that student-athletes should benefit from the use of their images. (There's much more to know about this lawsuit, which can be found on the internet.) The case went through the judicial system all the way up to the Supreme Court. After findings in favor of O'Bannon and subsequent appeals, finally, in 2021, twelve years after the action was first filed, the Ninth Circuit upheld the favorable ruling, and the Supreme Court unanimously affirmed the decision. On July 1, 2021, the NCAA capitulated and announced new rules that removed the absolute restrictions on college athletes for paid endorsements, sponsorship deals and the like. The name, image and likeness (NIL) era was born.

On the surface, the ability for a collegiate athlete to receive money during their college careers seems only fair, from all sorts of perspectives. But how fair? Nineteenth-century English poet Percy Bysshe Shelley observed, "the rich get richer, the poor get poorer." Will NIL perpetuate the tradition? Let's look at early results.

Raising Giants

There are college football players who have signed endorsement agreements with major brands worth millions of dollars. Who are they? The players one might expect. Quarterbacks. Wide receivers. One report from early 2023 listed the top twenty collegiate NIL deals. All were for football and basketball players. Of the top ten, six were from the gridiron and of those, four were quarterbacks and two were wide receivers. The second ten had five football players, all quarterbacks. The minimum deal was $1 million. All skill-position guys.

What about linemen, like Mitchell and Geoffrey? Early on the ceiling seemed to be $50,000 per individual. Recently I read about one offensive lineman signing a $1 million NIL deal, but that seems like an outlier. To bring greater clarity to the inequity of the NIL program, I read a *USA Today* article from two years ago. At that time, "the average transaction involving a college football player is $3,396," while "the median deal is just $53." (A quick math lesson. Average adds all the values and divides by the number of players involved, skewed by the higher dollar deals. Median is a midpoint. Half above, half below. Typically the lower value.)

I understand that viewers watch games to see the top QBs throw TDs to top wide receivers. However, are the skill-position guys any more committed to their trade than the guys who protect their well-being and make it possible to toss those touchdown passes? Nope. I wonder if the disparity will ever lead to resentment between position groups. Imagine the troubles that could create on the field.

Another implication of the new rules relates to player movement. When Geoffrey and Mitchell were in college, the transfer rules were quite rigid. In simplistic terms, athletes needed permission from their current school to make a move and, if granted, were required to sit out one year while attending classes at their new school as a penalty for transferring.

Imagine that. A "penalty" for switching. And a rather arbitrary decision process. If the coach deemed the athlete important to their program, he could simply deny the request. Or the coach could prevent movement if the transfer was to a team within their conference, not wanting to unleash talent to a competitor. There was an appeals process, but it was cumbersome at best. By the time an appeal might be resolved, the career could be over. But the coaches? They could, and still do, change jobs without any such one-year transfer penalties. Before recent transfer portal adjustments, a coach could depart a program soon after signing day.

The Changing Landscape of Collegiate Football

The committed athlete had no options. They couldn't move. What if they chose that program because of the connection with the departed head coach? Why the disparity? Are players chattel?

Possibly knowing that the O'Bannon case ruling was a *fait accompli* and soon to be adjudicated, two months before the landmark ruling was upheld and affirmed, the NCAA updated its prior protocols and established a "one-time transfer rule." Again, a triggering event was likely the fuel that led to change. It was not the NCAA voluntarily updating the rule because it was the right thing to do. As a result, athletes could enter the "transfer portal" and be allowed to move to a different school one time during their career and play immediately without getting permission from the coach or the institution. (Rules regarding the portal continue to change.)

I frequently wondered how Geoffrey and Mitchell might have handled their careers if the current transfer rule was in place back then. Given the success of Mitchell's career and what I know about his experience at Cal, my suspicion is that nothing would have been different. But Geoffrey?

One day I was listening to one of his radio shows when this exact question was asked of him. Good thing I was sitting down because the answer kinda floored me. I wrote earlier in the book about the issues he had with one of his Oregon coaches. Apparently, those issues, and possibly others, would have been enough reason for Geoffrey to seek a change. In no uncertain terms he offered that had the open transfer been in place during his time as a Duck, he would have entered the portal. Who knows, had he done so, if his career would have taken a different trajectory.

So often the grass seems greener elsewhere. Isn't that why people change jobs? Unhappy at their current company and believing that another organization would be a better situation. Yet, so often, having made the transition, the grass is not greener, but actually worse, spurring regrets for having made the move.

Statistics confirm that the transfer portal isn't always the magic elixir. According to RealResponse, a secure digital platform for student-athletes, more than 31,000 players entered the transfer portal in 2023 alone, with about 45 percent successfully moving to new schools. The 17,000 who weren't picked up by another team had to continue looking, transfer to a non-NCAA school or leave the sport completely. Was the grass greener?

Raising Giants

I could not find any statistics to inform me whether transfers saw more playing time at their new school after the switch. Wasn't that the underlying reason to make a change? Some, I'm sure, did not. So, instead of improving their lot in life, many found themselves worse off than while at their former university. Some athletes, who couldn't find a new team, requested reentry to their former school. Those requests are not always granted. The former team may have filled the position through recruiting, or maybe the transfer portal. Or maybe the coaching staff is vindictive. "You left me. Why should I take you back?"

Besides more playing time being a motivation to make a switch, a transfer might also be prompted by their perceived ability to receive NIL deal(s) that weren't available at their original school. That is happening all over the college landscape. Players are transferring to schools where the alumni organizations/collectives are stronger and are more inclined to open the door to NIL opportunities. The rich getting richer?

The NIL environment just doesn't make sense to me as a businessperson. Take this case. A Southern California high school quarterback was reported to have committed to an institution, likely spurred from inking an $8 million NIL deal...while not having played one collegiate down. How's that possible? Do those behind the deal truly expect to receive a return on their investment? The college team that was hoping to benefit from this early commitment had last won a national championship in the late 1990s. Since then they hadn't been relevant until recent years. It seems to me that unless this school jumps to consistent relevance and ranks toward the top of the polls during this QB's tenure, and possibly wins another national championship, the investors will be hard-pressed to see a return on their investment.

One other possible ramification from this new NIL environment. Let's hypothetically look at this scenario. An alumnus of an institution, or any collection of business folks, supports an NIL deal to an incoming freshman player. What are the expectations of this group? That the player sees immediate time on the field? And what if that doesn't happen? Will the investors feel they have the juice to exert their will on coaches to force playing time? G-d forbid that ever becomes a reality.

Another issue with the transfer portal for me is the ease of entrance or, viewed alternatively, the ease of leaving their "home" team. I think back to when Geoffrey agreed to play soccer with his neighbor friend. I don't think he had reached his tenth birthday by then. We learned that

Geoffrey was not cut out for soccer. Too big to be running up and down the field. His motivation was not genuine. He didn't care about the sport. Just seemed like something to do at the time. He quickly realized it wasn't his cup of tea and came to me with a request to bow out. I told him no. "You finish what you start."

Thousands of college football players have decided to jump ship and not finish what they started since the portal was made available. There's that old saying, "When the going gets tough, the tough get going." I don't believe that "get going" means jumping ship. Life, as we all know, is not always a pleasure trip. There are unanticipated challenges along the way. If the route to overcoming these character-building opportunities is so easily skirted, how does one build the fortitude to push through challenges? I understand that not all circumstances are the same and, therefore, in some cases, a change of scenery is necessary. But I would assert that change is not always the solution, as borne out by the statistics shared.

Conference Reorganization

Not only are players and coaches finding new homes, but so are teams, pulling roots from long-standing conference affiliations for bigger pay days. In July of 2021, the SEC, otherwise known as the Southeastern Conference, announced that the universities of Texas and Oklahoma were accepted as full members of the conference, effective four years hence. They will abandon the Big 12. About a year later, in response to the loss of the two teams, the Big 12 announced the expansion of their conference with four teams joining their conference in 2023. I gotta believe that the NCAA head honchos realized these moves were but the beginning of a major tectonic shift in conference realignment. If they didn't, they sure have learned otherwise.

Just a few weeks later, in a stunning move that caught most people by complete surprise, my alma mater, UCLA, along with the USC Trojans, announced their move from the Pac-12 Conference to the Big 10. Both schools have been affiliated with some version of the Pac-12 since the 1920s. One might ask, "Why jump ship?" The answer is rather simple and conforms to a theme that I've presented at other points in this book. As actor Cuba Gooding's football character Rod Tidwell in the movie *Jerry McGuire* demanded of his agent, played by Tom Cruise, "Show me the money!" There are some reports that suggest the two Los Angeles-based schools will receive an additional $30 million per year, possibly more, through their association with the Big 10 than they would have received remaining in the Pac-12.

The dominoes continued to fall. The Pac-12 is no more. Eight other teams have jumped to other conferences. Only Washington State and Oregon State remain, to be known as the Pac-2, having been forced into arrangements with less desirable conferences. And on a personal level, Geoffrey's gig with SiriusXM's *Pac-12 Today* daily radio show has gone bye-bye. He's now trying to find an opportunity with the SiriusXM radio Big 10 counterpart.

I continue to draw focus to the dollars and cents of sports, whether professional or collegiate. The move by UCLA and USC, done for financial purposes, might simply be the best affirmation. UCLA completed its 2021 fiscal year drowning in red ink. A $62.5 million deficit for the year. Over $100 million in the red for the three years ending in 2021. This move to the Big 10 was really their only way to dig out of the enormous hole before they were forced to slice other athletic programs. USC was the instigator of the move. UCLA's basketball and football programs hadn't been competitive nor top-flight for years. They wouldn't bring eyeballs and add value in the eyes of the networks. Also, the Big 10 didn't want to split the LA market, so if they wanted USC, because they believed USC would bring eyeballs, then they had to accept UCLA.

UCLA should forever be grateful that the Trojans opened this door to financial solvency, because there's no way the Big 10 was accepting UCLA without USC.

But let's dig deeper regarding the impact of this conference shift. The average distance from UCLA to a former Pac-12 school—not including USC—was about 735 miles. The average distance from Westwood to a Big 10 campus? 2,160 miles, ranging from a minimum of 1,537 to the farthest at 2,800, literally across the country. A five-hour-plus flight in the best of travel conditions. The descriptor the NCAA likes to use when referring to players is "student-athlete." I suspect this is an attempt to give the impression that the "student" element is the more important of the two. NOT!

Would you consider making athletes travel, on average, more miles by a factor of three to be a benefit for the students? No way. Longer flights. Different time zones. More time away from school. Less time available for studying. Football teams tend to charter planes, so less impactful to them, but what about most of the other programs? They fly commercial on, typically, full planes and are subject to the regular delays and disruptions with flights that are now the norm.

And what about parents and family who wish to support their son or daughter? I suspect few have the financial resources and/or the time to consistently traverse the country to attend games/matches. I've shared in a prior chapter how many games I attended over the course of the boys' careers. Livie wasn't far behind. While I can't say for sure these many years later, I would speculate that we would have attended fewer games in this new environment. Some weekends we could leave Saturday morning and be in our seats at kickoff. Other weekends we'd travel on Friday. But in all cases during college days, we were back home on Sunday. I just don't see that happening in this new world order for UCLA and USC, having to trek across country, particularly given flight availabilities. And, of course, the cost of tickets has dramatically increased.

And that's football. What about Olympic sports, such as baseball, soccer, volleyball, etc., etc.? They don't travel on charter flights. Baseball teams typically play a three-game series against their conference foes. Friday and Saturday nights. Sunday afternoons. Do they now travel five hours the morning of the opening series game? Likely not. Are they able to fly out Sunday afternoon if completing a Sunday contest at 4 p.m. EST? Maybe. If so, just imagine middle of the night arrival times in Los Angeles knowing Monday morning will arrive shortly, along with a class or practice. Not the most ideal. And this will be repeated about half a dozen times each conference season. Again, does this sound like the best interests of the students were considered?

One other consideration. Recruiting and college selection. Let's look at baseball again. There are Southern California–based programs outside of UCLA and USC that are very competitive. Would a prospective recruit choose to be a Bruin or Trojan knowing cross-country travel awaits or family participation might be limited? There are options.

This chapter was not intended to be a thorough, comprehensive exposé on the rules governing the NCAA, nor the merits of those rules. They're very fluid anyway. However, I have my opinions. For the purpose of this book, I reflect on today's environment compared with the realities that existed during the boys' experiences. Much has changed. Would the course of Geoffrey's and Mitchell's careers have been different back then with today's rules in place? Maybe yes. Maybe no. We can only speculate.

OVERTIME

22

FROM BOYS TO MEN—BUILDING CHARACTER

At sixteen years old a whole lot of teenagers believe they have the world by the tail. They believe they know all there is to know, even more than their parents. (There will come a time when, as young adults, they'll have an epiphany that their parents were a bit smarter than they gave them credit for when younger.) Many youths are quite competent and capable...for their age. But are they prepared to face the rigors of being a top-flight athlete, a prized collegiate prospect playing a game that demands so much? I would offer maybe, but not without the support of their elders.

I have always advanced the notion that parenting is the single most challenging responsibility that an individual could ever face, complicated by the fact that parents have zero real-life training to be one, and we receive little feedback as to our parental success until it is virtually too late to make meaningful changes. If a receiver drops catchable passes on a regular basis, everyone immediately knows that he isn't very good. An offensive lineman's porous pass protection leading to multiple sacks finds him quickly washed out. In the business world, properly run companies conduct annual reviews of their employees. There's no such feedback when parenting.

Livie and I tried our best to be good parents, learning from our childhood experiences to improve upon areas that we felt were less than ideal.

Humbly, I think we did an excellent job overall. We did have some early indications. The boys would enjoy play dates at their friends' homes. Livie and/or I would drive over to pick them up. We would likely engage in casual conversation with the friend's parents and then hear, "Geoffrey/Mitchell was so helpful. They cleaned up. They were very polite." Livie and I would, with a level of astonishment, eyeball each other and think to ourselves, "Are you talking about our son?" We weren't surprised about the politeness. That was a very important trait to instill in them from early on. But "helpful?" "Cleaned up?" Haha.

The boys' football journeys began at around age fourteen. By sixteen, the know-it-all age, they were thrust into the recruiting wars. And then from there it was college and the NFL. Each step up the ladder brought its own challenges and opportunities for emotional and mental growth. I'm proud of the way both guys met the challenges facing them and largely overcame their demons, but it wasn't always a smooth ride.

In Chapter 13, "Football Intelligence," I referenced Mitchell's single error on an elementary school spelling test that was catastrophic for him. Little did Livie and I realize back then that his reaction was an indicator as to how Mitchell viewed the world, and himself. I'm not telling anything "out of school," as Mitchell has publicly addressed his feelings. Saturdays in college and Sundays in the NFL were extremely anxiety-ridden days for him. He much preferred practice days with far less on the line than on game days. Who would have thought?

Apparently, the responsibility of having to protect his quarterback was very personal. He didn't want to be the one allowing a QB sack or, more impactfully, being the cause of an injury to the team's prized player. He was, and continues to be, a perfectionist. Fortunately, maybe driven by his anxieties, he developed into a top-tier player who protected his quarterbacks quite well...but still lived with his fears that never went away.

Geoffrey was the complete opposite. Gee whiz, the theme continues. Geoffrey lived for those days when he and his teammates charged out of the tunnel to the roaring cheers of their fans, or the boos cascading down when playing an away game. That got his juices flowing. He thought practices were mere drudgery. I know that Geoffrey was equally concerned with keeping his quarterback upright and healthy, but he emotionally dealt with his responsibilities in a manner quite different than Mitchell did.

From Boys To Men—The Building of Character

As a consultant mentoring some of my clients, I frequently spoke with them about the difference between confrontation and conversation. We all face times when we must have a "hard" conversation, one that makes us uncomfortable because what needs to be said is likely to cause the other person some degree of discomfort. I remember one incident for me that was my epiphany.

* * *

I had an employee who was horribly underperforming. Regardless of efforts to help her improve, nothing was getting better. My only option, ultimately, was termination. I spent days agonizing over my decision. The procrastination wasn't going to change anything, so I came to closure and said to myself, "Tomorrow morning." I arrived at work hardly able to control my nerves. I called the employee into my office and gave her the news. It was done professionally and calmly. When she walked out of the office, my whole body relaxed. It felt like a boulder had been removed from my shoulders. The nervousness flew away. I had the "hard" conversation that was necessary and was better for it.

I tried to instill this same attitude within Geoffrey and Mitchell when it came time to have a difficult conversation with a coach or other adult figures. "Why aren't I playing more?" "Sorry, but I will not be committing to your school." "I've selected another agent to represent me." These types of exchanges happened regularly during their football careers. When they were living at home during high school, Livie and I could work together with the guys on what needed to be said and how to say it. We could role-play. In college the same applied, other than we were hundreds of miles apart. By the time the guys entered the NFL, Mom and Dad were available if/when they wanted our input.

I can't say that the "hard" conversations ever became easy for either guy, but the conversations took place. Mitchell informing the one school to stop recruiting him. Geoffrey notifying the Arizona coach that he was committing to Oregon. There have been numerous other instances along the way. Geoffrey has publicly thanked me for "forcing" him to have the difficult conversations. I guess, in the end, Dad had something of value to impart.

I acknowledge I grew up at a different time. No 24/7 news cycles. No ESPN SportsCenter. No Internet or social media. Earlier in these pages I

Raising Giants

shared my admiration of Detroit Lions running back Barry Sanders. After scoring a touchdown, he never made it about him. Handed the ball to the nearest referee and ran to the sidelines. No slamming the pigskin to the turf in celebration. No gathering of teammates in the end zone for a group photo as happens in today's world. I do not understand why it's necessary for a wide receiver to pop up after a tough grab or a first down catch and go through all the gyrations that are common today. Screaming. Pounding one's chest. Pointing to the sky. Isn't making a catch what they get paid handsomely to do?

I remember an episode in our front yard years before the boys first laced up their football cleats. Geoffrey and Mitchell were playing their version of touch football on the front lawn. After scoring a touchdown, Geoffrey threw the ball to the ground in conquest. I jumped up and huddled with the boys, wagging my index finger side to side. "No, no, no! We don't do that." I explained why and told them I expected to never see that repeated.

Throughout the twenty years of Mitchell and Geoffrey playing football, I cannot think of one instance when their personal achievements took center stage. Actually, it was quite the opposite. Livie and I watched Mitchell time after time be the first to extend his arm to a tackled teammate to lift him from the turf, even when it was his block that sprung the running back.

Remember that amazing three-finger behind-the-head catch by Geoffrey's Giants teammate Odell Beckham Jr.—the one that some suggest is the greatest catch ever made? Remember it was Geoffrey who was the first one downfield to congratulate his teammate. And what did he do? Lifted him skyward such that Beckham was the point of focus for the crowd to toast. It was all about his teammate.

For Mitchell and Geoffrey, it's always been about their teammates, not themselves. When reporters asked questions that brought focus to either of them, their humility led them to deflect the answer, crediting their teammates. Geoffrey and Mitchell learned in their formative years of the importance of teamwork. More than perhaps any other major sport, football success comes from the synergies among the guys on the field. As an age-old idiom offers, "there's no 'I' in team." Quite a valuable lesson for them to have learned...and employed.

From Boys To Men—The Building of Character

Mental Health

Until recent years, talking about mental health was a taboo subject in professional sports. Athletes are supposed to be strong. Infallible. Admitting to some form of mental health challenge has been viewed as a sign of weakness. Thank goodness the openness to discuss one's mental health by professional athletes has taken a very positive turn. Mitchell, since retirement, has publicly shared his Sunday anxieties.

A research study suggests that anxiety and depression affect about 34 percent of current elite athletes and 26 percent of former elite athletes, with the trend line headed in the wrong direction. About 35 percent of elite athletes suffer a mental health crisis, which may manifest as stress, eating disorders, anxiety, depression or drug use. Furthermore, younger athletes are often the most vulnerable. They are held to the same standards as their adult counterparts; however, they don't possess the same level of mental maturity or judgment that their adult counterparts do.

During Geoffrey's junior year at Oregon, at the still-vulnerable age of twenty, he experienced his own mental health challenge. It wasn't a crisis but it was sure bogging him down. He felt unsupported by some of the Oregon coaching staff and didn't know how to deal with his feelings, didn't know how to go about resolving his anxieties. He and I would have conversations, but those talks weren't really helping him. I'm his dad, not a psychologist.

While Geoffrey was in high school, I was introduced to someone who privately trained basketball players, from high school through the professional ranks. Geoffrey worked with him—my goodness, did that improve his game—through high school. My relationship with this trainer carried on after Geoffrey left for Oregon. When Geoffrey's struggles seemed to require a professional touch, I reached out to him, asking if he had a referral. He did. An introduction was made to a psychologist who focused on athletes. His client list included several prominent professionals, the names of whom you'd easily recognize if I were to share. I talked with the psychologist. We then scheduled a second call to include Geoffrey.

Geoffrey took sessions with this psychologist, both in person and over the phone, into his NFL days, crediting him with providing clarity on how to manage his struggles in the football world, which I presume also cascaded to life outside of football. Without this support, I don't know how Geoffrey would have dealt with his mental and emotional issues.

I give Geoffrey so much credit for embracing this path. Doing so at that time was not very popular. Talking about it publicly was even more off-limits. But Geoffrey never hid his struggles. When the opportunity presented itself, he spoke very candidly about his experience. Maybe Livie and I normalized the practice for him, as we have used the services of psychologists throughout our adult lives.

In recent years, professional athletes have increasingly opened up about mental health and the struggles they have faced. Michael Phelps, holder of twenty-three Olympic gold medals, the most in Olympic history, has been quite public about his mental health struggles. Kevin Love, a college and professional basketball star, authored an article outlining his struggles with depression with the message, "You're not alone." Young tennis superstar Naomi Osaka turned to social media to explain her struggles with depression and social anxiety. Because of her condition, she once skipped all news conferences at a French Open tournament. Her openness to address her demons was "rewarded" with a $15,000 fine from the stewards of the Open.

Unfortunately, we still live in a world that lacks understanding of mental health struggles. Hopefully, through the likes of Geoffrey, Mitchell and other prominent athletes who courageously share their battles, the stigma causing athletes, and people in the general population, to conceal their need for help will be stripped away. To piggyback on Kevin Love's declaration, it is not necessary to ride this train alone.

Making the Tough Decisions

Decision-making doesn't always come easy, especially when the decision could be life altering. There are all sorts of books opining on decision-making practices. Both Mitchell and Geoffrey, as young adults, had such profound decisions to make. Their free-agent experiences, after Geoffrey's outright release by the Giants and Mitchell astonishingly having the rug pulled from beneath his feet by the Browns, stand out. I'll begin with Geoffrey's story, simply because it came first.

The Kansas City Chiefs, by nature of their low-ball contract offer, sent a message that they no longer wanted Geoffrey. He felt, as did Deryk, that he had more football to play, so Deryk went about pursuing free-agent opportunities.

From Boys To Men—The Building of Character

Saturday, March 8, 2014, was a truly momentous day in Geoffrey's life. That night he and Meridith were to tie the knot. The day would begin with the opening of Geoffrey's free agency.

Friends and family had descended upon Los Angeles for the nighttime festivities. Livie and I thought it would be fun to invite out-of-town guests and family to the house to enjoy lox, bagels, white fish and all the trappings of a Jewish breakfast. One of the guests was Deryk. He arrived sometime around 8:30 that morning. I remember all of us assembled around the kitchen table when the clock struck 9 a.m. PST, the official opening of free agency. Deryk's two cell phones began quivering nonstop. Deryk excused himself for some privacy, heading to our living room. Geoffrey followed like a puppy dog expecting some treats. The rest of us remained in the kitchen/family room area, respecting their privacy.

Some minutes later, Geoffrey invited me into the living room. He and Deryk began sharing the nature of the calls and the offers on the table. There were pros and cons to each offer. I asked Geoffrey where he was leaning. "The offer with the most money," he tells me. Hmm. Not sure that was the best way to make such an important decision. So I made this suggestion. Write down all the considerations in making a choice—money, location, offensive scheme, starting opportunity, team competitiveness, team history, coaching, etc., etc.—and then rank them in importance, from ten to one, top to bottom. Once done with that step, then, for each offer, assign a rating for each consideration. At the end, add up the numbers.

He did so for each team that had an offer on the table. When all was said and done, he scanned the results. The highest rating belonged to a team not offering the best money, as had been his original inclination. Deryk called the New York Giants to finalize a deal. Geoffrey has admitted several times over the airwaves that this exercise was a true learning experience for him about decision-making best practices.

Deryk spent the day negotiating with the Giants. We were all assembled at the wedding-site hotel later that afternoon with dusk almost upon us, signaling it was about time for Geoffrey and Mer to walk down the aisle. As Geoffrey passed Deryk on his way to prepare for the processional to the chupah, he simply asked of Deryk, "Are we good to go?" Deryk, beaming from ear to ear, nodded his head up and down and said, "Yep." Other than possibly the birth of our dear grandchildren, that had to be one of the best days in Geoffrey's life.

Raising Giants

⚽ ⚽ ⚽

As noted in the "It *Is* A Business" chapter, Mitchell and Brooke were visiting Los Angeles when he faced his lone free-agency experience. Interesting how two of the boys' biggest career experiences happened while in L.A. Imagine going to bed believing that a life-changing deal was in place, only to wake up and learn it wasn't. Mitchell was shattered.

Livie and I spent the day, along with Brooke, trying to console Mitchell, encouraging him to keep the faith, that all was not lost. It wasn't an easy period. Our hearts ached. Was Mitchell's career in jeopardy? But then, after Deryk and his colleagues vigorously pounded the pavement to identify other interested suitors, one surfaced. The Kansas City Chiefs were definitely in play. After some negotiation, an agreement was reached. We know the history. It was a momentous turn of events.

There are times during our stay on this earth when, in the moment, the worst seems to be taking place. The world seems to be caving in around us. All hope appears lost. However, benefiting from the passage of time with a chance to reflect, a look in the rearview mirror exposes the reality of what seemed so crushing. That day was actually a monumentally positive time in Mitchell's life. I truly hope Mitchell learned a life-sustaining lesson by that experience about fortitude, believing in oneself and the prospects of a positive outcome and that when the world around seems darkest, there typically is a beacon of light on the horizon.

These episodes just begin to tell the story of the lessons learned by the guys because of their affiliation with and participation in sports. There were certainly more.

- **Time management:** Both boys had to learn early on how to manage their time. A high school day began in the early morning with a slate of classes, followed by an afternoon of baseball, basketball or football practice. By the time they arrived home, it was dark, and they were tired and hungry. But homework awaited. Once they transitioned to college and the NFL, their lives were greatly scripted. When to arrive at the facility. Training timetables. Meetings. Practices. I still have Mitchell's weekend schedule when Cal faced off against USC. A four-by-two-inch-wide laminated card listing, in a font size that would require a magnifying glass for many, every activity beginning with Friday morning, ending after lunch on Monday.

From Boys To Men—The Building of Character

- **Perseverance:** I'm sure there were days when mentally and/or physically they were just not ready for the rigors of the day. But taking time off was not in the cards. They had to learn how to summon the fortitude to push through the mental and physical obstacles confronting them that day. When the going gets tough, the tough get going.
- **Being in the public eye:** I have had limited opportunity to be in front of a camera or to speak to a national audience, but I can assure you the experiences were nerve-racking. I can only imagine the nervousness felt by the boys as they sat in front of hordes of reporters firing question after question at them during, for instance, a postgame media frenzy. Little did we know at the time that those experiences were likely the foundation on which their post-football careers would be built.

And then there's this pre-football experience by Geoffrey as a sixth grader in middle school. Being the biggest kid on campus did not deter a quintet of students from accosting Geoffrey from behind while he stood at a urinal handling his business. In today's vernacular this incident might be described as bullying. Instead of confronting this group, he pushed his way through them and out the door.

When he got home Livie and I knew something was awry, but Geoffrey didn't want to share. We ultimately got him to spill the beans. We told him that this had to be reported to the principal, something he hadn't done while on campus. Again, he resisted. But this wasn't negotiable. We called the school and scheduled an appointment with the dean of discipline.

Geoffrey shared his story. The dean assured us that he would handle the situation without there being any retribution, something Geoffrey was very concerned about. The dean was true to his word. Two of the kids, as I recall, were suspended for a couple of days. That didn't sit well with their parents, as alternative day care had to be arranged for those days. There was no further clash. As a matter of fact, Geoffrey and a couple of the attackers found some common ground afterward.

I haven't talked with Geoffrey about this episode much since it happened three decades ago. I'm hopeful that it helped lay some foundational lessons that he's been able to apply in his life. Not shying away from traumatic experiences. Allowing higher authority to conduct their business and right any wrongs. Understanding. Forgiveness, which he granted his Oregon teammate who misguidedly shared that joke about Hitler and the Holocaust.

As I write this book, I have two thirty-something sons. (Since I'm only in my thirties myself, I have no idea how this happened. Haha.) But in all seriousness, I recognize and acknowledge that Livie and I are very fortunate parents. At any time during their formative years and into young adulthood, especially given the careers they both chose, it was possible for them to take the left fork in the road when the right was the appropriate decision. They always went right. Mitchell and Geoffrey have grown up to be outstanding people and citizens as a result of the lessons learned along the way.

They are wonderful husbands. Geoffrey has proven to be an amazing dad. I'm sure that Mitchell will also be as his family grows after the birth of Scottie in June 2024. They give back to their communities. They are generous with their time and resources, such as Mitchell's 'Que for a Cause charity event. It began in 2018. Hosted by Mitchell, the event has attracted hundreds of fans who wish to join him and his K.C. buddies—including titans Patrick Mahomes and Travis Kelce—"turning in their helmets for aprons and a night of charity."

I attended the first two years. Numerous local restaurants donated their specialties for attendees to dine on. Aprons with player numbers were auctioned off. Guests were able to mingle with Mitchell and his teammates. It was a win-win for all. Proceeds were donated to charities close to Mitchell's and Brooke's hearts. Unfortunately COVID interrupted the flow, but the special evening has since resumed.

What's great to see as parents is that Geoffrey and Mitchell live their lives ethically and morally. There are no two more important elements to one's character as far as Livie and I are concerned. We all have seen those who reach some level of fame, fortune and/or notoriety and then become a different person, having been changed by their newfound status. That hasn't been case with Mitchell or Geoffrey. They are no different as people today then when they walked out the door headed for college life. That makes Livie and I supremely proud.

As a very dear friend of mine, John Peterson, offered in an autobiographical piece he recently wrote for his family, "If I have any advice, now that I am in my eighth decade, it is simply that you should never stop learning." It is heartwarming to know that Mitchell and Geoffrey are

From Boys To Men—The Building of Character

such solid people who will continue to learn, building upon their sound foundation.

23
STORIES WITHOUT A HOME

As we get closer to returning to the locker room, here are several stories that are homeless, having not been included previously, but ones that I believe you may appreciate.

All Losses Are Not Equal

I remember this game like it was yesterday, watching from home. The Kansas City Chiefs, with Geoffrey as a starter, traveled to Indianapolis to face the Colts in an NFL Wild Card matchup. Ninety seconds into the third quarter the Chiefs had amassed what appeared to be an insurmountable lead, 38-10. The Colts then scored twenty-one points to the Chiefs' three to close the gap to only ten with about two minutes left in the third quarter.

Having played and watched sports for decades, there are times when one sees/experiences a singular play that becomes an omen for what's to come. The Colts were driving for another touchdown, the ball inside the five-yard line. The announcers commented that the Colts running back, Donald Brown, had never fumbled in his career. On the very next play, Colts' quarterback Andrew Luck took the snap and handed the ball to Brown. The back took one step and was blasted by a Chiefs' defender. The ball popped loose. As we know, a football is odd-shaped, known as a prolate spheroid. It can, and usually does, bounce weirdly.

In this case, the ball hit the ground and bounced backward toward Luck, who snatched the pigskin in midair. From there it was like the Red Sea parted. A gaping hole emerged in front of Luck. He waltzed into the end zone untouched. At that moment I knew, with almost absolute certainty, that the game was lost.

But former New York Yankee Hall of Fame catcher Yogi Berra, as manager of the New York Mets, is credited with proclaiming, "it ain't over 'til it's over." With about ten minutes left in the game and still holding a three-point lead, all was not yet lost for K.C. At least that's what I tried to tell myself. All the praying went for naught. Although the Chiefs added three more points on a field goal with five minutes left on the clock, Luck led Indianapolis to a last touchdown with only seventy-five seconds on the clock to win the game.

Geoffrey has told me that this game was the most agonizing loss for him in his NFL career. It was the second-largest comeback in NFL playoff history.

From Across the World

In the movie *A Few Good Men*, a riveting exchange takes place as Tom Cruise (playing a Navy lawyer) interrogates Jack Nicholson (as Marine Colonel Nathan R. Jessep) at a court-marshal for an alleged crime. Nicholson, in response to an answer provided to Cruise, wishing to affirm Cruise's understanding of the reply, asks, "Are we clear?" Before Cruise could respond, Nicholson repeats himself, raising the decibel level, "Are we clear?" Cruise calmly replies, "crystal." I'd like to think that by now I've made it crystal clear how important watching the boys' games was to me, even if I was to be halfway around the world.

In 2019 Livie and I, along with our regular traveling companions, cooked up the idea of visiting Israel. It was a bucket-list wish of mine, for sure. With three couples with different schedules to consider, we listened to our travel agent regarding best times to travel and finally agreed upon an October timeframe, although it was football season. The final travel schedule had me facing two possible viewing challenges.

Our departure date was a Thursday. That happened to be the same day the Chiefs played the Denver Broncos. I was a subscriber to an app that purportedly would allow me to view the game on my laptop while flying. I boarded the flight with some trepidation that the app wouldn't work. Thankfully it did. Helped to pass the time on our first leg, an eight-hour flight to England.

Our twelve-day trip extended through a second Chiefs' game. This one in Green Bay, Wisconsin, facing off against the Packers. It was a Sunday night contest. Accounting for the time difference between Green Bay and Israel, I awoke around 3 a.m. Israel time to set up my computer. I fumbled a bit with my laptop connection but soon accessed the broadcast. Livie and I watched the entire game before sunrise from our hotel room 6,086 nautical miles away. If there's a will, there's a way.

Not His Finest Moments

Geoffrey did not lift weights while playing high school football. Genetically speaking he was tall, solidly built, with natural brute strength. Weightlifting began in earnest when he arrived as a freshman at Oregon. But compared with his fellow teammates, he was well behind the eight ball. One day, early in summer camp, he found himself lined up against a freak of nature, Haloti Ngata. A Hall of Fame inductee in 2025, he is a huge person with amazing athleticism. Geoffrey didn't have a chance. The ball was snapped. Haloti came charging across the line of scrimmage. Before he realized what hit him, Geoffrey was prone on his back, tracking the clouds above. Being hit by a Mack truck couldn't have felt any worse. It wasn't one of Geoffrey's finest moments, but was an eye-opening experience for him. He knew right then and there that he needed to devote himself to getting stronger and improving his technique, and that he had graduated to the big time.

Julius Peppers is another freak of nature. He played seventeen years in the NFL, amassing 159.5 career sacks, the fourth-highest in NFL history. He is another fellow teammate who will wear a yellow jacket. Before Peppers decided to focus fully on football, he was a reserve on the North Carolina basketball team. Some athlete.

When Geoffrey arrived in the NFL, he was Peppers' teammate on the Carolina Panthers. Geoffrey, as a tackle, constantly lined up against Peppers during practices. Peppers was not only able to push Geoffrey around but also used his speed and athleticism to get by him in pass protection. Those reps were challenging enough but not game changing—just ego bruising.

Peppers ultimately left the Panthers, signing a free agent contract with the Chicago Bears. Geoffrey had ascended to be the Panthers' starting right tackle when the Bears and Peppers visited Carolina for an October 2010 contest. In preparing for the game, the Carolina coaches told Geoffrey that they would not put him in any compromising situations against Peppers. As I've alluded to elsewhere in the book, one just can't trust these coaches.

A pass play was called, requiring Geoffrey to cut the legs out from underneath Peppers so that the pass could be thrown right over where Peppers once stood. Cut blocks were never Geoffrey's forte. He made a valiant attempt, but Peppers' athleticism was on full display. When seeing Geoffrey begin the cut block, Peppers jumped backward, which caused him to bend at the waist but not fall to the turf. Knowing what was likely coming, Peppers instinctually rose and jumped. Remember, he was once a basketball player who had some hops.

Peppers tipped the ball skyward. So often tipped passes land harmlessly on the ground. Not this time. Peppers put out his big mitts and caught the ball for an interception. This was likely Geoffrey's most embarrassing moment on a football field. It was also a further demonstration that compared to his contemporaries, Geoffrey was definitely not the most athletically gifted, but then all the more impressive that through his knowledge of the game, strength development and determination he was able to fashion a career of which he could be proud.

Chance Meeting

Chip Kelly was Geoffrey's offensive coordinator during his senior season at Oregon. Because I attended practices and was able to access the locker room postgame, I got to know Chip on a casual basis.

In 2009 Mitchell and his Cal Bears played Oregon in Eugene. It was my first return to Autzen Stadium since Geoffrey's graduation. Instead of being decked out in Oregon yellow and green, I was wearing Cal's blue and gold. There's an area outside the stadium that was very familiar to me. It was the path from the Ducks' locker room to the tunnel leading to the stadium floor. A few yards away from that reference point was the parking lot used by the coaches on game day.

As I stood there looking toward the lot, I saw a familiar figure. It was Chip. Should I approach him? Would he remember me? As is my penchant, I thought, "What do I have to lose?" But in this case, I had a real purpose. Weeks earlier Geoffrey had received a box from Oregon. In it was all sorts of Oregon gear. A hoodie. T-shirts. Gym pants. And a note. The message apologized for shoes not being sent. Nike didn't produce size 18 in the style provided to the other alums playing in the NFL.

The message went on to wish Geoffrey good luck in the coming season, signed by Chip. I thought it was a great gesture by Chip and the Oregon staff and wanted to tell Chip so. As we walked toward each other, I heard from Chip, "Hi, Mr. Schwartz." I was shocked that he remembered me, particularly since I was representing Cal that day. Dispensing with the formalities, I thanked Chip on behalf of Geoffrey for sending the goodie box. Chip's response was, "It was nothing." No, it wasn't "nothing." It made quite an impression on Geoffrey and, as was intended, continued to cement the relationship he's forever carried forward with Oregon.

Love at First Sight

If it were not for football, there would be no Meridith or Brooke in our sons' lives.

Mitchell was playing for the Browns when he invited his best friend to attend a game in Cleveland. While sitting in the family section, his friend took notice of an attractive woman sitting next to him. This friend was already attached so his interest wasn't personal. He was looking out for his best friend.

Apparently, there was a person sitting in the section behind him acting rather crudely. This caused the best friend to catch the eye of this attractive woman and engage in conversation about the individual behind them. He pounced on the idea. "How would you like to go out with number 72 on the field?" It's important to note that the attractive woman to whom he was speaking knew nothing about football. She was attending as the guest of another player's significant other. There was some initial hesitation. Any wonder?

Mitchell's friend finally realized there was a missing piece to this puzzle. From her vantage point, all this woman could see was this fairly large individual running around the field, fully helmeted. She had no idea what Mitchell looked like. The friend accessed his trusty cell phone and brought up Mitchell's picture. After giving this proposition some careful consideration, she provided her phone number to Mitchell's buddy, who later shared the story and phone number with Mitchell. Just a day or two later Mitchell got up the courage to call Brooke. The rest, as they say, is history.

After being drafted, Geoffrey landed in Carolina waiting for camp to begin. The rookies were housed in a local hotel. Although I don't think barhopping has ever been Geoffrey's modus operandi, he found himself in a bar one night two or three weeks after arriving in Charlotte. There he spotted an attractive—there's a theme here—blonde. They began a conversation. I dare say love at first sight.

As I shared in a previous chapter, their relationship was blossoming so quickly that Geoffrey needed to be sure Meridith understood the importance of raising his kids Jewish, given Meridith was not. She understood. They continued to see each other regularly, moving about the country as Geoffrey changed teams, until they decided to tie the knot. Once again, as they say, the rest is history.

The Journey That Keeps on Giving

This story happened years after Geoffrey left the game—the journey that keeps on giving—but was so outstanding that it finds its way into the book.

Geoffrey has remained connected to Oregon. For three consecutive years he co-hosted Oregon's National Signing Day extravaganza when that year's recruiting class was introduced to the Oregon faithful. Mike Parr's family business, Parr Lumber, is the lead sponsor for these events. In late January of 2024, Mike invited me to attend that year's version. Geoffrey would be cohosting once again.

After some serious deliberation, I accepted. I knew I would see Geoffrey, always a great joy, and Mike. I also expected to see some of Geoffrey's former teammates, as I did that night at Nike World Headquarters. Jonathan Stewart. Haloti Ngata. Jeremiah Johnson. LeGarrette Blount. Adam Snyder. It was great seeing these guys and reminiscing.

But the highlight of the night was a chance meeting with Head Coach Dan Lanning. In the minutes leading up to the formal event, I was introduced to Coach Lanning. Very outgoing guy. He knew Geoffrey from his appearances on Geoffrey's *Pac-12 Today* radio show. Just weeks before, Coach Lanning was offered the opportunity to replace retiring Head Coach Nick Saban at the University of Alabama, a true "blue blood" program. A dream job for many. But Lanning turned down the offer.

After the initial pleasantries, I said, "Coach, I really need to compliment you on your handling of the Alabama opportunity." You see, before Alabama came calling, Lanning said he couldn't be swayed to leave Oregon for another coaching position. And when the moment of truth arose, he kept to his commitment. In today's world, that's almost never seen. For a variety of reasons, the pull is too strong. But not for Lanning. I felt I needed to offer recognition of his ethics in a world where character is often lacking. Kinda like other stories within the book, huh?

Coach Lanning continued to defer, offering, "Oregon makes it easy to stay." They may, but that doesn't override Coach's demonstration of basic principles and ethics.

Traveling in Style

I've shared stories along the way related to the recruiting trips taken by Mitchell and Geoffrey. All have detailed our on-site experiences. But there was one rather humorous experience, at least to me, that I think you'll appreciate.

Travels to these campuses were rather mundane. Where distance required, we'd all hop on a commercial flight. There was one exception though, involving Geoffrey and his trip to Oregon.

We live within a football field's distance from the boundary of the Santa Monica airport. Imagine, then, our amazement when one day we received a call from an Oregon staffer attempting to arrange transportation from our house to the airport. Geoffrey literally could have walked there. Or we could have driven the three minutes from our house to the airport. But no, they were adamant, and sent a stretch limo to our house to transport Geoffrey to the airport.

The staffer also asked about food. What would Geoffrey like to eat while traveling to the Northwest? Such personalized service. As I recall, he asked for pasta and shrimp.

When he arrived at the airport, a private jet was waiting for him. He boarded and then took off to the Pacific Northwest, treated like a king. That was December of 2003. He might have been one of the last to enjoy such pampered treatment. Nine months later the NCAA Board of Directors approved a reform restricting use of private jets to ferry recruits for visits. One of the task force members explained the need for a change thusly: "The intention is to bring prospects on campus and have their visits be as similar as possible to nonathletes when they visit." Huh? Is there anything remotely similar about how a scholarship athlete is treated compared with their nonathlete counterparts? I'll leave that answer up to you after, hopefully, consuming this book.

Living with a Mess

Being a highly recognized three-sport athlete at Pali High School, Geoffrey's accomplishments apparently caught the eye of a sports reporter working for the local NBC television station in town. Mario Solis reached out to the school to arrange an on-campus interview. He and Coach Blatt agreed on a time and set the plans in gear.

The interview itself was rather standard. What stood out, though, was the segment featuring the trunk of Geoffrey's car. The camera crew staged a few minutes with Geoffrey opening the trunk and explaining what the viewers were seeing. A mess actually!! The trunk was stuffed, seemingly with no rhyme or reason, with sports equipment from his three sports. Football cleats. Basketballs. Bats and gloves. It was a true reflection of Geoffrey, who, admittedly, is not a neatnik. Quite the contrary. And he's completely unaware. When Livie and I would visit him in Oregon, driving in this same car, and would comment—rather complain—about the car's messiness, in all earnestness he used to respond, "What mess?" It's like he had blinders on. We laughed hysterically.

Unfortunately, there was a hitch to this story. Coach Blatt agreed to the interview thinking it was great publicity for the school and for Geoffrey. And it was. However, the school's athletic director at the time thought otherwise, outraged that Coach hadn't first asked for approval. Coach thought he was doing the school and his athlete a good turn but instead was chastised for his efforts. I can't say for sure, but I believe that this experience was the catalyst for Coach's decision to leave Pali High.

🏈 🏈 🏈

Are there other stories involving Geoffrey, Mitchell, their lives and their careers? Indeed, there are many, but hopefully these few extras will serve to round out the big picture of my extraordinary journey with two NFL sons.

24
THE FINAL WHISTLE: ACKNOWLEDGMENTS

Before the final whistle is blown, I have some last-minute details to address.

Writing this book has been an extraordinary experience for me. I've been able to relive so many incredible moments. I find myself somewhat melancholy as I know the final words are about to be written. How blessed am I to have had this unique life experience.

There are so many people to thank. I'm going to start with the stars of this story, Geoffrey and Mitchell. The idea of writing the book hatched while they were still playing football. I innately knew that it was best for them to wait until they retired before telling the story. They didn't need "rabbit ear" coaches or team personnel acting against them because of my words. When I felt the timing was right, I approached the guys, telling them I'd like to begin writing. They both gave me a thumbs up, without hesitation. THANK YOU!

I also need to thank them for allowing me to be so involved in their careers. At times it was a real balance between my desire to be involved and their comfort level with my involvement. I'd like to think that I usually found a satisfactory balance between the two. I believe they knew that my intentions were *always* for their benefit.

However, I believe I flagrantly crossed that line one time.

Raising Giants

Geoffrey's 2003 Palisades High baseball team earned the right to play in the Invitational bracket of the city championship game at Dodger Stadium. Geoffrey was an indispensable part of that team, with his 1.56 earned run average (ERA) that season. He either started or relieved in the three playoff games leading up to the championship.

I'll spare you all the raw details as that afternoon at Dodger Stadium was not my finest moment. Pali won 10-0. For all intents and purposes, it should have been a glorious day. It wasn't for me. There was a ten-run mercy rule in place, meaning that if one team built a lead of ten runs or more by the end of the fifth inning, the game was called. When that happened, Geoffrey was the *only* player on the Pali roster who did not get to play...at Dodger Stadium. I felt Geoffrey was robbed of a once-in-a-lifetime experience. I went ballistic. I could feel the veins in my neck bulging. I started screaming at the coach from the stands.

You may remember that I had talked about Geoffrey working with a basketball trainer. Fortunately, that trainer was in the seat next to me that day. Seeing what was happening, he did his best to usher me away from the field, and from making an even bigger fool of myself—and possibly having a heart attack on the spot.

Love you guys so much.

Of course, none of the journey would have been possible without Livie. She was my first and only girlfriend and as of this publication has been my life partner for over forty-seven years. She has been incredible, balancing her legal career with being a committed mother to the boys. They would not have developed into the people they are today without her influences. THANKS! ILY/VM.

My brother Fred and I have been basically joined at the hip throughout the entire journey. I remember Geoffrey's early high school days when we'd toss around the idea of his playing in college. We've spent long hours on the phone evaluating every step along the way. He attended high school games, traveled to Oregon and Cal, and accompanied us to cities like New York, Kansas City and Cleveland. He has been a wonderful companion. THANKS, Fred!!

To the fan club, oh my, this journey would have been so lonely without all of you. Thanks for allowing me to share the comings and goings of the boys throughout their football careers. Maybe it was simply fear of being "the one" but, unbelievably to me, although I offered a chance to

The Final Whistle: Acknowledgments

be removed from the distribution list every year, only one person ever asked to be.

I suspect we all know how difficult it can be to stay in touch with friends. Life gets in the way. Sometimes distance interrupts communication. But through the fan club updates I have been able to remain in touch with dozens upon dozens of those who might have fallen off the radar. To each and every one of you, thank you for your continued interest in the boys and for your ongoing friendship.

My dear, dear friend John Peterson retired from his law practice about three years before I started writing the book. Maybe he had nothing better to do when he offered to be my unofficial editor. John has read every single word I've written, first and second draft, responding with corrections and suggestions that have been invaluable. Mere words alone can't convey my extreme gratitude for his contributions. THANKS, John!!

Not only was John overseeing my every word, but so was Livie—that is, after some intense negotiation with her. Livie has always been a remarkable writer, but her style, because of her training, is legally oriented. My style is quite the contrary. I write more like I talk and therefore I'm not necessarily traditional, shall we say, in my prose. Our agreement was this: She was welcome to correct spelling, punctuation and grammar. She was welcome to correct stories to ensure accuracy. She was welcome to remind me of tales not included. But what she could not comment on was my style of writing.

It has all worked out very well. She's read every chapter. Twice as well. Offered her observations. Having both her and John involved has been a tremendous benefit. Funny though, given they are both excellent writers and therefore top-notch editors, there have been times when, for instance, one would catch a "speling" mistake while the other would identify a punctuation gaffe. Curious how our minds work.

To my neighbor Chris Farnsworth, himself an American novelist and screenwriter, my heartfelt thank you for taking an interest in this project, for your words of encouragement, for guiding me through some challenging times, and for a huge assist with the selection of a publishing company. Your actions went beyond neighborliness.

Speaking of publishing this book, as those who know me would attest and those having read the book might surmise, I am a very process-oriented individual. So when it came time to evaluate how best to bring this book to life, I engaged in a very thorough evaluation. I am so pleased to have selected Michael Roney of Highpoint Executive Publishing as my partner in this project. Michael's professionalism, commitment to excellence and collaborative approach made this a truly fulfilling experience.

My niece Heather Schwartz is an extremely accomplished graphic artist. I could think of no one better than Heather to bring my cover vision to reality. And boy, did she ever. On top of creating an eye-pleasing—at least to me—visual, she was so, so easy to work with. Thanks, Heather, for bringing my idea to reality.

Was it simply a coincidence that I began writing the book soon after sliding into "almost" retirement? I still have the door open to gigs, but I'm much more strategic in what I take on. Therefore, there's much more time for a project like this. Once done, I'll need to find other activities—I've actually started a second book—to take the place of the time spent on this project. That won't be hard. Time for more S.K.I. vacations.

You'll notice the way I wrote "S.K.I." That's because I'm not talking about snow skiing. S.K.I. is an acronym, one which I can't take credit for coining. It stands for Spending your Kids' Inheritance. Livie and I are very fortunate. We didn't have to pay for eight years of college expenses. And we haven't needed to support either son post-college. Both Mitchell and Geoffrey, thank goodness, are financially sound and won't need any support from us. So the world awaits.

The clock is winding down. I could not complete this chapter or the book without a big THANKS to all of you who have set aside some of your precious time to read the book. I hope you have enjoyed the read and found moments of laughter along the way. I hope you are a more educated football fan. And I hope that, for those who may be living the dream or expect to live the dream like I have, this book has provided you with some insights to make your journey easier and more rewarding.

One final acknowledgment – this one dating back almost fifty years.

I began my freshman year at UCLA enrolled in English 101. Within the first day or two, the course professor proclaimed, "This is English for dummies!" What?!? I admit English was not my best, or favorite, subject in high school but that proclamation stigmatized me, scarring me for years. Writing papers during college was torturous. I thought I was incompetent.

Fast forward. I graduated from UCLA. Found my first professional job. About two years into my career, the company president asked me to write a letter for him. "Me?" "Yes. Get to it." So I returned to my desk and began scribbling. You might be familiar with the vision of someone writing on a pad of paper (yes, old school) and then, in a fit of frustration, tearing the sheet from the pad, crumpling it up and tossing it over a shoulder headed for the trash can. That was me. After seemingly discarding half a pad, I got up and ambled back into the president's office.

I explained my predicament. Very calmly he responded, offering that he and I have no problem communicating verbally. So he encouraged me to "write like you talk." Oh my goodness. I was unshackled from that point forward. To Joe Tremblay, may his memory be a blessing, THANK YOU for "unleashing the monster." Without those four words of encouragement, Raising Giants may never have seen the light of day.

00:05
00:04
00:03
00:02
00:01
00:00

GLOSSARY

- Athlon Sports: Publisher of preseason guides for more than 50 years. Merged with *Sports Illustrated* in October 2022.
- Audible: A play called aloud by the quarterback at the line of scrimmage to supersede the original play call as a result of a change in strategy.
- Bar/Bat Mitzvah: Rite of passage at age 13 for a Jewish boy or girl as they become adults in the eyes of Judaism.
- Blind side: The back side of a quarterback as he drops back to pass the football.
- Blue bloods: Athletic programs considered to be among the most elite.
- Bowl games: Postseason college football games to recognize seasonal achievement of at least six wins.
- Bull rush: A direct forceful rush by a defensive player against an offensive lineman.
- Cap hit: The amount of money a player's contract takes up in the annual salary cap calculations.
- Chupah: A canopy under which a Jewish couple stands during their wedding ceremony.

- Collective Bargaining Agreement (CBA): A document that details the terms of employment as agreed upon by a union and its members.

- Collective: Founded by prominent former athletes, boosters and donors of a university, a collective pools money and resources to create paid endorsement opportunities for student-athletes.

- Combine, NFL Scouting: Week-long showcase where college football players perform physical and mental tests in front of NFL coaches, general managers, and scouts.

- Compressed discs: Also known as herniated discs, a condition that affects the rubbery disks between the bones that stack to make the spine.

- Division 1: Formerly known as Division 1-A, the highest level of college football in the United States.

- Draft board: A ranking system applied to players by all NFL teams to prepare for draft selections.

- Drive block: A type of one-on-one block, specific to the run game, where at the snap, the blocker is responsible for taking a defender and "driving" him off the line of scrimmage.

- Edge rush: Pressure applied by defenders who line up on the outside edge of the line.

- FBS: Football Bowl Subdivision is the highest level of Division 1 football.

- Free agent contract: A contract signed by a player who previously was not under contract to any specific team.

- *Friday Night Lights*: Movie and TV show highlighting a Texas high school team in which attendance rivals college games.

- Google Alert: Notifications sent alerting recipient to a search inquiry match.

Glossary

- Grayshirt: An offer of scholarship only after the athlete is a part-time student and not part of team activities during their first semester. In your second semester, a full scholarship can be offered.

- Heisman Trophy: Annual award to recognize the most outstanding player in college football.

- Hogs: A nickname given to the offensive line of the Washington Redskins during the 1980s and early 1990s.

- *Lindy's*: Sports magazine that covers the NFL.

- Lombardi Award: Annual award recognizing the college football player "who best embodies the values and spirit of NFL's legendary coach Vince Lombardi."

- MCL: Medial collateral ligament located on the inner side of your knee that connects the thigh bone (femur) and the shinbone (tibia) providing knee stability.

- Mensch: A Yiddish word describing a person of integrity and honor.

- Mezuzah: A casement that contains a parchment inscribed with religious texts and is attached to the doorpost of a Jewish house as a sign of faith.

- Mikveh: Jewish ritual bath used, among other things, during a conversion ceremony to Judaism.

- Murderers' Row: Coined to describe the New York Yankees' top six players in their lineup that included Babe Ruth and Lou Gehrig.

- National Letter of Intent (NLI): The NLI is a document signed by a student-athlete representing their commitment to an NCAA college or university.

- National Signing Day (NSD): Traditionally the first day that a high school senior can sign a binding NLI.

Raising Giants

- Onside kick: An intentionally short kickoff required to travel ten yards, which the kicking team can attempt to recover.

- Outland Trophy: Awarded to the best college football interior lineman.

- Pancake: Usually performed by offensive linemen, it is the result of a well-executed block after which the defender ends up lying flat on their back, like a pancake.

- Passover Seder: Observed on the first and second nights, a traditional meal that is part of the Passover celebration.

- Phil Steele: A sportswriter and analyst who focuses exclusively on college and professional football and who produces the annual preseason magazine *Phil Steele's College Football Preview*.

- Pie chart: A circular statistical graphic which is divided into slices to illustrate numerical proportion.

- Play clock: Counts down the time the offense has to start the next play before it is assessed a penalty for delay of game: either 25 or 40 seconds depending on the situation.

- Practice squad: Also called the taxi squad or practice roster, a group of players signed by a team but not part of their main roster.

- Punch: A technique used by offensive linemen to maintain distance between them and their defensive counterpart.

- Redshirt: Decision made by college coaches to delay player participation in official games, granting them an extra year of eligibility to develop their skills, both physically and mentally.

- Rotoworld: An American fantasy sports and sports betting website.

- Scoliosis: Sideways curvature of the spine.

- Silent counts: Nonverbal cues prior to snapping a football that replace the typical verbal cadence used by quarterbacks.

Glossary

- Spotter: The act of assisting a weightlifter with their lifting exercise to help the athlete complete the lift, ensure proper technique, and prevent injury.

- Spread offense: An offensive scheme in football that by its formation typically "spreads" the defense horizontally using three-, four-, and even five-receiver sets.

- Stenosis: Back condition in which the space inside the backbone is too small.

- Two-point stance: Starting position with both feet on the ground and hands resting on thighs.

- Three-point stance: Starting position with both feet on the ground and one hand resting on the turf.

- Telephone booth: Phrase used to describe a small, confined space where an internal offensive lineman typically plays.

- Tendering: A contract offer for the upcoming season to a player who is under club control.

- Torah: Otherwise known as the *Five Books of Moses,* the written word of G-d that contains the laws and teachings of Judaism.

- Transfer portal: An NCAA application, database and compliance tool to manage and facilitate the process for student-athletes seeking to transfer between member institutions.

- Turducken: Thanksgiving fare combining turkey, duck and chicken made famous by former NFL coach John Madden.

- Twist: Movement by a pair of defensive players by which they exchange roles to better slip past blockers of the offensive team at the beginning of a play, in order to better rush the passer.

- Two-minute drill: A type of hurry-up offense instituted after the two-minute warning.

- War room: An NFL team's "draft room" where the clubs' decision-makers gather during the draft to finalize player selections.

INDEX

#
49ers (San Francisco), 47, 103, 107-108, 253, 260, 261, 320-321

A
ABC, 205
Abdul-Jabbar, Kareem, 49, 242
AFC Championship Game, 145, 255
Aikman, Troy, 104
Alabama, 65, 92-93, 122, 360
Alamo, San Antonio, Texas, 173-174
Alamodome, 173
Alcindor, Lew, 49, 242
Aloha Knights, 246-248
Aloha Stadium, 103
Alston, Walt, 225
Amazon, 314-315, 317, 330
America's Voices in Israel, 236
American Football League (AFL), 251-252, 264
Anaheim Angels, 108
Anaheim Stadium, 108
Andy Smith Award, 89
Angels (Anaheim), 108
Ann Arbor, Michigan, 41, 201, 202, 249
Appalachian State, 130
Aristotle, 202
Arizona Stadium, 153-154
Arizona State University (ASU) Sun Devils, 145, 167
Arizona Wildcats, 154, 169
Arrowhead Stadium, 138, 151, 215, 267

Associated Press (AP), 100, 104, 112, 209, 210
Astrodome, 49, 131
AT&T Park, 158, 197
AT&T Stadium, 141
The Athletic, 330
The Athletic Football Show, 217
Atlanta Falcons, 96
Auburn Tigers, 195
Autzen Stadium, 111, 113, 123, 134-135, 137-138, 140, 147-148, 170, 171, 193, 194, 196, 244, 245, 249, 358

B
Bainbridge Island, Washington, 174
Baker, Ted, 26-27
Baltimore Ravens, 12, 302
Bar/Bat Mitzvahed, 17, 101, 222, 226, 235-236, 323
Baseball Hall of Fame, 223
Bear Bets, 327
Bears (Chicago), 103, 105-108, 146, 357-358
Beavers (Oregon State University), 144-146, 148, 246, 338
Beaverton, Oregon, 246
Beckham Jr., Odell, 70, 346
Beegun, Eric, 32
Beegun, Norm, 32, 134
Bellotti, Mike, 36, 43-44, 66, 222-223
Bengals (Cincinnati), 238

Berkeley (California). *See* Cal Bears (University of California, Berkeley (Cal))
Berman, Chris "Boomer," 12–13
Berra, Yogi, 356
Beverly Hills, California, 53, 221
Bielema, Bret, 42
The Big House, 41, 123, 130, 137, 142, 172, 245
Blatt, Don, 24
Blatt, Jason, 25, 29, 64, 67, 175, 321, 362
Bleacher Report, 155
The Blind Side, 208
Blount, LeGarrette, 360
Blue Bloods, 242
Bob Tessier Award, 87
Bonds, Barry, 159
Bosa, Joey, 208
Boston Celtics, 5
Boulder, Colorado, 149
Bowlen family, 308
Bradley, Bill, 250
Bradshaw, Terry, 143, 211
Brady, Tom, 130, 145, 168, 217–218
Brick Muller Award, 88
Brigham Young University (BYU), 101
Broncos (Denver), 12, 97, 117, 209, 218, 308, 356
Brooks, Mel, 316
Brown, Donald, 355
Brown, James, 325
Brown, Jim, 150
Browns (Cleveland), 12–13, 41–42, 95–97, 120, 127–128, 136, 144, 150, 162, 166, 209, 229, 237, 283, 306–307, 348, 359
Bruins (University of California, Los Angeles (UCLA)), 15, 35–37, 39–40, 49–55, 89, 102–103, 108, 117–118, 121–124, 129, 137, 164, 172–173, 195, 201–202, 242, 245, 249, 273–274, 307, 333, 337–339
Buckeyes (Ohio State), 121–122, 142–143
Buffaloes (Colorado), 25, 64–65, 148–149
Bulldog Stadium, 135
Bulldogs (Fresno State), 135
Bulls (South Florida), 195

C

Caesars Superdome, 139
Cal Bears (University of California, Berkeley (Cal)), 32, 38–39, 46, 87–100, 114, 116–117, 119, 120, 134, 135, 143, 146, 147, 149, 155–158, 165, 170–173, 197, 199, 200, 211–212, 231, 277, 297–298, 350, 358–359
Camp Simcha, 228
Cannon, Kermit, 21
Canton, Ohio, 229, 287
Cardinal (Stanford), 34–35, 38, 44–47, 50, 52–53, 124, 156, 170, 212
Carolina Panthers, 69, 71, 77–80, 120, 124, 138–139, 143, 147, 150–151, 165, 243, 279–282, 302–304, 308
Carr, Lloyd, 40–41, 130
Catskill Mountains, 228
CBS Sports, 128, 325
Celtics (Boston), 5
Century City, Los Angeles, California, 53
Century Plaza Hotel, 53
Cepeda, Orlando, 197
Chanukah, 228–229, 233–234, 237
Chai Lifeline, 227
Chargers (San Diego), 117–118, 166
Charlotte, North Carolina, 141, 153, 228, 232, 233, 255, 267, 325, 360
Chicago Bears, 103, 105–108, 146, 357–358
Chiefs (Kansas City), 78, 96, 117–118, 120, 126–128, 136, 143, 145, 152–155, 162, 192–193, 207–209, 218, 224, 228, 236, 243, 254–256, 258, 260–268, 283, 285, 304–305, 307, 309, 348, 350, 355–357
Christian Youth Organization (CYO), 251
Cincinnati Bengals, 238
Clark, Ryan, 239
Clemens, Kellen, 112
Cleveland Browns, 12–13, 41–42, 95–97, 120, 127–128, 136, 144, 150, 162, 166, 209, 229, 237, 283, 306–307, 348, 359
CNN, 231
College Football News, 87
College GameDay, 32, 140
College Park, Maryland, 146
Collins, Gary, 13
Collinsworth, Chris, 218

Index

Colorado Buffaloes, 25, 64–65, 148–149
Colts (Indianapolis), 12, 68, 70, 74, 252, 291, 355–356
Columbus, Ohio, 143
Combine, NFL Scouting, 12, 59, 65, 68–75, 94–96, 284, 298, 302–303
Commanders (Washington), 290
Coples, Quinton, 93
Corso, Lee, 32
Corvallis Knights, 246–248
Corvallis, Oregon, 246
Cosell, Howard, 283
Cotton, DeWitt, 21–22
Cougars (Houston), 49
Cougars (Washington State), 111–113, 338
Countdown to Kickoff, 327
COVID, 41, 118, 253, 267, 352
Cowboys (Dallas), 94, 141, 225, 283, 308
Cowboys Stadium, 141
Cowherd, Colin, 108
Cow Palace, 250
Crawford, Jack, 94
Cruise, Tom, 337, 356

D

D1 Sports Training, 71, 72, 74, 94, 223
Dallas, Texas, 139, 228
Dallas Cowboys, 94, 141, 225, 283, 308
Denver Broncos, 12, 97, 117, 209, 218, 308, 356
Denver, Colorado, 152, 162
Detroit Lions, 106, 292, 302, 305, 346
DirecTV, 119
Disney, Walt, 149
Dixon, Dennis, 124, 153, 195, 297
Dodgers (Los Angeles), 223–225
Dolphins (Miami), 258
Don Antonio's, 193
Donald, Aaron, 238
Dorrell, Karl, 50–53
DOS For Dummies, 203
Doyle, Sir Arthur Conan, 289
Drysdale, Don, 223–225
Ducks (Oregon), 21, 27, 36, 39, 42, 44, 46, 48, 54, 59–61, 110–114, 120–125, 129–131, 134–135, 137, 140, 146, 147, 149, 154, 164, 170, 171, 192–197, 199, 201, 222, 242, 244–246, 248–249, 278–279, 333, 358

E

Eagles (Philadelphia), 95, 231
East-West Shrine Game, 65, 67, 78, 92–93
Eastwood, Clint, 133
Eat My Schwartz, 73, 196, 313–318
eDuck, 27
Eisen, Deborah, 12–13
El Paso, Texas, 84, 195
El Torito, 80
Emerald Bowl, 158
Emeryville, California, 198
Empire State Building, 140
English, Ron, 40–41
ESPN, 12, 32, 89, 94, 97, 101, 117, 140, 239, 298, 325, 345
Essig, Don, 147
Ewbank, Wilber Charles "Weeb," 252

F

Falcons (Atlanta), 96
Fallica, Chris "The Bear," 327
FanBuzz.com, 138
FedEx Field, 290
Fighting Irish (Notre Dame), 28, 103, 122, 124, 142
First Take, 239
Flo Rida, 266
Football for Dummies, 203, 206
For Dummies, 203
Fosnot, Suzi, 323
Fox Sports, 301, 305, 327
Fox, John, 79–80, 125
Franklin, Tennessee, 71
Fresno State Bulldogs, 135
Friday Night Lights, 39, 134
Fulmer, Phil, 38

G

Geoff Schwartz Is Smarter Than You, 217, 327
Get Your Own Damn Beer, I'm Watching the Game!, 206
Giants (New York), 70, 116, 120, 140, 143, 151, 153, 168–169, 208, 224–225, 227, 234, 236, 281, 284–290, 292–294, 302, 305–306, 325, 331, 346, 348–349
Giants (San Francisco), 158, 197, 223
Giants Stadium, 143
Gilmore, Camille, 256

Gilmore, Deryk, 63-65, 72-77, 79, 91, 95-96, 290, 292, 302, 306-307, 313-314, 321, 332, 348-350
Gladstones, 39, 53
Gladwell, Malcolm, 67, 285
Glendale, Arizona, 195
Goff, Jared, 153
Goodell, Roger, 13
Gooding, Cuba, 337
Goodkin, Olivia (Livie), 6, 11, 12, 17-20, 23-25, 28, 35, 38, 40-48, 50-53, 61-63, 74-75, 79-80, 82-83, 90-91, 98, 103, 106, 108-115, 121, 126, 127, 128, 133, 134, 136, 140, 142, 146, 148, 152-159, 163-164, 167-168, 171-175, 185, 187, 191-194, 197-198, 201, 206, 216, 222-223, 231-233, 236, 240, 241-242, 245, 247, 253-263, 265-268, 276, 277, 283, 287, 289, 290, 292, 317, 322-327, 330, 339, 343-352, 356-357, 362
Gould, Ron, 43, 46
Greatwood, Steve, 36, 60, 81, 83-84
Green Bay Packers, 105, 138-139, 264, 357
Green Bay, Wisconsin, 138-139, 357
Groh, Al, 43, 46
Gross, Jordon, 69
Guerrero, Dan, 54

H

Haden, Pat, 15, 59
Harbaugh, Jim, 46-47, 130
Hard Knocks, 205
Hard Rock Stadium, 258
Harris, Franco, 144
Harris, Les, 149
Harris, Walt, 45
Hayes, Elvin, 49
Hayes, Woody, 121
Hayward Field, 245
Heinz Field, 144, 283
Hill, Andy, 54
Hill, Tyreek, 261
Hink, Bob, 88
Hitler, Adolf, 230-231, 352
Holiday Bowl, 91
Hollywood Bowl, 242
Hornung, Paul, 139
The Horseshoe, 142-143
Horween, Arnold, 238
Horween, Ralph, 238
Houston Cougars, 49

Houston, Texas, 65, 67, 131
Houston Texans, 83 207, 254
Howard, Desmond, 130
Hunt, Clark, 264-265
Hunt, Lamar, 264
Hurricanes (Miami), 158
Huskies (Washington), 141, 174-175
Husky Stadium, 141-142

I

Immaculate Reception, 143-144
Indianapolis Colts, 12, 68, 70, 74, 252, 291, 355-356
Ingram, Melvin, 208
In-N-Out Burger, 172
Irvin, Michael, 150
Isenberg, Marc, 170, 309
Israel, 120, 236-238, 356, 357

J

Jackson, DeSean, 231
James, LeBron, 242
Jaroslovsky, Rich, 170
Jaworski, Ron, 325
Jerry McGuire, 337
Jets (New York), 252, 287
Jewish Family and Children's Service (JFCS), 229
Johnson, Cam, 94
Johnson, Don, 51, 53
Johnson, Jeremiah, 360
Jones, David "Deacon," 296
Jones, Jerry, 141, 308
Junior Day, 33-36, 50, 52, 155
JW Marriott Spa and Resort, 256

K

Kansas City Chiefs, 78, 96, 117-118, 120, 126-128, 136, 143, 145, 152-155, 162, 192-193, 207-209, 218, 224, 228, 236, 243, 254-256, 258, 260-268, 283, 285, 304-305, 307, 309, 348, 350, 355-357
Kansas City Royals, 309
Kaufman, Seth, 314-315
Kay, Jordon, 35
Kay, Neil, 35, 169
Kelce, Jason, 330
Kelce, Travis, 330, 352
Kelly, Chip, 66, 358-359
Kiper, Mel, 97
Knicks (New York), 250

Index

Knight Campus, 245
Knight, Penny, 245-246
Knight, Phil, 48, 125, 241-250
Knights (Aloha), 246-248
Koufax, Sandy, 223-227
Kurtzman, Hal, 16

L

Ladd-Peebles Stadium, 93
Lakers (Los Angeles), 212
Lambeau Field, 138-139
Landry, Tom, 94
Lanning, Dan, 360-361
Las Vegas, Nevada, 46, 118
Las Vegas Bowl, 46
Las Vegas Raiders. *See* Oakland Raiders
Lemming, Tom, 173
Lemon, Don, 231
Lindy's Sports, 87-88
Lions (Detroit), 106, 292, 302, 305, 346
Little League, 5, 16, 18, 20-22, 174
Live Bets, 327
Lombardi Award, 89
Lombardi, Vince, 264
Lombardi Trophy, 186, 264, 267
Longhorns (Texas), 91, 337
Los Angeles, California, 23, 50, 62, 102-103, 106, 108, 112, 118, 130, 139, 142, 163, 166, 169, 172, 192, 227, 233, 242, 256, 317, 322-323, 326, 337, 339, 349-350
Los Angeles Chargers. *See* San Diego Chargers
Los Angeles Coliseum, 50, 102, 108, 130-131, 139, 142, 153, 164, 171, 278
Los Angeles Dodgers, 223-225
Los Angeles Lakers, 212
Los Angeles Rams, 103, 106-108, 152-153, 238, 296, 299
Love, Kevin, 348
Lucas Stadium, 70
Luck, Andrew, 291, 355-356

M

Mack, Alex, 307
Mack, Kalil, 207-208
Macy's Thanksgiving Day Parade, 140-141
Madden, John, 205, 226
Madsen, Mark, 212
Magnum, P.I., 242

Mahomes, Patrick, 153, 218, 254, 261, 309, 352
Major League Baseball (MLB), 108, 246, 309-310
Major League Baseball Players Association (MLBPA), 309
Manning, Eli, 168, 290, 330
Manning, Peyton, 215, 330
Manyweather, Duke, 98, 119, 146, 216
Martindale, Marty, 27
Maryland Terrapins, 146
Matthew Knight Arena, 244
Mays, Robert, 217, 330
Mays, Willie, 197
McCartney, Bill, 64
McCartney, Mike, 64
McGuiness, Gordon, 127, 304
McHugh, Mike "Huge," 91
McKay, Jim, 205
Mead, Margeret, 175
Megee, Andy, 20
Memorial Stadium, 147, 155, 157, 174, 196-197, 297
Menafee, Curt, 325
Mercer County, New Jersey, 229
Meredith, "Dandy" Don, 283
MetLife Stadium, 143, 287
Messi, Lionel, 17
MetLife Stadium, 143, 287
Mexico City, Mexico, 152-153
Miami Dolphins, 258
Miami, Florida, 125, 255-256, 258-260, 309
Miami Hurricanes, 158
Michalczik, Jim, 45-46, 174-175, 212
Michigan State Spartans, 212
Michigan Wolverines, 40, 47, 121-122, 123, 130, 142, 201-202, 245
Miles, Les, 42
Miller, Marvin, 309
Miller, Von, 208-209, 218
Milwaukee, Wisconsin, 138
Minneapolis, Minnesota, 200, 208
Minnesota Twins, 223
Minnesota Vikings, 243, 280, 285, 304
Mobile, Alabama, 65, 92-94
Moeller, Andy, 41-42
Monday Night Football, 153, 330
Money Talks, 327
Montana, Joe, 103
Moscow, Idaho, 113
Moshofsky Center, 193

N

Namath, Joe Willie "Broadway Joe," 252
Nashville, Tennessee, 71
National Baseball Congress (NBC) World Series, 247
National Collegiate Athletic Association (NCAA), 20–21, 25, 37–39, 42–43, 49, 54, 63–64, 90–91, 100, 134–135, 282, 314, 327, 329, 332–333, 335, 337–339, 361
National Football League (NFL), 5–6, 11–13, 15–16, 27, 29, 36–37, 41, 48, 52, 59–70, 73–81, 85, 88, 90, 92–97, 99–101, 103–108, 115–119, 121–123, 126–130, 133, 135–136, 138, 145, 150, 152–155, 162–163, 169, 205–211, 213, 216–218, 226, 228–229, 231, 237–238, 243, 251–253, 255, 258, 261, 264, 277–278, 282–283, 285–286, 289, 296–297, 299–305, 307–311, 313–316, 318, 320–321, 324–325
National Football League Players Association (NFLPA), 300, 309
National Letter of Intent (NLI), 15, 47,
National Signing Day (NSD), 47, 360
NBC news station, 218, 362
Netanyahu, Benjamin, 236
New England Patriots, 145, 168–169
New Orleans, Lousiana, 42, 131, 139, 153, 196
New York, New York, 136, 168, 220, 225, 302, 315, 322, 325
New York Giants, 70, 116, 120, 140, 143, 151, 153, 168–169, 208, 224–225, 227, 234, 236, 281, 284–290, 292–294, 302, 305–306, 325, 331, 346, 348–349
New York Knicks, 250
New York Jets, 252, 287
New York Times, 314
Newton, Cam, 195
Newton, Sir Isaac, 214
NFL Boot Camp, 325
NFL Films, 325
NFL Hall of Fame, 207, 208, 211, 215, 216, 217, 229, 243, 252, 286–287, 296, 320, 324, 357
NFL Network, 68, 324
NFL Sunday Ticket, 319
Ngata, Haloti, 357, 360

Nicholson, Jack, 356
Nike, 244, 359, 360
Nimoy, Leonard, 175
Nitschke, Ray, 139
Norman, Oklahoma, 111, 243–245
Notre Dame Fighting Irish, 28, 103, 122, 124, 142

O

Oahu, Hawaii, 103
Oakland, California, 154, 162
Oakland Coliseum, 158
Oakland Raiders, 102, 115, 117–118, 143–144, 154–155, 158, 207
O'Bannon, Ed, 333, 335
Ohio State Buckeyes, 121–122, 142–143
OL Masterminds, 216
Olive Garden, 98
Oklahoma Sooners, 111, 116, 149, 153, 242, 256, 337
Oregon Ducks, 21, 27, 36, 39, 42, 44, 46, 48, 54, 59–61, 110–114, 120–125, 129–131, 134–135, 137, 140, 146, 147, 149, 154, 164, 170, 171, 192–197, 199, 201, 222, 242, 244–246, 248–249, 278–279, 333, 358
Oregon State University Beavers, 144–146, 148, 246, 338
Orgeron, Ed, 37–38
Osaka, Naomi, 348
Outland Trophy, 89
Oxford, England, 250

P

Packers (Green Bay), 105, 138–139, 264, 357
Pacific Palisades, Los Angeles, California, 23
Pali High School, 23–25, 31–33, 36, 39, 40, 51, 53, 62, 110, 116, 133, 161, 192, 321, 362, 364
Palisades Post Cup Award, 192
Palo Alto, California, 34
Panthers (Carolina), 69, 71, 77–80, 120, 124, 138–139, 143, 147, 150–151, 165, 243, 279–282, 302–304, 308
Paramus, New Jersey, 228
Parr, Mike, 135, 144, 193, 244, 360
Pasadena, California, 39, 137, 165, 202, 273
Patriots (New England), 145, 168–169

Index

Pauley Pavilion, 50, 245, 249
The Peddlers, 157
Peete, Holly Robinson, 206
Peete, Rodney, 206
Pellum, Don, 43
Penn State University, 94
Peppers, Julius, 357-358
Perry, William "Refrigerator," 105
Peterson, Adrian, 242
Peterson, John, 352, 365
Peterson, Karen, 168
Phelps, Michael, 348
Philadelphia Eagles, 95, 231
Phil Steele College Football Preview, 87-89
Phoenix, Arizona, 20-21, 46, 145, 167, 169, 195
Phoenix Stadium, 195
Pitbull, 266
Pitino, My Story, 314
Pitino, Rick, 314
Pittsburgh Steelers, 96, 101, 139, 143-144, 211, 253, 283
Police Activities League (PAL), 21
Pop Warner Youth Football, 101
Priority Sports and Entertainment, 63-64, 71, 75, 90, 91, 94
Pro Bowl, 103-104, 209-210, 286
Pro Day, 12, 75, 95-96
Pro Football Writers Association, 78
ProFootballFocus (PFF), 126-127, 285, 304
Puget Sound, Washington, 174
Pullman, Washington, 111-113, 200

Q

Qualcomm Stadium, 91

R

Raiders (Oakland), 102, 115, 117-118, 143-144, 154-155, 158, 207
Ralphie the Buffalo, 148-149
Rams (Los Angeles), 103, 106-108, 152-153, 238, 296, 299
Rams (St. Louis), 11-12
Ravens (Baltimore), 12, 302
Reagan, Ronald, 170
RealResponse, 335
Redskins (Washington), 290
Reid, Andy, 151, 162, 264
Reliant Stadium, 131

Reno, Nevada, 115, 228
Rice, Jerry, 104, 320-321
Richardson, Trent, 12
Rodgers, Aaron, 156
Rose Bowl, 40, 50, 53, 108, 121-123, 129, 137, 164-165, 193, 202, 273
Rosh Hashanah, 221, 225
Rotoworld, 285
Roy, Dorrick, 25
Royals (Kansas City), 309

S

Saban, Nick, 360
Saenger, Gary, 123
San Antonio, Texas, 142, 173
San Diego, California, 91, 118, 162, 166, 256, 290
San Diego Chargers, 117-118, 166
San Jose State University, 49
Sanders, Barry, 217, 346
Sanders, Deion "Prime Time," 150
San Francisco 49ers, 47, 103, 107-108, 253, 260, 261, 320-321
San Francisco Giants, 158, 197, 223
Santa Monica, California, 80, 221, 361
Santa Rosa, California, 102, 147, 251, 256
Schembechler, Bo, 130
Schwartz, Alex, 19, 122, 140, 185, 233, 236, 255, 290-291
Schwartz, Amanda, 98
Schwartz, Brenda, 98
Schwartz, Brooke, 151, 156, 185, 258, 262, 267, 306, 307, 350, 352, 359
Schwartz, Emmy, 19, 185, 233, 255, 290
Schwartz, Fred, 98, 144, 164-166, 173
Schwartz, Heather, 98, 366
Schwartz, Meridith, 98, 140-141, 147, 153, 185, 187, 228, 232-234, 255-259, 261-263, 265-266, 284, 289-291, 349, 359-360
Schwartz, Norman (Papa), 5, 25, 46, 80, 82, 101-102, 109, 129, 164-166, 184, 185, 187, 222, 230, 236, 250, 251, 319
Schwartz, Paul, 46
Schwartz, Rachel, 46
Schwartz, Rebecca, 46
Schwartz, Scottie, 352
Schwartz, Tammy, 46
Seahawks (Seattle), 138-139, 174-175
Sears Directors' Cups, 34

Seattle Seahawks, 138-139, 174-175
Selleck, Tom, 242
Seneca, 175
Senior Bowl, 65, 92-94, 96
Sirius Radio, 218, 327, 338
Smith, Stephen A., 239-240
Smith, Trey, 78
Snyder, Adam, 360
SNYNY, 325
Soldier Field, 105, 107
Solis, Mario, 362
Sooners (Oklahoma), 111, 116, 149, 153, 242, 256, 337
South Florida Bulls, 195
Spaceballs, 316
Spartans (Michigan State), 212
Spokane, Washington, 112-113
Sports Illustrated, 99-100, 130, 211
SportsCenter, ESPN, 298, 345
SportsNet New York, 325
St. Louis Rams, 11-12
St. Martin's Press, 315
Stanford Cardinal, 34-35, 38, 44-47, 50, 52-53, 124, 156, 170, 212
Starr, Bart, 139
Steele, Phil, 87-89
Steelers (Pittsburgh), 96, 101, 139, 143-144, 211, 253, 283
Steil, Kevin "Chief," 61
Stewart, Jonathan, 77, 243, 360
Stoops, Mike, 44, 46-47
Sun Bowl, 84, 195-196
Sun Devils (Arizona State University (ASU)), 145, 167
Sun Devil Stadium, 145, 167
Super Bowl LIV, 125-127, 251-268, 307
Super Bowl, 5-6, 27, 88, 103, 105, 118, 145, 172, 192, 211, 286, 324
Switzer, Barry, 242

T

Taylor, Jim, 139
Taylor, Lawrence, 208
Tedford, Jeff, 45-46, 155-157, 174
Teevens, Buddy, 34
Tempe, Arizona, 167, 169
Tennessee Titans, 254
Tennessee Volunteers, 38, 44, 78
Terrapins (Maryland), 146
Texans (Houston), 207, 254
Texas Longhorns, 91, 337
Thomas, Joe, 277, 330
Three Rivers Stadium, 144

Thurmond, Nate, 250
Tigers (Auburn), 195
Times Picayune, 42
Titans (Tennessee), 254
Transportation Security Administration (TSA), 152
Trojans (University of Southern California (USC)), 27, 37, 50, 52, 59, 82, 102-103, 114, 116, 123-124, 130, 134, 137, 142, 162, 164, 166, 170-171, 248, 274, 277-278, 337-339, 350
Tucson, Arizona, 169, 200
Twins (Minnesota), 223
Twitter (X). *See* X (Twitter)

U

Unger, Cynda, 172
Unger, Cynnie, 172
Unger, Keith, 172
Unger, Max, 172
Unger, Ray, 172
Unitas, Johnny, 252
University of California, Los Angeles (UCLA) Bruins, 15, 35-37, 39-40, 49-55, 89, 102-103, 108, 117-118, 121-124, 129, 137, 164, 172-173, 195, 201-202, 242, 245, 249, 273-274, 307, 333, 337-339
University of California, Berkeley (Cal) Bears, 32, 38-39, 46, 87-100, 114, 116-117, 119, 120, 134, 135, 143, 146, 147, 149, 155-158, 165, 170-173, 197, 199, 200, 211-212, 231, 277, 297-298, 350, 358-359
University of Georgia (Former USSR), 34
University of Southern California (USC) Trojans, 27, 37, 50, 52, 59, 82, 102-103, 114, 116, 123-124, 130, 134, 137, 142, 162, 164, 166, 170-171, 248, 274, 277-278, 337-339, 350
University of Virginia, 38-39, 43-44, 94
Up Close and Personal, 205
Upshaw, Courtney, 93
U.S. Army All American Game, 173
U.S. News and World Report, 38, 44, 211

Index

V

Vikings (Minnesota), 243, 280, 285, 304
Volunteers (Tennessee), 38, 44, 78
VSiN, 327

W

Wall Street Journal, 170
Washington D.C., 232, 317
Washington Huskies, 141, 174-175
Washington Redskins/Commanders, 290
Washington State Cougars, 111-113, 338
Watt, J.J., 207-208
Weber, Mark, 51-52
Weeden, Brandon, 12
Weinstein, Joel, 12-13, 198
West Los Angeles, California, 20, 23, 28-29, 71, 221, 256
Westwood, California, 102, 172
White, Ed, 88
Wikipedia, 301
Wild Card, 254, 355
Wildcats (Arizona), 154, 169
Wilkinson, Bud, 242
Williams, DeAngelo, 243
Willingham, Tyrone, 28
Wolverines (Michigan), 40, 47, 121-122, 123, 130, 142, 201-202, 245
Women's National Basketball Association (WNBA), 64
Wonderlic Test, 94
Wondery, 330
Wooden, John, 54, 188
WSJ.com, 170

X

X (Twitter), 206, 217, 234, 238, 293-294, 327

Y

Yankee Stadium, 5
Yom Kippur, 221-223, 228-229
Young, Steve, 104, 108

Z

Zeta Beta Tau, 102
Zoumboukos, Neal, 60, 222

www.ingramcontent.com/pod-product-compliance
Lightning Source LLC
Chambersburg PA
CBHW060106170426
43198CB00010B/786